FROM THE *CANCIONEIRO DA VATICANA* TO THE *CANCIONERO GENERAL*: STUDIES IN HONOUR OF JANE WHETNALL

Edited by

ALAN DEYERMOND

&

BARRY TAYLOR

Department of Hispanic Studies
Queen Mary, University of London
2007

The PMHRS logo on the half-title is from
the *Cancionero d'Herberay des Essarts*

Typeset by Ian Macpherson
Printed and bound by KKS Printing

ISBN 0 902238 50 7
ISSN 1460–051X

Papers of the Medieval Hispanic Research Seminar

60

FROM THE *CANCIONEIRO DA VATICANA*

TO THE *CANCIONERO GENERAL:*

STUDIES IN HONOUR OF

JANE WHETNALL

Contents

Abbreviations

AH	Clásicos Universales Planeta: Autores Hispánicos
BAE	Biblioteca de Autores Españoles
BFH	Biblioteca Filológica Hispana
BHS	*Bulletin of Hispanic Studies*
BRAE	*Boletín de la Real Academia Española*
BSS	*Bulletin of Spanish Studies*
C	*La Corónica*
CSIC	Consejo Superior de Investigaciones Científicas
CT	Colección Támesis
ENC	Els Nostres Clàssics
HR	*Hispanic Review*
HSMS	Hispanic Seminary of Medieval Studies
MÆ	*Medium Ævum*
MRTS	Medieval & Renaissance Texts & Studies
PMHRS	Papers of the Medieval Hispanic Research Seminar
RAE	Real Academia Española
RFE	*Revista de Filología Española*

Preface

Jane Whetnall took early retirement from her Senior Lectureship at Queen Mary at the end of August 2007, so as to concentrate on research. The vigour and quality of that research were instantly recognized by her appointment as an Honorary Research Fellow. She had decided on retirement only ten months earlier, so we have had to move quickly to prepare this Festschrift, with the inevitable result that some of those invited to contribute were unable to do so in the short time available. This is, like the Willkommenschrift for Ian Macpherson, published eight years ago (PMHRS, 11), a domestic tribute to a great *cancionero* scholar. All of the contributors are, or were recently, active members of the Medieval Hispanic Research Seminar, and they represent several generations, from graduate student to professor emeritus (more than fifty years separate the birth dates of the youngest and oldest contributors). We know that many other scholars — in Britain, in the rest of Western Europe, and in the Americas — would have wished to contribute to this volume, for Jane is a popular and admired participant in both *cancionero* and wider medieval conferences. The latest evidence of that is her election, while most of this volume was in proof stage, as a member of the executive committee of the Asociación Hispánica de Literatura Medieval. But to invite contributions from the wider world of *cancionero* scholars would have delayed publication excessively, and would also have taken the book far beyond the length limit of PMHRS. That wider world is, however, represented here by Giuseppe Mazzocchi's tribute to Jane, which stands alongside Barry Taylor's (these tributes are complemented by what Julian Weiss says of her work, pp. 245–47, below).

The sixteen essays in this volume study aspects of the Castilian, Catalan, and Galician-Portuguese poetry written from the midthirteenth to the early sixteenth centuries, collected in *cancioneros*, *cançoners*, and *cancioneiros*. Two deal with the poetry of the Galician-Portuguese *Cancioneiro da Vaticana* and *Cancioneiro Colocci-Brancuti* (or *da Biblioteca Nacional*): Stephen Reckert compares the female-voice *cantigas de amigo* with women's love poetry in medieval Japan, and Julian Weiss studies the satire directed, in the *cantigas d'escarnio e de mal dizer*, against the most famous of the *soldadeiras* (singers, and probably in some cases authors of songs), Maria Pérez, known as 'a Balteira'. The imagery of the earliest Castilian *cancionero*, the *Cancionero de Baena*, is the subject of Alan Deyermond's essay on the ostrich in three poems by Alfonso Álvarez de Villasandino and one by Ruy Páez de Ribera, and Barry Taylor's on the garden in a poem by Fray Pedro de Valencia. The three great poets of the first half of the fifteenth century — the Valencian Ausiàs March, the Castilian Íñigo López de Mendoza, Marqués de Santillana, and the Andalusian Juan de Mena — and their older contemporary Andreu Febrer are studied by Robert Archer, Francisco Bautista, and Lluís Cabré, respectively. Archer revises his interactive approach to March's similes in the light of cognitivist theory, choosing poem CXVII to illustrate his argument; Bautista studies the concept of poets laureate in the fifteenth century, with special reference to Mena's *Coronación*; and Cabré discusses Febrer as a reader of poetry in several languages. Carlos Conde Solares studies the *Declamación de Lucrecia*, a short prose work in one of the next generation of *cancioneros*, *Herberay des Essarts*, giving special attention to the author's use of classical literature.

Three Catalan poems in praise of the Virgin Mary are included in a Barcelona manuscript of the 1430s (contemporary with Febrer and March); David Barnett studies and edits the two that are found only in this manuscript. Another religious poet, Íñigo de Mendoza, exemplifies the change from script to print, and Dorothy Sherman Severin sorts out the first three, manuscript, recensions of his *Vita Christi*, and the fourth recension which constitutes the printed tradition, and she transcribes thirty-two hitherto unpublished stanzas. Fully in the printed tradition is the 1508 *Cancionero* of Juan de Luzón, better known as the *Suma de las virtudes*; Andrew M. Beresford studies Luzón's treatment of John the Baptist and John the Evangelist. Much the best-known *cancionero* is, of course, the vast *Cancionero general* compiled by Hernando del Castillo, and two essays examine groups of poems in this anthology. Roger Boase tackles the knotty problem of the identity of three ladies addressed or mentioned in two poems by Pinar and one by Francisco Vaca, and Kirstin Kennedy argues that some poets (for instance, Tapia, Luis de Bivero, and the Vizconde de Altamira) allude to impotence, and she relates this to the use of the crossbow as an image by Garci Sánchez de Badajoz and the Conde de Oliva.

The background to *cancionero* poetry is explored in essays from three disciplines. Martin J. Duffell provides a guide to the poets' metrics, elucidating problems in the scansion of both *arte mayor* and octosyllabic verse. Edward Cooper draws on his historian's background to study two castles, el Real de Manzanares (Madrid) and

Cogolludo (Guadalajara), associated with the most prominent literary family of the fifteenth-century aristocracy, the Mendozas. And Xelo Sanmateu studies the reception in the cinema of Isabel la Católica, a major presence in the background (and in some cases in the text) of many poems.

Contributors were free to choose their topic. As we had hoped, they have covered almost the full range of Jane Whetnall's *cancionero* interests (only the *Cancioneiro Geral* and Catalan poetry of the later fifteenth century are missing). They have also covered a wide variety of verse-forms, genres, themes, and critical approaches. In form, both the parallelistic and the non-parallelistic Galician-Portuguese *cantigas* are covered (Reckert and Weiss, respectively). So are the Catalan forms inherited from Provençal (Archer and Cabré), the short-line *canción* (Boase and Duffell), the *invención* (Kennedy), the octosyllabic *dezir* (Duffell, Severin, and Taylor, with *pie quebrado* in Beresford), and *arte mayor* (Bautista, Deyermond, and Duffell). In genre, we have panegyric (Bautista), satire (Kennedy and Weiss), love lyric (Archer, Boase, Kennedy, Reckert, and Taylor), allegory (Deyermond), religious lyric (Barnett), and religious narrative (Beresford and Severin). Critical approaches are equally varied: analysis of imagery (Archer, Deyermond, Kennedy, Reckert, and Taylor), metrical analysis (Duffell), thematic study (Bautista), biography and history (Boase and Cooper), comparative literature (Reckert), literary theory (Archer), identification of lost literature (Weiss), literary relationships (Bautista and Cabré), film studies (Sanmateu), and edition of texts (Barnett, Beresford, and Severin).

In the hope that Jane, having read the book, may from time to time wish to consult it, Alan Deyermond has prepared five indexes. The remaining editorial tasks have been shared between the editors, except for those undertaken by Ian Macpherson. Ian, having reluctantly decided that he could not contribute an essay in the time available, because it would have required a visit to Spanish archives, generously offered to typeset the book. He has done so meticulously, despite the rogue formatting introduced by some contributors, but he has gone beyond that: in at least two cases he has read the first draft of an essay and helped to reshape it, and he has given advice on details of a number of the contributions. Editors, contributors, and readers are greatly indebted to him and, although his name is absent from the title-page at his insistence and despite the editors' wishes, it is unlikely that without his help the book would have appeared on time.

GIOVANE in vna notte oscura, vestita di color turchino, nella de-
stra mano tiene vna lampada piena d'olio accesa, & nella sinistra
vn Libro

Si dipinge giouane, perche hà dominio sopra le stelle, che non l'inuec-
chiano, ne gli tolgano l'intelligenza de secreti di Dio, i quali sono viui,
& veri eternamente.

La lampada accesa, è il lume dell'intelletto, il quale per particolare
dono di Dio, arde nell'anima nostra senza mai consumarsi, ò sminuirsi;
solo auuiene per nostro particolare mancaméto, che venga spesso in gran
parte offuscato, & ricoperto da vitij, che sono le tenebre, le quali sopra-
bondano nell'anima, & occupando la vista del lume, fanno estinguere la
sapienza, & introducono in suo luogo l'ignoranza, & i cattiui pensieri;

Ee 3   Quin-

Publications of Jane Whetnall

A. Books edited

1. *Hers Ancient and Modern: Women's Writing in Spain and Brazil* (with Catherine Davies), Manchester Spanish & Portuguese Studies, 6 (Manchester: Dept of Spanish and Portuguese, Univ. of Manchester, 1997).
2. *Proceedings of the Eleventh Colloquium* (with Alan Deyermond), PMHRS, 34 (2002).
3. *Proceedings of the Twelfth Colloquium* (with Alan Deyermond), PMHRS, 35 (2003).
4. John Gornall, *The 'Invenciones' of the British Library 'Cancionero'*, PMHRS, 41 (2003).
5. *Proceedings of the Thirteenth Colloquium* (with Alan Deyermond), PMHRS, 51 (2006).

B. Articles

1. '*Lírica femenina* in the Early Manuscript *Cancioneros*', in *What's Past Is Prologue: A Collection of Essays in Honour of L. J. Woodward*, ed. Salvador Bacarisse et al. (Edinburgh: Scottish Academic Press, 1984), pp. 138–50 & 171–75.
2. 'Songs and *Canciones* in the *Cancionero general* of 1511', in *The Age of the Catholic Monarchs, 1474–1516: Literary Studies in Memory of Keith Whinnom*, ed. Alan Deyermond & Ian Macpherson (Liverpool: UP, 1989), pp. 197–207.
3. 'Isabel González of the *Cancionero de Baena*, and Other Lost Voices', C, 21.1 (1992): 59–82. Awarded the John K. Walsh Prize.
4. 'El *Cancionero general* de 1511: textos únicos y textos omitidos', in *Medioevo y literatura: Actas del V Congreso de la Asociación Hispánica de Literatura Medieval (Granada, 27 septiembre–1 octubre 1993)*, ed. Juan Paredes (Granada: Universidad, 1995), IV , pp. 505–15.
5. 'A Question of Genre: *Roncesvalles* and the *Siete Infantes* Connection', in '*Al que en buen ora nacio*': *Essays on the Hispanic Epic and Ballad in Honour of Colin Smith*, ed. Brian Powell & Geoffrey West, Hispanic Studies, Textual Research and Criticism, 12 (Liverpool: UP & Modern Humanities Research Association, 1996), pp. 153–69.

6. 'Mayor Arias's Poem and the Early Spanish *Contrafactum*', in *The Medieval Mind: Hispanic Studies in Honour of Alan Deyermond*, ed. Ian Macpherson & Ralph Penny, CT, A170 (London: Tamesis, 1997), pp. 535–52.

7. 'Unmasking the Devout Lover: Hugo de Urriés in the *Cancionero de Herberay*', BHS (Liverpool), 74 (1997): 275–98.

8. 'Adiciones y *enmiendas* al *Cancionero del siglo XV*', in '*Cancionero*' Studies in Honour of Ian Macpherson*, ed. Alan Deyermond, PMHRS, 11 (1998), pp. 195–218.

9. 'Editing Santillana's Early Sonnets: Some Doubts about the Authority of SA8', in *Santillana: A Symposium*, ed. Alan Deyermond, PMHRS, 28 (2000), pp. 53–80.

10. '*Cancioneros*', in *Castilian Writers 1400–1500*, ed. George Greenia & Frank A. Domínguez, Dictionary of Literary Biography, 286 (Detroit: Thomson Gale, 2003), pp. 288–323.

11. 'John Gornall (1932–2003)' (with Barry Taylor), C, 32.1 (2003): 344–55.

12. 'Mayor Arias' and 'Poetry, Vernacular, Popular, and Learned: *Cancioneros* of Spain', in *Medieval Iberia: An Encyclopedia*, ed. E. Michael Gerli (New York: Routledge, 2003), pp. 110 & 666–69.

13. '*Veteris vestigia flammae:* a la caza de la cita cancioneril', in *I canzonieri di Lucrezia — Los cancioneros de Lucrecia: Atti del Convegno Internazionale sulle Raccolte Poetiche Iberiche dei Secoli XV–XVII (Ferrara 1992)*, ed. Andrea Baldissera & Giuseppe Mazzocchi (Padova: Unipress, 2005), pp. 179–92.

14. 'Las transformaciones de Petrarca en cuatro poetas de cancionero: Santillana, Carvajales, Cartagena y Florencia Pinar', *Cancionero General*, 4 (2006 [2007]): 81–108.

15. 'Mayor Arias, "¡Ay, mar brava, esquiva!"', in *Seis siglos de poesía española escrita por mujeres: pautas poéticas y revisiones críticas*, ed. Dolores Romero López et al., Perspectivas Hispánicas, 26 (Bern: Peter Lang, 2007), pp. 11–25.

C. Reviews

In *BHS* (Glasgow), *BHS* (Liverpool), *C*, *Celestinesca*, *Modern Language Review*, *Portuguese Studies*, and *Tesserae*.

La señora de los cancioneros

GIUSEPPE MAZZOCCHI

(Università di Pavia)

Las señoras, y no me refiero sólo a las lectoras sino también a las filólogas, siempre se han movido entre los cancioneros. ¿Cómo olvidar a Dona Carolina, a quien no le faltó algún que otro compañero tan indiscreto como para achacarle lo lúbrico de ciertos textos gallego-portugueses que trabajaba? Gracias a Dios, la siguieron muchas más, aunque pocas con la clase de *lady* (le tomo prestado el término a Barry Taylor) de Jane Whetnall.

La primera vez que la vi (y ya había leído varios trabajos suyos), lo que me impresionó fue la pinta de mujer perennemente ajetreada y con la cabeza ocupada por cientos de pensamientos y preocupaciones, que a pesar de esto tenía una base irrebatible de valores y puntos de referencia. Como padre de tres hijos noté algo familiar en esta unión de la solidez y el caos, el agobio y el entusiasmo, y sobre todo, reconocía esa capacidad de no perder el rumbo a pesar de todo que todavía no deja de admirarme en la madre de mis churumbeles.

Nos había reunido en Padua otra señora de los cancioneros, Patrizia Botta, y cuando le tocó hablar a Jane, la primera impresión de desconcierto (en un revoloteo aparentemente incontrolable de fichas y citas, dentro de una sintaxis hispana algo anacolútica) dejó rápidamente lugar al asombro, mío y de toda la asistencia, ante la solución brillante de un problema tan y tan variamente trillado como el petrarquismo de la lírica cancioneril. Corría el año del Señor 2000, y ya no recuerdo cuántas veces he tenido la necesidad de citar este trabajo como en prensa, o de insistir con Jane para que se publicase. Leerlo en el último tomo aparecido de *Cancionero General* (2006) me ha avivado el recuerdo imborrable de este primer encuentro, y me ha brindado finalmente en lo concreto de la página impresa, la aclaración de un nudo de la historia literaria del siglo XV castellano que entre avanzadas y retiradas (todo es Petrarca, nada es Petrarca) lleva ocupando desde hace muchos años a la crítica. Baste con ver cómo cambia la perspectiva en las tres ediciones (1948, 1968, 1985) de *La trayectoria poética de Garcilaso* de Rafael Lapesa: en la tercera don Rafael vuelve a introducir, 'obligado por los convincentes artículos de Francisco Rico', un párrafo de la primera que había suprimido en la segunda, y que viene a decir: 'Recuerdos tanciales y menciones [del *Canzoniere*] son índice de nutrida incorporación de conceptos, posturas espirituales y maneras de sentir.' Ahora, con el artículo de Jane a la vista, todo casa de forma cristalina. Los *Rerum vulgarium fragmenta* están bien presentes en poetas cancioneriles de diferente talla, ambiente, formación y generación, sin que estos mismos poetas renuncien a su gusto y su poética. Era una idea que ya había asomado en el trabajo espléndido sobre los problemas de edición de los sonetos de Santillana (donde la autoridad del testimonio salmantino SA8 se ponía en discusión pre-cisamente a raíz de su discordancia respecto a la fuente italiana); y que con anterioridad se había propuesto de forma más bien intuitiva, pero que no había cuajado todavía de forma tan definitiva ni tan convincente. No se nos indican simplemente citas de Petrarca, sino toda una forma de aprovecharle. ¡Gracias, doña Jane!

En este trabajo, que no va a ser el último, sino el primero de la larga serie que lo seguirá y que todos esperamos de la autora, notamos por otra parte dos aspectos constantes en su trayectoria de investigadora, es decir el asedio progresivo y obstinado al tema de estudio, con aproximaciones y ataques sucesivos (véase la constelación de estudios sobre la voz femenina y las poetas de los cancioneros); y la capacidad de volver a considerar lo ya estudiado por otros para interpretarlo de forma diferente y desaforada. Las verdaderas señoras saben desarrollar una capacidad fuera de lo común (y, por supuesto, poco masculina) para escuchar y reflexionar. A la señora (y que lo haga de mujer, de madre, de profesora o de filóloga es igual), le interesa más comprender que el que se la comprenda. Eso sí: cuando abre la boca, perdón, cuando escribe un artículo, toda la reflexión acumulada obliga a quien ya habló (a lo mejor de forma poco considerada o un tanto apresurada) a callarse. En las páginas sobre lírica tradicional y lírica femenina, alrededor del poema de Mayor Arias y otros textos, a las cuales acabo de aludir, por ejemplo, se habla con un planteamiento novedoso de *contrafactum* de la lírica popular en textos cultos (*contrafactum*, que no glosa); mientras que el problema de la escasez de voces femeninas y autoras en la lírica cancioneril se explica, de forma muy poco ideológica (lo cual se agradece), no como un problema de ausencia, sino como una omisión en la recopilación y una restricción de la difusión producidas por la mentalidad dominante, según sugieren unos textos reveladores que se comentan en su pleno sentido por primera vez. En estas mismas páginas, asombra la capacidad de centrarse en los aspectos formales de los textos para comprender su sentido y las coordenadas en las que nacieron. Nada más alejado de la línea de investigación de Jane que un historicismo con poca atención por la palabra literaria, o que un formalismo sin sensibilidad histórica. Examinando los textos con lupa es como Jane sabe modificar el sentido que los mismos tienen en la historia de la cultura. Sólo la gran sensibilidad con la que sabe leer el texto y relacionarlo con los que lo acompañan, puede explicar la sorprendente atribución de ciertos poemas del *Cancionero de Herberay* a Hugo de Urriés (y ya quedan superados tanto el atribucionismo total del primer editor, Charles V. Aubrun, como el negacionismo de otros), realizada con una técnica modélica de análisis intertextual, que no deja nada a la impresión o a tesis preconcebidas. Y la misma capacidad es la que lleva a enfocar como problema de género literario la relación entre el lamento de Gonzalo Gústioz y el *Roncesvalles*, una de las pocas ocasiones en las que Jane ha salido del jardín cancioneril: romance y cantar son dos formas diferentes que exigen un tratamiento formal diferente ('coexisting but functionally alternative of the same heroic material'), lo cual lleva a asumir las posturas del neotradicionalismo, aunque de forma renovada, una vez que se niega la posibilidad que los dos textos sean fragmentos de textos épicos más amplios.

Como se ve en todos los ejemplos aducidos hasta ahora, en la aproximación al hecho literario entendido como sistema, hay una atención importante por parte de Jane a la dialéctica colectivo-individual, que sobresale también en el trabajo que se presentó en un congreso ferrarés, trasladado, según espero, al buen recuerdo de todos los participantes. Ver una canción musicada francesa reflejarse en textos castellanos ayuda a derrumbar barreras culturales inexistentes, y a aprender que la forma de un texto y la historia de su circulación no se pueden separar. Es evidente que un descubrimiento como éste exige una atención extremada a los testimonios antiguos, una abertura de mira fuera de lo común, una cultura amplísima, y también gran paciencia y humildad. Por otra parte, ¿cómo no admirar aquí la capacidad de evitar el iberocentrismo, una de las distorsiones más peligrosas de la historiografía literaria ibérica, según apuntaba Keith Whinnom? Jane sabe salvar este riesgo, y también es notable en ella (se me disculpará lo políticamente incorrecto) que evite siempre ciertos límites del empirismo insular que a veces le chocan a la *forma mentis* continental. Jane no hace nada sin datos, pero los datos se interpretan constantemente; los datos no son un fin en sí, y por muy exactamente reconstruida que esté, una realidad necesita una interpretación. No quisiera pasarme de psicólogo, pero no me extrañaría que hubiese que ver aquí un reflejo más de la capacidad general de Jane de ver más allá de las cosas, de captar el sentido profundo de lo que nos rodea y de lo que hacemos, de trascender las apariencias.

Y en la base de esta misma dialéctica entre lo individual y lo colectivo, está el hecho mismo de que un cancionero llegue a constituirse como tal. Las páginas sobre los 'textos únicos y los textos omitidos' del *Cancionero general* de 1511 rechazan las ideas de Antonio Rodríguez-Moñino (a quien, por respeto, no se le nombra) sobre la antología medieval como colección sin seleccionar de todos los textos que el antólogo tenía a su disposición, para resaltar que la novedad era el aspecto determinante del criterio de inclusión: así se evitaba volver a proponer al lector obras que ya habían conocido los tórculos. Esta dialéctica es tanto más interesante porque no ve al destinatario como una entidad pasiva, todo lo contrario, según ilustran también las canciones del *Cancionero general*. Aquí nuestra *lady* mantiene como sólida base de su andadura el trabajo clásico de Whinnom sobre la forma de este género métrico en la gran antología valenciana, aunque lo supera en el enfoque todo *reader-oriented*, y una mirada muy atenta a la repercusión que la recepción tiene en la transmisión textual, hasta la letra de cada pieza. El nexo entre el éxito de un texto (valorado por el número de citas que tiene), el anonimato (o la pluralidad de atribuciones) que a menudo cubre el nombre del autor, la falta de correspondencia que a veces se da entre el número de citas y el número de copias del texto integral, nos llevan, según nos enseña la profesora, a la difusión musical de las piezas.

¿Pero no será, precisamente, esta dialéctica entre lo individual y lo colectivo el atractivo mayor que debió sentir por la realidad de los cancioneros nuestra amiga? Henri-Irénée Marrou, en su *De la connaissance historique*, nos demuestra que entre el historiador y el objeto de sus estudios hay una relación más fuerte de lo que podría pensarse. ¿No será éste también el caso de Jane? Quien, en una dialéctica compleja entre presente y pasado, en el bendito florecimiento de los estudios sobre cancioneros de las últimas décadas, en la amplitud de su horizonte de investigadora, ha sido capaz de aclarar, profundizar y enseñar. Y todo esto, con el máximo de discreción, y a la vez la solidez, cuando no la firmeza, a la hora de mantener sus posiciones y afir-mar una línea de coherencia intelectual absoluta, la que debe caracterizar a una señora de los cancioneros. ¡Muchas gracias, doña Jane!

Whetnall and I

The secrecy which surrounds the Festschrift genre means that for once I am publishing a piece of work that has not been scrutinized by Jane Whetnall.

It was 1 March 1984, around 1 p.m. Carlos Alvar was that day's speaker at the Medieval Hispanic Research Seminar at Westfield, and Alan Deyermond entertained him and his wife, Pilar Palanco, to lunch at the now defunct Finch's in Finchley Road. At lunch I met a lady: I gathered that she was a hispanist who had been out of circulation for some time. I also got the vague impression that she was the mother of a large family. (Two girls and a boy at the time, plus another boy later, but to an only child like myself this seemed a multitude.) In conversation I learned she had been a lecturer at the University of Exeter, where I had later taught. That summer I left Westfield for a post at the British Library, 'permanent and pensionable', and Alan chose Jane (for it was she) to replace me as assistant hispanomedievalist at the College. The rest is history: Westfield eventually became Queen Mary and Westfield (now abbreviated to Queen Mary) and Jane and I have been the best of friends for over twenty years.

Various qualities distinguish Jane as a teacher. At a time when concern for students as individuals seems to be diminishing, she is generous in the time she devotes to discussing students' work. Concerned that the only students who left university capable of writing critical essays were those who had learned how to do so at school, she developed various courses in writing skills.

During her years outside the university devoted to raising a family Jane worked as a copy-editor and proof-reader, and this left its mark. We editors get to see the academic gods *en chemise*, but Jane's copy is always immaculate. Her sharp-eyed and meticulous editing of other people's work, and the breadth of knowledge she brings to bear on the task, have been much appreciated by colleagues.

Her linguistic range is remarkable (although of course it should be the norm). School trained her in French, Latin, and Greek (indeed at one stage she entertained the possibility of a career as a Latin teacher). Her gap year was spent as an au pair in Italy. Her St Andrews degree included Spanish, Portuguese, and Catalan. At Exeter she acquired a reading knowledge of Arabic. After holidays in the Low Countries and the Czech Republic she felt that given a little time she could have made rapid progress in their languages. But time for Jane (more so than for most colleagues) has always been scarce.

The poetry of the *cancioneros* has suffered a bad press since the eighteenth century, being dismissed as cerebral and lifeless. Jane's approach is not to make exaggerated claims for its poetic quality, but to study an aspect of the archeology of taste. Her thesis, by examining which poems were most quoted in other poems, established which were the most appreciated. This enabled her to quantify that commonplace, all too frequently stated but never scrutinized, that the most popular poems were songs.

More than most people, I think, Jane has a large store of papers given but never published. (Now of course is the time for her to put this right.) One subject on which she has worked is the depiction of women readers in literature and art. To a degree she published on it in 'Isabel González of the *Cancionero de Baena* and Other Lost Voices' (B3), which won the first ever John K. Walsh Prize for the best *La Corónica* article of the year. But wouldn't you like to read her paper on women readers in Lope and *La Regenta*?

Jane and I agree on various things, one of them the language in which hispanomedievalist work should ideally be written, although force of circumstances may often prevent us from following this through. We are connoisseurs too of the obituary, although the only obituary we have written is that of John Gornall (B11). A related minor genre is the book review, which can be composed with varying degrees of dedication. Another question: should editors silently improve the copy they receive, or let poor work fend for itself? I think we both erred on the side of kindness.

One reason why Jane's works are much stronger in quality than quantity is that her work is so original that each study, rather than beginning with a literature survey on which she builds, has to start from first principles. This explains why her work on *cancioneros* forms a consistent whole. Often a critical study has necessitated a re-editing of the text to be criticized, as in her 'Editing Santillana's Early Sonnets' (B9).

The contributions to this Festschrift reflect the range of Jane's *cancionero* interests, and we trust that the volume may not be wholly unworthy of her.

The Art of Experience:
Ausiàs March and the Similitudes of Love

ROBERT ARCHER

(King's College London)

The manuscript transmission of the work of Ausiàs March is one of the most complex in medieval Hispanic literature, and is in itself an object-lesson in necessary respect for later witnesses.[1] There are eighteen poems by March that do not appear in the fifteenth-century manuscripts where all the other 111 are first documented; for these eighteen we have to rely on copies made in the 1540s, and some of them problematic ones at that, as well as three passages that have come down only through the editions of 1539 to 1560 (March 1997: I, 22; Beltran 2006).

One of the poems transmitted by these later witnesses is CXVII. A version of 240 lines is found in manuscripts *BDE* (1541, c. 1540?, and 1546 respectively). Another version of 244 lines, however, appears in two of the sixteenth-century editions, namely those of Valladolid 1555 (prepared by Juan de Resa) and of Barcelona 1560. As Pagès argues (1912–14: I, 74–78), the latter edition, published by Claudi Bornat like the two earlier Barcelona editions of 1543 and 1545, seeks to consolidate the efforts undertaken on behalf of Ferrando Folch de Cardona in recovering March's work (Folch is behind both the earlier Barcelona editions and the two sixteenth-century manuscripts *BK*). The Valladolid edition of 1555 had represented a fresh challenge to those efforts, in so far as it contained new texts, the most significant of which is: 1) the *tornada* of CXXVI (a *resposta* which conventionally required a *tornada*), 2) a 28-line version of LXVIII (all other sources contain the twenty-line version), 3) the *tornada* of CXVII. It is important to bear in mind that the

---

[1] For the perplexity of the transmission of March's work see Pagès 1912–14: I, 9–83 & 117–49); March 1997: II, 11–39; and the recent important monograph of Beltran 2006.

From the 'Cancioneiro da Vaticana' to the 'Cancionero general': Studies in Honour of Jane Whetnall, ed. Alan Deyermond & Barry Taylor, PMHRS, 60 (London: Department of Hispanic Studies, Queen Mary, University of London, 2007), pp. 21–38. ISSN 1460–051X. ISBN 0 902238 50 7.

compiler of the Valladolid edition. who is also the author of a Castilian vocabulary of words in March's text, was clearly not a native speaker of any form of Catalan: he can thus hardly be charged with inventing any of the additional material.

In his critical edition of 1912–14 Amédée Pagès prints the lines in italics, as if to indicate that they have a different status from the rest of his text, but makes no comment about their inclusion either in his edition or in his *Commentaire* (Pagès 1925). Pere Bohigas, on the other hand, in his edition of 1952–59 (Bohigas 2000) excludes them from his text, referring to them only in the *apparatus criticus*; Joan Ferraté (1979) also excludes them, without comment. My own solution (Archer 1997) was to give the lines equal status with the preceding 240 (for the *tornada* I used the version of the edition of 1560 since it is free of the obvious error in line 242 found in the text of 1555).

In this poem, rather as in CXVI which precedes it in the canonical order, March analyses his contradictory relationship with love. In CXVI March had focused on the question of love and hate in this relationship, but here he stresses the importance of habit or custom in ensuring that the lover, and concretely the poet, remains subject to love in spite of his rational understanding of the undesirability of this relationship.

The *tornada* of this poem, which begins with the apostrophe *Amor, Amor* that is also found in eleven other compositions, endows it with the kind of ending that we see in similarly discursive poems: in all these March keeps his poetic persona keenly to the forefront and concludes with the kind of concise I-centred statement for which *tornades* are largely designed to be the vehicle. While the final whole stanza contains a general statement about the nature of love, in the *tornada* March stresses the need to accept the bitter with the sweet in love, and then makes a final claim for authority in matters of love, much as he does in other poems:

Amor, Amor, qui vostre amarg no tasta
no porà dir lo dolç que en si mescla;
jo bé ho puc dir puix tinc experiença,
que de les arts és la que més profita.[2]

The poet cites unique *experiença* as the basis for his authority, in this way bringing the poem back to the sense of its initial opening statement that a lifetime of error has finally led to his illumination

[2] All quotations are from Archer 1997.

(ll. 1–8). In the particular area of life that is human love — so March claims in this final half-stanza — only the subjective form of knowledge (*art*) that is derived from direct and life-long experience is of any real value.

What I want to explore here is the relationship between this emphasis on experience and the extensive use of long similes. No other poem of March's contains so many of them.[3] In its thirty stanzas there are fifteen comparisons, most of them arranged in sequence, one after another, the majority taking up a whole stanza in each case. They draw on a range of human activities and on the larger world as their point of comparison. All of them are related to the question of habit in moral behaviour and, at an implicit rhetorical level, to the related matter of the poet's relative responsibility for his own moral behaviour. All but five of them — those that appear in a section of general and depersonalized discussion about love in ll. 113–85 (similes numbers 7 to 9 below) and the final one of ll. 233–40 — are applied to the poet. The comparisons and their basic analogical application to the context in which March uses them are as follows (the text is given in the Appendix):

1   a man who hates his own sinful nature whenever he recalls the fact that he is the work of God ↔ poet feels remorse when his actions in love fail to measure up to the *gentils fets* he imagines (57–64);

2   a man who has been imprisoned since childhood and has grown used to life in his cell ↔ habit, in the same way, keeps the poet tied to love (67–68);

3   [here in the form of a metaphorical statement: 'Jo só aquell'] a man who has been brought up to earn his living in a despised profession only half understands that it is such because he takes pleasure in it and has grown accustomed to it ↔ the poet only partially comprehends the ugly nature of his service to love because of the force of habit and the pleasure it affords (77–78);

4   a man is subject to fits of demoniacal possession when he loses all respect for God and all sense of honour, and returns

---

[3] And this is not the first time that he has made heavy use of similes in the context of claims about authority in matters of love: there are five such similes in the more personal second half of his long LXXXVII and four in a similar position in CXIII.

to sanity once they pass ↔ the poet loses his reason when he gives himself over to carnal love, but realizes his error later (89–94);

5   a man who loses his sight after a long period in darkness ↔ the poet whose desire to act virtuously fades with the effect of habit (97–100);

6   the quality of arms is determined by the nature of the alloy used to make them ↔ the form that love takes depends on the relation of its constituent elements (carnal and spiritual) (125–28);

7   in man the dominant humour constantly varies and the relationship between the humours is never stable ↔ the nature of love is that it varies constantly and is never stable (141–44);

8   heat is latent in steel and is brought out when the steel is exposed to fire ↔ love may be dormant in man, but because of the power of habit, it can suddenly be revived (169–76);

9   no element exists without the small admixture of another element that the senses cannot detect ↔ human love is sensual but never simple since there is always a spiritual element, and it is ugly or beautiful according to how strong the spiritual element is (177–84);

10 a man under siege who is able to hold out until the enemy sends in its strongest combatant, one who then easily vanquishes him ↔ the poet can hold out in his moral resistance to love until habit easily overpowers him (ll. 185–92);

11 the madman believes himself a king until the fit passes and his thoughts of grandeur evaporate ↔ the poet glories in thoughts of love until he remembers its true nature (193–200);

12 a miser loves money for its own sake, not for what it can buy, and can think of no context in which spending might be necessary ↔ the poet loves unthinkingly and for love's own sake, without asking himself whether it is of any benefit to him (201–08);

13 a man feels displeasure at the foolish and sinful behaviour of his son, in spite of natural paternal love ↔ the poet has come to feel displeasure in the ways of love, even though, by force of habit, it seems natural to love (209–16);

14 a man loves his friend for the good deeds he has done rather

than what he might do now ↔ the poet loves because of the noble deeds (*actes nobles*) love has performed, and seeks no other justification for loving (217–20);

15   the science of medicine is beautiful in itself and in its capacity to heal, but medical practice involves much that is repellent ↔ love is in essence noble, but in practice both hateful and terrifying because of its heinous effects on body and soul (233–40).

I have studied March's use of similes extensively during the last three decades (1985 and 1996). My position on them has been that the 109 long-image similes (with images of at least four lines) used by March in some 80 of the 128 attributed poems, together with the 68 comparisons with two-line images, function as elements of discourse in surprising ways. I have tried to show that they do not merely explain or elucidate the meaning set out in the rest of the stanza where the explicit context appears (the 'referent'), or simply add an emotional charge to what is said, but in fact are set to work in a whole range of functions. They frequently are given the following tasks: to prefigure the occasion of the poem later revealed in the *tornada* (and this itself is a function under which several further poetic aims have to be subsumed); to persuade the reader to a certain viewpoint by means which include the purely devious one of sophistical argument; to introduce a moral perspective where none is otherwise evident; to deflect and redirect moral responsibility away from the poet in a way which must make the reader question the apparent detachment of the moral voice; or to contradict outright the poet's own sporadic advocacy of sensual love. The identification of these various functions derived from the idea that the meaning of the similes was not confined to the immediate context in which they appear in the poem. Rather, such meaning was seen to extend pervasively, to varying degrees and with different levels of emphasis, over the entire poem, thus affecting its meaning as a whole.

This reading of March's similes has its theoretical basis in the 'interactive' theory of metaphor developed from the work of I. A. Richards (1976) by Max Black (1977), Paul Ricoeur (1978), and others. The theory centres on the way that metaphorical meaning is produced, that is, the mental processes by which a metaphor comes into being either for its creator or for one who hears or reads it. It develops the idea that metaphorical meaning is created through the interaction of a primary and a secondary subject (the 'focus' and the 'frame'), where the secondary subject is an 'implicative complex' consisting of the commonly held associations which are invoked by the word or words used in it. Once it is seen that the metaphorical statement does not make sense literally (when a 'logical absurdity' is perceived), then certain of the associated 'implicative complexes' of the secondary subject are projected upon the primary; the implications taken up by it are limited to those that are predicable of it. Features of the primary subject are selected, emphasized, and organized (or suppressed) so that they become 'predicable', forming a parallel 'implicative complex' consisting of elements that are isomorphic with those of the secondary subject. Then — crucially for the interactive theory — the thus modified primary subject induces parallel changes in the secondary subject. Significantly too, it is impossible, as Black says, 'to set firm bounds to admissible interpretations; ambiguity is a necessary by-product of the metaphor's suggestiveness' (1977: 441).

This concept of metaphor — here drastically summarized — served as the basis for developing a theory with which to explain what goes on in the reader's mind when he reads a poem by March that is full of similes (Archer 1985 and 1996: 149–200). The two parts of the simile — what I called its 'referent' and 'image' — interact in the same way as metaphor, but there is one important modification to the process. Since in practice the explicit part of the correlation of primary and secondary subjects ('referent' and 'image' respectively) tends to be very limited in March's similes, elements of the image that are not taken up in the immediate process of correlation as well as other projected associations of the image, are projected into the body of the poem's discourse, to be taken up (or dismissed) at a later point. In this way, the associative power of the simile pervades the whole poem, throwing out 'interactable' elements that may come into play at a point at some remove from the actual stanza in which they explicitly interact with the referent.

What the interactive approach uncovers is the rhetorical power of March's use of similes: the way in which they serve decisions about what particular effect the poem is meant to have. This is a conscious and subtle art of persuasion (including persuasion towards an attitude of questioning).

But what my interactive approach to the similes has overlooked is that this is not the only level at which the simile-poems come to have meaning. The most important of these other levels of meaning has to do with the way that the images themselves open out the limited terms of reference of *amor* in which March develops the greater part of his work so as to encompass other areas of experience. It does this by alluding to the larger world of men, and to other aspects of the created world. It is in this context that another approach to simile than the 'interactive' one just described comes into its own, while at the same time it challenges the validity of interactionism. Since my book of 1985, the ground has shifted considerably in the study of metaphor, and one theory in particular, developed from a variety of angles by George Lakoff and his collaborators, has come to occupy much of the foreground (Lakoff & Johnson 1980). This approach to metaphor cuts across all previous ones — at times rather too dismissively (Jackendorff & Aaron 1991; Musolff 2004).

It does this in two important ways. Firstly, it posits the operation of a large number of what are termed conceptual metaphors that are deemed to underlie the way that the cultures of many societies and periods of linguistic practice perceive the world through language. Such conceptual metaphors, expressed in the sloganized form that cognitivists work with, can be very general, such as PURPOSES ARE DESTINATIONS, STATES ARE LOCATIONS, EVENTS ARE ACTIONS, or they may be related to the most vital parts of our existence as in the case of metaphors for life and death, such as LIFE IS A JOURNEY, DEATH IS A DEPARTURE, PEOPLE ARE PLANTS, A LIFETIME IS A YEAR, DEATH IS SLEEP, LIFE IS A FLUID (Lakoff & Turner 1989: 52). Many of these conceptual metaphors are related to the pervasive cultural model of THE GREAT CHAIN OF BEING which turns out to be, as the cognitivists convincingly demonstrate, not simply a fundamental concept in the medieval and early-modern world-view, but one which still pervades the way we think about the world, even if we are not medievalists and have never heard of the Great Chain of Being. By means of this cultural model, such conceptual metaphors as those just mentioned — the basis of countless other lexicalized metaphorical expressions, both in their everyday and poetic forms — bear upon the process by which we are able to relate to what March is saying.

The second important way in which the cognitive theory has changed thinking about metaphor is by identifying a process in the production of meaning in which a 'source domain' maps onto a 'target domain' ('sueño' maps onto 'la vida' in the title of Calderón's play). The major difference from the interactionist view is

that, whereas interaction supposes a reciprocal, but not symme-
trical, modification of the two subjects, the cognitivist theory posits
a superimposition and 'mapping' of one domain onto the other:
'sueño' modifies 'la vida', but not the other way round.

Lakoff & Turner do not address the extended simile (there is no
obvious reason why they should), but their approach to poetic metaphor has clear implications for it. Above all, it implies a
modification of the role of interaction in the process by which
March's similes come to mean or, as Lakoff & Turner argue, a
complete discarding of the notion of interaction (1989: 131–33). We
can see something of the impact that the cognitivist theory could
have in this regard if we take as an example the simile of ll. 185–92
of the poem:

> Semblant me trop de l'assetjat en plaça
> on és lo burg e fort castell e vila
> e, armejant, perdent forces, lo'n meten
> fins al pus fort on no fa ne tem armes.
> Així amor mos pensaments lo llancen
> fora de mi d'un acte aprés l'altre,
> fins que roman en l'hàbit sol de pensa
> e en lo voler com a correu se'n passa.

An 'interactionist' reading (following the method developed in
my 1985 book) would begin by setting the image and referent alongside one another, following the narrative structure of the image, to
identify the main explicit and implicit correlatives (the latter is
shown below in brackets):

IMAGE (man under siege: 185–88)	REFERENT (poet: 185, 189–92)
a) holds out from a strong position	rejects love through the exercise of his *pensaments*
(b) enemy struggles vainly to overcome him (*armejant, perdent forces*)	[love assails him ever more feebly]
(c) but then sends in his last but strongest combatant,	habit of thought
(d) one who neither wields arms nor fears them	[overpowers all *pensaments*]
(e) [and who quickly overpowers him]	and swiftly takes hold of the will

The metaphor of the assault of love as the besieging enemy has a
long tradition. In Giraut de Bornelh, for instance, it provides the

basis for the long simile of the besieged castle (Giraut de Bornelh 1910–35: poem XII, 40–50) where it is used to describe the position of the poet assailed by the *fortz senhors Amors* and by the lady. Characteristically, in March the conflict depicted through the metaphor is a moral one. This is the sense in which he uses it in another poem (XVI.17–32), where it is developed into an allegory of the 'mixed' type, according to the distinction made by Quintilian, that is, one in which elements of the primary subject mingle explicitly with the secondary (Archer 1985: 63 and 1996: 155–72).

In this development of the siege metaphor as a simile, elements of the image are projected as a coherent narrative towards the referent. March's simile-images always operate metaphorically from the first, given that the reader comes to expect that the primary subject will be almost invariably 'I, the poet'; here this is made explicit from the first line where the poet identifies as the object of the following comparison: 'Semblant me trop' (l. 185). As we read the stanza in its entirety, structural elements of the image (those that make up the narrative outlined in the schema above), together with all the associative complexes of each of those elements, are projected towards the remainder of the referent. It is as we read the referent of ll. 189–92 that the modified form of metaphoric interaction comes fully into operation. By the end of the stanza, by means of the interactive process, the elements of the narrative formed by the image have been correlated, either explicitly or implicitly, with the referent, to reveal the grounding analogies that are at the core of what the simile means in a discursive sense. These grounding analogies, as can be seen from the schema, are not produced by a simple matching of explicit elements of image and referent. Thus, elements b) and e) involve inferences from image to referent, while f) requires a similar inference from referent to image. But nor do the grounding analogies constitute all the simile means. Rather, the image in the interaction of its 'implicative complexes' with those of the referent has the same power as that which we find in the more inventive kinds of metaphoric statement, opening up the correlative sense to further 'horizons' of meaning, uncovering further analogies, or pointing to dissimilarities that may be meaningful in themselves. Some of this aura of further meaning surrounding the simile would include the following: the notion of the poet's command of the complex citadel of the moral self (he commands the defence), the power of this moral defence and the extent of the poet's responsibility for his own well-being (the castellan's power and responsibility in *lo burg e fort castell e vila*), and the potential conflict in terms of the fifteenth-century mode of life of the lower classes of knights between military strength and moral weakness in questions of love.

Much of this meaning may also be perfectly explicable in terms of cognitivist theory. But we should then have to seek to explain the Marchian simile by positing a process of meaning that involves the mapping of the source domain (the image) onto the target domain (the referent). This would also involve 'metaphorical entailments', that is, the 'rich knowledge' that people have about source domains that are carried over in the process of mapping to the target domain, a concept close to that of the implicative complex of the secondary subject in the interactive view of metaphor. The basic cognitivist stance is that both the mapping and the entailments operate only from source to target domain and are not bidirectional, contrary to the interaction view (Lakoff & Turner 1989: 31–35). If the cognitivists are right, then the interactionist assumption that the 'implicative complexes' of both the referent and the image are modified in the process would have to be discarded. And yet perhaps there is some potential for development towards a position which is less dismissive of interactionism: more recently the notion has been explored that in certain metaphorical expressions there is a 'blended space' in which it becomes more appropriate to conceive of two 'input domains' rather than mappings from source to target (Kövecses 2002: 228–29). This is a question that requires more space than I have here, but there are some similes, for instance that of 89–94 in this poem, that suggest that the concept of a unidirectional mapping would not account for the way all images and their referents come to mean, since in them two-way adjustments seem to be essential. In this simile it is easy enough to see that even the brief referent of ll. 93–94 contains information about the basis of the analogy that is not transmitted by the image of ll. 89–93: the referent stresses the poet's insensitivity to the harm that carnal love produces, while the image focuses largely on the idea of the loss of reason during the madman's fit. This idea originating in the referent has to be incorporated into the overall sense of the simile, and this can happen only if the image is modified by the information provided by that idea. This may prove to be more a shortcoming of March's handling of the simile than a flaw in the theory, but it is something that will need to be

explored at a later date when trying to develop cognitivist per-
ceptions in relation to extended simile.

Where the cognitivist approach may be more immediately useful
is in relation to the underlying presence of conceptual metaphors.
While an interactive reading appropriately addresses the problem
of how the similes operate as forces of meaning in a poem, leading
us away from the restrictive idea that their role is simply that of
explicative or emotive rhetorical devices, it leaves unanswered a
more basic problem. This is the fundamental question behind the
work of Lakoff and Turner, namely: how are we able to understand easily and naturally that metaphorical meaning is intended
by a poet? This question arises in the simile we have just seen, for
instance, as soon as we start to read the image. We know at once
that when March describes the castellan in the stronghold under
siege he is describing not a piece of military history but an emotional and psychological state. We are aware of this before any of
the implicit or explicit workings-out of the analogy that is an-
nounced with the phrase 'Semblant me trop' have begun. Even
before the actual interaction with the referent, there is metaphorical meaning in the image — specifically the meaning arising from
the action of the underlying conceptual metaphor STATES ARE
LOCATIONS. By means of this metaphor we know from the start,
and prior to any explicit or implicit interaction, that the place
March describes (and the action in it) refers to a human state. Certainly, our reading of medieval allegory of various kinds will also
suggest specific antecedents for the image, but these themselves
also depend on the same conceptual metaphor and derive from it.
And as the referent develops, it is the same conceptual metaphor
(now transmuted into CHANGE OF STATE IS CHANGE OF LOCATION)
that makes that development possible, while another very general
conceptual metaphor, EVENTS ARE ACTIONS, accounts for the way
that abstractions (*pensaments, hàbit, voler*) become personifications,
supporting our instinctive understanding that events such as the
poet's moral collapse are actions by a world he cannot control (Lakoff & Turner 1989: 37 & 72–80). At the level of conceptual
metaphor it becomes possible to relate the similes of March's poem
to the basic metaphorical mechanisms by which we, as readers,
perceive the world in a way that is much closer to our own than
the social and ideological framework of his work might immediately suggest. It is at this level that the cognitivist approach to
metaphor can take our reading of the similes in a quite different,

but perhaps not necessarily contradictory, direction from the inter-active approach.

It is not difficult to identify the underlying conceptual metaphors of the fifteen comparisons in this poem:

1   SAD IS DOWN (i.e. after looking up to God), HAPPY IS UP, BEING HAPPY IS BEING IN HEAVEN.
2   ABSTRACT DEVELOPMENT IS NATURAL PHYSICAL GROWTH.
3   ABSTRACT DEVELOPMENT IS NATURAL PHYSICAL GROWTH.
4   LOVE IS A RAPTURE.
5   KNOWING IS SEEING, ABSTRACT DEVELOPMENT IS NATURAL PHYSICAL GROWTH
6   THE FUNCTIONING OF AN ABSTRACT COMPLEX SYSTEM IS THE WORKING OF A MACHINE (here 'arms').
7   ABSTRACT COMPLEX SYSTEM IS THE HUMAN BODY, GREAT CHAIN OF BEING.
8   GREAT CHAIN OF BEING.
9   GREAT CHAIN OF BEING.
10 STATES ARE LOCATIONS.
11 KNOWING IS SEEING.
12 KNOWING IS SEEING (NOT SEEING IS NOT KNOWING).
13 LOVE IS A BOND.
14 LOVE IS A BOND.
15 INTERNAL IS EXTERNAL, THE MIND IS THE BODY.

It is because of the presence of such conceptual metaphors that we can identify at once the essential basis of similitude between image and referent, at a level of perception that is more instinctive than rational, and at a cognitive stage that precedes any other meta-phorical action. Such metaphors are not the result of interaction between the image and the referent, but rather the underlying mechanism that subsequently allows us to perceive the world through a multitude of linguistic metaphorical expressions (or modified forms of them like the Marchian simile). In interactionist terms, we might say that it is the presence of conceptual meta-phors that sets the interaction between image and referent in the similes (respectively their secondary and primary subjects) into operation.

This aspect of the cognitive approach concerns the production of meaning at what we might call the 'macro metaphorical level', rather than the 'micro' level we have just been discussing (the process of interaction versus mapping). This is the level at which all linguistic metaphorical expressions (including extended similes) derive from conceptual metaphors which are grounded in, or motivated by, human experience. The perception of metaphor of all kinds, even fifteenth-century forms of it, as something 'we live by', to use the title of one of Lakoff's books, at the root of the way we construe the world, just might help explain the enduring anomaly of our readerly habitation of poetic worlds constructed with the literary language of much earlier centuries, as I have suggested in a recent article on March and Góngora (Archer 2007). We can assume the presence of a considerable area of overlap between what is in March's text and what we as later readers bring to it. We tend to take that overlap for granted. This suggests, vitally, that there exists a mode of perceiving the world and of referring to it that is at least partly shared by poets like March and those of us who read their work today. Readerly competence must be assumed, of course: we have to know sufficient about the context of the poem to be able to avoid making grossly false assumptions and, thanks to such knowledge, we are able to jettison irrelevant parts of our own conceptual and cultural baggage. But such readerly competence — essentially, intellectual knowledge — does not explain in itself how we are able to relate on an extra-intellectual level to a poem written in a period far distant from our own. The cognitive processes in all the metaphors underlying the similes of CXVII open up a world of human experience and knowledge of the world that is immediately accessible to us.

The similes of March's poem, like many other forms of metaphor, operate, even for us today, as a way of knowing the world. By 'knowing the world' I refer to a level of meaning beyond the context in which March conceived his poem (the context of love and its relationship to habit). Each of the comparisons not only maps a similitude but also releases the power of conceptual metaphors in order to universalize the particular discourse of the poem on *amor* and *hàbit*. They are able to do this since they address, as Lakoff & Turner put it, 'central and indispensable aspects of our conceptual system' (1989: 215). While the *tornada* brings the poem conventionally back at its close to the familiar Marchian context of *amor*, its similes have opened it up towards a more universal meaning, one which is supported by the presence of one of the fundamental general conceptual metaphors, GENERIC IS SPECIFIC. By means of this conceptual metaphor together with all the others that underlie the similes, we map, as it were, the specific context of *amor* onto the world we are always in the process of perceiving. It is this that may well explain how a poem set temporally and culturally at such a distance from our own can yet be, for the suitably prepared modern reader, eerily meaningful. If there is a sense of experience in the reading of such poems, it is likely to be in large part because of the shared experiential basis of conceptual metaphor. As medievalists, especially, we tend to be blinded by the demands of philology and literary history to the astonishing fact that certain of the texts we study, March's among them, can still mean something directly relevant to the person behind the medievalist. In a dimension of meaning that extends far beyond that of March's ideas about love and the various ways it affects the persona he adopts when he writes, the final *experiença* to which the poem alludes is ultimately always ours.

APPENDIX

Poem CXVII: comparisons

1. Així me'n pren com aquell qui contempla
    l'ésser de l'hom, e com és de Déu obra,
    e puix ell ve a contemplar sos actes:
    tant avorreix trobar-se en lo món home!
    Com de amor son ésser imagine
    e·ls gentils fets que en l'entend·rem romanen,
    jo m'adelit, e com al voler passe,
    per llur excés e qualitat m'agreuge.   (57–64)

2. Entenc no bé los mals que amor atraça,
    perquè altres béns no sentí en ma vida:
    qui en carçre viu del començ d'infantea
    ab dol se n'ix puix en hàbit li torna.   (65–68)

3. Jo só aquell qui en lleig ofici·s cria:
    sap e no sap que és mal e no·n pren altre,
    car no pot ser hàbit sens delit reste.   (77–79)

4. Semblant a aquell qui ha mal de diable
    e, quan lo pren, Déu no coneix ne honra,
    perquè és d'aquell qui té ses virtuts preses,
    e puix, jaquit, torna en sa coneixença,
    quan per la carn amor me passiona
    n·om sent raó, ne mal que per ell vinga.   (89–94)

5. Sí com se perd lo poder de la vista
    si l'hom està llongament en tenebres,
    així·l voler se perd si no executa
    los fets aquells d'on havia costuma.   (97–100)

6. Així com és tota arma bona o mala
    segons que pren d'acer e ferre tempre,
    amor és tal que, segons és composta,
    sa valor pren lo tal e qual la honren.   (125–28)

7. Sí com en l'hom una humor predomina
    que no és u que per egual les haja,
    e ve per temps que·s canvia·l domini,
    així amor pratica en nosaltres.   (137–44)

8. Tot enaixí com lo foc no és en acte
    en lo acer mas l'obra és en potença
    e, mes al foc, la calor lo desperta,
    car, si en l'acer no hi fos, no escalfaria,
    amor en temps està en l'hom com defuncta,
    e puix reviu, mostrant-se en part o tota,
    d'on se veu clar que restava en l'hàbit,
    prest en obrar, mogut per son consemble.   (169–76)

9. Tot element elementat no és simple,
    ans és compost d'un altre son contrari,
    mas és tan poc lo que de l'altre s'ampra
    que bé no·s pot açò pels senys conéixer;
    tal és amor, que·ls actes no ha simples,
    car sensuals són, e d'esperit toquen,
    mas una part a l'altra sobremunta,
    que ella·s diu tot, segons qual, bella o lleja.   (177–84)

10. Semblant me trop de l'assetjat en plaça
    on és lo burg e fort castell e vila
    e, armejant, perdent forces, lo'n meten
    fins al pus fort on no fa ne tem armes.
    Així amor mos pensaments lo llancen
    fora de mi d'un acte aprés l'altre,
    fins que roman en l'hàbit sol de pensa
    e en lo voler com a correu se'n passa.   (185–92)

11. Sí com lo foll en pensa rei se forja
    fins que percep que no ha de rei actes,
    e dura tant estar en ignorança
    com ell roman en pensa de rei ésser,
    així amor en pensa m'adelita
    fins que la fi pens que se'n deu atényer.
    Ans que jo pens a qui amar, jo ame;
    quan l'imagín, de la millor m'espante.   (193–200)

12. Sí com l'avar los diners per ells ama,
    que no veu res per què aquells despenga
    (a si mateix no diu que no se n'ampre,
    mas non sap cas, ne pensa que ésser pusca),
    així amor·no veig a què·m profite:
    en tant me plau que de la fi no pense.
    Jo no esper ne en desesperar baste;
    entre lo mig d'aquests extrems alleuge.   (201–08)

13. Un hom és tal que ama per natura
    son fill en tant que avorrir n·ol poria,
    e si és foll, de sos fets se desalta
    perquè·l veu tal e ple de cabdals vicis;
    així amor ses penses me deliten,
    per l'hàbit pres, que natural repute;
    mas per mon temps de sos fets me desalte,
    car totalment lo trop a mi dessemble.   (209–16)

14. Amor me plac tant per sos actes nobles
    que de per si jo l'am sens esguard altre,
    semblant a aquell qui son bon amic ama
    pel que ha fet e no per lo que faça.   (217–220)

15. Així com és la ciença del metge
    bella en extrem segons si e on guarda,
    així en extrem és la pràtica lleja
    e tots los senys quasi fastig ne senten,
    tal és amor, que·l seu ésser és noble,
    lo praticar odiós e terrible,
    car l'esperit ne pren molt gran angoixa
    e lo cos fam, i en fastig volant passa.   (233–40)

There are also shorter analogical devices in the poem that are not considered here: 'Al grau primer, bo, del pecant me trobe/ que del mal fet ha coneixença fosca' (21–22); 'Mi e mos fets jo mir ab vista fosca,/ no pas com orb ne ab la vista clara' (81–82).

WORKS CITED

ARCHER, Robert, 1985. *The Pervasive Image: The Role of Analogy in the Poetry of Ausiàs March*. Purdue University Monographs in Romance Languages, 17 (Amsterdam: John Benjamins).

——, 1996. *Aproximació a Ausiàs March: estructura, tradició, metàfora* (Barcelona: Empúries).

——, ed., 1997. *Ausiàs March. Obra completa*, 2 vols, (Barcelona: Barcanova).

——, 2007. 'El concepto como forma metafórica en los siglos XV a XVII', in *Exploración y proceso: investigando la cultura hispánica*, ed. Catherine Boyle et al. (Valencia: Biblioteca Valenciana), pp. 309–19.

BELTRAN, Vicenç, 2006. *Poesia, escriptura i societat: els camins de March* (Castelló: Fundació Germà Colón Domènech; Barcelona: Publicacions de l'Abadia de Montserrat).

BLACK, Max, 1977. 'More about Metaphor', *Dialectica*, 31: 431–57. Repr. in his *Perplexities. Rational Choice, The Prisoner's Dilemma, Metaphor, Poetic Ambiguity, and Other Puzzles* (Ithaca: Cornell UP, 1990), pp. 47–76.

BOHIGAS, Pere, ed., 2000. *Ausiàs March, Poesies*, 2nd ed., ed. Amadeu-J. Soberanas & Noemí Espinàs, ENC, B19 (Barcelona: Barcino).

FERRATÉ, Joan, ed., 1979. *Les poesies d'Ausiàs March* (Barcelona: Quaderns Crema).

GIRAUT DE BORNELH, 1910–35. *Sämtliche Lieder des Trobadors Giraut de Bornelh*, ed. Adolf Kolsen, 2 vols (Halle: Niemeyer).

JACKENDOFF, Ray, & David AARON, 1991. Review of Lakoff & Turner 1989, *Language*, 67: 320–38.

KÖVECSES, Zoltán, 2002. *Metaphor: A Practical Introduction* (Oxford: UP).

LAKOFF, George, & Mark JOHNSON, 1980. *Metaphors We Live By* (Chicago: University of Chicago Press).

——, & Mark TURNER, 1989. *More than Cool Reason: A Field Guide to Poetic Metaphor* (Chicago: University of Chicago Press).

MUSOLFF, Andreas, 2004. *Metaphor and Political Discourse: Analogical Reasoning in Debates about Europe* (Basingstoke: Palgrave Macmillan).

PAGÈS, Amédée, ed., 1912–14. *Les obres d'Auzias March*, 2 vols (Barcelona: Institut d'Estudis Catalans).

——, 1925. *Commentaire des poésies d'Auzias March* (Paris: Honoré Champion).

RICHARDS, I. A., 1976. *The Philosophy of Rhetoric* (Oxford: UP).

RICOEUR, Paul, 1978. *The Rule of Metaphor: Multi-Disciplinary Studies of the Creation of Meaning in Language*, tr. Robert Czerny et al. (London: Routledge & Kegan Paul).

Fol ii.

LES OBRES DE MOSSEN AV
SIAS MARCH.

Ceuf

Vi no es trist/de mos dictats no
bo'n algū tēps/que sia trist, estat
e lo qui es/demals passionat
p fer se trist/no cerq loch scur
lija mos dits/mostrāts pēssa torbada
sens algū art/exits d'hó fora sēny
e la raho/que'n tal dolor me'npeny
amor ho sab/quin es la causa'stada;

Alguna part/he molta es trobada
de gran delit/enla pensa del trist
be si les gents/ab gran dolor m'an vist

Arma per
anima.
de gran delit/m'arma fon companyada
quant simplament/amor ab mi habita
tal delit sent/que nom cuyt ser al mon

De pgon
per prima
ment.
e com sos fets/vul veure de pregon
mescladament/ab dolor me delita.

Milsper
millor.
Prest,es lo temps/que fare vida b'rmita
per mils poder/d'amor les festes colre
de'st viure'strany/algu nos vula dolre
car per sa cott/amor me vol, hem cita
be yo quil am/per fi,tant solament
no denegant/lo do quem pot donar
a sa tristor/me plau abandonar
e per tostems/viure'n tristadament.

A

Two Devotional Poems to the Virgin in a Barcelona Manuscript

DAVID BARNETT

(Queen Mary)

I

Barcelona Cathedral Archive, MS 6, copied between 1430 and 1439, contains a collection of prose miracles of the Virgin.[1] It also includes three anonymous poems of praise, or *llaors*, to the Virgin: *Vierge de les viergens*, *Flor de paradís*, and *Enterpretació del nom de Maria*.[2] There are four manuscript witnesses to the second poem, *Flor de paradís*, but the first and third are unique to the Barcelona manuscript, and it is therefore on these two that I shall focus here.[3]

The *llaòrs* occur about three-quarters of the way through the manuscript (folios 89r–97r out of a total of 118), after a first sequence of 102 miracles followed by the legend of Joan Garí (folios 1–89r), and before a second and final sequence of 25 more miracles (folios 97v–118r), including two by Ramon Llull. Four folios are missing from the manuscript, one of which (folio 92) truncates the

[1] The rubric on fol. 1 gives the date when the manuscript was given to the archive as 18 November 1439. Pere Bohigas rightly points out that internal dating shows it must have been copied after 1430 (1956: 10–11): the miracle on fol. 77v is said to have taken place in Barcelona 'lo jorn de Carnestoltes any mill cccc xxx'. The script indicates that it was copied in the early fifteenth century (Massó Torrents 1914: 146).

[2] The poems have been edited before by Barbara Spaggiari (1977) and by the cathedral's current archivist, Josep Baucells i Reig (2003a and 2003b). Of the miracles, seventeen have been edited by Bohigas (1956) as an appendix to his edition of another collection of Catalan Marian miracles, and two Llullian ones by Joan Santanach i Suñol (2005).

[3] See Oroz Arizcuren 1972: 430 and Spaggiari 1977: 314–15 for details of the other manuscript witnesses to *Flor de paradís* (two from the Bibliothèque Nationale in Paris, one from the Biblioteca Comunale, Siena, and one from the Laurenziana in Florence). See Massó Torrents 1932: 261 and Valls y Taberner 1912: 349 for details of a further Catalan manuscript witness to *Flor de paradís* that has not survived.

From the 'Cancioneiro da Vaticana' to the 'Cancionero general': Studies in Honour of Jane Whetnall, ed. Alan Deyermond & Barry Taylor, PMHRS, 60 (London: Department of Hispanic Studies, Queen Mary, University of London, 2007), pp. 39–54. ISSN 1460–051X. ISBN 0 902238 50 7.

first poem.[4] The three poems provide a break in form and content within the manuscript, but maintain its exclusively Marian focus.

The manuscript is written in a single hand, except for four folios (1, 2, 17, & 18) which the book's previous owner, a notary who gives his name as Juliá dez Roure in the rubric on folio 1, copied and replaced in his own hand (Baucells 2003a: 45) before he donated the codex to the Cathedral Archive on 18 November 1439. The first two lines of *Vierge de les viergens* are rendered in a more formal display script (*textualis formata*) than the largely cursive script used elsewhere in the manuscript.[5] The whole of *Enterpretació del nom de Maria* is in *textualis formata*.[6] This seems to indicate an intention by the scribe to make the poems stand out from the rest of the manuscript.

The greater level of decoration in the poems supports this idea. Most of the miracles start with pen-flourished *litterae notabiliores*, in one of two colours — red or blue — while the flourish is in the other. This two-tone combination alternates throughout.[7] In *Vierge de les viergens*, there are three levels of decoration used for initial letters. The first initial of the poem is the largest, is coloured red, but has no further decoration. The initials of subsequent stanzas almost all of which begin with a large letter 'V' have yellow-brown highlighting, perhaps orginally golden, and are decorated with *paragraphus* symbols in red or blue, alternately. The initial letters of the second, third, and fourth lines of each stanza are slightly larger, have no additional decoration, and are highlighted in the same golden colour. The initial letters of the five stanzas of *Enterpretació del nom de Maria* are the largest of any in the manuscript and are coloured in red and blue alternately.

The scribe who did the decoration clearly spent proportionately more time on the poems than on the prose miracles. The poems

[4] The other missing folios are 95 (in the middle of *Flor de paradís*), 109, and 116.

[5] I am following the paleographic nomenclature in Brown 1990. The Catalan Gothic script that predominates in the manuscript is similar to a hand from the late 1420s (lámina 206) in Ibars Mateu & Ibars Mateu 1991: I, 897–900.

[6] *Textualis* is also used for the titles of three miracles in the collection, the two by Ramon Llull (folios 97v–98 and 106v–107), and one entitled 'Del Rey Rubert' (fol. 113v).

[7] There are no *litterae notabiliores* on the four folios copied by the manuscript's donor (1, 2, 17, 18). There are ten in the much longer legend of Joan Garí. The level of decoration in the final sequence of 25 miracles is less uniform: only seven follow the same pattern as in the first 89 folios; the remainder have much smaller initials (that hardly extend above or below a single line) which have the same yellow-brown highlighting used in the poems.

alone display all three colours used in the manuscript's decoration. The level of decoration, combined with the use of the more careful display script, distinguishes the final poem, *Enterpretació del nom de Maria*. The fact that the decoration and script are maintained at a uniformly higher level in this poem may be due to its length: at only five stanzas it occupies just one folio.

II

Vierge[8] de les viergens, flor de les fflors,
regina del ciel, porta de *pe*radis,

Senyora del mon, redolent mes que·l lirs,
de vostres laus e sant consabiment,
5   ab mans junctes e en tierra prostat,
ffa·*us* he *us* offrich li present violeta.

Vierges, vos fues *per* Dieu predestinada,
anans que·l mon haguies comensament,
de esser mayra e filla e nodrissa
10   del Rey dels reys e Senyor om*n*ipotent.

Vierges,[9] li jorns que lo Satan malvats
li n*os*t*r*es p*r*imers payres hac decebuts e enganats,
ffon revalat *per* Dieu que vos, Vierges, naxaries
qui al dit Satan la tiesta hi rompriets.

15   Vierges, vos fues *per* Balam pr*o*fetada
e *per* li patriarcha de la antiga ley
e a Joachim *per* l'angel nunciada
e a sant'Ana de part del Rey del ciell.

Vierges, abans que vos essets consabuda,
20   vos fues votada *per* li v*os*t*r*es parients
en *ser*vir Dieu e star en lo tiempla
ffins vos essets en edat covinents.

---

[8] The text is a diplomatic transcription with the following editorial changes: regularization of the use of *u* and *v*, *b* and *v*, and *i* and *j* (with the exception of 'Ia' in line 13 of *Enterpretació del nom de Maria*, to preserve the acrostic); addition of modern punctuation and capital letters; resolution of paleographic abbreviations, given in italics; modern separation of words in cases where there is no elision; elisions indicated by *punts volats* and apostrophes according to whether the elision occurs in the first or second word in the pair, respectively; acute accents on final stressed syllables of polysyllabic words ending in a vowel or vowel + 's'.

[9] MS: 'Virges'.

Vierges, vos nasqués e fues consabuda
pura e neta de original pecat
25 car ja d'aquiell per Dieu fues preservada
abans que eyl hagués lo mon format.

Vierges, en aysí con en la creació del mon
Dieu fi·en la luy en resplandor del dia
axsí, Vierges, en vostra neximent
30 vos reluys e ets dels fisels guia.

Vierges, quant vos hagués tres anys passats,
vos, Vierges, fues al timpla presentada
e los .xv. grahons qui eran en aquiell
moytás fort leus sens ajuda humana.

35 Vierges, molt sa meravellaren li vostres sants perients,
e li sacerdots qui en lo tiempla eren,
de vos, Verge, qui en ten paucha edat
los dits grahons montar-vos·i vayeren.

Vierges, en laus d'aysó lla Sgleya Romana
40 hay ordonat diser lo Canticum Gradum
en les maytines qui a honor de voy
per li clerch en cascun jorns sa dison.

Vierges, apriés .v. anys que vos fues en lo tiempla,
vos ets lausada de vostra nuyriment
45 mes que nul altre qui en aquiel hi fos
per li sacerdots e tota altre gient.

Vierges, quant fues en edat costituida
de tritza anys, volents vos dar marit,
vos respongués que haviets votat
50 en servir Dieu tostemps en castedat.

Vierges, per aysó li sacerdots del tiempla
ffueran pausats en grant perplexament,
per que acordaren fues supplicat a Dieu
que sobra aysó lus das avisament.

55 Vierges, en la nuyt fou per Dieu revelat
a Isachar, lo sacerdot del tiempla,
que essets sposada de aquiell de vostra trips
al qual la vierga secha en les seus mans florís.

Vierges, no s·i atroba sinó lo prosom Josep

60 al qual la vierga secha florís, segons es dit,
    per que fues sposada de eyll molt santament
    qui us mana en sa casa he us tiench devotament.

Vierges, aprés de pauch, l'angell sen Gabriell
    vos viench he us saluda, disent 'Ave, Maria!'
65 notifficant a voy que en vos sa encarnaria
    lo Fill de Dieu, Jhesús, qui lo mon salvara.

Vierges, vos al angel humilment respongués:
    'Con sa poria faser que verga consabés?'
    car vos havieu votada de tenir castadat
70 a Dieu omnipotent ab tota puritat.

Vierges, a vos replica lo dit sen Gabriell
    dient que vos consabriets per la virtut de Dieu,
    tostemps stant vierge e sens macula de peccat,
    segons per la essencia divina era stat ja ordonat.

75 Vierges molt excellent, en aysó vos respongués:
    'Vet la sirventa de Dieu: sia·m fet segons dit es.'
    Per que encontinent lo Sant Sperit vos a ombra
    e lo fill del Altisma en vos, Vierga, sa encarna.

Vierges, aprés de aysó, vos vesitar anés
80 sancta Elisabet, en lo set mes prenyada,
    la qual encontinent de vos profititza,
    e beneyta sobre totes, Vierga, vos apela.

This first poem, *Vierge de les viergens*, has an explanatory prologue:

En lo seguent compendi aperen e son contenguts tots los actes seguits en e per la gloriosa Verga Maria del comensament del mon fins en la nativitat del gloriós Ffill seu. (fol. 89ʳ)

As Joan Coromines points out, 'compendi' retains the sense of its Latin root, *compendium*, an abridgement or abbreviation (1981: II, 885). This is therefore a perfectly apposite designation for a poem of no more than 28 four-line stanzas, and a two-line initial invocation, that claims to cover 'tots los actes seguits en e per la gloriosa Verga Maria'.[10]

---

[10] The absence of folio 93 from the manuscript cuts the poem short. The missing stanzas would have included a conclusion to the narrative and, if the poem followed the pattern typical of *oraciones narrativas*, a final petition (Gimeno Casalduero 1975: 12). The final stanza in the manuscript on folio 92ᵛ introduces the Visitation. The missing folio could have contained a maximum of eight stanzas, four on each side.

What is striking about this preliminary description of the poem's narrative is the start date, 'el comensament del mon', echoed in lines 8 and 26 of the poem itself. This immediately indicates the poem's immaculist agenda: one of the cornerstones of the argument in favour of the doctrine of the Immaculate Conception was that 'Mary was conceived in the mind of God [...] before the fall and before sin entered the world' (Mayberry 1991: 213-14).[11] This is the first of several immaculist indicators in the poem: in the opening invocation, the poet offers praise to the Virgin's 'sant consabiment' ('holy conception'); in the second line, the poet addresses the Virgin as 'porta de peradís', an immaculist allusion to Genesis (Mayberry 1991: 212) that also occurs in the second line of *Enterpretació del nom de Maria*; and line 14, 'qui al dit Satan la tiesta hi rompriets', refers to the *Protoevangelium* (Genesis 3.15), a key text that was used to support the idea that Mary was exempt from original sin. The stanza that begins on line 23 is addressed to the Virgin who was conceived free from original sin because God had preserved her from it before the Creation.

The poem's immaculist message is echoed elsewhere in the manuscript: the miracle on folios 71r-71v, usually referred to as the Helsinus miracle, relates the story of the English abbot whose ship is hit by a storm on the way back from a peace mission. He prays to the Virgin and a man in bishop's attire appears telling him to celebrate the Feast of the Conception. He promises to do so and the storm abates.[12] The miracle on folios 72v-73v, which tells of the Virgin's gift of an alb and throne to Ildefonso of Toledo, is prefaced by a short biography of the bishop, who:

However, as Baucells points out, there is no way of knowing whether the poem might be missing only four stanzas, finishing on a recto, with the verso either being left blank (unlikely given that the second poem finishes on a verso with no blank space left before the third poem), or taken up with an additional shorter poem, now lost in its entirety (2003a: 48).

[11] For a general history of the doctrine of the Immaculate Conception, see Graef 1963-65, I, chapters 5 & 6. For the history of the doctrine in the Crown of Aragon, see Gazulla 1905-06 and Twomey 1995: 36-39. Ecclesiasticus 24.9, 'Ab initio et ante saecula creata sum', was first used by the Franciscan Petrus Thomae in Barcelona in 1320 to support the doctrine (Stratton 1994: 55).

[12] The miracle also features in Alfonso X's *Cantigas de Santa Maria*, but without any reference to the Feast of the Conception (Mettmann 1986-89: I, 149-50). For its significance as an immaculist indicator in miracle collections, see Bayo 2004: 858 and Twomey 1995: 19.

ordona que en son archabisbat quescu*n* hany lo .xviii. die abans de la nativitat del gloriós Jhes*ús* fill seu, fos[13] feta e celebrada en cascuna sgleya
solempnitat de la Concepció *de* la gloriosa Verge Maria. (fol. 73ʳ)

This is one of the most popular Marian miracles and features in
most collections, including the *Cantigas de Santa Maria* (number 2)
and Berceo's *Milagros de Nuestra Señora* (number 1). Alfonso makes
no mention of the Toledan bishop establishing any feasts. Berceo
does refer to Ildefonso instituting a feast 'en deciembre mediado'
(Berceo 1989: 79), but this is the feast of the Annunciation which he
moved from its unfestively Lenten day in March to 18 December.
The idea that Ildefonso was the first to establish the Feast of the
Immaculate Conception (which is not thought to have been celebrated in Spain until the fourteenth century) is undoubtedly
apocryphal, but confirms the immaculist intent of the Barcelona
manuscript.[14]

Furthermore, the inclusion of two Marian miracles from one of the
earliest writers to be associated with the doctrine, Ramon Llull, although they make no reference to the doctrine, further enhances the
codex's immaculist credentials.[15] The period when the manuscript
was being compiled (between 1430 and 1439) saw considerable debate about the dogma within the Church. The Council of Basle
(1431–49), after lengthy and extensive deliberations, voted to ap-
prove the doctrine in 1438.[16]

On the question of language and sources, Jaume Massó Torrents
suggests that the poem is a translation 'catalano-aprovençalada' of a
French original. He adds that the translator seems to have understood the sense of his source, but not the rhymes, almost all of which
are imperfect. His first impressions were that it was a translation of

[13] The original 'fou' has been corrected to 'fos'.

[14] Confusion between the Feast of the Annunciation and the Feast of the Immaculate Conception 'was frequent because of the similarity of the names *conceptio
Virginis* and *In conceptione Virginis'* (Twomey 1995: 73). See Fernández Conde 1982:
304 for details of the adoption of the Feast of the Immaculate Conception in Spain.

[15] 'The Immaculate Conception of the Virgin is discussed in a number of late-
thirteenth-century treatises that have been attributed to Llull. The earliest that is
surely by Llull himself is the *Liber principiorum theologiae*, which was completed no
later than 1274 and in which he refers unequivocally to the "beatae Virginis Mariae
sine labe conceptae" [blessed Virgin Mary spotlessly conceived]' (Stratton 1994: 6).
See Domínguez Reboiras 1990 for the role that Llullian and pseudo-Llullian texts
played in the debate between the Franciscans and Dominicans over the doctrine.

[16] The Basle decree was later declared invalid as the Church was in schism (Mayberry 1991: 208). The doctrine was not officially accepted by the Church until 1854.

a Provençal poem — which begins 'Vergena de la verges, francha res e grasida!' but is penitential rather than narrative — before he opted for 'un original francès que desconeixem' (1932: 263). Neither Spaggiari (1977) nor Baucells (2003a) comments on possible sources. Spaggiari analyses the rhyme scheme, and the language which is 'fondamentalmente catalana' but with characteristics 'tipiche del catalano con intenti provenzaleggianti' (1977: 300). Baucells inter- prets the reference to the *Canticum Gradum* (line 40) as an indication that the poet was from the clergy, 'ben segur un prevere o almenys algú que havia rebut un orde sagrat' (2003a: 48–49).

In the light of these possible Provençal and French sources, it is legitimate to point to further parallels in those languages. A four- teenth-century Provençal penitential poem opens with a similar invocation:

> Flor sor totas las autras flors,
> Gemma sor totas preciosa,
> Car es maire de deus e sposa,
> Et es porta de paradis.
> (Levy 1887: 71)[17]

This Provençal translation of a French book of devotion written in 1254, like the poem originally suggested by Massó Torrents, indi- cates similarities in the opening invocational elements of the Catalan poem and earlier Provençal and French verses. The way the poet addresses the Virgin in the following stanza is similar to the opening of a thirteenth-century French poem on the *Ave Maria:*

> AVE virge Marie, je vous salueray
> Et devant vostre ymage je m'agenoulleray,
> Jointez mains, a genoux, je vous depreieray:
> Ayes mercey de moy et je m'amanderay.
> (Långfors 1906: 351–52)[18]

The description of the author's prayerful posture of humility in- troduces the idea that the poem may well have been recited before an image of the Virgin. There are many examples of penitential poems that open each stanza by addressing the Mother of God as Virgin, a further indication of a possible Provençal or French source,

---

[17] The poem is from Wolfenbüttel, MS Extravag. 268, fol. 30[r].
[18] This is from a 24-stanza poem in Paris, BN franç. 1555, fol. 120[r].

at least for some structural elements.[19] *Vierge de les viergens*, however, is devotional and narrative rather than penitential. As such it is closer in many respects to one of the most popular subgenres of poems in praise of the Virgin: *goigs* ('joys of the Virgin').

Los VII Gautz de Nostra Dona, which praise the Virgin by highlighting a number of episodes in her life, are considered by many to be the earliest examples of the subgenre. They were composed by the troubadour Gui Faucoi le Gros, who later became Pope Clement IV (1265-68). The Catalan tradition is thought to have stemmed from a Latin paraphrase of the original Provençal (Romeu i Figueras 2000: 201).[20] From the late thirteenth century, the *Joys* were to become a standard form of Marian poetry. They were especially popular in the eastern kingdoms of Spain.[21] Typically, the poems open with a devotional invocation to the Virgin, followed by a chronological listing of the joys, each one assigned a number and, usually, just a single stanza. The most common episodes in Catalan *goigs* are the Annunciation, Nativity, Epiphany, Resurrection, Ascension, Pentecost, and Assumption. It is clear that they are based on canonical episodes in the Virgin's life (with the exception of the Assumption) and do not stray into her earlier years, accounts of which are found only in the Apocryphal Gospels.

Vierge de les viergens, therefore, although using a chronological narrative as the basis of its praise, differs from the *goigs* in its coverage of the Virgin's life. It starts before the Creation, covers the Fall, and then moves on to the Annunciation to Joachim and Anna, the Virgin's parents. The earliest episode in any medieval *goigs* is the birth of the Virgin and there is none, as far as I am aware, that features any joys chronologically earlier than that.[22] Furthermore,

---

[19] A six-stanza poem in the same manuscript follows this pattern (Levy 1887: 78–79), as does the second poem in the Barcelona manscript, *Flor de paradís*, also penitential and dating from the thirteenth century.

[20] Some scholars believe that the earliest joys were only five in number: certainly the earliest examples in the French tradition include five (Gros 2004: 33), as does Alfonso's *Cantiga* 1. For the significance of the number five in Marian devotion, see Beltrán 1984–85: 331.

[21] The earliest surviving Catalan *goigs* are *Los set gotxs recomptarem* from the *Llibre vermell* of Montserrat. See the entry for *goigs* in Molas & Massot i Muntaner 1979: 294–95 for an overview of the history of the subgenre in Catalan and related bibliography.

[22] The Nativity of the Virgin is the first joy in a poem in the Bodleian, Bodley 9, fols 53ᵛ-54ʳ, a mid-fifteenth-century collection of prayers and poems in Latin, French, and English for a religious woman (Gros 2004: 38).

the poem in the Barcelona manuscript lacks the formal structure that characterizes the *goig* subgenre: there is no numbering or listing of the events narrated.

While there are indications that our poem may be a translation from Provençal or French, it is also possible that its source is Latin. One of the earliest narrative biographical poems to the Virgin is to be found in a Barcelona papyrus dating from the fourth century (Roca-Puig 1965). The opening invocation is to God the Father and Christ's conception, but the following stanzas trace the Virgin's life, starting with Old Testament prophecies, followed by several apocryphal episodes including the Virgin's birth, her Presentation at the Temple at the age of three, and her marriage to Joseph after leaving the Temple aged twelve. This coverage of the Virgin's infancy is very similar to the account in *Vierge de les viergens*. Nevertheless, the time between these two poems and the distinctive treatment of the episodes in each is sufficient to rule out any direct link. The survival of the earlier one, though, is evidence of a tradition in Latin that may indicate a possible source for *Vierge de les viergens*.

III

Enterpretació del nom de Maria

Mayre de Diu, stiell del albe pura,
dompna del mon, porta de paradís,
vos consabés lo Fill de Deu, Jhesús,
5   romanent vierge e sens tota lesura.

Advocata ests dels fisells en dretura,
qui en vos haien bona devocion,
e al nevegant, homayer, e mal hom
a vos reclamets, aydats en lur pressura.

10 Regina etz de angelical natura,
sobrepujant en laus e valor gran
tots quants natz son en aquest mon uman[23]
e no es res a vos par en valura.

Ia a Luciffer, princep de la foscura,
15 rompies lo cap e a tots sos seguasses
qui a vostra fill posaven enbarasses,
per que d'ell a ell son prostratz en tortura.

---

[23] MS: 'irnan'.

A vos, Verga, ten humil criatura,
offir mos ditz de vostra nom composts,
20 supplicant-vos que·s vullatz dar repós
en lo regna hon es gaug sen tristura.

Amen

Enterpretació del nom de Maria occupies just a single folio (97ʳ). It has five four-line stanzas, each beginning with one of the five letters that make up the Virgin's name. These initials are the largest and most heavily decorated in the manuscript: the reader cannot, therefore, fail to notice the acrostic. The alternate use of red and blue, decorated with golden highlights, calls to mind a miracle story from Alfonso's *Cantigas*. In *Cantiga* 384, a devout monk who delights in reciting the Hours and reading the 'Vidas dos Santos Padres', is also a scribe. He is whisked off to heaven after his death because whenever he came to write the Virgin's name, he did so in three colours: gold (because it is so precious), blue (because it is the colour of the heavens), and rose (because it is red).[24]

There are two other *cantigas* — both *loores* — that focus on the name 'Maria' in a similar way to *Enterpretació del nom de Maria*. *Cantiga* 70 is headed 'Esta é de loor de Santa Maria, das çinque leteras que á no seu nome e o que queren dizer' and has five four-line stanzas, each dedicated to a letter. It is also an acrostic poem, with one of the five letters of the Virgin's name beginning each of the five stanzas. *Cantiga* 410, entitled *Prologo das cantigas das cinco festas de Santa Maria*, is not an acrostic. It has eight stanzas, the first three introducing the final five, each of which glosses one of the letters of the Virgin's name. Only the final four stanzas begin with the corresponding letter.

The way in which each letter is interpreted, however, is significantly different in the *Cantigas* from the way they are interpreted in the Barcelona poem. The first stanza of *Cantiga* 70 demonstrates this clearly:

---

[24] 'A primeyra era ouro, coor rrica e fremosa / a semellante da Virgen nobre e mui preçiosa; / e a outra d'azur era, coor mui maravilllosa / que ao çeo semella quand'é con sas [e]splandores. // A terçeyra chamam rosa, porque é coor vermella; / onde cada ũa destas coores mui ben semella / aa Virgen que é rica, mui santa, e que parella / nuna ouv'en fremosura, ar é mellor das mellores.' (Mettmann 1986–89: III, 282). This implies that the monk used real gold when writing the Virgin's name, rather than the gold colour used by the scribe of the Barcelona manuscript.

M mostra MADR' e MAYOR
e mais MANSA e mui MELLOR
de quant' al fez Nostro Sennor
nen que fazer poderia.
(Mettmann 1986-89: I, 235)

It supplies four words that also begin with 'm' that could apply to
the Virgin. By beginning 'M mostra', it makes it clear that the verse
is an interpretation of the significance of that particular letter. *Cantiga* 410 is equally explicit: the third stanza tells how the Church
established five Marian feast days because there are five letters to
her name; the fourth stanza begins 'A primeira, que M é, / mostra'
(Mettmann 1986-89: III, 325), an explanatory formula similar to the
one used in *Cantiga* 70.

The poem in the Barcelona manuscript does not employ this explicit signposting, where the poet names the letter that is to be
glossed. Instead, the first stanza begins 'Mayre de Diu, stiell del
albe pura'. The clue that the 'm' of *mayre* is also the first letter of
the Virgin's name is given in the title — *Enterpretació del nom de
Maria* — and in the heavily decorated initials.

An untitled song of praise to the Virgin by Thibaut de Cham-
pagne (1201-53), who later became King Teobaldo I of Navarre
(1234-53), also focuses on the five letters of the Virgin's name. This
is not an acrostic poem, though, and is closer to the *Cantigas* versions in its overt explanation of the rationale:

Dou tres douz non a la virge Marie
Vos espondrai .v. letres plainement.
La premiere est *M*, qui senefie
Que les ames en sont fors de torment
Quar par li vint ça jus entre sa gent
Et nos gita de la noire prison
Diex, qui por nos en sosfri passion.
Iceste *M* est et sa mere et s'amie.
(Järnström & Långfors 1927: 43–44)

Here the poet is introducing each letter in turn, but in addition to
offering another word that begins with that letter (*mere*, 'mother',
in line eight), he uses a pun: the pronunciation of *M* in line three is
the same as *ames*, 'souls', in line four, and the first syllable of *amie*
in line eight. His ingenuity is particularly striking in the fourth
stanza when he compares the Virgin to the letter 'i' which is 'toz
droiz, genz et de bele taille'.

There are at least six manuscript witnesses to Thibaut de Cham-
pagne's poem, five of which include the musical setting. It seems

fair to conclude, therefore, that it was disseminated relatively widely, and that it was performed to music. *Cantigas* 70 and 410 were also set to music (Fernandes Lopes 1985: 19) and, it can be assumed, performed. However, in a performance of the Barcelona poem, the reference to the five letters of Mary's name would not necessarily be conveyed: although the opening words of the first three stanzas, *mayre*, *advocada*, and *regina*, might suggest the acrostic, the final two stanzas, beginning as they do with an adverb and a preposition, do not stand out. The declaration in the final stanza that the verses are 'de vostra nom composts' comes too late to alert the audience to the use of the five letters.

Both the Old French poem and *Cantiga* 70 are written in the first person plural, a further indication of their communal, performative tone. The other *cantiga* is in the first person singular, but is clearly addressed to an audience: in the third stanza, the poet says the Church established the five feasts because Mary's name has five letters 'como vos quero depa[r]tir' (Mettmann 1986–89: III, 325). *Enterpretació del nom de Maria* is written in the first person singular but the 'vos' being addressed is the Virgin herself rather than the audience. It is therefore a more personal poem.

The level of explanation, the performativity, and the poet's voice indicate a difference in the audience. The more explanatory ones lend themselves more to being performed, whereas the reliance on the visual highlighting of the name in the Barcelona manuscript indicates that it was designed with a readership rather than aural audience in mind. If Massó Torrents's hunch is correct that the translator of the (unknown) original French version of *Vierge de les viergens* understood the sense but not the rhyme scheme, this also has implications for the audience of that poem. If it is the sense and not the rhythm that the translator has chosen to privilege, it seems reasonable to assume that this was because the Catalan version was to be read and not sung. The devotional first-person-singular invocation (lines 5 and 6) adds further weight to the argument that this poem, like the *Enterpretació del nom de Maria*, was to be read by an individual rather than performed before an audience.

These two early-fifteenth-century *llaors* belong to a tradition that stretches back through Provençal poetry to early-medieval French Marian lyric and, before that, to popular Latin songs in praise of the Virgin. The inclusion of immaculist material in *Vierge de les viergens* and, to a lesser extent, *Enterpretació del nom de Maria*, illustrates how

popular religious lyric adapted to incorporate the strong support
for the doctrine in the Crown of Aragon, and Barcelona in particular, at the time. However, it is not only the content that reflects
change: the personal tone of these poems and their target audience
— ocular rather than aural — suggest that devotional practices
were increasingly individual rather than collective.

WORKS CITED

BAUCELLS I REIG, Josep, 2003a. 'Disset poesies catalanes medievals de l'Arxiu
de la Catedral de Barcelona (II)', *Teologia Actual*, 51: 45–65.
——, 2003b. 'Disset poesies catalanes medievals de l'Arxiu de la Catedral de
Barcelona (III)', *Teologia Actual*, 52: 33–38.
BAYO, Juan Carlos, 2004. 'Las colecciones universales de milagros de la Virgen
hasta Gonzalo de Berceo', *BSS*, 81: 849–71.
BELTRÁN, Luis, 1984–85. 'Texto verbal y texto pictórico: las cantigas 1 y 10 del
Códice Rico', *Revista Canadiense de Estudios Hispánicos*, 9: 329–43.
BERCEO, Gonzalo de, 1989. *Milagros de Nuestra Señora*, ed. Michael Gerli, Letras
Hispánicas, 224 (Madrid: Cátedra).
BOHIGAS, Pere, ed., 1956. *Miracles de la verge Maria: col·lecció del segle XIV* (Barce-
lona: Biblioteca Catalana d'Obres Antigues).
BROWN, Michelle, 1990. *A Guide to Western Historical Scripts from Antiquity to
1600* (London: British Library).
COROMINES, Joan, 1981. *Diccionari etimològic i complementari de la llengua catala-
na* (Barcelona: Curial & La Caixa).
DOMÍNGUEZ REBOIRAS, Fernando, 1990. 'Els apòcrifs lul·lians sobre la Immacu-
lada: la seva importància en la història del lul·lisme', *Randa*, 27 (*Del frau a
l'erudició: aportacions a la història del lul·lisme dels segles XIV al XVIII*, ed. Lola
Badia): 11–43.
FERNANDES LOPES, Francisco, 1985. *A música das 'Cantigas de Santa Maria' e ou-
tros ensaios* (Olhão: Câmara Municipal de Olhão).
FERNÁNDEZ CONDE, J. ed., 1982. *Historia de la Iglesia en España*, Biblioteca de
Autores Cristianos, Maior, 22, II.2: *La Iglesia en la España de los siglos VIII al XIV*
(Madrid: Editorial Católica).
GAZULLA, Fr. Faustino D., 1905–06. 'Los Reyes de Aragón y la Purísima Con-
cepción de María Santísima', *Boletín de la Real Academia de Buenas Letras de
Barcelona*, 3: 1–18, 49–62, 143–50, 224–32, & 257–64.
GIMENO CASALDUERO, Joaquín, 1975. *Estructura y diseño en la literatura castella-
na medieval* (Madrid: José Porrúa Turanzas).
GRAEF, Hilda, 1963–65. *Mary: A History of Doctrine and Devotion* (New York:
Sheed & Ward).
GROS, Gérard, 2004. *Ave Vierge Marie: étude sur les prières mariales en vers fran-
çais (XIIe–XVe siècles)* (Lyon: Presses Universitaires).
IBARS MATEU, Josefina, & M. Dolores IBARS MATEU, 1991. *Colectánea paleográfica
de la Corona de Aragón: siglos IX–XVIII* (Barcelona: Universitat de Barcelona).

JÄRNSTRÖM, E., & A. LÅNGFORS, ed., 1927. *Recueil de chansons pieuses du XIIIe* *siècle* (Helsinki: Suomalaisen Tiedeakatemian Toimituksia).

LÅNGFORS, Artur, ed., 1906. '*Li Ave Maria en roumans* par Huon le Roi de Cambrai', *Mémoires de la Société Néo-Philologique à Helsingfors*, 4: 319–62.

LEVY, Emil, ed., 1887. *Poésies religieuses provençales et françaises* (Paris: Maisonneuve & Charles Leclerc).

MASSÓ TORRENTS, Jaume, 1914. 'Catàleg dels manuscrits catalans de la Biblioteca Capitular de Barcelona', *Butlletí de la Biblioteca de Barcelona*, 1: 145–53.

——, 1932. *Repertori de l'antiga literatura catalana*, I: *La poesia* (Barcelona: Institut d'Estudis Catalans).

MAYBERRY, Nancy, 1991. 'The Controversy over the Immaculate Conception in Medieval and Renaissance Art, Literature, and Society', *Journal of Medieval and Renaissance Studies*, 21: 207–24.

METTMANN, Walter, ed., 1986–89. *Cantigas de Santa María*, Clásicos Castalia, 134, 172, & 178 (Madrid: Castalia).

MOLAS, Joaquim, & Josep MASSOT I MUNTANER, ed., 1979. *Diccionari de la literatura catalana* (Barcelona: Edicions 62).

OROZ ARIZCUREN, Francisco J., 1972. *La lírica religiosa en la literatura provenzal antigua* (Pamplona: Diputación Foral de Navarra & Institución Príncipe de Viana).

ROCA-PUIG, R., ed., 1965. *Himne a la Verge Maria: papir llatí del segle IV* (Barcelona: Asociación de Bibliófilos de Barcelona).

ROMEU I FIGUERAS, Josep, ed., 2000. *Corpus d'antiga poesia popular*, ENC, B18 (Barcelona: Barcino).

SANTANACH I SUÑOL, Joan, 2005. 'Dos exemples de Ramon Llull inclosos en un recull de miracles', *Randa*, 55 (*Homenatge a Jordi Carbonell*, I, ed. Josep Massot i Muntaner): 7–13.

SPAGGIARI, Barbara, 1977. 'La poesia religiosa anonima catalana o occitanica', *Annali della Scuola Normale Superiore di Pisa (Classe di Lettere e Filosofia)*, 3rd ser., 7: 117–350.

STRATTON, Suzanne L., 1994. *The Immaculate Conception in Spanish Art* (Cambridge: UP).

TWOMEY, Lesley K., 1995. 'The Immaculate Conception in Castilian and Catalan Poetry of the Fifteenth Century: A Comparative Thematic Study', PhD thesis (University of Hull).

VALLS Y TABERNER, F., 1912. 'Manuscrit literari del monestir de St Pere', *Estudis Universitaris Catalans*, 6: 347–50.

Verges molt sa ma nettare li bres sants pren te
E li sacdots qui en lo tiempla eren.
De bos verge qui enten paucsa edat
los dus grahons montar bosi bayeren

Verges en sag dayspolla sylera romana
vay ordonat diser lo canticu gradum
En les maynnes qui a honor de boy
li clerch en capti jorns sa dyson

Verges apries b ays que bos fues en lo tiempla
Vos ets lausada de bra myximent
mes que nulsaltre qui en agiyel hi fos
li sacerdots e tota altre gient

Verges quant fues en edat costituyda
Detriga ays bolents bos dar mayt
Vos respongues que hayyets votat
En siyr dieu tostemps en capt edat

Santillana, Mena, y la coronación de los poetas

FRANCISCO BAUTISTA

(Universidad de Salamanca)

1. Principio

Pocos, al decir de Dante, tanto príncipes como poetas ('o Cesare o poeta'), contemplaban en su tiempo el laurel de Apolo como una adecuada insignia de sus trabajos y sus triunfos (*Paradiso*, I.25-33). Y él, que perseguía tal galardón, sólo llegaría a ser coronado de forma póstuma o alegórica. Había recibido una invitación de la Universidad de Bolonia con la condición de que escribiera algunos versos en latín, pero para entonces Dante no sólo había tomado ya partido por el romance, sino que además el único lugar en el que deseaba recibir la corona era Florencia.[1] Es, sin embargo, la coronación de Petrarca en 1341 el acontecimiento que habría de marcar un hito decisivo para este tipo de ceremonias. Se trata, como escribió Ernest H. Wilkins, del episodio más espectacular en la vida del poeta, y también de uno de los homenajes más sonados que se tributaron a la poesía (1943: 155). Petrarca, que preparó cuidadosamente el evento y lo glosó con profusión en su obra, le dio también un significado trascendental, desconocido de la tradición anterior, que le ofreció, en cualquier caso, el esquema básico de su desarrollo. La coronación constituyó el símbolo de su proyecto de recuperación de la antigüedad clásica, y el discurso pronunciado en tal ocasión ha sido considerado a menudo, según había diseñado el propio autor, como la inauguración de un nuevo periodo cultural y como un manifiesto para la misma (Trapp 1958: 239). La

---

[1] Sobre la coronación de Dante, véase Ernest H. Wilkins 1943: 164-65, y para el motivo de la coronación de los poetas, Trapp 1958 (sobre Dante, pp. 237-38). En *Paradiso*, XXIV, san Pedro somete al poeta a un riguroso examen sobre la fe, tras el que recibe su bendición. Tal pasaje está modelado, como la ceremonia de coronación en Italia, sobre las pruebas universitarias para la obtención del grado de doctor (Wilkins 1943: 164; Wenzel 1995). Para las coronaciones imperiales de los poetas, véase ahora el exhaustivo trabajo de John L. Flood 2006 (referencia que debo a Barry Taylor).

From the 'Cancioneiro da Vaticana' to the 'Cancionero general': Studies in Honour of Jane Whetnall, ed. Alan Deyermond & Barry Taylor, PMHRS, 60 (London: Department of Hispanic Studies, Queen Mary, University of London, 2007), pp. 55-74. ISSN 1460-051X. ISBN 0 902238 50 7.

fama de Petrarca pareció ligada insistentemente a este episodio, y la corona de laurel se convirtió en una imagen casi automática para referirse a la excelencia de los poetas, pero ninguna coronación, ni como ceremonia real ni como construcción alegórica, alcanzó la densidad y el significado de la de aquel momento. No parece que en Castilla llegaran a tener lugar ceremonias reales de este tipo, aunque el *topos* dio pie a dos textos bastante significativos, y también a una fugaz polémica, asuntos que no han sido aún conside-considerados en conjunto. Mi propósito es, pues, explorar las tradiciones que se dan cita en tales textos, sus significados, y el sentido que arroja la evolución general en torno a este motivo.

2. Corona y memoria

Los primeros usos y alusiones de Petrarca en la Península Ibérica se documentan, como es bien sabido, en el reino de Aragón, y en ellos su nombre aparece ya unido indisociablemente a su condición de poeta laureado. Hacia 1386, Pere Des-Pont le explica a su maestro, interesado por el particular, que Petrarca fue 'digne laureatus poeta et maximam habet reputacionem', y un formulario de la época escrito por un notario catalán se refiere también a 'magistro Patrarca [sic] poeta laureato'. Francisco Rico, que ha estudiado ejemplarmente éstas y otras alusiones (2002: 157 & 168), ha observado cómo el autor que se revela en ellas sirvió como semillero de citas y florilegios, pero apenas como el modelo cultural que se propuso para una percepción distinta del pasado. Lo mismo que sucederá en Castilla hasta bien entrado el siglo XV (Deyermond 1992). Es más, a la hora de comprender o de recrear la coronación de Petrarca no parecen haberse tenido en cuenta sus premisas ni conocido sus detalles, puesto que las noticias no van mucho más allá de la mención estereotipada del laurel y la corona, de manera que tal momento se diría contemplado a la luz de unos ceremoniales y unos presupuestos que le eran completamente ajenos. El 20 de febrero de 1393, Juan I de Aragón (1387–96), acogiendo favorablemente una propuesta de Jaume March y Lluís d'Averçó, decretó que se celebrara cada año en Barcelona un concurso dedicado a los creadores de poesía trovadoresca, a imagen del que venía teniendo lugar en Toulouse desde 1324.[2] El documento regio elogia el amor

---

[2] Para el Consistori tolosano, véase ahora Valerie M. Wilhite 2005; y para su implantación en Cataluña, Giuseppe Tavani 1996; ambos trabajos ofrecen además amplias indicaciones bibliográficas.

como la esencia de la poesía, y establece la pertinencia de su cultivo, para lo que se establece el concurso, que sería dirimido por
aquellos que lo habían solicitado.[3] La creación del Consistori, en el
que como en el de Toulouse se premiaban con una violeta las mejores composiciones sobre un tema previamente establecido, tuvo
unos comienzos difíciles, y poco después las fiestas, según escribe
Enrique de Villena en su *Arte de trovar* (c. 1430), se interrumpieron
a la muerte de Martín el Humano (1396–1410). Fue merced al propio Villena, que nos ha dejado en la obra mencionada una
privilegiada historia y descripción del Consistori, como se recupe-
raron las actividades en 1413, en el marco de un reinado, el de
Fernando I, al que interesaba resaltar la continuidad con el periodo
anterior.

Pero la restitución del Consistori tuvo mucho también de rein-
vención. Ya no se trataría de reuniones anuales, sino de tantas
como fueran oportunas; y no sólo se entregaría una violeta al trovador, sino que la obra en cuestión habría también de ser
coronada: 'E aquella [la obra premiada] ya la traía el escrivano del
consistorio en pergamino bien illuminada e ençima puesta la corona de oro' (Cátedra 1994–2000: I, 358).[4] Hay en esta duplicación del
trofeo, muy probablemente, un indicio de la creciente presión ejer-
cida por la corona de Petrarca y un indicio también de que ambos
acontecimientos se contemplaban como algo indistinto. Es lo que
sucede no mucho después con la traducción castellana y la exposición del soneto 116 de Petrarca, entendido como la expresión del
deseo del autor de 'optener la poesía e ser en aquélla laureado'
(Cátedra 1994–2000: I, 374).[5] El comentarista, al imaginar las circunstancias del soneto ('la istoria'), reproduce una situación muy
similar a las del Consistori: propuesto un tema ('diziendo cada uno

---

[3] El texto puede leerse en Roger Boase 1981: 125–27. Su autor, Bartolomeo Sirvent,
es justamente el destinatario de la carta de Pere Des-Pont mencionada anterior-
mente. Véase un breve análisis de éste y de otros documentos que mencionaré a
continuación en Josep Pujol 1994: 74–82.

[4] A la corona ('laudis corona') se refiere también el documento de Fernando I, del
17 de marzo de 1413, por el que se reestablece el Consistori (Boase 1981: 139). Para
sus actividades en este momento, véase también Pujol 1996, donde se editan los
sermones de Felip de Malla sobre la gaya ciencia pronunciados a lo largo de ese
año durante las ceremonias.

[5] La traducción y comentario parecen efectuados hacia 1428, muy probablemente por
el propio Enrique de Villena, como ya defendió Derek C. Carr 1980–81, el primer
editor del texto. Ha sido objeto de un excelente estudio a cargo de Julian Weiss 1991,
cuyos datos y argumentos recoge puntualmente Joaquín Rubio Tovar 2005.

lo que más deseava de las feliçidades temporales'), se producen varias respuestas ('unos nombravan riquezas, otros honras, otros victoria de enemigos, otros cumplimiento de amores, e así cada uno segúnd sus appetitos e affecçiones'), hasta que finalmente 'miçer Françisco' se aparta del resto y escribe su soneto, en el que coloca la poesía como su aspiración suprema, que fue elogiado por todos; entonces 'mostráronlo al rey dicho e con plazer que d'él ovo, mandólo escrevir en el registro de sus obras' (379).[6] Si la escena inventada se desarrolla aquí en la 'cámara del rey', cabe recordar también que el Consistori había acabado siendo una iniciativa fundamentalmente regia, y que en la descripción de Villena el rey ocupa (o había de ocupar) un lugar primordial en las ceremonias. Corrobora la sintonía entre el comentario y las prácticas del colegio barcelonés el que en uno y otro caso el destino de la obra premiada sea el mismo, pues según el *Arte de trovar*, 'la obra coronada [...] era asentada en el registro del consistorio, dando authoridat e liçençia para que se pudiese cantar e en público dezir' (358). Eso es lo que quiere significar el comentario al perseguir el destino del soneto, donde se muestra abiertamente de qué manera los versos de Petrarca tratan de acomodarse aquí a las experiencias y los usos recreados en el propio *Arte* de Villena.

No hay constancia de que algo similar al Consistori tuviera lugar en Castilla. Sin embargo, cabe la posibilidad de que en la confección de ese registro poético que es el *Cancionero de Baena* hayan influido algunas de las ideas relacionadas con ese ambiente. El compilador, Juan Alfonso de Baena, que usa el término de 'gaya ciencia' para referirse a la poesía, parece familiarizado de alguna forma con los textos ligados al Consistori tolosano, como las *Leys d'amors*, que tuvieron una importante difusión en el reino de Aragón, pues su prólogo evidencia ciertas sintonías en cuanto a su función y sus cometidos.[7] En ambos casos, la poesía va encaminada a dar placer y distracción, en especial a aquellos ocupados en altos

---

[6] Es esta anécdota la que parece estar detrás de la referencia que Santillana hace de Petrarca en su *Prohemio e carta* (Gómez Moreno 1990: 56), en donde además se sitúa al italiano en la transición de los antiguos a los modernos, índice de la relevancia, al menos simbólica, que el autor le concedía. Para el petrarquismo de Santillana, véase Jane Whetnall 2000: 65-68 y 2006: 82-89.

[7] Para el prólogo, véase Weiss 1990: 25-54, que recoge y discute la bibliografía anterior. También Mark D. Johnston 1996, que destaca la presentación de la poesía como una práctica cortesana, y Vicenç Beltran 2001, para las características de la compilación.

trabajos, al tiempo que se dota a ésta de un significado moral.[8] Pero en el *Cancionero* no nos encontramos ante un 'arte', sino ante un verdadero registro; no pretende ser doctrina poética (de ahí que no figuren indicaciones al propósito) sino sobre todo objeto de lectura, de utilización cortesana, como en la descripción del registro del Consistori que ofrece Villena: 'dando authoridat e liçençia para que se pudiese cantar e en público dezir'. Es quizá por eso también, por su vinculación al pasado, a la memoria poética, por lo que Baena se sirve en el prólogo del paradigma de la historia, que se sitúa igualmente entre los divertimentos de la corte pero que tiene además un inmediato e insoslayable sentido moral.[9] Junto a ello, Baena parece inspirarse en prácticas análogas a las del Consistori cuando se refiere a Alfonso Álvarez de Villasandino, en la rúbrica que presenta sus obras, como 'esmalte e luz e espejo e corona e monarca de todos los poetas e trobadores que fasta oy fueron en toda España' (Dutton & González Cuenca 1993: 11; ID 1147). Manuel Alvar se ha referido al propio *Cancionero* como un consistorio poético (1989: 4 & 13), y Mark D. Johnston ha señalado que Baena establece una ecuación por la que iguala la poesía de Villasandino con la perfección en la gaya ciencia, de forma que la jerarquía establecida aquí respondería implícitamente a la de los concursos descritos por Villena (1998: 247). La corona, como signo de la excelencia poética, se sitúa como principio estructurador del *Cancionero*, y junto a ello permite también prestigiar una tradición a la que se debe el propio compilador. Se ha desplazado la idea de la corona del mero ceremonial de una fiesta cortesana al eje de la historia, de la tradición, en donde la operación sirve asimismo para validar una corriente estética, para contextualizar la propia opción de Baena, y para dejar a un lado, en una discreta segunda fila, otras variantes.

---

[8] No se han enfrentado detenidamente aún los textos de las *Leys* con el prólogo de Baena (compárese, para lo que menciono aquí, Gatien-Arnoult 1841–43: I, 8–10; también Anglade 1919–20: I, 7–9). Se refiere su autor a estas obras en el *Dezir de don Juan II* (Dutton & González Cuenca 1993: 743; ID 0285), y cabe la posibilidad de que haya tenido conocimiento de las prácticas descritas en el *Arte de trovar* (por más que Baena parezca haber estado enfrentado a Villena) y quizá de algunos de los documentos relacionados con el Consistori barcelonés. Se trataría en cualquier caso de un bagaje sobre todo del compilador, más que del propio *Cancionero*.

[9] No tanto, como señala Beltran 2001: 16–17, porque el *Cancionero* recoja un legado que pertenece exclusivamente al pasado (lo que lo reduciría a mera antigüedad ya en su momento), sino porque construye un discurso sobre la tradición, y con él una genealogía del presente.

Que así fue al menos entendido desde muy pronto se hace evidente en el *Prohemio e carta* del Marqués de Santillana, que pretende tejer una historia distinta para la poesía castellana, y en donde el autor, sin mencionarlo abiertamente, parece discutir el dictamen de Baena, a quien por otra parte no menciona en absoluto. En efecto, tras referirse a Villasandino en términos elogiosos, pero considerándolo siempre como un trovador, escribe:

> E así por esto, com(m)o por ser tanto conosçidas e esparzidas a todas p(ar)tes sus obr(a)s, passaremos a miçer Françisco Inperial, al q(ua)l yo no llamaría dezidor o trobador mas poeta, com(m)o sea çierto q(ue), sy alguno en estas p(ar)tes del occaso meresçió premio de aquella triunphal e láurea guirnalda, loando a todos los otros, éste fue. (Gómez Moreno 1990: 63)

La corona se ha convertido ya en una imagen perfectamente reconocible dentro de la historia literaria y del canon poético.[10] Y es, de nuevo, un expediente que señala la excelencia de una corriente, en este caso de la tradición italianizante iniciada por Imperial, al establecer al primero de sus representantes como el mayor de los poetas, como aquel que ha alcanzado en general las mayores cotas dentro del cultivo de la poesía en Castilla. Este uso del motivo de la corona, que reaparecerá en otros textos, revela una tensión por establecer una imagen de la poesía castellana y por fijar unos términos que a su vez figuraran como criterios de excelencia para valorar la nueva poesía, con lo que tanto Baena como Santillana trataban de asegurarse una posición de privilegio merced a su inserción dentro de una tradición ya por ellos prestigiada. Se trata, en buena medida, de una pugna por el establecimiento de una tradición reinventada desde el presente, como era de esperar en un contexto de cambio y en un momento en el que entre las diversas opciones ninguna ha obtenido todavía una sanción más o menos definitiva. Pero tal pugna tenía también un sesgo sin duda excluyente, pese a todos sus paliativos, por lo que acabó generando polémicas como las protagonizadas por estos dos autores.[11]

---

[10] Que se liga a su vez a la caracterización de Imperial como poeta en lugar de trovador, distinción muy significativa para Santillana (Gómez Moreno 1990: 142–44). Justamente por ello Santillana designa como poeta también a Jordi de Sant Jordi en su *Coronación*, que comento más abajo.

[11] Santillana, vale la pena recordarlo, no figura en el *Cancionero de Baena*, y aunque ello pueda ser debido a su edad en el momento en que se compiló la colección y a las propias características de ésta, que no concede espacio a las nuevas corrientes poéticas de hacia 1425–30 (no aparece, por ejemplo, Álvaro de Luna; véase Beltran 2001: 16–17, y arriba, n9), la posición literaria de Baena no dejaba por ello de representar

3. El laurel de Venus

Implicaciones muy similares había tenido ya la *Coronación de Jordi de Sant Jordi* del propio Santillana, compuesta después de la muerte del poeta catalán, sucedida en 1424.[12] Para su autor la corona se había convertido en una imagen recurrente de la excelencia literaria, a raíz de los textos que le suministraba Villena y de la prestigiosa memoria de Petrarca: así, al margen del *Prohemio* y del texto construido sobre este motivo, nombra también la corona de laurel en la *Defunsión de don Enrique de Villena* (vv. 147–48) y en la *Comedieta de Ponça*: 'e non se ignorava la su perfecçión [dice a propósito de Boccaccio] / ca de verde lauro era coronado' (vv. 75–76; también v. 224). La *Coronación*, que alude a Dante (v. 13) y a la *Eneida* (v. 32), está elaborada justamente a partir de recuerdos de la *Commedia* y del texto virgiliano. Se basa en la primera para la descripción del amanecer (vv. 1–16; *Purgatorio*, IX.1–18), para la escena final de los poetas (vv. 185–92; *Infierno*, IV.100–05) y quizá también para la descripción del *locus amoenus* (vv. 17–24; *Purgatorio*, VII.70–81 & XXVIII), y en general para el marco del sueño.[13] De la *Eneida*, que Santillana usa a partir de la traducción y glosas de Villena, como ha demostrado Pedro M. Cátedra (1996: 155–59), procede la descripción del cortejo de Venus (vv. 25–40). Por lo demás, para la propia escena de la coronación, Santillana podría haberse apoyado libremente en la exposición sobre el soneto 116 de Petrarca ya mencionada, que formó, recogida en el mismo códice que la *Commedia*, parte de su biblioteca, y también en las prácticas del Consistori, quizá nuevamente a través de la descripción que le proporcionaba el *Arte de trovar* y que Villena había redactado por encargo suyo. Con todos estos materiales, ni siquiera sería necesario suponer el conocimiento de la *Amorosa visione* de Boccaccio, propuesto por Chandler R. Post (1915: 60), y que presenta no pocas diferencias con

---

una opción muy distinta a la suya. Sin embargo, la situación es otra cuando escribe el *Prohemio*, pues para entonces sus palabras certifican un cambio de rumbo que no había hecho sino afianzarse desde la compilación de Baena.

[12] Cito el texto por la edición de Ángel Gómez Moreno & Maximilian P. A. M. Kerkhof 1988: 101–08. Por las fuentes que maneja debió escribirse después de 1430, aproximadamente. Si se acepta el modelo que propongo más abajo, el texto habría de ser aún algo posterior a esa fecha, en torno a 1434.

[13] El primer paralelo fue señalado por Lapesa 1957: 110, y el segundo lo ha sido por Riquer & Badia 1984: 57. El uso de la *Commedia* se haría a partir del códice que contiene la traducción llevada a cabo por Villena junto a la copia del original italiano (véase Cátedra 1994–2000: III, xi-xiii).

el nuestro.[14] Así las cosas, más que un tributo a Virgilio (Cátedra 1996: 156), e incluso más que una exaltación de Jordi de Sant Jordi, el poema se diría un secreto y exhaustivo homenaje a las labores de Villena, pues casi todos los ingredientes que lo constituyen habían salido de su escritorio.

Se trata de un texto que, en opinión de Rafael Lapesa, posee 'el encanto de la facilidad', en el que 'los versos fluyen con soltura' (1957: 109), y en el que la simplicidad de la escena compensa con creces el leve artificio del lenguaje. La imagen más sorprendente, la de la aparición de Venus en una torre a lomos de un elefante, parece ser una invención del poeta, que funde dos motivos bien comunes en la época merced a la llegada de la diosa desde Oriente: el de la torre sobre la que asoma una dueña, frecuente por ejemplo en la representación de los Castillos de Amor (Loomis 1919), y el del elefante que porta un castillo, abundante en todos los textos e imágenes ligados a las maravillas del Este (Heckscher 1947: 158–68).[15] Tras esta imagen, el poeta contempla la fiesta de la diosa y su cortejo; a continuación alcanza a ver a tres varones de 'grand estado' (v. 92) y a un caballero, que se encaminan hacia Venus. Les pregunta ésta a dónde se dirigen, y uno de los tres hombres, tras elogiarla, le dice que desean solicitarle 'la corona / de los prudentes letrados' (vv. 159–60) para el cuarto: 'Mossén Jorde'. Venus se la concede, y ellos, Homero, Virgilio y Lucano, se lo 'dan por sirviente' (v. 176). El hecho de que sea la misma Venus quien ha de otorgar la corona al poeta implica que los versos de éste la han tenido por 'materia' (v. 150), pero el elogio de la diosa (vv. 137–52) podría conectarse en particular con las sesiones del Consistori, en las que, según explica el *Arte de trovar*, 'levantávase el maestro en theología, que era uno de los mantenedores, e fazía una presuposiçión con su thema y sus alegaçiones e loores de la gaya sciençia e de aquella materia que se avía de tratar en aquel consistorio' (Cátedra 1994–2000: I, 357). Así, la coronación elaborada por Santillana es de nuevo expresión y muestra de la combinación de dos tradiciones, la del Consistori, representada por la descripción y por el motivo mismo de la obra, y la italianizante, que proporciona el

[14] Como ya indicó Lapesa 1957: 109–10; véase, en cambio, un posible, aunque muy débil, paralelo con esta obra señalado recientemente por Miguel Ángel Pérez Priego 2001: 487.

[15] Lapesa 1962 propuso que podría haberse basado ya en una figuración similar previa, pero hasta donde sé no se ha documentado ninguna análoga en la Edad Media.

marco alegórico y un nutrido número de referencias, combinación que se había dado ya antes con Enrique de Villena y aun con el mismo Jordi de Sant Jordi. No deja de ser significativo, a este respecto, que los poemas suyos recordados por Santillana en el *Prohemio*, la *Cançó d'opòsits* y la *Passio amoris*, traduzcan precisamente esta misma mezcla: la primera evidencia el influjo de Petrarca y la segunda es una construcción alegórica mediante la que se van engarzando citas poéticas de otros trovadores.[16]

Chandler R. Post defendió que la obra se basaba finalmente además en el motivo de la Corte de Amor: 'In its essence the composition is plainly connected with the Court of Love' (1915: 58). A pesar de que Post no tenía en cuenta la experiencia del Consistori, el paralelo no debería menospreciarse. Más aún si reparamos en que Santillana participó en abril de 1434 en una justa organizada por Álvaro de Luna y relacionada justamente con las Cortes de Amor: dos compañías de caballeros se combatirían bajo ciertas disposiciones, y tres jueces, que habrían de representar al 'dios de Amor', dictarían sentencia sobre los mejores de entre ellos. Uno de aquellos jueces no fue otro que 'Íñigo López de Mendoça, señor de Fita' (Carriazo 1946: 154). La presencia del Dios de Amor, 'asentado por tribunal en la nuestra alta sylla de justiçia', pudo inspirar la descripción de la silla de Venus en el poema (vv. 74–88), desde la que la diosa concede la corona al poeta. Asimismo, la súplica de Homero y los suyos ('suplican a tu persona', v. 158) podría emparentarse con las súplicas de Amor al final de su sentencia, donde pide a las dueñas 'rremuneraçión y galardón' para sus justadores: 'Lo qual afectuosamente, como dicho es, suplicamos' (160). Es más, el hecho de que los poetas entreguen a Jordi de Sant Jordi como siervo de la diosa al final del poema se corresponde con un motivo común en este tipo de fiestas caballerescas. Sea como fuere, el poema combina elementos poéticos y cortesanos muy concretos, con la intención de promocionar un tipo de poesía en la corte, allí justamente donde la tradición que representa el poema de Santillana no parecía haber tenido la mejor fortuna hasta estos mismos momentos. Es, de esa forma, también una apología, que anuncia la implantación de unos usos y unos gustos que irán dejando atrás paulatinamente las opciones más características del *Cancionero de Baena*.

[16] Sobre estas referencias, véase también Lluís Cabré 1998: 30–33.

4. *Insignia Apollinis*

En un sugerente ensayo, Ernst H. Kantorowicz (1965) mostró cómo a fines de la Edad Media, hacia 1400, se desarrolla la representación de Apolo portando al mismo tiempo el arco y la lira, limitando así sus insignias y centrándolas en una expresión de la ideal concordia entre las armas y las letras. No se trataría ya de sugerir los diversos poderes del dios, ni las varias facetas de sus actuaciones, sino la tensión dialéctica entre la sabiduría y el gobierno, el libro y la espada, cuya conjunción se convierte en la esencia y en la personificación de la virtud. No sabemos si Juan de Mena llegó a tener noticia de alguna de estas representaciones, porque lo cierto es que en su *Coronación del marqués de Santillana* el dios Apolo figura fundamentalmente como una imagen del conocimiento y de las artes (117), pero no todavía de la 'militar diçiplina', que se relaciona con Hércules (108).[17] Sin embargo, el texto en conjunto es en realidad un buen representante de la ética apolínea descrita por Kantorowicz, que se resuelve aquí en una encendida alabanza de la combinación del conocimiento y del poder. El propio Santillana había defendido esta concepción en el prólogo a sus *Proverbios*, donde critica a aquellos que desprecian el cultivo del saber en los hombres de armas y refiere con orgullo la opinión de un amigo, según el cual 'la sçiencia non enbota el fierro de la lança, nin faze floxa la espada en la mano del cavallero' (Gómez Moreno & Kerkhof: 218–19). No parece casualidad que el propio Santillana precise a propósito de Jordi de Sant Jordi en su *Coronación* que se trata de un caballero (v. 97), sugiriendo ya allí un elogio del ejercicio simultáneo de las armas y las letras. Da la impresión de que este motivo acompañó a Santillana, así, a lo largo de toda su carrera, por lo que hubo de sentirse particularmente halagado cuando Mena escribe este elogio en el que le ofrece una corona compuesta de laurel y de roble, para celebrar su excelencia en el saber y en la guerra.[18]

Ahora bien, en el texto de Mena la poesía queda, referida a Santillana, solamente como un telón de fondo, mientras que por su propia forma, fundamentada en el autocomentario, la *Coronación*

---

[17] Cito la *Coronación* a partir de la edición de Miguel Ángel Pérez Priego 1989, indicando sólamente la página. Para las fuentes del poema, véase Pilar Berrio Martín-Retortillo 1996, con la bibliografía allí mencionada.

[18] Sobre el motivo de las armas y las letras en la Castilla del siglo XV, es esencial todavía el estudio de Peter E. Russell 1978; véase también, entre otros trabajos, la bibliografía mencionada en Weiss 1990: 12–13n27.

viene a constituir una alabanza refleja de Mena como poeta, según él mismo indica en su prólogo: 'a sí mismo glorifica e da gloria el que alaba al alabado' (106; véase Weiss 1990: 142). Como señaló Post (1912: 260), la poesía no es importante aquí desde un punto de vista temático (lo es, como digo, desde el punto de vista estructural a través del comentario), y Santillana es coronado no como un servidor de Venus, según lo había sido Jordi de Sant Jordi, sino como un ejemplo de sabiduría versátil. Mena pudo haberse inspirado en la coronación de Fernando I para hacer de las cuatro Virtudes las damas que coronan a Santillana (como señaló también Post 1912: 261), pero la escena en cualquier caso resulta indesligable de su proyecto, y esencial para entender su significado.[19] El poeta que se elogia aquí es sobre todo el autor de los *Proverbios*, y no resulta casual que sea precisamente Salomón el primero de los escritores que comparecen en el Parnaso (copla 26): 'en esta parte pone la copla una de las obras que Salamón fizo [los *Proverbios*], por dar a entender que dizía por Salamón e por glorificar la su sabiduría faziendo mención de la su obra' (187). Es más, si la de Santillana es una corona de laurel y de roble, la ocasión del poema, el hecho que está en su origen, la conquista de Huelma, se liga solamente a la faceta militar, y en gran medida como subordinada a ella parece figurar la literatura; no, por tanto, como algo digno de elogio en sí mismo, sino en su dimensión práctica, en cuanto que favorece o se ve avalada por el ejercicio de las armas. Podría tal vez deducirse de aquí una especie de cicatería de Mena, que trata de regatearle al homenajeado sus valores literarios, pero nada estaría más lejos de la realidad. Se trata sin duda de una construcción apologética, deudora de la autopresentación que Santillana propone, justamente, en los *Proverbios*, y hay que contemplarla como una defensa de las actividades literarias del magnate, que se habrían visto brillantemente confirmadas en su victoria contra los moros. La imagen de Santillana en la *Coronación* es una respuesta más a los que podrían haber criticado sus aficiones literarias (la alusión a posibles críticos es abundante en el poema), y tal defensa determina la construcción de su imagen. Determina, por ello, también la imagen de la poesía, que se agota en el conocimiento, en su relación directa con la virtud, en la vertiente, en suma, que representan en particular los *Proverbios*.

---

[19] Para la coronación de Fernando I, véase Roser Salicrú i Lluch 1995; el texto sobre la representación alegórica en la que intervienen los pecados y las virtudes puede leerse en Pérez Priego 1997: 240–46.

Si, de acuerdo con Post (1912: 264), el propósito del poema es, efectivamente, mostrar la excelencia en la virtud, no en la poesía, lo cierto es que este desplazamiento del elogio tiene no sólo un contexto personal (esas supuestas críticas a Santillana), sino también un marco cultural y un significado político. Santillana se con- convierte en el perfecto cortesano, y en un modelo para los nobles de su tiempo, 'que por Íñigo López podemos entender qualquier omne virtuoso' (204). Representa, así pues, la quintaesencia de la 'política vida, que es puerta de buenas costunbres, [y] se contorna e rebuelve e rige por estas quatro virtudes, las quales dan corona de gloriosa fama a qualquier omne virtuoso' (203). Precisamente esta alusión permite conciliar las interpretaciones política y moral del poema, que han propuesto Inez Macdonald (1939) y Julian Weiss (1981–82), respectivamente.[20] Como ha demostrado Jeremy Lawran- ce (2000: 9–12) a partir de un rastreo por los textos de este momento, la 'vida política' se entiende en ellos siempre como una categoría subor-dinada a la ética. Escribe, por ejemplo, Alfonso de la Torre:

> La terçera manera de vida es segund qu'el omne es omne; e segunt aquésta le conviene usar e comunicar con los otros omnes, e le convienen las virtu- des morales para ordenar a sý mesmo e a su casa e para ordenar el estado que ha de tener en el lugar do vive. E aquesta tal vida es llamada vida polí- tica. (García López 1991: I, 249)

De la misma forma, en la *Coronación* las virtudes explican y corro- boran retrospectivamente el éxito militar de Santillana, y con ello lo que su figura y tal victoria representan: en primer lugar, la búsqueda de la sabiduría, a través de la unión de armas y letras, y en segundo lugar la búsqueda del bien común y la defensa de unos intereses generales, cifrados por el poema en la conquista de Huelma. Macdonald (1939: 131–34) incidió sagazmente en el hecho de que el paso de Mena por el infierno mostraba casi exclusiva- mente ejemplos de vicios políticos, en la medida en que mencionaban cómo ciertos reyes y grandes hombres habían ante- puesto sus propios intereses a los de su tierra, olvidando sus responsabilidades y abandonándose al lujo, la pereza o la avaricia. Santillana, en cambio, antes que trabajar para sí, lo ha hecho por su rey, por su tierra y por su fe:

[20] Quizá Macdonald limita demasiado el texto al entenderlo fundamentalmente como una apología de la Reconquista (1939: 130), pero está lejos de ser también, en mi opinión, sólo una alegoría sobre la vida moral del hombre (Weiss 1981–82: 137).

trabajando de día e velando de noche por acresçentar el serviçio de Dios e del su rey e señor, e por ensanchar los sus reinos e poner allende los padrones de sus límites [...] e parando preçiosas margaritas al regio çetro e española corona. (197)

El contraste entre Santillana y los condenados en el infierno no puede ser mayor, y es dicho contraste, moral y político a un tiempo, el que Mena construye cuidadosamente en el poema. Pues el infierno es el lugar de la noche y la 'ignorança nephanda' (116-19), y la sabiduría, según el poeta, la clave que permite apartarse del vicio y alcanzar la virtud. Es por ello, finalmente, por lo que tal sabiduría se presenta también como una categoría ética y política, que debe dejar a un lado las señas menos prácticas o útiles de la poesía.

Pero el contexto en el que se escribió la *Coronación* daba al texto también un significado inmediatamente político, no ya desde un punto de vista ideal o teórico, sino en el marco de los conflictos que se producen en Castilla justo en el momento de la victoria de Santillana. Es elocuente, en este sentido, el relato de la *Crónica de Juan II*: en el año 1438, tras narrar la conquista de Huelma, se refiere inmediatamente la fuga de Pero Manrique, que acabaría desembocando en una revuelta de buena parte de la nobleza, resuelta sólo años después con la batalla de Olmedo en 1445 (Rosell 1877: 547-49).[21] Situado, como escribe Juan de Mena, 'en la frontera de los infieles moros guerreador e capitán de los obispados de Córdova e Jahén e sus términos por mandado del serenísimo e muy alto e esclaresçido rey e señor don Juan de Castilla e de León' (197), la figura de Santillana se coloca en el polo opuesto de quienes se vuelven en Castilla contra la autoridad de su rey.[22] En este sentido, las alusiones en el poema a la virtud y a la fama expresan la ideología contra la que esos nobles se habrían rebelado, al no aceptar que la primera fuera una aspiración en sí misma, y la segunda una apropiada recompensa de su fidelidad al rey y su sometimiento al bien común.[23] El monumento a la fama en el que se resuelve el poema, que se abre y se cierra con sendas invocaciones a

[21] Para el contexto histórico y político del poema, me permito remitir a Francisco Bautista 2005: 122-23, con bibliografía.

[22] La *Coronación* prepara así el terreno para un poema abiertamente político como el *Laberinto de Fortuna*, sobre el que debe verse en este sentido el trabajo de Alan Deyermond 1983.

[23] El estudio de María Rosa Lida de Malkiel 1952 ilustra bien las diversas actitudes de los hombres del siglo XV hacia la fama (en concreto, para Juan de Mena, pp. 278-90), aunque habría que insistir quizá en las connotaciones políticas de este motivo.

esta diosa (106 & 204-06), pretende quizá servir como una defensa indirecta también de la recientemente amenazada posición regia y de los contenidos de óptima política que conformarían su relación con la nobleza y con el resto de los naturales del reino. Así, mediante la coronación de Santillana el poema construye una vasta alegoría que pretende mostrar cómo la defensa del rey y del reino define la virtud política y constituye la causa y el contenido de la fama. Es posible que sea desde esta perspectiva también como haya que entender las alusiones de Mena a las posibles críticas de su poema, que vendrían de aquellos nobles decididos a rechazar esa relación y esa ideología. En todo caso, la composición de Mena nos aleja ahora de las implicaciones específicamente literarias que habían tenido los textos anteriores sobre la coronación de los poetas. La corona pertenece aquí al dominio de la fama, de la virtud política, y éste al de una ética para los nobles que se cifraría en su sometimiento a la autoridad del rey y su persecución de unos intereses generales. Sólo el texto, en cuanto tal, con sus pretensiones abiertamente canónicas y su extenso comentario, se erige en sí mismo ya como emblema de la excelencia poética.

5. Polémica y olvido

Por lo demás, la *Coronación* se liga con una serie de referencias y textos en torno a la aspiración intelectual como un componente necesario para la nobleza (Weiss 1990: 158-64) y a la virtud como el ideario de ésta. Tales ideas, y en especial la de una relación causal entre virtud y nobleza, tienen entre 1430 y 1440 a Álvaro de Luna como uno de sus principales defensores y promotores, dentro de una política que pretende reducir la influencia de ciertos magnates y favorecer la ascensión de individuos afectos a su persona, y frente a ellas se alza hacia 1440 una obra como la *Cadira de honor* de Juan Rodríguez del Padrón.[24] Discute el autor varias formas de nobleza, dentro de las cuales su atención principal se dirige a la nobleza política, pero al repasar brevemente la nobleza moral, a la que trata de presentar como un sinónimo de la 'virtud moral' (Hernández Alonso 1983: 266), se refiere con cierto pormenor a la coronación de los poetas, lo que indicaría que el autor entiende este tipo de nobleza como una cualidad intelectual.[25] De la misma

---

[24] He discutido las ideas y los textos en los que se desarrolla la polémica al respecto por estos años en Bautista 2005.

[25] Puede que la consideración de las coronaciones en el contexto de la nobleza moral permita entrever un pretendido uso de la poesía como expediente, al menos

manera que un caballero, escribe, aunque haya llevado a cabo hechos portentosos, no puede disfrutar de los privilegios de la caballería 'fasta que por algund otro que pueda la orden resçiba' (267), los poetas sólo pueden recibir la corona de manos del príncipe:

> E así de un poeta, aunque a Omero e a Publio Maro pase en eloquençia, non traerá la aureola fasta que por el príncipe a quien pertenesçe dar el laurel o yedra, segund fueron los antiguos, e Petrarca en nuestra (h)edat, sea laureado. Onde no poco ofenden la magestad del príncipe algunos poetas vulgares, que de su propia abtoridad a otros coronan. E por verdad dezir, solo temor de errar por modo semejable, retraer me fizo de laurear, segund mi propósito era, al varón constante, generoso, bien enseñado Maçías, de loable e piadosa recordaçión; ningund otro seyendo en nuestros días meresçer las frondas de Danne. E no menos de un estudiante que las divinas e humanas leyes, las mathemáticas e naturales çiencias tenga en la memoria, se pueda exenplificar; el qual non es doctor fasta que devida mente de aquel que puede el grado resçiba. (267-68)

La cita es interesante por varios motivos. Primero, porque Rodríguez del Padrón parece estar mucho mejor informado que sus contemporáneos acerca de las ceremonias de coronación, ya que indica la intervención del príncipe, la presencia del laurel y de la hiedra, y la analogía con las graduaciones universitarias.[26] La crítica tiene, en principio, un contenido directamente literario: no sólo se refiere con cierto desdén a los 'poetas vulgares' (probablemente Santillana y Mena), sino que también propone una genealogía distinta para la poesía castellana, en cuyo centro habría de colocarse la figura de Macías. Volvemos aquí, entonces, a una reflexión sobre la tradición literaria, y al uso de la imagen de la corona como un instrumento destacado dentro de tal discurso.[27]

Pero hay asimismo en las palabras de Rodríguez del Padrón, y en su negativa a valerse de este motivo, una sutil ironía literaria ('aunque a Omero e a Publio Maro pase en eloquençia'), y también una calculada ironía política, al indicar que los 'poetas vulgares' habrían dañado la autoridad del príncipe con sus coronaciones, pues es sólo éste quien puede entregar la corona. Ahora bien, ni las

---

simbólico, de ennoblecimiento, aunque en todo caso se trata de una nobleza secundaria dentro de la discusión de la *Cadira*. Sobre las ideas en torno a la nobleza intelectual en la Edad Media, véase ahora Andrea A. Robiglio 2006, con abundante bibliografía.

[26] Sobre este último asunto, véase Trapp 1958: 242 & nn59-60, y arriba n1.

[27] Este uso responde al hecho por los poetas anteriores en el mismo sentido, aunque Rodríguez del Padrón se desmarca de esta corriente al declinar la escritura de un nuevo texto.

ceremonias a las que se refiere el autor, las aquí estudiadas, eran ceremonias reales, por lo que la censura resulta un tanto improcedente, ni la *Cadira* es un texto que defienda la autoridad del rey, sino todo lo contrario. Lo que se pretende aquí sugerir con esa alusión maliciosa es que los autores de las coronaciones, que pertenecen al entorno del rey (en especial Juan de Mena) habrían socavado, conscientemente o no, su figura al usurparle estas competencias, todo lo cual alcanza en fin un punto mayor de sarcasmo referido a un rey como Juan II, particularmente sensible hacia la literatura. Por último, más allá de esta ironía, es probable que las precisiones de Rodríguez del Padrón sobre la incorrección de la ceremonia coadyuvaran a su olvido, pues a partir de este momento no encontramos ya textos construidos sobre este motivo.[28] Solamente es equiparable la *Coronación de las quatro virtudes cardinales*, de Fernán Pérez de Guzmán, texto dirigido además nuevamente al Marqués de Santillana (Foulché-Delbosc 1912: 664-71; ID 4324). Pero aquí la referencia a la coronación es ya exclusivamente simbólica: ni se describe ninguna ceremonia ni el texto gira en torno a la poesía. Es simplemente un elogio de las virtudes cardinales, que se apoya temáticamente en el poema de Juan de Mena, en donde las virtudes coronaban al poeta, pero en el que se desliga ahora el cultivo de la virtud de las aspiraciones poéticas o intelectuales.[29]

6. A modo de conclusión

El olvido de este motivo significaría, así pues, el abandono también de una forma un tanto estereotipada de representar o defender la excelencia poética e incluso el desinterés, al menos inmediato o directo, por definir una historia literaria y la propia posición dentro de ella. Supondrá, en definitiva, el alejamiento de unas prácticas ligadas muy estrechamente a una corriente y a unos individuos concretos: a la corriente que recoge el legado de Enrique de Villena y a un escritor como Santillana que parece haber poseído una aguda conciencia sobre la situación histórica de la poesía y un persistente deseo de construir y asegurarse un lugar dentro de ella. La burla de Rodríguez del Padrón al respecto, planteada por alguien que conoce bien la ceremonia y que está muy

[28] Sobre la idea de buen y mal ritual, a partir de textos altomedievales, véase Philippe Buc 2001: 15-50.

[29] Es más, como han sugerido Lapesa 1957: 275-76 y Weiss 1990: 180-81, cabe la posibilidad de que el final del poema represente en realidad una crítica del interés de Santillana, para Pérez de Guzmán equivocado, por una poesía no didáctica.

lejos de haberla mitificado, vino a significar el golpe de gracia sobre este motivo, que acabó quedando en cierta forma como el
distintivo de algunos 'poetas vulgares', de esas pretensiones tan
voluntariosas como insuficientes que otros intelectuales posteriores criticarán también en Santillana (Russell 1978: 225). Es
significativo que la reivindicación de Macías procediera de alguien
mejor familiarizado con las corrientes que llegaban desde Italia, y
que, quizá por ello, se decide con plena independencia de criterio
por la tradición gallego-portuguesa, justamente por aquella que
habían ido ensombreciendo la influencia catalano-provenzal y la
moda italianizante.[30] Se trata asimismo, en efecto, de una disputa
en la que se alían literatura y política, y en cuyo marco Rodríguez
del Padrón pasaría además a ocupar un lugar análogo, pero contrario, al de Juan de Mena. Sea como fuere, sin correlato
institucional y sin prestigio cultural, el motivo de la coronación de
los poetas estaba llamado a desaparecer junto a algunos de los rasgos más singulares que definen la herencia de Villena y la
personalidad literaria de Santillana. Tal motivo, en suma, abre y
cierra un momento estético, y podría considerarse sin duda como
uno de sus más definitivos emblemas.

OBRAS CITADAS

ALVAR, Manuel, 1989. 'La "nueva maestría" y las rúbricas del *Cancionero de Baena'*, en *Miscellanea di studi in onore di Aurelio Roncaglia a cinquant'anni dalla sua laurea* (Modena: Mucchi Editore), I, pp. 1–24.

ANGLADE, Joseph, ed., 1919–20. *Las Leys d'amors*, Bibliothèque Méridionale, 17–20 (Toulouse: Édouard Privat).

BAUTISTA, Francisco, 2005. 'Nobleza y bandos en la *Cadira de honor'*, en *Juan Rodríguez del Padrón: Studies in Honour of Olga Tudorică Impey*, ed. Alan Deyermond & Carmen Parrilla, I: *Poetry and Doctrinal Prose*, PMHRS, 48, pp. 103–35.

BELTRAN, Vicenç, 2001. '"La poesía es un arma cargada de futuro": polémica y propaganda política en el *Cancionero de Baena'*, en *Juan Alfonso de Baena y su cancionero: Actas del I Congreso Internacional sobre el 'Cancionero de Baena' (Baena, del 16 al 20 de febrero de 1999)*, ed. José Luis Serrano Reyes & Juan Fernández Jiménez (Baena: Ayuntamiento), pp. 15–52.

BERRIO MARTÍN-RETORTILLO, Pilar, 1996. 'Orfeo en la *Coronación* de Juan de Mena', *Dicenda*, 14: 21–46.

---

[30] María Rosa Lida de Malkiel, que incidió tal vez en exceso en el carácter medieval de Rodríguez del Padrón, señaló ya su fisonomía singular entre los letrados de la corte de Juan II (1977: 76). Por supuesto, de más está decirlo, que la obra de Santillana resulta mucho más amplia y compleja de lo que sugeriría la crítica de la *Cadira*.

BOASE, Roger, 1981. *El resurgimiento de los trovadores: un estudio del cambio social y el tradicionalismo en el final de la Edad Media en España*, trad. José Miguel Muro (Madrid: Pegaso). Original inglés, 1978.

BUC, Philippe, 2001. *The Dangers of Ritual: Between Early Medieval Texts and Social Scientific Theory* (Princeton: UP).

CABRÉ, Lluís, 1998. 'Notas sobre la memoria de Santillana y los poetas de la Corona de Aragón', en *Cancionero Studies in Honour of Ian Macpherson*, ed. Alan Deyermond, PMHRS, 11, pp. 25–38.

CARR, Derek C., 1980–81. 'A Fifteenth-Century Castilian Translation and Commentary of a Petrarch Sonnet: Biblioteca Nacional, MS 10186, fols 196ʳ–199ʳ', *Revista Canadiense de Estudios Hispánicos*, 5: 123–43.

CARRIAZO, Juan de Mata, ed., 1946. *Crónica del Halconero de Juan II, Pedro Carrillo de Huete*, Colección de Crónicas Españolas, 8 (Madrid: Espasa-Calpe).

CÁTEDRA, Pedro M., ed., 1994–2000. Enrique de Villena, *Obras completas*, 3 vols. (Madrid: Turner & Fundación José Antonio de Castro).

——, 1996. 'El sentido involucrado y la poesía de siglo XV: lecturas virgilianas de Santillana, con Villena', en *Nunca fue pena mayor: estudios de literatura española en homenaje a Brian Dutton*, ed. Ana Menéndez Collera & Victoriano Roncero López, Colección Varios, 4 (Cuenca: Universidad de Castilla-La Mancha), pp. 149–62.

DEYERMOND, Alan, 1983. 'Structure and Style as Instruments of Propaganda in Juan de Mena's *Laberinto de Fortuna*', *Proceedings of the Patristic, Medieval and Renaissance Conference*, 5: 159–67.

——, 1992. 'The Double Petrarchism of Medieval Spain', *Journal of the Institute of Romance Studies*, 1: 69–85.

——, ed., 2000. *Santillana: A Symposium*, PMHRS, 28.

DUTTON, Brian, & Joaquín GONZÁLEZ CUENCA, ed., 1993. *Cancionero de Juan Alfonso de Baena*, BFH, 14 (Madrid: Visor).

FLOOD, John L., 2006. *Poets Laureate in the Holy Roman Empire: A Bio-Bibliographical Handbook*, 4 vols. (Berlin: Walter de Gruyter).

FOULCHÉ-DELBOSC, R., ed., 1912. *Cancionero castellano del siglo XV*, I, Nueva Biblioteca de Autores Españoles, 19 (Madrid: Bailly-Baillière).

GARCÍA LÓPEZ, Jorge, ed., 1991. Alfonso de la Torre, *Visión deleytable*, Textos Recuperados, 6–7 (Salamanca: Ediciones Universidad de Salamanca).

GATIEN-ARNOULT, M., ed., 1841–43. *Las Flors del gay saber, estier dichas las Leys d'amors*, Monuments de la Littérature Romane, 1–3 (Toulouse: Bon et Privat). Reimpr. Genève: Slatkine, 1977, 2 vols.

GÓMEZ MORENO, Ángel, ed., 1990. *El prohemio e carta del Marqués de Santillana y la teoría literaria del s. XV*, Filológica, 1 (Barcelona: PPU).

——, & Maximilian P. A. M. KERKHOF, ed., 1988. Íñigo López de Mendoza, Marqués de Santillana, *Obras completas*, Clásicos Universales Planeta: Autores Hispánicos, 146 (Barcelona: Planeta).

HECKSCHER, William S., 1947. 'Bernini's Elephant and Obelisk', *Art Bulletin*, 29: 155–82.

HERNÁNDEZ ALONSO, César, ed., 1982. Juan Rodríguez del Padrón, *Obras completas*, Biblioteca de la Literatura y el Pensamiento Hispánicos, 48 (Madrid: Editora Nacional).

JOHNSTON, Mark D., 1996. 'Poetry and Courtliness in Baena's Prologue', *C*, 25.1: 93–105.

——, 1998. 'Cultural Studies on the *Gaya Ciencia*', en *Poetry at Court in Trastamaran Spain: From the 'Cancionero de Baena' to the 'Cancionero General'*, ed. E. Michael Gerli & Julian Weiss, MRTS, 181 (Tempe, AZ: MRTS), pp. 235–53.

KANTOROWICZ, Ernst H., 1965. 'On Transformations of Apolline Ethics', en sus *Selected Studies*, ed. Michael Cherniavsky & Ralph E. Giesey (Locust Valley, NY: J. J. Augustin), pp. 399–408. 1ª publ., 1957.

LAPESA, Rafael, 1957. *La obra literaria del Marqués de Santillana* (Madrid: Ínsula).

——, 1962. 'Sobre la *Coronación de Mossén Jordi de Sant Jordi*: Venus y los elefantes', en *Estudis Romànics*, 19 (*Estudis de literatura catalana oferts a Jordi Rubió i Balaguer en el seu setanta-cinquè aniversari*, ed. R. Aramon i Serra): 273–76.

LAWRANCE, Jeremy, 2000. 'Santillana's Political Poetry', en Deyermond 2000: 7–37.

LIDA DE MALKIEL, María Rosa, 1952. *La idea de la fama en la Edad Media castellana* (México: Fondo de Cultura Económica).

——, 1977. 'Juan Rodríguez del Padrón', en sus *Estudios sobre la literatura española del siglo XV*, ed. Yakov Malkiel (Madrid: José Porrúa Turanzas), pp. 21–144. 1ª publ., *Nueva Revista de Filología Hispánica*, 6 (1952): 313–51; 8 (1954): 1–38, & 14 (1960): 318–21.

LOOMIS, Roger Sherman, 1919. 'The Allegorical Siege in the Art of the Middle Ages', *American Journal of Archaeology*, 23: 255–69.

MACDONALD, Inez, 1939. 'The *Coronaçión* of Juan de Mena: Poem and Commentary', *HR*, 7: 125–44.

PÉREZ PRIEGO, Miguel Ángel, ed., 1989. Juan de Mena, *Obras completas*, Clásicos Universales Planeta: Autores Hispánicos, 175 (Barcelona: Planeta).

——, ed., 1997. *Teatro medieval, 2: Castilla*, Páginas de Biblioteca Clásica (Barcelona: Crítica).

——, 2001. 'Boccaccio en la obra literaria de Santillana', en *La Recepción de Boccaccio en España: Actas del Seminario Internacional Complutense (18–20 de octubre de 2000)*, ed. María Hernández Esteban = *Cuadernos de Filología Italiana*, vol. extraordinario, pp. 479–95.

POST, Chandler Rathfon, 1912. 'The Sources of Juan de Mena', *Romanic Review*, 3: 223–79.

——, 1915. *Mediaeval Spanish Allegory*, Harvard Studies in Comparative Literature, 4 (Cambridge, MA: Harvard UP). Reimpr. Hildesheim: Georg Olms, 1971.

PUJOL, Josep, 1994. '"Gaya vel gaudiosa, et alio nomine inveniendi sciencia": les idees sobre la poesia en llengua vulgar als segles XIV i XV', en *Intel·lectuals i escriptors a la baixa Edat Mitjana: treballs del Seminari de Filologia Catalana (Universitat de Barcelona, 1988–94)*, ed. Lola Badia & Albert Soler, Textos i Estudis de Cultura Catalana, 36 (Barcelona: Curial & PAM), pp. 69–94.

——, 1996. '"Psallite sapienter": la gaya ciència en els sermons de Felip de Malla de 1413 (estudi i edició)', *Cultura Neolatina*, 56: 177–250.

RICO, Francisco, 2002. 'Petrarca y el "humanismo catalán"', en sus *Estudios de literatura y otras cosas* (Barcelona: Destino), pp. 147–78. 1ª publ., 1983.

RIQUER, Martí de, & Lola BADIA, ed., 1984. *Les poesies de Jordi de Sant Jordi*, Biblioteca d'Estudis i Investigacions, 7 (Valencia: Tres i Quatre).

ROBIGLIO, Andrea A., 2006. 'The Thinker as a Noble Man (*bene natus*) and Preliminary Remarks on the Medieval Concepts of Nobility', *Vivarium*, 44: 205–47.

ROSELL, Cayetano, ed., 1877. Lorenzo Galíndez de Carvajal, *Crónica de Juan II* (Logroño, 1517), en *Crónicas de los reyes de Castilla desde don Alfonso el Sabio hasta los Católicos don Fernando y doña Isabel*, II, BAE, 68 (Madrid: Rivadeneyra), pp. 273–693.

RUBIO TOVAR, Joaquín, 2005. 'El soneto CXLVIII de Petrarca traducido por Enrique de Villena: ¿original o traducción?', en *El 'Canzoniere' de Petrarca en Europa: ediciones, comentarios, traducciones y proyección*, ed. María Hernández Esteban = *Cuadernos de Filología Italiana*, vol. extraordinario, pp. 87–102.

RUSSELL, Peter E., 1978. 'Las armas contra las letras: para una definición del humanismo español del siglo XV', en su *Temas de 'La Celestina' y otros estudios del 'Cid' al 'Quijote'*, trad. Alejandro Pérez, Letras e Ideas: Maior, 14 (Barcelona: Ariel), pp. 207–39. Original inglés, 1967.

SALICRÚ I LLUCH, Roser, 1995. 'La coronació de Ferran d'Antequera: l'organització i els preparatius de la festa', *Anuario de Estudios Medievales*, 25: 699–759.

TAVANI, Giuseppe, 1996. 'Tolosa i Barcelona: dos consistoris per a una poesia', en su *Per una història de la cultura catalana medieval* (Barcelona: Curial), pp. 53–81. 1ª publ., 1989.

TRAPP, J. B., 1958. 'The Owl's Ivy and the Poet's Bays', *Journal of the Warburg and Courtauld Institutes*, 21: 227–55.

WEISS, Julian, 1981–82. 'Juan de Mena's *Coronación*: Satire or *Sátira*?', *Journal of Hispanic Philology*, 6: 113–38.

——, 1990. *The Poet's Art: Literary Theory in Castile, 1400–60*, Medium Aevum Monographs, ns, 14 (Oxford: The Society for the Study of Mediaeval Languages and Literature).

——, 1991. '"La affección poetal virtuosa": Petrarch's Sonnet 116 as Poetic Manifesto for Fifteenth-Century Castile', *Modern Language Review*, 86: 70–78.

WENZEL, Siegfried, 1995. 'Academic Sermons at Oxford in the Early Fifteenth Century', *Speculum*, 70: 305–29.

WHETNALL, Jane, 2000. 'Editing Santillana's Early Sonnets: Some Doubts about the Authority of SA8', en Deyermond 2000: 53–80.

——, 2006. 'Las transformaciones de Petrarca en cuatro poetas de cancionero: Santillana, Carvajales, Cartagena y Florencia Pinar', *Cancionero General*, 4: 81–108.

WILHITE, Valerie M., 2005. 'The Loss of Love's Emotions: The Urban Consistori and the Reconceptualization of the Court's Love Lyric', en *Emotions in the Heart of the City (14th–16th Century)*, ed. Elodie Lecuppre-Desjardin & Anne-Laure Van Bruaene, Studies in European History (1100–1800), 5 (Turnhout: Brepols), pp. 203–22.

WILKINS, Ernest H., 1943. 'The Coronation of Petrarch', *Speculum*, 18: 155–97.

Saints John the Baptist and John the Evangelist in the *Cancionero* of Juan de Luzón

ANDREW M. BERESFORD

(University of Durham)

The *Cancionero* of Juan de Luzón (08JL), most commonly known as the *Suma de las virtudes*, was printed in Zaragoza by Jorge Coci on 12 October 1508.[1] The collection, which contains the only extant examples of the poet's works, has been available in the facsimile edition prepared by Antonio Rodríguez-Moñino since 1959, but in common with a number of other branches of late-medieval religious writing, it has not received the attention that it deserves. Its major poem, the *Suma de las virtudes* (ID 4698), a work comprising some 395 stanzas of *arte mayor*, has yet to become the subject of serious academic enquiry, and it would perhaps now be appropriate for Rodríguez-Moñino's rather offhand description of it as an 'interminable y pesada cabalgata' (1959: viii) to be either dismissed or substantiated by a detailed analysis of the poem's content and structure. The remaining poems have fared little better, and what little is known about them is complicated by the fact that some of them have been catalogued incorrectly. In his *Cancionero del siglo XV*, for instance, Brian Dutton (1990–91: V, 109–10), records eleven poems in addition to the *Suma de las virtudes*. In the majority of instances his judgements are unproblematic, but a misunderstanding

---

[1] Much of what is known about the poet and his work is taken from the colophon, which explains that it was completed in Burgos on 31 July 1506 and printed just over two years later along with an extensive series of glosses. His occupation is given as 'criado de la muy excelente y muy cathólica señora, la señora doña Juana d'Aragón, duquesa de Frías, condessa de Haro' (fol. n5ᵛ), and it is in her honour that the collection is dedicated. Quotations are from Rodríguez-Moñino's facsimile edition (1959): abbreviations have been expanded in italics, the use of c/ς, i/j, and u/v regularized, and punctuation and capitalization adapted to make them conform to modern practice. For ease of reference the seven poems on the two Saint Johns are edited in an appendix.

From the *'Cancioneiro da Vaticana'* to the *'Cancionero general'*: *Studies in Honour of Jane Whetnall*, ed. Alan Deyermond & Barry Taylor, PMHRS, 60 (London: Department of Hispanic Studies, Queen Mary, University of London, 2007), pp. 75–88. ISSN 1460–051X. ISBN 0 902238 50 7.

affects the interpretation of ID 4707 ('*Domine* ante te omne desideriu*m* meum'), which is catalogued as a poem of four stanzas.[2] A
second Latin incipit placed at the start of the third stanza, however, marks the beginning of a fresh composition based on a
different Latin gloss ('Memorare novissima tua in omnibus operi-
bus tuis'), and in view of this, it should be classified in future as
two poems rather than one.[3]

The remaining problems of classification affect the interpretation
of a series of poems dealing with two of the poet's namesakes: the
common hagiographic pairing of Saints John the Baptist and John
the Apostle and Evangelist.[4] The first, *Gozos del nascimiento de señor
San Juan Bautista* (ID 4702) is classified by Dutton (V, 109) as a
poem of seventy-five lines divided into a series of nine stanzas of
varying length (4, 5x8, 12, 9, 10). The apparent irregularity of its
form, however, indicates only that it should be categorized more
appropriately as a sequence of three poems on related themes. The

[2] The rubrics of the eight poems catalogued correctly are: 'Contemplaciones sobre
la passión de Nuestro Señor, las quales embió San Bernardo a un devoto religioso'
(ID 4699), 'Comiença el psalmo de "Miserere mei deus"' (ID 4700), 'Otra oración
sobre el salmo "De profundis" por diálogo entre Nuestro Señor y el peccador' (ID
4701), 'Otra oración sobre el hymno "O gloriosa domina"' (ID 7394), 'Elegi abiec-
tu*m* esse in domo d*o*mini magis qua*m* habitare in tabernaculis peccatoru*m*' (ID
4705), 'D*o*mine doce me facere volu*n*tate*m* tuam quia deus meus es tu' (ID 4706),
'D*o*mine ante te omne desideriu*m* meum' (ID 4707), and 'Multi pacifici sunt tibi et
co*n*siliariu*s* sit tibi un*us* d*e* mille' (ID 4708).

[3] The distinction between the two is emphasized by the fact that although they are
both octosyllabic, their form is different — the first rhyming ABBBA-CDDDC /
EFFFE-GHHHG, and the second, ABBBA-CDCCD / EFFFE-GHGGH. Equally
noticeable is a distinction in subject matter, with the first offering a personal reflec-
tion on the relationship between the individual and the divine, and the second
adopting a didactic tone, counselling readers on the inevitability of death: 'al
mundo dexa, mesquino, / qu'es muy breve y es camino / del cielo que siempre
dura' (fol. n5rb; lines 18–20).

[4] The most significant comment in early Castilian on the rivalry between the two
Johns can be found in Clemente Sánchez de Vercial's *Libro de los exenplos por a.b.c*
under the rubric *De los sanctos non es de disputar / qual dellos sera mas de alabar* (no.
57): 'Grandes maestros en theologia, el uno alabava a Santo Johan Baptista e dezia
que era mejor, e el otro alabava a Santo Johan Evangelista entendiendo que era
mejor. E acordaron de aver disputacion solenpne sobre esta question. E cada uno
estudiava con grand deligencia de buscar abtoridades e rrazones suficientes para
alabar cada uno al que era devoto e que era mayor. En la noche ante del dia de la
disputacion cada uno destos sanctos aparescio al su devoto que tenia su parte e
dixole: "Nos en el çielo bien somos concordes e vos en la tierra non seades discor-
des". Estonçes anbos concordes publicaron esta rrazon e esta vision al pueblo e
dieron laudes a Dios' (Keller 1961: 63–64).

first, which begins 'Gozos den más regozijo / este día que otros días', is a Castilian version of a traditional Catalan *goig*, with a four-line *estribillo* followed by five stanzas of eight lines and a concluding twelve-line *Oración* in which the speaker's voice is more prominent.[5] The second, a gloss of Luke 1.63 beginning 'Joannes, porqu'est más glorioso / nomen que los otros nombres', is a poem of nine lines that offers a fine scholarly blending of Latin and Castilian, with the words of the gloss ('Joannes est nomen eius') spelled out not only within the poem itself, but also in the margin. This is a technique duplicated by the last of the three, 'Inter natos con el manto, / mulierum de santidad', as it offers a reworking of Christ's words to the multitude ('Inter natos mulierum non surrexit mayor Joanne Baptista') in Matthew 11.11.

The confusion between the poems could be attributed in part to the fact that they share a number of features, the most obvious being the use of octosyllabic lines.[6] A more significant potential problem, however, can be seen in the poet's idiosyncratic approach to rhyme, with the first of the three employing an apparently random series of consecutive and alternating patterns, used (it would seem) as a result of linguistic necessity rather than of deliberate planning.[7] The second and third poems are superficially similar, and although there is a difference in stanza length (with nine lines in the former and ten in the latter), it is noticeable that they are also founded on a four-part rhyme scheme. Even more confusing is that the first five lines of each are structured according to the same formula.[8]

Formal characteristics aside, however, it is difficult to see how

---

[5] The *goig* has been studied by a number of critics, but of particular interest in relation to Luzón's approach to hagiography is the fifteenth-century collection known as the *Cançoner sagrat de vides de sants*, which contains a series of fifty-nine poems, the majority of which are devoted to the legends of the saints. For further information, see Foulché-Delbosc & Massó y Torrents 1912.

[6] The only section to depart from this is the *Oración*, which introduces *pie quebrado* in every third line, producing the pattern ABcABcDEfDEf.

[7] The first stanza contains alternating rhymes only in the first quatrain (CDCD–BCCB), while the second and third have them only in the second (EFFE–EBEB / GHHG–GBGB); the final stanzas, in contrast, consist entirely of alternating rhymes (IJIJ–JBJB / KLKL–LBLB). The complexity of this scheme can be attributed to the fact that each stanza concludes with a rhyme based on the second and fourth lines of the *estribillo*.

[8] The two poems differ only in their concluding sections, the former rhyming ABAAB–CDDC, and the latter, ABAAB–CDCCD.

the three could have been confused. The first, a panegyric designed to be read on the feast of the saint's birth (24 June), offers a
lyrical treatment of his posthumous significance, and is comparable to a number of other works composed during the period.[9] Its
content, which achieves a degree of thematic unity by reflecting
not merely on the celebration of John's feast but on the various
other joys with which he is associated, is peppered with a series of
fleeting but evocative allusions to Scripture, the most important of
which are the Visitation (Luke 1.39–42) and the meeting between
Christ and John in the desert (John 1.29).[10] These sections are complemented by a reference to the popular tradition (with the feast of
the saint celebrated by the adornment of entrances to houses with
flowers and greenery) and by a concluding prayer in which the
speaker addresses him on behalf of his fellow Christians, invoking
his powers as an intermediary while soliciting protection from 'el
mal enemigo' (I, line 55).[11] The poem in this respect succeeds in
giving an impression of his status in the pantheon of saints, commenting not only on the fact that he was an important precursor of
Christ — capable of cleansing the one who could not be cleansed
— but that he was the most 'escogido santo / que los otros que

[9] The study of hagiography in *cancionero* poetry is in its infancy, but it is noticeable that
Luzón's poem shares much with a number of other compositions. These include Juan
Martínez de Burgos's 'Ante santo que nascido / excelente pregonero' (ID 3663; Severin
1976: 43–46), and two poems by Fray Ambrosio Montesino: 'De tus virtudes, Baptista /
no hago largo prohemio' and 'Cante la nación cristiana / el favor esclarescido' (ID 6022
and ID 6009; Rodríguez Puértolas 1987: 187–88 & 77–93). A third Montesino composition, 'Nuevas te traygo, Baptista / de llorar' (ID 6042; 1987: 213–14), is a
contrafact version of a traditional lyric in which the saint discusses his impending
death with his jailer (see Wardropper 1958: 140, Álvarez Pellitero 1976: 151–52, and
Crosbie 1989) and is in this sense more obviously related to the two glosses. For an
edition of the poems of the 1531 poetic joust that took place in Seville in his honour
(many of which were incorporated into the 1535 edition of the *Cancionero general*),
see Montoto 1955: 75–130.

[10] Luzón follows poetic tradition in his depiction of the meeting between John and
Christ by commenting specifically on the former's outstretched finger: 'pide al que
más amaste / y al de quien diste testigo / con el dedo' (lines 51–53). This can be
compared to a number of other treatments including Berceo's *Del sacrificio de la Misa*,
where we are told that 'Jhesú fue est cordero, bien parece por vista, / mostrólo con su
dedo san Johán Baptista' (Cátedra 1992: 997; st. 153ab).

[11] 'todo el mundo / goza con rosas y flores, / claro, verde y rubicundo / con
matizes y colores' (lines 29–31). For further information on the relationship between John and the popular tradition, see Sánchez Romeralo 1969: 64–65 and
Pedrosa 2001.

escogidos / son de Dios' (I, lines 45–47).[12]

The second and third poems, in contrast, are more occasional pieces that assume the form of learned glosses dominated by the display of linguistic wit. The integration of Latin and Castilian gives an impression of scholarly *gravitas*, and one imagines as a result that they were composed not for the benefit of ordinary believers (as is the case in the previous poem), but for an educated elite, able to understand and appreciate the depth of the author's erudition.[13] At times the technique is both daring and entertaining, particularly in the formation of compound hybrids such as 'porqu'est' (II, line 2) and in the reiteration of themes developed elsewhere, a good example being the speaker's comments on John's special status: 'mayor fue y más escogido / Joanne Baptista que todos' (III, lines 6–7). As is common in compositions of this type, however, the integration of specific Latin glosses establishes an additional (and perhaps unnecessary) level of poetic complexity that leads almost inevitably to a certain degree of dullness, even predictability. A major exception is in the conclusion to the second of the two pieces, as the speaker fashions an intriguing and novel comparison drawn from Spain's past, affirming that John remains 'en el cielo más subido / que fueron acá los godos' (III, lines 9–10).

An equally noticeable misunderstanding affects the interpretation of a sequence of three pieces dealing with Saint John the Apostle and Evangelist.[14] Dutton (V, 109), who amalgamates the three into a single poem (ID 4703), classifies it as a work of fifty-six lines, broken once again into a series of stanzas of varying length (2x10, 2x18). Rodríguez-Moñino's facsimile edition, however, contains only thirty-

---

[12] John's status can be seen in the fact that in addition to the feast of his birth, his martyrdom was celebrated in the sanctoral calendar on 29 August. A number of prose accounts of his nativity and martyrdom were reworked into Castilian in the late fourteenth and early fifteenth centuries, but only one of these (Biblioteca Ménendez Pelayo MS 8, fols 35va–37va) has been edited (see Baños Vallejo & Uría 2000: 179–82). For versions of the two accounts in Catalan, see Maneikis Kniazzeh & Neugaard 1977: III, 24–36 & 239–46.

[13] For a discussion of bilingualism in the *cancioneros*, see Deyermond 1998.

[14] John the Apostle is another rare example of a saint with two feasts (27 May and 6 December) in the sanctoral calendar, and it is partly on account of this that he is so often paired with his namesake. A series of prose accounts of both feasts was reworked into Castilian in the late fourteenth and early fifteenth centuries, but only one of these (Biblioteca Ménendez Pelayo MS 8, fols 24va–35ra) has been edited (see Baños Vallejo & Uría 2000: 147). For versions of the two accounts in Catalan, see Maneikis Kniazzeh & Neugaard 1977: II, 87–95 & 467–68, and for an edition of the poetic joust that took place in 1531 in Seville in his honour, Montoto 1955: 33–73.

six lines, and shows that it should be regarded as a second trilogy of independent compositions. The first poem is prefaced by the words 'De señor San Juan evangelista' and is a gloss of 'Joannes apostolus et evangelista virgo est electus a domino inter ceteros magis dilectus'. This piece, with two stanzas of ten lines, is the most extensive of the three, and paves the way for two further compositions, both of which assume the form of glosses of familiar biblical citations. The first, which begins 'Joannes, pues que más pujaste / con Dios, ecce que en la cruz', is based on John 19.27 ('Joannes ecce mater tua'), while the second, 'Mulier que sin hijo madre / hoy serás por culpa ajena', is derived from the wording of the preceding passage ('Mulier ecce filius tuus') in John 19.26.

As with the author's poems on John the Baptist, it is difficult to see how the arrangement of the second trilogy could have been misinterpreted. The three poems are cast once again as octosyllables, and there are clear affinities in the use of rhyme, particularly in the second and third compositions, which adopt identical patterns.[15] The sequence of stanza forms and the presence of individual incipits, however, show that there are three compositions rather than one, each of them taking a related aspect of John's legacy as its subject matter. The closest textual relationship is between the two short glosses, which focus on the bond between John and Mary at the height of the Crucifixion. Reasons for the inversion of the chronology of Scripture are not forthcoming, but the success of both can be attributed to the fact that they enliven the content of the gospel narrative by focusing on the power and significance of family bonds. The development of this theme allows them to be read as companion pieces, with some of the content of the former ('pues ser hijo alcançaste / de la virgen madre suya, / sirve la que en madre tuya / la dexa', V, lines 5–8) restated in a more direct fashion in the latter: 'ecce Juan en quien más fío, / filius tuus de oy más sea' (VI, lines 5–6). Their approach in this respect is deeply traditional, and it could be that they were inspired by the intersecting monologues that are a fundamental characteristic of the *Planctus Mariae* tradition.[16]

---

[15] The structure of the longer poem is unusual, but its rhyme scheme (ABAAB-ACAAC / DAAAF–EFEEF) suggests that its form is deliberate. The second and third poems adopt the same formula, rhyming ABBA–CDDC.

[16] The *Planctus Mariae* is perhaps best known in the late-medieval Castilian dramatic tradition, familiar examples being Gómez Manrique's *Lamentaciones hechas para la Semana Santa* and Alonso del Campo's *Auto de la Pasión*. For further information, see

The most important treatment of the saint, however, is in the first of the three compositions, which offers a more extensive encomium of his accomplishments. Its first stanza is devoted to his function as part of the tetramorph, an image drawn from Ezekiel 1.4–11 and 10.14, but developed also in relation to Revelation 4.6– 8. According to tradition, the tetramorph is a winged creature with four faces representing the evangelists: a man or an angel for Matthew, a lion for Mark, an ox for Luke, and an eagle for John.[17] Luzón's poem, which builds on a series of earlier Castilian representations, is based on a paradox, with the saint's lofty interpretative ability raising him high above the world, but also, as a result of his talent, from immediate physical contact with Christ. The development of this paradox paves the way for the introduction of a more emotional second stanza and to a reference to his relationship as an adoptive son of the Virgin: 'en la cruz le encomendó / su querida virgen madre' (IV, lines 14–15). On this occasion, however, the image is combined with a fleeting allusion to the Last Supper and to the popular assumption that he was favoured above all others because he was allowed to sleep on Christ's bosom: 'y todos le obedecieron / pues durmió en los sanctos pechos' (IV, lines 19–20). This view, which is at odds with the words of John 13.23 (where he merely reclines next to Christ), provides an aptly emotional conclusion that in some ways prepares the reader for the content of the poems that follow.[18]

The structuring of the two trilogies shows that their arrangement is not random. The first begins with a lyrical treatment of John the Bap-tist and is followed by two short glosses that shed further

Pérez Priego 1997.

[17] John is traditionally represented as an eagle on account of the depth of his erudition and the number of unique insights within his Gospel. Fray Ambrosio Montesino praises him in this respect, on one occasion placing him on a par with the cherubim and seraphim, the highest of the nine orders of angels: 'Dinos, águila, que vuelas / mejor que los querubines, / por qué fines te consuelas / en las eternas escuelas / de los serafines' (ID 2391; Sancha 1855: 403a). The clearest definition of the tetramorph, however, is in Berceo's *Loores de Nuestra Señora*: 'Matheo empeçó en la encarnación, / píntanlo con faz d'omne por tal entenciïon; / Luchas á faz de buey, ca diz' de la pasión / cóm se feço tu fijo, Señora, oblación. / Marcho diz' sobre todos de la resurrectión, / por essa fortaleza riñe como león; / Juhan en Trinidat empieza su lectión, / por esso tomó d'águila sotil comparación' (Salvador Miguel 1992: 913; st. 164–65).

[18] Fray Ambrosio Montesino also follows popular tradition: 'Celebrando el rey la cena / del cordero figurado, / sobre el corazón de Cristo / San Juan está reclinando' (ID 6035; Rodríguez Puértolas 1987: 201, lines 1–4).

light on his legacy. The focus then shifts to the second John, who is dealt with in a similar manner, the only substantive difference being the adoption of an erudite rather than a popular register in the initial poem of the sequence. The strength of the relationship between the two groupings is reinforced by the fact that they are presented physically on the page as prayer-like acts of homage that conclude with the word 'Amén'. This, to some extent, makes it easier to understand the rationale for Dutton's judgement, but more telling is the fact that the following poem (which is classified correctly) returns to the beginning of the cycle by taking John the Baptist as its subject matter. This work, 'Fuit un gran mensajero, / homo de mucha excelencia', is prefaced by the words 'Más de señor San Juan Bautista' and is a gloss of John 1.6: 'Fuit homo missus a deo cui nomen erat Joannes'. The way in which this seventh hagiographic poem provides a conclusion to the sequence is fascinating, for by framing one John within the other (and, furthermore, using the words of his own Gospel in order to do so), it enters into the longstanding medieval debate on superiority, suggesting that the achievements of Saint John the Evangelist are surpassed by those of John the Baptist.[19] Equally noticeable is the completion of a sophisticated and esthetically appealing pattern of numerical symbolism, with the numbers three and four now combining to make seven, in this way bringing to mind images of the Trinity, the Gospels, and the Evangelists, and ultimately of the Creation. This careful patterning, which plays also on a series of folkloric connotations embedded into the popular consciousness, shows that Luzón's poetry is by no means lacking in literary merit and that a full-scale reassessment of his life and works is long overdue.

APPENDIX: JUAN DE LUZÓN'S HAGIOGRAPHIC POEMS

[fol. n2ᵛᵇ]   [I] *Gozos del nascimiento de señor San Juan Bautista*

Gozos den más regozijo
este día que otros días,
que hoy nació el muy sancto hijo

---

[19] An impression of circularity is generated by a series of lexical reminiscences of the first poem, notable examples being the discussion of joy ('nacido en gran regozijo / de una prima de su madre', VII, 7–8), and the description of the meeting in the desert: 'él començó a descubrillo / con el dedo entre la gente' (VII, 13–14).

4   de Ysabel[20] y Zacharías.

            Gozóse el verbo divino
            quando su primo saltava
            en el vientre viejo dino
8   que su madre visitava;
            y tú, Virgen, que estarías
            al parto de tal sobrino,
            gozo sin tiento ni tino
12   recibe con Zacharías.

            Dios padre tan bien embía
            sus ministriles del cielo,
            que den gozos y consuelo
16   a la de Dios hijo tía;
            y el luzero que salía
            declarando profecías,
            'ecce agnus dei' dizía,
20   dando gozo a Zacharías.

            Goze, goze el mar sagrado[21]
            con las aguas del Jordano,
            pues que d'ellas y la mano
24   d'éste el limpio fue lavado;
            que Dios por él bautizado
            y él también fue por Messías,
[fol. n3ra] gozo pues regozijado
28   del hijo de Zacharías.

            Este día todo el mundo
            goza con rosas y flores,
            claro, verde y rubicundo,
32   con matizes y colores;
            y pues dio de sus favores
            Dios a éste mejorías,
            gozos, gozos y loores
36   del hijo de Zacharías.

            De gozo dentro se vista
            y fuera toda la gente,
            que hoy nasció San Juan Bautista

---

[20] Ysabel : Ylabel
[21] sagrado : saglado

40   de Dios precursor potente;
y pues que es muy mereciente
de loores y alegrías,
gozos, gozos juntamente
44   del hijo de Zacharías.

Oración

Muy más escogido santo
que los otros que escogidos
son de Dios,
48   porque cobiertos con manto
del pecado y muy perdidos
somos nós,
pide al que más amaste
52   y al de quien diste testigo
con el dedo,
que no sufra el mal contraste
que nos busca el mal enemigo
56   y ande quedo.

[fol. n3rb]   [II] *Joannes est nomen eius*

Joannes, porqu'est más glorioso   [Joannes est]
nomen que los otros nombres,   [nomen]
ést'es el d'éste más dichoso,
4   justo, santo y glorioso
que ningún hijo de hombres;
eius del qual queda a nós   [eius]
ser su santa madre tía,
8   de Christo hi de María
y el primo de nuestro Dios.

[III] *Inter natos mulierum non surrexit[22] mayor Joanne Baptista*

Inter natos con el manto,   [Inter[23] natos]
mulierum de santidad,   [mulierum]
non surrexit nadie tanto   [non surrexit]
4   ni dio nunca ningún santo
tanta lumbre y claridad;
mayor fue y más escogido   [mayor]

[22] surrexit : surerxit
[23] Inter : Iter

8	Joanne Baptista que todos, antes santo que nascido y en el cielo más subido que fueron acá los godos.	[Joanne Baptista]

Amén

[fol. n3va]   [IV] *De señor San Juan evangelista*

Joannes apostolus et evangelista virgo est electus
a domino inter ceteros magis dilectus

	Joannes fue quien más privó (apostolus et evangelista)	[Joannes] [apostolus et

Evangilista]

4	con Dios, pues lo sublimó y entre los quatro boló con las alas y la vista; virgo, que solo alcançó los secretos encubiertos,	[virgo]
8	al qual Dios le prometió que pues tanto lo preció, no morría entre los muertos.	

	Est electus de Dios padre	[est electus]
12	y a domino quien siguió porque nunca lo dexó; en la cruz le encomendó su querida virgen madre;	[a domino]
16	inter ceteros que fueron de Dios siervos en sus hechos	[inter ceteros]
	magis dilectus no vieron, y todos le obedecieron	[magis dilectus]
20	pues durmió en los sanctos pechos.	

[fol. n3vb]   [V] *Joannes ecce mater tua*

	Joannes, pues que más pujaste con Dios, ecce que en la cruz	[Joannes] [ecce]
	su vida, su bien y luz	
4	te da aquél que más amaste; y pues ser hijo alcançaste de la virgen madre suya,	
	sirve la que en madre tuya	[mater tua]
8	la dexa, pues nol' dexaste.	

[VI] *Mulier ecce filius tuus*

	Mulier que sin hijo madre	[Mulier]
	hoy serás por culpa ajena,	
	por que nadie te dé pena	
4	nin te muerda, aunque te ladre,	
	ecce Juan en quien más fío:	[ecce]
	filius tuus de oy más sea	[filius tuus]
	por que te sirva y te[24] lea,	
8	que lo dexo en lugar mío.	

Amén

[VII] *Más de señor San Juan Bautista*

Fuit homo missus a deo cui nomen erat Joannes

	Fuit un gran mensajero,	[Fuit]
	homo de mucha excelencia,	[homo]
[fol. n4ra]	capitán, que con potencia	
4	divina vino primero;	
	missus a Deo del padre	[missus a deo]
	con vanderas de Dios hijo,	
	nacido en gran regozijo	
8	de una prima de su madre.	
	Cui a este gran caudillo	[cui]
	nomen erat sublimado,	[nomen erat]
	Joannes, más sanctificado	[Joannes]
12	que nadie puede dezillo;	
	él començó a descubrillo	
	con el dedo entre[25] la gente;	
	quiso el agnus innocente	
16	del bautismo recebillo.	

Amén

[24] te : se
[25] entre : entra

WORKS CITED

ÁLVAREZ PELLITERO, Ana María, 1976. *La obra lingüística y literaria de fray Ambrosio Montesino*, Colección Castilla, 5 (Valladolid: Departamento de Lengua y Literatura Españolas, Univ. de Valladolid).

BAÑOS VALLEJO, & Isabel URÍA MAQUA, ed., 2000. *'La leyenda de los santos': 'Flos sanctorum' del ms. 8 de la Biblioteca de Menéndez Pelayo*, Estudios de Literatura y Pensamiento Hispánicos, 18 (Santander: Asociación Cultural Año Jubilar Lebaniego & Sociedad Menéndez Pelayo).

CÁTEDRA, Pedro M., ed., 1992. *'Del sacrificio de la Misa'*, in Gonzalo de Berceo, *Obra completa*, ed. Isabel Uría, Clásicos Castellanos, ns [unnumbered] (Madrid: Espasa-Calpe), pp. 933–1033.

CROSBIE, John, 1989. *'A lo divino' Lyric Poetry: An Alternative View*, Durham Modern Language Series: Hispanic Monographs, 5 (Durham: Univ. of Durham).

DEYERMOND, Alan, 1998. 'Bilingualism in the *Cancioneros* and its Implications', in *Poetry at Court in Trastamaran Spain: From the 'Cancionero de Baena' to the 'Cancionero general'*, ed. E. Michael Gerli & Julian Weiss, MRTS, 181 (Tempe, AZ: MRTS), pp. 137–70.

DUTTON, Brian, ed., 1990–91. *El cancionero del siglo XV, c. 1360–1520*, Biblioteca Española del Siglo XV, Serie Maior, 1–7 (Salamanca: Biblioteca Española del Siglo XV & Universidad).

FOULCHÉ-DELBOSC, R., & Jaume MASSÓ Y TORRENTS, ed., 1912. *'Cançoner sagrat de vides de sants': segle XV* (Barcelona: Societat Catalana de Bibliòfils).

KELLER, John Esten, ed., 1961. Clemente Sánchez de Vercial, *Libro de los exemplos por ABC*, Clásicos Hispánicos, 2.5 (Madrid: CSIC).

MANEIKIS KNIAZZEH, Charlotte S., & Edward J. NEUGAARD, ed., 1977. *'Vides de sants rossellonesas': text català del segle XIII*, Publicacions de la Fundació Salvador Vives Casajuana, 48, 51, & 53 (Barcelona: Fundació Salvador Vives Casajuana).

MONTOTO, Santiago, ed., 1955. *Justas poéticas sevillanas del siglo XVI* (Valencia: Castalia).

PEDROSA, José Manuel, 2001. 'La canción de San Juan Verde: del análisis textual al análisis cultural', in *Canzonieri iberici*, ed. Patrizia Botta, Carmen Parrilla, & Ignacio Pérez Pascual, II, Biblioteca Filológica, 8 (Noia: Toxosoutos; A Coruña: Università di Padova & Universidade da Coruña), pp. 101–15.

PÉREZ PRIEGO, Miguel Ángel, ed., 1997. *Teatro medieval, II: Castilla*, Páginas de Biblioteca Clásica (Barcelona: Crítica).

RODRÍGUEZ-MOÑINO, Antonio, ed., 1959. Juan de Luzón, *Cancionero* (Madrid: n.pub).

RODRÍGUEZ PUÉRTOLAS, Julio, ed., 1987. *Cancionero de Fray Ambrosio Montesino*, Estudios Literarios, 1 (Cuenca: Diputación Provincial).

SALVADOR MIGUEL, Nicasio, ed. 1992. *'Loores de Nuestra Señora'*, in Gonzalo de Berceo, *Obra completa*, ed. Isabel Uría, Clásicos Castellanos, ns [unnumbered] (Madrid: Espasa-Calpe), pp. 859–931.

SANCHA, Justo de, ed., 1855. *Romancero y cancionero sagrados: colección de poesías cristianas morales y divinas*, BAE, 55 (Madrid: Rivadeneyra).

SÁNCHEZ ROMERALO, Antonio, 1969. *El villancico: estudios sobre la lírica popular en los siglos XV a XVI*, Biblioteca Románica Hispánica, 2.131 (Madrid: Gredos).

SEVERIN, Dorothy S., ed., 1976. *The 'Cancionero' of Martínez de Burgos: A Description of its Contents, with an Edition of the Prose and Poetry of Juan Martínez de Burgos*, Exeter Hispanic Texts, 12 (Exeter: University).

WARDROPPER, Bruce W., 1958. *Historia de la poesía lírica a lo divino en la cristiandad occidental* (Madrid: Revista de Occidente).

The Name that Ends in A and the Countess of Quirra (Toda Centelles, Violant Carròs, and Costanza d'Ávalos)

ROGER BOASE

(Queen Mary)

Canción suya [Pinar] *a Doña Toda Centellas* (ID 6654; 11CG– 882)[1]

Quien encendió mis querellas,	She who kindled my complaints,
sin saber lo que será,	not knowing what would be,
el renombre es de Centellas,	Sparky is her name and fame
y su nombre acaba en .a.	and her first name ends in A.
Y las llamas d'este fuego,	And the more I attempt to quell
quanto más quiero apagallas,	these fierce consuming flames,
ell amor me cresce luego,	the more does my love then swell,
raviando por abivallas.	craving to kindle them again.
Y aunque me pierda por ellas,	Although they may lead me astray,
una fe me salvará,	a pledge of love will save me,
pues salló d'estas centellas	since these were the sparks that gave me
el nombre que acaba en .a.	the name that ends in an A.

Little is known about Pinar, the author of this *canción*, except that he and his sister Florencia Pinar were poets of the late fifteenth century associated with the court of the Catholic Monarchs (Fulks 1989, Perea Rodríguez 2007: 234n4). Even less is known about Toda Centellas, the lady to whom this poem is addressed. I believe that she and the Countess of Quirra, for whom Pinar composed a gloss of the song 'Desconsolado de mí' (ID 0780, 11CG-881), were half-sisters and members of the Catalan-Aragonese aristocracy of Sardinia. The Countess of Quirra addressed by Pinar was Violant Carròs i de Centelles (1456–1510), and the lady named Toda Centellas in the above rubric was Violant's illegitimate half-sister Toda Senesterra-Carròs (1469–1547), whose son Guillem Ramon de Centelles became Count

---

1 The poem ID numbers and cancionero reference numbers used in this article are those established by Brian Dutton (Dutton 1990–91). I am grateful to Ian Macpherson for useful comments, including some improvements to the translation of ID 6654.

From the 'Cancioneiro da Vaticana' to the 'Cancionero general': Studies in Honour of Jane Whetnall, ed. Alan Deyermond & Barry Taylor, PMHRS, 60 (London: Department of Hispanic Studies, Queen Mary, University of London, 2007), pp. 89–102. ISSN 1460-051X. ISBN 0 902238 50 7.

of Quirra in 1512. But the picture is confused by the existence of another contemporary Countess of Quirra, or Chirra, Costanza d'Ávalos, a member of the Spanish-Neapolitan aristocracy.

The *canción* 'Quien encendió mis querellas', which is found in the *Cancionero general,* does not qualify for admission in the fifteenth-century popularity charts.[2] It is not mentioned in quoting poems and the only gloss of it is by Pinar himself. Nor, by any criterion, does it deserve to be highly rated. Nevertheless, there are other reasons why it is well worth discussing: it deliberately flouts the courtly convention of secrecy, and thus helpfully illustrates how the names of ladies were often concealed in verse, perhaps enabling us to decode other poems that allude to this same lady; furthermore, it sheds some light on the historical context of *cancionero* poetry at the end of the fifteenth century.

The style of the *estribillo* of this *canción* resembles that of a typical *letra* of an *invención*, or jousting device, and yet Pinar is consciously subverting the principle that one should allude to a lady's identity by referring to the first, not the last, letter of her name. This is one of the typical, although not essential, features of an *invención*: 'fue común estilo en nuestra España (y no creo que es de todo punto olvidado), que la imbención ha de ser que la primera letra della sea conforme [a] aquella en que comienza el nombre de la dama a quien se endereza' (Fernández de Oviedo 1983–2002: II, 244–45). Indeed it is possible that Pinar was inspired to compose his *canción* for Toda Centellas by an *invención* addressed to a lady whose name begins (and ends) with the letter *A* (ID 0986, 11CG–575):

> Otro sacó una .a. de oro, porque su amiga avía nombre Aldonça, y dixo
> Diziendo qu'es y de qué,
> ésta d[a] quien cuyo só;
> dize lo que hago yo.

As Ian Macpherson explains, 'Only when the literal device is pronounced aloud — *a de oro > a d'oro* — is the figurative sense revealed: 'este galán adora a Aldonza' (1998: 93). But one can take this procedure a step further. The *letra* is an instruction manual on what questions need to be asked to discover hidden meanings. If one asks '¿De qué?', the answer is 'De A', or *dea*, goddess. Therefore the concealed text is: 'Adoro a una dea'. Furthermore, the

---

[2] The popularity of a *canción* may be assessed by the number of times it is cited, glossed, copied, or printed. This was the general approach adopted by Jane Whetnall when compiling a list of most-quoted lyrics from 1465 to 1516 (Whetnall 1986 and 1989).

letter *A* may be written in the shape of a staple, *aro*, in which case the answer to the question '¿Qué es?' is: 'Es un *A* de aro', which means her name is Aldonza de Haro.

Aldonza de Haro was the only daughter of the poet Diego López de Haro (1453–1523), Señor del Carpio, and Leonor de Ayala, daughter of Pedro López de Ayala, I Count of Fuensalida, and María de Silva, sister of Juan López de Ayala, I Count of Cifuentes. Diego López de Haro, a native of Toledo and a member of an old aristocratic family of Basque origin, was one of the most ambitious and talented of the young courtiers in the service of the Catholic Monarchs: a gifted poet, a wise counsellor, a brave soldier, and a skilled diplomat (Marcello 1995). It was Leonor de Ayala's untimely death in childbirth in 1473 that led her bereaved husband to compose the *canción* 'Desconsolado de mí' (ID 0779). The unnamed jouster was probably the gentleman who became Aldonza's husband: Pedro Laso de Castilla, an illegitimate son of the magistrate Pedro de Castilla 'el Mozo' (a nephew of Alonso de Fonseca, the Archbishop of Seville, and a great-grandson of King Peter the Cruel) and Catalina Laso de Mendoza, Countess of Medinaceli, who was a granddaughter of the poet Íñigo López de Mendoza, Marquis of Santillana (Fernández de Oviedo 1983–2002: III: 211–15 & 237). Note also that the word *aro* is the first person singular of a verb that, since biblical times, has had a sexual connotation: she is the lady whom the jouster 'ploughs', or would wish to 'plough'. The letter *A* is made of gold not only because gold is yellow, the colour of despair, but also because, as a metal that does not rust or become tarnished, it is a symbol of constancy in love, and of course love, *amor*, begins with *A*.

The *canción* 'Desconsolado de mí' is attributed to Diego López de Haro in the British Library *Cancionero* (LB1–440), but it is published anonymously elsewhere. It was glossed by Pinar with the rubric *Otras suyas a la condesa de quirra porque le demandó la glosa de la canción que después d'estas verná* (11CG–881). It was also glossed by Rodrigo d'Ávalos, and cited by Diego de San Pedro, Comendador Román, Pinar, and Afonso Valente. It is generally assumed that the LB1 manuscript is much less reliable than the 1511 edition of the *Cancionero general*. However, in this case, if one compares the variants, it becomes clear that the more authentic version of the text of this song must surely be that which is found in LB1 in the section devoted to the poetry of Diego López de Haro, where it has the rubric *canción suya* (LB1–440). I suspect that Pinar was responsible for the alteration of the sequence of lines 6 and 7, so that the line 'perdí toda mi alegría' (11CG–881, 11CG–178, line 6) replaces 'tener toda mi alegría' (LB1–440, line 7), an alteration which may be explained by his love for Doña Toda Centellas:

Desconsolado de mí,	Desconsolado de mí,
no hallo quien me consuele;	no hallo quien me consuele;
çedo mi vida s'assuele,	çedo mi vida se asuele
pues tal pérdida perdí.	pues tal pérdida perdí.
Perdí mi consolación,	Perdí mi consolación,
perdí toda mi alegría,	perdí más con quien solía
y perdí con quien solía	tener toda mi alegría
consolar mi coraçón.	y consolar mi coraçón.
De ser ledo como suele	De ser ledo como suele
yo, triste, me despedí;	yo, triste, me despedí;
çedo mi vida s'assuele,	çedo mi vida se asuele,
pues tal pérdida perdí.	pues tal pérdida perdí.
(Text: 11CG–881, cf. 11CG–178)	(Text: LB1–440)

Each version above has the rhyme scheme *ABBA CDDCABAB*, whereas in the version accompanying the gloss by Rodrigo d'Ávalos the last four lines are rearranged to produce greater symmetry (*ABBA CDDCABBA*), perhaps reflecting a general trend towards formal perfection in the *canción* at the end of the fifteenth century (Whinnom 1970: 370).

At this point it is necessary to supply some biographical details about the Countess of Quirra and Toda Centellas (Costa 1973, Brook et al. 1984: 398–409). Quirra is a rugged region in the southeast of Sardinia. The title of Count of Quirra was first conferred on Berenguer II Carròs i de Ribelles (d. 1372) in 1363. The title passed to his daughter, Violant Carròs (d. 1408), in 1383, and to her son Berenguer III (d. 1427), Viceroy of Sardinia, who took his mother's name Carròs, and then to his son Jaume Carròs i Manrique (c. 1420–69), Viceroy of Sardinia (1452–54) and royal chamberlain, who in 1447 married Violant de Centelles (d. 1459), daughter of Aymeric de Centelles and Brunissenda de Perellòs.

The Countess of Quirra addressed by Pinar was almost certainly Violant Carròs i de Centelles (1456–1510), daughter of Jaume Carròs, IV Count of Quirra, and Violant de Centelles. Her father was one of the wealthiest men in Sardinia — not as rich as the Marquis of Oristany, but richer than his distant cousin and rival Nicolau Carròs d'Arborea (who later became Violant's father-in-law) — with estates extending over a quarter of the island; he had a house at Càller, or Cagliari, and a castle at Sant Miquel, which was his main residence.[3] He was a man of some culture, with a taste for music and poetry: he had two flutes, a viola, and an organ with three bellows.

On 3 January 1469, in the castle of Sant Miquel, Jaume Carròs died from burns that he had received at Christmas in a fire, leaving his estates to his one surviving legitimate child, Violant Carròs i de Centelles, who was then only about twelve years of age. One of the three executors of her father's will was Nicolau Carròs d'Arborea i de Mur (d. 1478), Baron of Terranova (1460), Majordomo of Queen Juana Enríquez (1463–65), and Viceroy of Sardinia (1460–78). This gentleman immediately took control of Violant's affairs, seized her property and, in 1471, forced her to marry his son Dalmau Carròs d'Arborea. In May 1478 Dalmau Carròs was killed at Macomer, a battle that brought to an end a rebellion against Aragonese rule in Sardinia, led by Leonardo de Alagón, Lord of Oristany, and at the end of that year Dalmau's father Nicolau Carròs became sick and died.

By this time, not long before her first husband's death, Violant, who was now about twenty years of age, had fallen in love with Dalmau's cousin, Felip de Castre Pinós i de So, son of Guillem Ramon de Castre So and Estefania Carròs d'Arborea, Nicolau's sister. Violant's mother-in-law, Brianda de Mur (d. 1487), formerly a lady-in-waiting at the Aragonese court, had barred the gates of the castle to prevent Felip from entering, but he managed to gain admittance by means of a rope ladder, and early in 1479, before the customary year of mourning had elapsed, Felip and Violant were man and wife. Her happiness, however, was short-lived because, within little more than a year, and certainly by 1482, her second husband had also died (Costa 1973: 53).

Violant Carròs had two sons, Jaume and Felip de Castre-So, but they

---

[3] He had at least twenty beds and more than sixty mattresses upholstered in red and yellow calico; two or three Neapolitan chests filled with clothes made of silk, velvet, and fur; two swords with gilt and enamelled hilts; two cuirasses covered in black leather and white velvet; two cross-bows; and a prayer-book with illuminations bound in gold and inscribed with his coat-of-arms. He had one thousand head of cattle, three thousand pigs, three thousand sheep, sixty or seventy Sicilian horses, and ninety horses of Irish pedigree. He had over a hundred servants in his household, including half a dozen Moorish slaves. He owned two galleons for importing and exporting merchandise, that were capable of engaging in combat with pirates. At the time of his death, his estate was worth about 372,000 lire and he had an annual income of 10,725 lire.

both predeceased her in 1503. She also had three younger illegitimate step-siblings, born after her mother's premature death: Carles (born c. 1463), who died as an infant; Isabel (born c. 1465), who in 1485 married Pere de Besalù in Catalonia; and Toda Senesterra-Carròs (1469–Barcelona 1547), who in 1497 had the extraordinary good fortune to marry her cousin Lluís de Centelles, eldest son of Guillem Ramon II de Centelles (d. 1490), heir to the Catalan estates of both his father and his father's half-brother Crisògon Andreu de Centelles (who had died without issue in 1470). Toda's eldest son, Serafí de Centelles, eventually inherited the title of Count of Centelles, with a castle near Vic, and her second son, Guillem Ramon de Centelles (d. 1565), a child of about twelve years of age, was formally proclaimed VI Count of Quirra with King Ferdinand's permission on 28 April 1512.

Violant Carròs had initiated a lawsuit against her sister-in-law, Beatriu Carròs d'Arborea, Senyora de Moixent in the Kingdom of Valencia, and her husband Pere Maça de Liçana, in order to recover her dowry and the property that she claimed had been stolen from her and mismanaged while she was a minor under the guardianship of her deceased father-in-law Nicolau Carròs. The court proceedings began in Cagliari on 1 September 1492 and dragged on, with various interruptions, until 1510. It is as a result of this trial that so much is known about her life.[4]

During the course of the lawsuit, between 1495 and 1500, Beatriu died, but her son Pere Maça Carròs d'Arborea, with the support of his wife Angela de Centelles, niece of Serafí de Centelles, II Count of Oliva, to whom the *Cancionero general* (1511) is dedicated, took up the defence against Violant's allegations. Then, in 1503, when Violant's two sons died, Pere Maça aggressively renewed another long-running court case concerning the rightful location of the ancestral tombs of the two rival branches of the Carròs family in the church of the Franciscan monastery at Cagliari.

On 15 April 1504 King Ferdinand ordered Joan Dusay, the Viceroy of Sardinia (1491–1501, 1502–07), to wind up the two cases, but personally reserved the right to pass judgement. Although the trial over the ancestral tombs was resolved in her favour, the trial over her inheritance was inconclusive. Dusay was obviously sympathetic to Violant's plight, but Fernando Girón de Rebolledo, who

---

[4] Archivo de la Corona de Aragón, Real Audiencia, Procesos Patrimoniales, leg. 138, 139; see Costa 1973. She was, it seems, a very litigious lady: in early October 1479, she was involved a lawsuit with Baltasar de Casasagia (ACA, Cancillería reg. 3630, vols 19–21; Cocozzella 1991: 34n71).

was Viceroy of Sardinia from 1508 to 1515, supported the claims of Pere Maça. On 10 August 1509, Miquel Aragall, the governor of Cagliari, arrested her and imprisoned her in a small room in her own house. All her servants were dismissed, except for two ladies and a page; and she was forbidden to speak to her friends and relatives. But somehow she managed to escape from her detention and sailed to Barcelona with some servants and members of her household. She travelled from there to Valladolid, where the royal court was residing, to appeal to King Ferdinand for help.[5] Ferdinand said that he considered her and those who had assisted her in her flight from Sardinia to be free of blame, and he ordered the viceroy to drop the charges against her, saying that his treasurer would pay the expenses. However, a month later Violant complained to the king that the officials in Sardinia had extorted rent-money from her vassals and had arrested and tortured her servants to persuade them to reveal the whereabouts of their mistress's jewellery and money. Again the king ordered that Violant should be fully compensated for her losses and that all those detained should be released. The Royal Council examined the trial proceedings and finally the Countess of Quirra was fully reinstated on 2 March 1510 (Costa 1973: 59–60).

The reason or pretext for Violant's detention was the suspicion that she was implicated in the death of a priest, named Joan Castanya, who had been hanged from the window of one of her houses in the Valley of Alès. It is by no means certain that the countess was innocent of this charge, but it is hard to separate fact from fiction. Before leaving Sardinia to seek King Ferdinand's help, she had obtained a letter signed by members of the deceased man's family, absolving her of any blame. There is, however, a tradition in Sardinia that this priest was Violant's chaplain and that she had arranged for him to be killed. It is reported that the cathedral of Alès was built at her expense to atone for her sin, and it is said that she did penance by retiring to a small room at the entrance to the cloister of the Franciscan monastery of Stampace, leaving instructions in her will that she should be buried outside the church and that the friars should be the beneficiaries of an annual endowment of wheat and money.[6]

[5] This would probably have been in late August 1509. During the months of August and September, the court was at Valladolid (Rumeu de Armas 1974: 354–55).

[6] See <http://www.cagliaridascoprire.it/natura/castellosmichele.htmquotations>.

Violant Carròs died at Cagliari in the winter of 1510 or early in 1511; she was about fifty-five years of age. Estefania Carròs, Baroness of Posada, the only remaining child of Nicolau and Brianda, died as a spinster in Barcelona on 16 March 1511, renouncing her rights to the county of Quirra in favour of Toda's son Guillem Ramon de Centelles (Costa 1973: 60–61). However, her nephew Pere Maça, son of Pere Maça de Liçana, pursued his case against the new heir, and in 1511, after Estefania's death, at the request of Miguel Ximénez de Urrea, Count of Aranda (1508), the viceroy Girón de Rebolledo took control of the County of Quirra, and it was only through King Ferdinand's intervention that Guillem Ramon was eventually declared the rightful heir.

Toda Senesterra-Carròs, who acquired renown by marrying Lluís de Centelles, was almost certainly the lady to whom Pinar addressed his *canción* 'Quien encendió mis querellas'. The Countess of Quirra, for whom Pinar composed a gloss on 'Desconsolado de mí', was obviously Violant Carròs. The gloss is preceded by a visionary prelude in the style of Dante, or in the manner of the ballad of the 'caballero de amor', banished to 'tierras estrañas' by the force of his unrequited love.[7] Although the whole poem is a lament by the despairing lover, there are, it seems, allusions to the dispute over the inheritance of Quirra: the proverbs 'Yo puse mis pensamientos / en obrar ciertos castillos' (ll. 1–2) and 'La cobdicia rompe el saco' (l. 75); and the statement that venial sins are not judged in criminal lawsuits (ll. 114–16). The *canción* for Toda may have been composed in 1497 on the occasion of her wedding, and it is likely that the gloss of 'Desconsolado de mí' dates from the same period.

What is puzzling, however, is that there is another Countess of Quirra in the *Cancionero general*: it is evident from the rubric and the text of Francisco Vaca's eulogy, addressed to the Marquis of Pescara, that he is describing Doña Costanza d'Ávalos, not Violant Carròs.[8] The poet-narrator, wandering through a thicket, chances

---

The archaeologist Canon Giovanni Spano, in *Guida alla città e dintorni di Cagliari*, states that Violant ordered the chaplain to be killed because he had openly condemned her for her secret liaison with Berenguer Bertran. It was thus that, in Sardinian mythology, she acquired the epithet 'la sanguinaria'; see <http://www.villasimiusweb.it/mostre/carroz/tombe.htm>.

[7] See anon. *romance* 'Maldita seas ventura' (ID 0756), glossed by Pinar (ID 0757, LB1-65), and Boase 1991: 57–58.

[8] *Otras suyas* [Francisco Vaca] *en loor de la condesa de la cherra dirigidas al marqués de la pesquera* (ID 6106, 11CG-128); it is clearly stated in the text: 'dávalos doña costan-

to meet the goddess Nature, who asks him if he has been to Naples; he replies that he has been there and will be returning soon; Nature then asks if, when he was there, he saw a lady whose highly flattering portrait she proceeds to give. This lady, the most perfect of Nature's creations, is tall, with lips like a rose, beautiful eyes, and a white face of a crystalline complexion; her hands, breasts, and neck are such that, if Venus were mortal, she would die of envy to behold them; and her hair makes the rays of Phoebus look dull.[9] She is so pure and charming and so graceful in her conversation, laughter, and general bearing that those who go to meet her do so more out of a desire to see her than to engage in business with her:

> Tan medida en su hablar
> que nunca a nadie desplaze,
> muy graciosa en razonar,
> en reyr y en passear,
> y en quanto comiença y haze.
> ¿Qué te podré dezir d'ella
> que no sea de admirar
> si quien negocia con ella
> muy más vezes va por vella
> que no va por negociar? (ll. 61–70)

This lady has been identified as Costanza d'Ávalos (c. 1460–1507), Duchess of Francavilla (1496), the daughter of Íñigo d'Ávalos (d. 30 September 1503); the poet Rodrigo d'Ávalos may have been her younger brother, who inherited from his father the title of Count of Monteodorisio and fought in Italy with Gonzalo Fernández de Córdoba.[10] Her elder brother was Alfonso d'Ávalos, II Marquis of Pescara, to whom the poem by Francisco Vaca, cited above, may be addressed.[11]

Costanza's father, Íñigo d'Ávalos, was one of the eleven children

---

ça, / la condessa de la cherra' (ll. 94–95).

[9] There is a hypothesis, proposed by the art historian Adolfo Venturi, that she was the model for Leonardo da Vinci's Mona Lisa (Clark 1973).

[10] Perea Rodríguez 2004: 289–90 and 2007: 27. Macpherson identifies him as a citizen of Guadix, a constable of the Inquisition in Jaén, married to Leonor de la Cueva, and the son of Pedro d'Ávalos Fajardo, Alcalde de Caravaca, and Juana Galve (2004: 41). But it seems more likely that he was a member of the Italian branch of the family, bearing in mind the fact that Rodrigo d'Ávalos composed a gloss of 'Desconsolado de mí', and that the author of this canción, Diego López de Haro (1453–1523), was ambassador to Rome in 1493, and that another gloss of this canción was addressed to Costanza d'Ávalos.

[11] Another of her brothers was Íñigo d'Ávalos d'Aquino, Marquis of el Vasto and Count of Monteodorisio, who married Laura Sanseverino, daughter of the Prince of Bisignano.

of Ruy López d'Ávalos (1357–1428), the Constable of Castile, who
had been stripped of his titles and estates because he had supported
the Infantes de Aragón against Álvaro de Luna in the civil wars of
Castile in the reign of John II (1406–54). He had entered the service
of Alfonso the Magnanimous of Aragon in the Kingdom of Naples
and had married Antonella d'Aquino (d. 1493), Marchioness of
Pescara, Countess of Loreto and Satriano, a member of the Sicilian
branch of the Catalan family of Cardona. Costanza's first husband,
whom she married in 1477, was Federico del Balzo (c. 1455–ante
1487), Count of Acerra, Prince of Altamura, and Duke of Andria.
Her second husband, whom she married at some time between
1496 and 1501, was Don Giovanni Battista (d. 1508), IV Duke of
Sessa, II Duke of Squillace, Count of Montalto and Alife, Count of
Carinola, and many other territories.

Costanza d'Ávalos was for several years the de facto governor of
the island of Ischia near Naples where she had set up a little Aragonese court in a castle which Alfonso the Magnanimous had built
for his young mistress Lucrezia d'Alagno in 1433. When Louis XII
of France invaded Italy in 1499, Costanza d'Ávalos gave refuge in
Ischia to Frederick IV (1496–1504), the last of the Aragonese rulers
of Naples, with other aristocratic refugees from the mainland, and
in 1503 she defended the island successfully from French attacks
for about four months. One of her pupils and protégés was the
beautiful and gifted poet Vittoria Colonna (1490–1547), a close
friend of many artists and writers, such as Michelangelo, Bembo,
and Castiglione. Vittoria married her cousin Francesco Ferrante
d'Ávalos on 27 December 1509.

Costanza d'Ávalos would have inherited a claim to the county of
Quirra from her aunt Polixena de Centellas, who was the daughter of
Antonio de Centellas-Ventimiglia, Prince of Santa Severina, and the
wife of Arrigo d'Aragona (d. 1478), Marquis of Gerace. Polixena's sister was Leonor de Centelles (d. 1504), the Marchioness of Cotrone, the
author of a subtle jousting device (ID 0940; 11CG–535, 14CG–574),
whose husband and son both died in Constantinople after being cap-
tured by pirates in 1502, and to whom Juan del Encina addressed four
compositions when she was a widow (ID 6579–82).[13]

---

[13] Other members of the family had died or entered holy orders. The eldest son of Polixena de Centelles was Luigi d'Aragona, who in 1492 married Battista Usodimari, the
niece of Pope Innocent VIII. The marriage was annulled in 1494 when Luigi d'Aragona
took holy orders: he became Bishop of León and Aversa, and later Cardinal.

Vittoria Colonna. Michelangelo addressed some sonnets to her and drew her many times. This fine pen and ink drawing, showing her looking startled, innocent, and intense, is taken from http://upload.wikimedia.org/wikipedia/commons/0/08/Vittoria_Colonna.jpg>.

It is likely that Costanza d'Ávalos received the title of Countess of Quirra from Ferdinand II (Ferrante) of Naples between 1494 and 1496. If the Marquis of Pescara to whom Francisco Vaca addresses his eulogy was her brother Alfonso d'Ávalos, a close friend of the Catalan poet Benet Garret, 'Il Cariteo', then it is likely that this poem was composed after the death of his mother, Marchioness of Pescara, in 1493, and before 7 September 1495 when he himself died (Fenzi 2002: 130). What is certain is that Costanza d'Ávalos did not retain the title of Quirra for long. She sold it to Fernando de Cárdenas, a relative and *criado* of Gutierre de Cárdenas, the Comendador Mayor of León, who had become very rich as deputy governor of Almería. Gonzalo Fernández de Oviedo, who knew this gentleman well because he himself had entered the service of King Frederick IV of Naples after the death of Prince Juan in 1496, states that Fernando de Cárdenas married a Neapolitan lady of high rank named Lucrezia.[14] It is evident from royal accounts, which give information on construction work on the dungeon at Almería, that Fernando de Cárdenas was indeed absent in Naples in 1496-97 (Cooper 1991: I, 213). This means that Francisco Vaca's poem in praise of Costanza d'Ávalos was probably composed between 1493 and 1496. It was exactly during these years that Violant Carròs was fighting for her legal right to the title of Quirra. Costanza d'Ávalos was certainly a shrewd businesswoman because it must have been evident, certainly by 1497, that her title to Quirra was of little use to her: King Ferdinand of Aragon controlled Sardinia and it looked likely that Violant Carròs would win her lawsuit to recover her full rights.

Pinar's gloss of 'Desconsolado de mí', addressed to Violant Carròs, and his *canción* for Toda Centelles were probably composed two or three years later, in 1497 or shortly afterwards.[15]

---

[14] 'Ese caballero que decís era pariente e criado del comendador mayor, e hízole su teniente de alcayde en Almería, donde se hizo muy rico de dinero; e sin venir a las Indias, llevó tantos a Nápoles, que compró de aquella muy hermosa e notable condesa de la Cherra, doña Costanza de Ábalos e de sus herederos, la Cherra; e de otros, a Layno; e el rey le dio esos títulos de conde de Layno e marqués de la Cherra. Casóse en Nápoles con una señora poderosa, llamada doña Lucreçia, que fue una de las bien dispuestas e gentiles damas de aquel reyno' (Fernández de Oviedo 1983-2002: I, 409; cf. Fernández de Oviedo 1989: 27).

[15] There are several other poems associated with these ladies, but the present article is still very much work in progress. Francesc Moner (1463-92), during the period when he lived in Valencia at the court of Ramon Folch de Cardona, Constable of Catalonia and Duke of Cardona, between 1485 and 1491, composed a *canción* in Castilian, 'Mis esfuerzos se mantienen', with a Catalan commentary in

WORKS CITED

BOASE, Roger, 1991. '*Rabia de amor*: Garcilaso's Critique of the Late-Fifteenth-Century Cult of Amorous Despair', in *Golden Age Spanish Literature: Studies in Honour of John Varey by his Colleagues and Pupils*, ed. Charles Davis & Alan Deyermond (London: Westfield College), 49–62.

BROOK, L. L., F. C. CASULA, M. M. COSTA, A. M. OLIVA, R. PAVONI, & M. TANGHERONI, 1984. *Genealogie medioevali di Sardegna*, ed. Francesco Cesare Casula (Cagliari: Due D Editrice Mediterranea).

CLARK, Kenneth, 1973. 'Mona Lisa', *The Burlington Magazine*, 115, no. 840 (March): 144–51.

COCOZZELLA, Peter, 1991. 'Introducción', in Fray Francesco Moner, *Obras castellanas, I: Poemas menores* (Lewiston, NY: Edwin Mellen Press).

COOPER, Edward, 1991. *Castillos señoriales en la Corona de Castilla*, 3 vols in 4 (Salamanca: Junta de Castilla y León).

COSTA, Maria-Mercè, 1973. *Violant Carroç, una comtessa dissortada* (Barcelona: Rafael Dalmau).

DUTTON, Brian, ed., 1990–91. *El cancionero del siglo XV, c. 1360–1520*, Biblioteca Española del Siglo XV, Serie Maior, 1–7 (Salamanca: Universidad de Salamanca).

FENZI, Enrico, 2002. '"Et havrà Barcellona il suo poeta": Benet Garret, il Cariteo', *Quaderns d'Italià*, 7: 117–40

FERNÁNDEZ DE OVIEDO, Gonzalo, 1983–2002. *Batallas y quinquagenas*, ed. José Amador de los Ríos & Juan Pérez de Tudela y Bueso, 4 vols (Madrid: Real Academia de la Historia).

——, 1989. *Batallas y quinquagenas*, ed. Juan Bautista de Avalle-Arce, Lengua y Literatura, 4 (Salamanca: Diputación de Salamanca).

FULKS, Barbara, 1989. 'The Poet Named Florencia Pinar', *C*, 18.1: 33–44.

MACPHERSON, Ian, 1998. *The 'Invenciones' and 'Letras' of the 'Cancionero general'*, PMHRS, 9.

——2004. '*Motes y glosas' in the 'Cancionero general'*, PMHRS, 46.

MARCELLO, Elena Elisabetta, 1995. 'Diego López de Haro, poeta cancioneril:

prose, addressed to Violant Carròs, Countess of Quirra (Moner 1970: 113–19, 23–24; Cocozzella 1991: 15). There is a eulogistic poem addressed by Juan de Cardona, 'Busco esfuerço a mi desmayo' (ID 6702, 11CG-926), with the rubric *Coplas de don juan de cardona en loor de doña ysabel y doña brianda y doña ana maças*. Brianda and Isabel are the two younger sisters of Pere Maça Carròs d'Arborea; the third young lady, Ana Maças, is probably his wife Angela Maça. This poem must have been composed before 1501 because Isabel Maça died in that year while still very young, and her sister Brianda died at about the same time (Brook et al. 1984: 398–409). Juan de Cardona, the author of several compositions in the *Cancionero general*, was, like Villafaña and Perálvarez de Ayllón, a member of the military retinue of César de Borja, Duke of Valentinois (Macpherson 1998: 70); his title was Lord of Guadalest; he was a brother of Alonso de Cardona, Admiral of Aragon; he was associated with the Aragonese court in Naples and Valencia; and he died at the Battle of Ravenna in 1512 (Perea Rodríguez 2004: 428 & 524; 2007: 249n27). Note the key word *esfuerço* in the first line of these two poems.

profilo storico-biografico,' *Il Confronto Letterario*, 12: 105–29.

MONER, Francesc, 1970. *Obres catalanes*, ed. Peter Cocozzella, ENC, A100 (Barcelona: Barcino).

PEREA RODRÍGUEZ, Óscar, 2004. 'Las cortes literarias hispánicas del siglo XV: el entorno histórico del *Cancionero general* de Hernando del Castillo (1511)', doctoral thesis (Universidad Complutense).

——, 2007. *Estudio biográfico sobre los poetas del 'Cancionero general'*, Anejos de la *RFE*, 98 (Madrid: CSIC).

RUMEU DE ARMAS, Antonio, 1974. *Itinerario de los Reyes Católicos 1474–1516* (Madrid: CSIC).

WHETNALL, Jane, 1986. 'Manuscript Love Poetry of the Fifteenth Century: Developing Standards and Continuing Traditions', doctoral thesis (University of Cambridge).

——, 1989. 'Songs and *Canciones* in the *Cancionero general* of 1511,' in *The Age of the Catholic Monarchs, 1474–1516: Literary Studies in Memory of Keith Whinnom*, ed. Alan Deyermond & Ian Macpherson (Liverpool: UP), pp. 197–207.

WHINNOM, Keith, 1970. 'Hacia una interpretación y apreciación de las canciones del *Cancionero general*', *Filología*, 13 (1968–69 [1970]: *Homenaje a don Ramón Menéndez Pidal*): 361–81.

Andreu Febrer, *fabbro* i lector

Lluís Cabré

(Universitat Autònoma de Barcelona)

El coneixement de la història de la poesia hispànica medieval ha progressat molt en les últimes dècades. Recollida en cancioneros i en cançoners, aquesta producció s'ha beneficiat de la investigació a l'arxiu (sota el savi principi *cherchez la cour*) i l'anàlisi codicològica de les miscel·lànies poètiques. Aquests dos instruments s'han revelat imprescindibles. Resulta igualment necessària, però, la lectura detallada d'aquestes obres, sovint menors, si volem trobar pautes d'història literària que ens orientin també la interpretació dels poetes majors, és a dir, que ens ajudin a establir la tradició. Els acurats, incisius, estudis de Jane Whetnall ho han demostrat a bastament: al domini dels cancioneros, que ja porten sovint a les corts d'Aragó, hi ha sumat acumen i un generós coneixement del conjunt de les líriques romàniques, catalana inclosa.[1] Les pàgines que segueixen només són una modesta torna: voldria tractar d'un poeta català aparentment secundari, però bon lector, els versos del qual ens remeten, no pas per atzar, a obres cabdals de la lírica romànica medieval.

Andreu Febrer (ca. 1375–1440/44) ha viscut a l'ombra de Jordi de Sant Jordi, com un precedent, i figura de fa temps en la història literària al costat del cavaller valencià Gilabert de Pròixida. (Les obres de Febrer i Pròixida, compostes a tot estirar no gaire més enllà del canvi de segle, es conserven en còpia única fent part d'un primer estrat del cançoner Vega-Aguiló (Alberni Jordà 2002a: 150–55), un recull acabat a mitjan dècada de 1420.) La valoració és prou parcial, perquè Febrer, com és sabut, també va traduir en tercines decasil·làbiques la *Commedia* de Dante, i una empresa d'aquesta

---

[1] Vegeu, per exemple, Whetnall 2005: una lliçó d'història que descobreix la petja de Christine de Pizan en *La glòria d'amor* passada per l'essencial moda musical de les corts quatrecentistes.

From the 'Cancioneiro da Vaticana' to the 'Cancionero general': Studies in Honour of Jane Whetnall, ed. Alan Deyermond & Barry Taylor, PMHRS, 60 (London: Department of Hispanic Studies, Queen Mary, University of London, 2007), pp. 103-14. ISSN 1460–051X. ISBN 0 902238 50 7.

envergadura (acabada en plena maduresa l'agost de 1429) pressuposa una preparació lingüística considerable i una inusual confiança en l'exercici de la ploma. És natural que el marquès de Santillana, que havia rebut la versió en prosa d'Enrique de Villena (1428), subratllés al *Prohemio e carta* vint anys després la gosadia del poeta català: 'Mosén Febrer fizo obras nobles, e algunos afirman aya traído el Dante de lengua florentina en catalán no menmenguando punto en la orden del metrificar e consonar' (1997: 22, amb un lleuger canvi de puntuació).

Aquesta confiança s'entén millor si tenim present, com s'ha fet no fa gaire, que Febrer era un home de lletres: de jovenet va rebre la primera tonsura i, cal suposar, l'educació escolar pertinent; abans de 1393 va ingressar a la cort com a escrivà (com ho havia fet Bernat Metge el 1371) i va servir molts anys com a funcionari abans de passar al servei del jove rei Alfons I de ser posteriorment adobat a cavaller, probablement en edat força avançada (Parera 2006: 5-13). Aquesta formació — ben diferent a la d'un fill de cavaller — potser no és estranya a la seva capacitat lingüística.

Febrer va gosar traduir la *Commedia* per a Alfons perquè s'havia establert a Sicília (ja era castellà d'Ursini el 1418 i va morir deixant família a Palerm); en aquests anys devia adquirir un domini complet de la llengua italiana, però el 1398 les seves cobles ja imiten amb subtilesa uns versos de l'*Inferno* (Riquer 1951: 55; Parera 2006: 9). D'altra banda, havia pertangut a l'escrivania de Joan I, el rei que era 'tot francès', i havia exercit missions diplomàtiques a França, per a Martí I (1407) i particularment al servei de la reina vídua Violant de Bar durant la crisi de successió — Febrer defensava el dret del nét de Violant, Lluís d'Anjou, i l'àvia va elogiar el 1410 la manera de les cartes del seu domèstic: 'larch, distint et clar scriure' (Vendrell Gallostra 1992: 189).

Aquesta perícia també troba correspondència en el vers. Febrer va incorporar la *ballade* (XI, ed. Riquer 1951) i va adaptar per primera vegada el *lay* (XIV i XV) segons l'estil del mestre de l'*ars nova*, Guillaume de Machaut, i ho va fer amb plena consciència de la dificultat i el sentit del gènere. La música francesa era molt apreciada a la cort de Joan i Violant (Pagès 1936: 28-30 i *passim*); la nova formulació havia convertit el lai (líric) en la joia de la corona dels gèneres de forma fixa, com advertia Eustache Deschamps abans d'establir-ne la preceptiva a *L'Art de dictier* el 1392: 'c'est une chose longue et malaisiee a faire et trouver' (1994: 94). S'ha tendit a subratllar (Pagès 1936: 159) que Febrer en va simplificar la versificació, i és ben cert, però també s'ha de tenir present que ni el mateix Machaut, ni Deschamps o Jean Froissart, s'ajustaren sempre a la preceptiva, i que Febrer, adaptant 'Loyauté, que point ne delay' (I, ed. Chichmaref 1909: 279–93), va saber veure-hi més d'un principi clau de composició. Al seu lai 'Amors, qui tost fér, quant li play' (XIV), per exemple, els rastres clars de la dicció francesa corresponen a l'inici i al final de la peça de Machaut, a un sistema de rimes molt reiterades gràcies als monosíl·labs (que cultivarà després Jordi de Sant Jordi), i als motius d'exordi i cloenda que delimiten el trajecte de la llarga queixa que és un lai (Cabré 1986: 187–88). Seguramente el poeta català ignorava *L'Art de dictier* de Deschamps, però amb el coneixement, almenys, de 'Loyauté, que point ne delay' en va tenir prou per ampliar l'espai de la lírica cortesana pròpia.

La mateixa capacitat literària s'observa, finalment, en relació a la tradició més inmediata. Febrer va escriure en la llengua poètica híbrida del seu temps — l'occità ja catalanitzat que anomenaven 'llemoví' (llemosí) — a finals del segle XIV, a l'època en què documentem a Barcelona la creació de concursos literaris a imitació dels tolosans. Als seus versos, però, hi va saber incorporar alguns dels millors trobadors del segle XII, com ara Raimbaut d'Aurenga i Arnaut Daniel, i el trobador local más destacat, Cerverí de Girona (Riquer 1951: 36–49). Una mostra d'aquesta voluntat és el conreu (i probable introducció) dels estramps, gènere ben estudiat per Josep Pujol (1988–89) i Costanzo di Girolamo (2003).[2] Tots dos treballs ens han confirmat que Febrer inaugura un gust poètic arrelat en la familiaritat amb el *trobar ric*, i que en fixar els estramps — la composició escrita de dalt a baix amb mots finals que no rimen però comporten una estètica de la dificultat — en un elogi a Maria de Sicília (I, ed. Riquer 1951) va donar lloc a un gènere nou de la poesia catalana, com es comprova en els *Stramps* (IX) de Jordi de Sant Jordi per a la reina vídua Margarida de Prades i en els que va escriure Ausiàs March per lloar Alfons el Magnànim (LXXII) o exaltar l'amor honest (XVIII, XLV o XCIV).

Tot comptat, la primera frase de l'elogi de Santillana tampoc no sembla gens gratuïta: certament Febrer 'fizo obras nobles'. (I deixo en el tinter altres novetats potser encara més pertinents, com la peça 'Sobre·l pus naut element de tots quatre' (I), no sols pels estramps

---

[2] Cito aquest treball per facilitar-ne la consulta; la part sobre els estramps reprodueix (amb correccions) Di Girolamo & Siviero (1999). Vegeu també Billy (2005).

sinó pel contingut astrològic i al·legòric, tan habitual en exhibicions de saviesa cortesana al segle XV des de Francisco Imperial.[3])

El retrat que he esbossat és el d'un artífex: salvant les distàncies, el d'un 'fabbro' de la llengua, com va dir Dante d'Arnaut Daniel (*Purgatorio* XXVI.127). Part d'aquesta dimensió s'ha començat a apreciar gràcies als estudis recents que he anat citant, de manera que hom ha arribat a escriure que Febrer potser 'fou la veritable eminència grisa de la poesia catalana durant més de trenta anys' (Di Girolamo & Siviero 1999: 37). No m'atreviria a dir tant, però una conclusió segura de tots aquests treballs és que no va ser un simple precedent sinó el mestre de Jordi de Sant Jordi.[4] En la mesura que el coneixement de la poesia catalana quatrecentista progressa, aquest mestratge conjunt va arribant més enllà.[5]

La revaloració de l'obra lírica de Febrer ha vingut, sobretot, pel costat de la versificació: el lai i els estramps. És mèrit de Di Girolamo (2003: 53–58) haver observat un altre factor literari: la necessària presència de la *sestina* de Dante en els *Stramps* (IX) de Jordi de Sant Jordi i la possible influència prèvia del conjunt de les *rime petrose* dantesques en els versos estramps de Febrer (I) i en la seva cançó 'Combas e valhs, puigs, muntanyes e colhs' (X), escrita en rims dissoluts al dictat de Raimbaut d'Aurenga i sobretot d'Arnaut Daniel.[6] No insistiré gaire, doncs, en els models formals. Però voldria matisar que un bon poeta — i Febrer ho era — quan pren un patró és perquè ha llegit bé el text, com hem vist en el cas del lai. Llavors pot recrear la tradició i dialogar-hi. Ho il·lustraré a continuació.

---

[3] En aquest text de Febrer s'enregistra per primera vegada en poesia catalana el terme 'calitat' (I, v. 21), val a dir el temperament o composició humana natural que resulta de la determinació astral. En poetes posteriors esdevindrà un terme clau de la teoria sobre l'amor, com vaig mirar d'explicar (Cabré 1997: 64–66) a propòsit d'Ausiàs March i Pere Torroella (per al qual vegeu ara Rodríguez Risquete 2003: clxix-clxxvi & 69–70). Aprofito per corregir la cronologia: el 1997 confiava que la peça més antiga a tractar el motiu era de Jaume March, l'oncle d'Ausiàs; ara el seu antic editor ha proposat (i no n'hi ha dubte) que és obra d'un nét homònim, posterior, doncs, a Ausiàs (Pujol en premsa).

[4] Així s'anota amb detall en l'edició de Fratta (2005: e.g. 185–86 i notes a XII, vv. 2–6 i XVII, vv. 30 & 157). Per al context històric del virtuosisme formal de Jordi de Sant Jordi, i les tries literàries, vegeu Riquer & Badia (1984: 13–80).

[5] Jaume Torró ha tingut la bondat de mostrar-me la notable presència de Febrer i Jordi de Sant Jordi en Martí Garcia, l'edició del qual prepara en un volum per a Els Nostres Clàssics (Torró en premsa).

[6] Vegeu les notes de Riquer (1951), així com Pujol (1988–89: 65–69) i Di Girolamo (2003: 55).

La cançó x de Febrer és un homenatge a la sextina arnaldiana 'Lo ferm voler qu'el cor m'intra' (Pillet-Carstens 29.14; 6, ed. Riquer 1994). La rima dissoluta, és a dir, l'ús de mots a final de vers que no rimen dins de la cobla sinó entre cobla i cobla, era un recurs corrent en moltes peces d'Arnaut Daniel.[7] És possible que Febrer pensés que la sextina n'era una variant sofisticada, ja que la sextina el que fa és establir a final de vers sis mots (que no rimen entre ells) i que es van repetint a cada cobla (com els rims dissoluts), amb la diferència que ara cal repetir el mot íntegre (no sols la rima) i que la repetició (limitada als sis mots) no és vers a vers de cada cobla sinó que, seguint una combinatòria tancada, produeix sis cobles amb un ordre de mots finals diferent. En tot cas, Febrer devia considerar la cèlebre sextina com una part integrant de l'estil ric d'Arnaut Daniel, i devia observar-hi, de ben segur, que algunes de les sis paraules a final de vers eren de rima quasi impossible (així *oncle* i *ongla*). Això aproximava la sextina als estramps cars i, en especial, al que Jaume March n'havia dit 'rims de fènix' el 1371 (Pujol 1988–89: 47 & 55; Billy 2005: 533 & 541–42), entre els quals ja hi trobem 'ungla' (Griera 1921: 74).[8]

Si atenem a aquesta raons, potser entendrem millor que Febrer triés 'ungla' com un dels rims dissoluts de la cançó x, i, encara més, que el tractés com un *mot refranh* i el repetís al final de cada estrofa (perquè cap altre mot no podria rimar-hi i doncs el destacava com a mot íntegre, a la manera de la sextina). Però la raó potser és més profunda. El *mot refranh* no servia tant per singularitzar un mot per la riquesa de la rima com per subratllar una paraula que a voltes podia sintetizar un gènere (per exemple, 'alba' en el cas d'una alba) o el sentit d'una peça (així 'aver' en el *Vers verdadier* de Cerverí de Girona, Pillet-Carstens 434a.11), com si fos una cèl·lula primera del contingut de l'obra.[9] Penso, doncs, que el *mot refranh* 'ungla' en la cançó de Febrer comportava la noció de gènere, la marca d'estil del trobar difícil d'Arnaut Daniel, però segurament també remetia al contingut passional de la sextina,

[7] Per exemple, 'Doutz braitz e critz' (Pillet-Carstens 29.8; 1, ed. Riquer 1994), peça recordada a la cançó de Febrer (Riquer 1951: 45).

[8] Ni els 'estramps cars' de la preceptiva tolosana, ni els vocables 'yrsuta' de Dante (Di Girolamo 2003: 52), no acaben d'explicar la terminologia de Jaume March, que posa la condició dels 'rims de fènix' en la seva singularitat. Els vint anys que separen el *Llibre de concordances* de Jaume March de les obres de Febrer són, ara com ara, un enigma (però recordem que la producció catalana dels anys 1370–90 ha sobreviscut en casos molt comptats).

[9] Per al text de Cerverí, i el joc de paraules entre la rúbrica i el *mot refranh* (situat al final de la cobla), vegeu M. Cabré (1999: 43–45).

que deia: 'de lieis serai aisi cum carn e ongla' i 'mos cors no·s part de
lieis tan cum ten l'ongla' (vv. 17 & 30, ed. Riquer 1994). Aquesta imatge la repeteix Febrer: 'e·ns amarem tant com la carn e l'ungla' (v. 16,
ed. Riquer 1951), i la recrearà, seguint aquest trajecte, Jordi de Sant
Jordi als *Stramps*: 'no·s part mon cors de vos tant com dits d'ungla' (v.
40, ed. Riquer & Badia 1984).[10]

Tota la cançó de Febrer és un exercici d'exaltació del desig, de la
mateixa manera que ho és 'Lo ferm voler', que amb el mot 'cambra' centra l'espai del desig eròtic des del vers 'jauzirai joi dins
vergier o dins cambra' (v. 8, ed. Riquer 1994). Febrer en calca el
futur: 'jausirem tant lo joy d'amor, que drut / me dirà sieu tota
gen' (vv. 14–15); el terme 'drut' no pot ser més explícit.[11] La violència d'aquest desig, expressat feliçment en la unió de la carn i
l'ungla, devia colpir, i Febrer va saber recrear-la amb una imatge
carnal encara més potent: 'no me'n destulh [sc. separo] plus que de
carn fay lops' (v. 12). El poeta català, conclouria, va voler reprendre a la cançó x la manifestació del desig físic expressat a la sextina
d'Arnaut Daniel i, com els bons poetes, ho va fer sense dissociar la
marca d'estil de la força del contingut.

El que sorprèn d'entrada en la cançó de Febrer és l'inici, i no en
ell mateix (ja que recorre al *topos* de la naturalesa primaveral invertit), sinó perquè no troba correspondència en la sextina de Daniel.
Diu la primera cobla:

> Combas e valhs, puigs, muntanyes e colhs
> vey ja vestitz de comblachs e de neus,
> boys e jardís tots despulhats de rams,
> l'ayre cubert de vents plugs e de grops,
> e·l mar tot blanch d'escuma per mal temps
> e tuyt l'auselh stan en terra mut,
> qui per l'ivern no movo xants ne crits;
> mas yeu suy caltz quan l'altri búfon l'ungla
> (vv. 1–8, ed. Riquer 1951: 93)

El darrer vers, forçat per 'ungla', gairebé com un estirabot, és la
millor prova de la simpatia del poeta català amb l'estil de la sextina d'Arnaut. Els anteriors són una altra cosa. Riquer (1951: 95–96)

---

[10] Jordi de Sant Jordi també té en compte 'qu'aitan vezis cum es lo detz de l'ongla'
(v. 21, ed. Riquer 1994).

[11] De nou, Jordi de Sant Jordi reprèn el mot clau de Daniel en el vers més eròtic del
seu elogi: 'que·m retenyats en vostra valent cambra' (v. 47, ed. Riquer & Badia
1984); notem la perífrasi amb què s'al·ludia a la condició de *drutz* i comparem amb
Daniel: 'e cossentis m'a celat dins sa cambra' (v. 13, ed. Riquer 1994).

va anotar que Febrer, en descriure l'hivern com a contrast, recordava Raimbaut d'Aurenga, que ja dibuixava amb aspror aquest paisatge i remarcava la inversió a 'Er resplan la flor enversa' (Pillet-Carstens 389.16):

> Er resplan la flor enversa
> pels trencans rancx e pels tertres.
> Quals flors? Neus, gels e conglapis,
> que cotz e destrenh e trenca,
> don vey morz quils, critz, brays, siscles
> pels fuels, pels rams e pels giscles;
> mas mi te vert e jauzen joys,
> er quan vey secx los dolens croys.
> (vv. 1–8, ed. Riquer 1975: I, 445–47)

Aquesta *canso* està escrita, precisament, amb una tècnica semblant a la sextina, ja que les veus finals es repeteixen (amb inflexió) a cada cobla. L'expressió 'Neus, gels e conglapis' no deixa marge al dubte (cf. 'de comblachs e de neus'); l'estructura tampoc: descripció de l'hivern i adversativa amb 'mas' en tots dos casos. El poeta català, es pot concloure, hauria sobreposat els dos trobadors.

Recordem, tanmateix, que Febrer partia de la sextina d'Arnaut Daniel, on aquest paisatge hivernal i la noció d'inversió eren del tot inexistents. Al meu entendre, la connexió entre els dos textos trobadorescos li devia venir donada per una altra lectura, que Costanzo di Girolamo lògicament tenia present (perquè havia comparat els mots-rima de les *petrose* amb Febrer i Jordi de Sant Jordi).[12] Es tracta de la sextina de Dante 'Al poco giorno e al gran cerchio d'ombra', que comença així:

> Al poco giorno e al gran cerchio d'ombra
> son giunto, lasso, ed al bianchir de' colli,
> quando si perde lo color ne l'erba:
> e 'l mio disio però non cangia il verde,
> sí è barbato ne la dura petra
> che parla e sente come fosse donna.
> (vv. 1–6, ed. Contini 1965: 158)

Fixem-nos en tres qüestions: el contrast entre el paisatge hivernal i el 'verde' del poeta, que Dante reprèn de 'mas mi te vert' de Raimbaut d'Aurenga; el fet que és una sextina, òbviament arnaldiana, i

---

[12] Di Girolamo (2003: 56): 'Observons au passage que, s'il est exact que *Combas e valhs* évoque le paysage glaciale de la chanson de la *flors enversa* de Raimbaut (P.-C. 389.16), cela ne rappelle pas moins le scénario hivernal, désolé et brumeux, des *petrose* de Dante.'

que el text es dedica enterament a l'expressió ultrada del 'mio disio', com en el model; finalment, que s'hi troben els dos components del text de Febrer aliats a l'exordi. Si no volem temptar la poligènesi sobre un motiu tan concret, semblarà acceptable pensar que Febrer va trobar inspiració en la sextina dantesca. Ho confirma almenys un detall: 'puigs, muntanyes e colhs', el primer vers, porta el mot rima de 'al bianchir de' colli', el segon vers de la *sestina* (i Raimbaut d'Aurenga només esmentava 'tertre', puigs).[13] En Dante, crec, Febrer hi va trobar la lectura combinada dels dos trobadors, un model prestigiós que orientava, o almenys avalava, la seva pràctica d'artífex literari — la pràctica que confirmen tries tan eloqüents com el *trobar ric* de Cerverí de Girona o el *lay* de Machaut, sempre en cerca de la dificultat.

Pel cap baix, l'exemple de la cançó X ens ensenya que l'adopció d'un gènere l'emmarca la lectura, en aquest cas d'Arnaut Daniel i Raimbaut d'Aurenga i, si la interpretació proposada és correcta, a través de Dante. Sense aquesta lectura ben digerida, dificilment hi ha recreació (per molt que a vegades ens esforcem a separar les formes, o els trets d'estil, de la perícia literària). Com que aquesta lectura existia, la sextina d'Arnaut Daniel — i ara sense cap influència formal — va deixar una empremta ben diferent en la cançó III de Febrer 'Lo fol desir qu·Amor ha fayt intrar', composta en cinc canòniques octaves creucreuades (i capcaudades) amb tornada.

El vers inicial i un sintagma posterior ('ab ferm voler', v. 15, ed. Riquer 1951) deixen clar el punt de partida: 'Lo ferm voler qu'el cor m'intra' d'Arnaut Daniel (v. 1, ed. Riquer 1994). Ara, però, el text de Febrer es configura com una rèplica diametralment contrària a la peça del mestre: no exaltarà el desig, sinó que oposarà a consciència 'Lo fol desir' a 'Lo ferm voler', l'obertura dels versos inicials respectius. Tots dos desitjos els fa *intrar* Amor en l'enamorat però l'actitud ha canviat: segons Febrer, 'tant com poray lo vulh de mé lunyar' (v. 4). Aquesta aparent heterodòxia, en termes de fina amor, s'entén perquè el poeta vol, precisament, anul·lar el desig sensual: 'Dons, pus complir no pux mon desirer, / sen desirar yeu la·ntén a servir' (vv. 7–8), de manera que contra 'Lo ferm voler' de Daniel, que és el desig sensual (i.e. 'Lo fol desir' de Febrer), ara ens dirà que vol servir la dama 'ab ferm voler, sens esperar que·m don / joy ne s'amor' (vv. 15–16). La contesta a Daniel

---

[13] Més endavant, Febrer situa de nou el temps: 'eres en los jorns breus' (v. 26), potser recordant 'Al poco giorno'.

no pot ser més clara: el 'ferm voler' del poeta català és d'una altra naturalesa. Per aquesta raó, si seguim la ficció, Febrer vol fer la pau amb els envejosos que el denunciarien: 'Ab lausangiers faray yeu patz adés / e·z ab tots celhs qui·s fan devinadors, / qu·yeu no·ls entén donar nulha caysós /d'are enant de mé parler jamés' (vv. 33–36). Com que el seu amor serà cast — als antípodes del desig que és com el del llop per la carn, segons la cançó X —, pot renunciar al secret preceptiu i deixar d'encobrir la dama sota *senhal*: per això escriu directament el nom de l'estimada, 'Na Beatriu, qu·és sus totes valén' (v. 41). La promesa de castedat s'expressa en fórmula cristiana a la resta de la tornada: a la dama, no li ha faltat ni li faltarà de pensament, paraula ni obra ('anch no us felhí en nagun fayt ne dit, / mas si·n pençant vos he nulh temps felhit, / mercè us deman de mon folh penssamén', vv. 42–44).[14] Per al negatiu d'aquesta exposició d'un desig cast, només caldria recordar que Arnaut Daniel, a banda d'imaginar el gaudi 'dins cambra' (v. 6) i la unió 'aisi cum carn e ongla' (v. 17), començava la sextina dient que 'Lo ferm voler' no el podia malmetre cap 'lauzengier' (v. 2), i que la seva perspectiva era entrar en un paradís d'hipèrbole sagrada ('qu'en Paradis n'aura doble joi m'arma, / si ja nulhs hom per ben amar lai intra', vv. 35–36). Febrer ha invertit el codi amorós.

A la cançó III de Febrer, concloent, podem observar-hi tres novetats. El trencament de la convenció del *senhal*, que tornarem a trobar en la Isabel de Jordi de Sant Jordi (XI.41, ed. Riquer & Badia 1984). La declaració de lloança a una dama per la castedat, motiu que s'imposarà a partir de Melcior de Gualbes, amb clars ressons dantescos (Alberni Jordà 2002b: 163–164), i que trobarà una expressió prou neta a la poesia *Midons* (V) de Jordi de Sant Jordi i en els cicles marquians a Plena de seny i Llir entre cards. I, sobretot, la manifestació d'una plena consciència literària: la mateixa consciència que a 'Combas e valhs' li feia recrear i honorar la sextina d'Arnaut Daniel per la passió i l'estil (sintetitzats en el mot 'ungla'), li permet replicar-hi obertament a 'Lo fol desir'. Potser és aquesta consciència, aquest ofici literari madurat en la lectura de tres caps d'escola com Arnaut Daniel, Guillaume de Machaut i Dante, el que al capdavall ens explica que Febrer gosés traduir més tard la *Commedia* 'no menguando punto en la orden del metrificar e consonar'.[15]

---

[14] Aquesta dama s'acosta molt a la *midons* de Jordi de Sant Jordi: 'car leys es tal que no consen la taca / del parlamen, ne de fayts ne de fama' (V, vv. 22–23, ed. Riquer & Badia 1984).

[15] Quan aquest treball ja estava en fase de paginades, m'ha arribat una important contribució d'Isabel Grifoll (2006). El seu excel·lent estudi, complementari del present, ofereix

OBRES CITADES

ALBERNI JORDÀ, Anna, 2002a. 'El *Cançoner Vega-Aguiló* (BC, mss. 7–8): estructura i contingut', tesi doctoral (Universitat de Barcelona).

——, 2002b. 'El *Cançoner Vega-Aguiló*: una proposta de reconstrucció codicològica', dins *Literatura i cultura a la Corona d'Aragó (segles XIII-XV)*, ed. Lola Badia, Miriam Cabré, & Sadurní Martí (Barcelona: Curial & PAM), pp. 151–71.

BILLY, Dominique, 2005. 'Remarques inédites sur les *estramps* catalanes', dins *Études de langue et de littérature médiévales offertes à Peter T. Ricketts*, ed. Dominique Billy & Ann Buckley (Turnhout: Brepols), pp. 531–43.

CABRÉ, Lluís, 1986. '*Los enuigs* de Jordi de Sant Jordi i l'adaptació del lai líric a la poesia catalana medieval', dins *Estudis de literatura catalana en honor de Josep Romeu i Figueras*, ed. Lola Badia & Josep Massot i Muntaner, 2 vols. (Barcelona: PAM), I, pp. 183–206.

——, 1997. 'From Ausiàs March to Petrarch: Torroella, Urrea, and Other *Ausimarchides*', dins *The Medieval Mind: Hispanic Studies in Honour of Alan Deyermond*, ed. Ian Macpherson & Ralph Penny, CT, A170 (London: Tamesis), pp. 57–73.

CABRÉ, Miriam, 1999. *Cerverí de Girona and his Poetic Traditions*, CT, A169 (London: Tamesis).

CHICHMAREF, V., ed., 1909. Guillaume de Machaut, *Poésies lyriques*, 2 vols. (Paris: Honoré Champion).

CONTINI, Gianfranco, ed., 1965. Dante Alighieri, *Rime* (Torino: Einaudi).

DESCHAMPS, Eustache, 1994. *L'Art de dictier*, ed. & trad. Deborah Sinnreich-Levi (East Lansing, MI: Colleagues Press).

DI GIROLAMO, Costanzo, 2003. 'La versification catalane médiévale entre innovation et conservation de ses modèles occitanes', *Revue des Langues Romanes*, 107: 41–74.

——, & Donatella SIVIERO, 1999. 'D'Orange a Beniarjó (passant per Florència): una interpretació dels estramps catalans', *Mot so razo*, 1: 32–39.

FRATTA, Aniello, ed., 2005. Jordi de Sant Jordi, *Poesies*, ENC, B26 (Barcelona: Barcino).

GRIERA, Antoni, ed., 1921. *Diccionari de rims de Jaume March* (Barcelona: Institut d'Estudis Catalans).

GRIFOLL, Isabel, 2006. '*Combas e valhs, puigs, muntanyes e colhs*: Andreu Febrer i els trobadors', in *Trobadores a la Península Ibérica: homenatge al Dr Martí de Riquer*, ed. Vicenç Beltran, Meritxell Simó, & Elena Roig (Barcelona: Publicacions de l'Abadia de Montserrat), pp. 195–221.

PAGÈS, Amédée, 1936. *La Poésie française en Catalogne du XIIIᵉ siècle à la fin du XVᵉ* (Toulouse: Privat; Paris: Didier).

una visió de la presència d'Arnaut Daniel en la poesia catalana i una lectura de 'Combas e valhs' amb especial referència a Jaufre Rudel. No he pogut, però, revisar el meu treball a la llum del seu.

PARERA, Raquel, 2006. 'La versió d'Andreu Febrer de la *Commedia* de Dante: estudi del manuscrit i edició de l'*Infern*, I-XI', treball de recerca (Universitat Autònoma de Barcelona).

PILLET, A., & Henry CARSTENS, 1933. *Bibliographie des Troubadours*, Schriften des Königsberger Gelehrten Gesellschaft, 3 (Halle: KGG).

PUJOL, Josep, 1988-89. 'Els versos estramps en la lírica catalana medieval', *Llengua i Literatura*, 3: 41-87.

——, en premsa. 'L'atribució de les cançons amoroses de Jacme March', dins *Actes del XIIIè Col·loqui Internacional de Llengua i Literatura Catalanes (Universitat de Girona, 9-12 de setembre de 2003)*, ed. Sadurní Martí, Miriam Cabré, Francesc Feliu, Narcís Iglesias, & David Prats (Barcelona: AILLC & PAM), III, pp. 305-18.

RIQUER, Martí de, ed., 1951. Andreu Febrer, *Poesies*, ENC, A68 (Barcelona: Barcino).

——, 1975. *Los trovadores: historia literaria y textos*, 3 vols. (Barcelona: Planeta).

——, ed. & trad., 1994. Arnaut Daniel, *Poesías* (Barcelona: Quaderns Crema).

——, & Lola BADIA, ed. & trad.,1984. *Les poesies de Jordi de Sant Jordi, cavaller valencià del segle XV*, Biblioteca d'Estudis i Investigacions, 7 (València: Tres i Quatre).

RODRÍGUEZ RISQUETE, Francisco Javier, 2003. 'Vida y obra de Pere Torroella', tesi doctoral (Universitat de Girona).

SANTILLANA, Marqués de, 1997. '*Comedieta de Ponza*', sonetos, serranillas y otras obras, ed. Regula Rohland de Langbehn, Biblioteca Clásica, 12 (Barcelona: Crítica).

TORRÓ, Jaume, ed., en premsa. Lluís de Requesens, Bernat Miquel, Martí Garcia, Rodrigo Díeç, Lluís de Vilarasa i Mossèn Sunyer, *Poesies* (Barcelona: Barcino).

VENDRELL GALLOSTRA, Francisca, 1992. *Violante de Bar y el Compromiso de Caspe* (Barcelona: Real Academia de Buenas Letras).

WHETNALL, Jane, 2005. '*Veteris vestigia flammae*: a la caza de la cita cancioneril', dins *I canzioneri di Lucrecia / Los cancioneros de Lucrecia: Atti del Convegno Internazionale sulle raccolte poetiche iberiche dei secoli XV-XVII, Ferrara, 7-9 ottobre 2002*, ed. Andrea Baldissera & Giuseppe Mazzochi (Padova: Unipress), pp. 179-92.

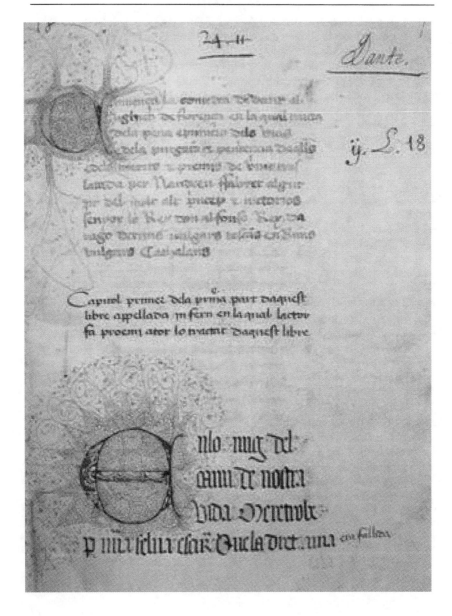

La *Declamación de Lucrecia*

CARLOS CONDE SOLARES

(*Queen Mary*)

Son varios los aspectos que hacen de la *Declamación de Lucrecia* (LB2-0$_a$, ID 2140) un texto de especial interés desde el punto de vista filológico. El primero de ellos salta a la vista: se trata del fragmento de prosa que abre el *Cancionero de Herberay*. Comienza en el folio 2^r y enlaza con la *Epístola de la Madreselua a Mansol* en el 5^r. Charles V. Aubrun le dedica escasa atención en su edición del manuscrito, que se centra mucho más en la parte poética y no dedica ninguna sección del estudio preliminar a la presencia de las prosas al inicio del cancionero. Sin embargo, en la sección de notas y variantes, Aubrun da noticia de la existencia de otra versión castellana de la *Declamación de Lucrecia* en el manuscrito 6a-2 de la sección restringida de la Biblioteca Nacional de Madrid, en la actualidad Vitrina 17-4 (Aubrun 1951: 205). Por otra parte, en la magna obra de Brian Dutton, no se transcriben ni éste ni ninguno de los fragmentos que encabezan el *Cancionero de Herberay* (Dutton 1990–91).

María Rosa Lida de Malkiel se refiere tangencialmente a la *Declamación*, citándola como exponente de la supuesta boga de que gozaría la 'epístola literaria puesta en boca de un personaje antiguo' a mediados del siglo XV (1954: 13). Su ejemplo, en todo caso, no resulta convincente, ya que la *Declamación* no es en absoluto una epístola: se trata de un intercambio semidramático de monólogos entre el padre de Lucrecia y su hija. El género literario del pasaje es uno de los puntos más interesantes, puesto que la presencia de breves acotaciones del narrador y de un resumen introductorio lo acerca bastante a lo teatral. Así reza la introducción que lo precede en el folio 2^r del manuscrito LB2:

> Lucrecia, fiia de Spurio Lucreçio, muger de Colatino Tarquino, forçada por Sexto Tarquino, fijo del rey Tarquino, dando ella lugar contra

From the 'Cancioneiro da Vaticana' to the 'Cancionero general': Studies in Honour of Jane Whetnall, ed. Alan Deyermond & Barry Taylor, PMHRS, 60 (London: Department of Hispanic Studies, Queen Mary, University of London, 2007), pp. 115–26. ISSN 1460–051X. ISBN 0 902238 50 7.

su voluntat a la fuerça solo por themor de infamia, por quanto Tarquino menazaua de echar un sclauo suyo degollado en la propria cama della. Clamando al padre e a su marido, contóles el caso, e fizo con ellos que le prometier[a]n vengança. E depués queriéndose ella matar, el padre e marido ge lo vedaron segunt se contiene en lo de yuso scripto.[1]

Como vemos, esta larga rúbrica funciona como una acotación introductoria al modo de las de los guiones teatrales. También hay otras breves intervenciones narrativas que separan los diálogos, a la manera de ésta del folio 3ᵛ: 'Síguese la declamación, conuiene a ssaber de Lucrecia en contrario.'

En cuanto a la procedencia directa del texto en castellano, el manuscrito de la Biblioteca Nacional de Madrid ofrece una pista impagable, una rúbrica final que dice lo siguiente: 'Fenescen las declaraciones de Colluçio chanceller de Florençia çerca de Lucreçia.' En efecto, la *Declamación de Lucrecia* que abre el *Cancionero de Herberay* es una traducción bastante fiel de la *Declamatio Lucretiae* de Coluccio Salutati. De este hombre sabemos que fue gobernador de Florencia entre 1372 y 1406, cargo desde el cual auspició una importante actividad cultural: se le considera uno de los padres del humanismo. Para el estudio de la *Declamatio* es fundamental la edición, con traducción al inglés, y el estudio de Stephanie H. Jed (1989).[2]

Podríamos valorar varias hipótesis a la hora de enjuiciar por qué la *Declamación* ocupa ese lugar de privilegio dentro del *Cancionero de Herberay*. Sorprendentemente, muy poco se ha dicho o escrito acerca de estas prosas, y nadie ha tratado de explicar el porqué de su situación en el manuscrito. Sin duda, el trabajo más esclarecedor de cuantos se han publicado acerca de la ordenación de contenidos en LB2 es el de Vicenç Beltran (2005). Beltran considera que entre los componentes del partido aragonés en Castilla se habría formado, antes de 1445, un pequeño cancionero amoroso ampliado con obras de la corte de Juan II de Navarra y con unos pocos poemas castellanos: éste sería el que Beltran llama el *primer arquetipo navarro-aragonés*, del que procedería LB2. Por otro lado, la aparición de un cierto cancionero individual de Juan de Mena habría impulsado la

[1] Utilizo mi propia transcripción de LB2, que aparecerá en mi tesis, dirigida por Jane Whetnall, 'The *Cancionero de Herberay* and the Literary Court of John II of Navarre'.

[2] Jed ofrece una excelente edición facsímil del texto del humanista italiano (basada en el manuscrito 93.6 de la Newberry Library de Chicago) con transcripción paleográfica. Para la transmisión textual interesa el ensayo de Enrico Menestò (1979). Únicamente tengo noticia de una edición, ya muy antigua, de sus 'epístolas' conservadas, la de Francesco Novati (1891–1911).

reordenación de sus obras y las de Torroella, que habrían pasado a concentrarse en un *segundo arquetipo navarro-aragonés*, del que procedería el *Cancionero de la Biblioteca Estense de Módena*.

Esta hipótesis, muy operativa en lo referido a los poemas, no parece ofrecer una explicación a la presencia del bloque inicial de siete obras en prosa: las hay anónimas, de Hugo de Urriés, de Pere Torroella, del Marqués de Santillana y de Rodríguez del Padrón. Tan sólo una de ellas, la *Complaynta sobre la muerte de dona Ynés de Cleves, princesa de Navarra, descrita por Pere Torrella*, deja evidencias internas claras de su procedencia: 1448 en el Reino de Navarra (la princesa murió en abril de ese año). Si damos por bueno que la transmisión textual de las siete prosas se hizo de forma simultánea, resulta entonces imposible que la *Declamación* (junto con las otras seis obras), formara parte del pequeño cancionero primigenio del que procede LB2. Sin embargo, sí que resulta razonable pensar que las prosas aparecen en esa supuesta ampliación que, acaso en 1448, dio lugar al *primer arquetipo navarro-aragonés*: las tres obras de Torroella se debieron escribir en ese reino durante esos años y es notorio que Hugo de Urriés es el destinatario de las *Leyes de amor* de Torroella y uno de los candidatos a traductor de la *Declamatio Lucretiae*. Por lo tanto, la *Declamación* debió unirse a la tradición textual que daría lugar al *Cancionero de Herberay* en torno a 1448 en el Reino de Navarra y con la participación de Hugo de Urriés (ya fuera como traductor, con su encargo o por su selección).

Por otra parte, independientemente de su procedencia del *primer arquetipo navarro-aragonés*, la individualidad del *Cancionero de Herberay* es innegable, merced a la intencionalidad del hipotético compilador del arquetipo de LB2 a la hora de ordenar los materiales. En este sentido, la presencia de la *Declamación* como obra de apertura cumple una función múltiple: establecer un programa cortés y humanista, culto y a la vez popularizante, algo que es una constante en el manuscrito LB2, tan alejado del prurito moralizante de, por ejemplo, el *Cancionero de Baena*. A propósito de LB1, Manuel Moreno (2005) considera que el papel de copistas y compiladores fue mucho más activo de lo que hasta ahora se había considerado. Éste parece ser el caso de LB2 y del supuesto compilador del arquetipo, un Hugo de Urriés que si abre su volumen con la *Declamación de Lucrecia*, no lo hace de forma casual, sino a sabiendas de que la misión de estas siete obras en prosa es la de justificar la selección de materiales en el resto del manuscrito: la ejemplaridad de la castidad de Lucrecia serviría como declaración de intenciones del responsable del cancionero. Urriés impregnó sus obras de una fuerte carga de decoro (véase, por ejemplo, *De los galanes*, LB2-42, ID 2188), marcando las distancias con los excesos de la *religio amoris* y distinguiéndose como el poeta del amor conyugal (el caso de Lucrecia es uno de fidelidad conyugal llevado al extremo). Profundizando algo por esta vía, y habida cuenta de que Jane Whetnall ha ofrecido convincentes indicios de que una parte considerable de los poemas anónimos de LB2 son obra de Urriés, no sería de extrañar que esta traducción también lo fuera (Whetnall 1997).

Podría objetarse que el poeta que en más ocasiones alude a Lucrecia en el corpus cancioneril es el Marqués de Santillana.[3] El hecho de que una de las prosas que siguen a la *Declamación* sea la *Lamentación de Spanya* podría incidir en esa sospecha. Sin embargo, una posible autoría de Santillana resulta poco verosímil: las obras del Marqués rara vez aparecen sin rúbrica y, por otra parte, dudo mucho que el ego literario de Íñigo López de Mendoza se conformara con hacer una traducción, y más de una fuente poco prestigiosa (por contemporánea) como Coluccio Salutati. Sin embargo, sí sabemos que Hugo de Urriés, de espíritu polifacético renacentista, se dedicó a traducir textos de todo tipo, ya fuera por gusto personal o por encargo (véase Marino 1977). En el supuesto de que el traductor de la pieza fuera, efectivamente, un poeta, la autoría de Urriés debería ser seriamente considerada.

Otro factor que apoya la autoría de Hugo de Urriés es su vida itinerante como embajador y su presencia en la península itálica. En la corte del rey Magnánimo, los cortesanos ibéricos entraron en contacto directo con la cultura humanista italiana. Existen trabajos muy ilustrativos del nivel de interacción cultural entre los poetas de cámara de Alfonso y los humanistas italianos de su corte. Una de las primeras alusiones a esta relación la realiza Francesca Vendrell Gallostra en su tesis doctoral (1933). Pocos años después vería la luz el artículo de Eugenio Mele sobre las relaciones entre Pere Torroella y Giovanni Pontano (1938). Pero la monografía más ilustrativa sobre el tema es la de José Carlos Rovira (1990): en ella se documenta la presencia de al menos ocho humanistas italianos que habrían servido como nexo de unión entre los poetas españoles y el florecimiento renacentista imperante en Nápoles; sus nombres

---

[3] Francisco Crosas López contabiliza ocho alusiones a Lucrecia la Casta en las obras del Marqués. Aunque Crosas no ambiciona ofrecer un panorama completo de la presencia de materia clásica en los cancioneros, su obra resulta una guía muy útil, sobre todo a la hora de estudiar a Mena y Santillana (1995: 328).

eran Antonio Beccadelli, Leonardo Bruni, Bartolomeo Fazio, Francesco Filelfo, Giorgio da Trebisonda, Guarino Veronese, Giannozzo Manetti y Matteo Palmieri. Las peticiones de copias de libros antiguos están reflejadas en cédulas de pagos realizados por el propio rey y por sus súbditos más cercanos, la mayoría de los cuales eran poetas cancioneriles. El conocimiento de algunos topoi clásicos por parte de la mayoría de poetas españoles se produce en principio a través de los humanistas, tanto contemporáneos como de siglos pasados (casos de Giovanni Boccaccio o, en menor medida, del propio Coluccio Salutati). Esto es relevante en el caso de la *Declamación de Lucrecia*, ya que la narración original (al menos la más original de que disponemos) es la de Tito Livio en su magna obra *Ab urbe condita libri*.[4] La historia de Lucrecia se cuenta al final del primer libro (capítulos 57 y 58) de la primera de las 'décadas' en las que se divide la obra del historiador romano. Se trata del mito fundacional de la República Romana o, más bien, del mito de la abolición de la monarquía de los Tarquinos.

La obra de Livio, narrada en tercera persona, es de vocación eminentemente histórica. Por contra, la de Salutati (y, por extensión, la traducción castellana) está presentada en forma de intercambio dramático de monólogos, con una finalidad marcadamente literaria. La historia, según Livio, comienza con un 'concurso de castidad' en el que Colatino (esposo de Lucrecia), el propio Tarquino y otros hombres examinan a las mujeres de la corte. Lucrecia es aclamada por todos como la más casta y virtuosa, lo cual, unido a su belleza, enciende una pasión criminal en el príncipe, que la viola sirviéndose de amenazas. El posterior suicidio de Lucrecia, que en vano tratan de impedir sus allegados, resulta ser la llama que, azuzada por Bruto, concluya con el repudio de la monarquía tarquina y con el advenimiento de la república romana (Livio 2005, I: 57–58). Se trata, por lo tanto, de una trama con una finalidad política clara: el mito fundacional que apuntala la legitimidad del sistema republicano en Roma (Jed 1989: 105–09).

Como era de esperar, esta intencionalidad se diluye casi totalmente en la obra de Coluccio Salutati, que se centra en la dramaticidad y el efectismo de los discursos de Lucrecia y su padre y

---

[4] Para el seguimiento global de esta ingente obra, existe una excelente edición online, en http://www.intratext.com/X/LAT0142.HTM#fonte (Livio 2005). Como bien es sabido, las ediciones en latín de los trabajos de Livio suelen ser parciales, por lo que recomiendo hacer uso de esta novedosa fuente, que ofrece además la posibilidad de consultar en qué partes de la obra se repiten alusiones a cada personaje.

concluye su versión del mito con la muerte de la ultrajada, que pasa de ser un instrumento político a constituir un fin en sí misma. Salutati es un buen exponente de cómo los humanistas seleccionan y procesan los materiales clásicos para crear mitos literarios a partir de ellos. Es bastante probable que el traductor español de la *Declamatio* tuviera sólo un conocimiento indirecto de la fuente original, a través de la obra de Salutati. Es muy común que los poetas utilicen fuentes de este tipo, mucho más accesibles aunque menos prestigiosas, sin ningún pudor, puesto que al humanista se le atribuye simplemente la función de transmisor del legado clásico.[5] Pero también parece realista pensar que la lectura de obras de los humanistas sirvió de acicate a los cortesanos españoles del rey Magnánimo para consultar las fuentes originales. En el caso de la obra de Tito Livio, sabemos que ya en 1418 (catorce años antes de su partida hacia Italia), Alfonso solicita a su tío Enrique de Villena una copia de las *Décadas*, nombre con que se conocía la obra completa de *Ab urbe condita* (ver Rovira 1990: 21).[6]

Ya fuera a través de unas fuentes o de otras, lo cierto es que en el siglo XV peninsular los intelectuales y poetas estaban familiarizados con la parte mítica de la violación y suicidio de Lucrecia. A un nivel más popular, sabemos que esta historia se había hecho un hueco en el canon de romances (Welles 2000: 51). En este sentido, el mito tuvo facilidad de penetración intercultural en el mundo hispánico, pues aún es posible recoger testimonios orales del llamado *Romance de Tarquino y Lucrecia* entre los judíos sefardíes provinientes del norte de África:

> Aquel rey de los romanos
> que Tarquino se llamaba
> enamoróse de Lucrecia,
> la noble y casta romana
> (Weich-Shahak 1997: 115).

En cuanto a los autores cultos, el Marqués de Santillana, cuya erudición es muchas veces superficial, cita a Lucrecia en la estrofa 36 del *Infierno de los enamorados*, aunque lo hace en el contexto de amantes cazadores (precedida por Hipólito, Diana y Céfalo):

---

[5] Crosas López habla de 'fuentes manifiestas y fuentes ocultas' que surten de motivos a los poetas cancioneriles. A pesar de lo riguroso de su estudio, se echa en falta alguna pista sobre cuáles son esas fuentes 'ocultas', que parecen tener un peso mucho más importante que las 'manifiestas' (1995: 211).

[6] Rovira documenta cómo Alfonso hace esta solicitud a su tío a través del poeta Pedro de Santa Fe.

Otros que hovo en Greçia
que la tal vía siguieron,
e, segund fizo Lucreçia,
por castidad padesçieron
(Rohland de Langbehn 1997: 87)

Mejor contextualizada, entre mujeres romanas, aparece en la estrofa 105 de la *Comedieta de Ponza*, aunque el que sale descolocado en esta ocasión es Tarquino (presumiblemente su marido Tarquino Colatino, no su violador Sexto Tarquino), a quien el Marqués 'casa' con Rea, personaje mitológico, madre de Rómulo y Remo:

Allí vi a Rea, muger de Tarquino,
Marçia e Lucreçia, Ortensia e Paulina
(1997: 179)

No es en absoluto de extrañar que Lucrecia se convirtiera en cita casi obligada de los poetas y tratadistas participantes en la eclosión de la *querelle des femmes* en el cuatrocientos hispánico.[7] La figura de Lucrecia venía siendo objeto de controversia a nivel occidental ya desde época antigua. Su imagen casi siempre fue la de un auténtico símbolo de castidad y belleza, dando lugar en no pocas ocasiones a un debate sobre la compatibilidad de ambas cualidades. Sin embargo, hay opiniones cuanto menos curiosas, fundadas en el cristianismo ascético, como la de San Agustín, para quien Lucrecia no es ni casta ni heroica, al interpretar que su suicidio se produce por sentimiento de culpabilidad, nunca de vergüenza (Welles 2005: 53). El *Roman de la Rose* de Jean de Meun, de finales del siglo XIII, también condena a Lucrecia a través de la mencionada incompatibilidad entre castidad y belleza, lo que provocaría la respuesta airada de Christine de Pizan más de un siglo después (Pizan 1999).[8] Es muy posible que los autores españoles tuvieran conocimiento tanto de la *Cité des dames* y de la *Epistre au dieu d'amours* (obra en la que Pizan ataca directamente a Meun) como del *De claris mulieribus* de Boccaccio, tres obras que sin duda marcaron la visión que

---

[7] Sobre este tema ha aparecido una obra fundamental que viene a cubrir la falta de monografías dedicadas enteramente a este importante debate: *The Problem of Woman in Late-Medieval Hispanic Literature*, de Robert Archer (2005). En ella se nos da una visión a la vez global y detallada de los diferentes participantes en la *querelle* hispánica.

[8] Para una panorámica histórica (que cubre desde la antigüedad clásica hasta el final de la Edad Media) del debate sobre las mujeres en Occidente, ver Blamires 1992. También de interés resulta Blamires 1997, centrado en la defensa de las mujeres como topos medieval.

sobre el mito de Lucrecia hubo en la Península Ibérica.[9] El traductor español de la *Declamatio* debió conocer sin duda estos trabajos.
Si tuvo acceso a la obra de Salutati, resulta casi impensable que no
lo tuviera a las obras de Boccaccio y Pizan, de una difusión enorme
a nivel europeo, como atestigua el gran número de manuscritos
que las contienen y las muchas alusiones a ambas en el seno de la
querelle des femmes (Brown 2001).[10]

Al comparar la versión castellana con el original de Coluccio Salutati, nos queda la impresión de que el texto hispánico ha debido
ser pergeñado por un traductor experto y muy hábil. Se trata de
una traducción muy fiel al espíritu del original, pero sin caer en la
literalidad o en el hieratismo rígido de que a veces adolecen las
traducciones del latín. La *Declamación de Lucrecia* es un texto con
vida propia, muy dinámico, con un estilo elegante que no rehuye
la crudeza cuando la situación lo requiere y que sabe pasar de ésta
al tono solemne con mucha naturalidad. El siguiente pasaje es ilustrativo de cómo el traductor castellano utiliza un tono más florido,
respetando la esencia de los hechos pero ofreciendo más detalles, y
con unos periodos oracionales más largos y acordes con los usos
de la lengua romance. Esto refuerza la hipótesis del traductor-
poeta, dada la evidente ambición creativa del texto de LB2; el respeto a la literalidad se conjuga a la perfección con una incipiente
voluntad de estilo:

Quam poenam expectas eiusque ultro quod cellare poteras accuses? Hoc adiuvat vita praecedens tuaque non solum in hominum oculis sed in secretis domus penetralibus et frugalitatem et pudicitiam coluisti. (Jed 1989: 145)	Pues ¿por qué quieres, o speras, *que* te sea dada pena de aq*ue*ste fecho, más de la que mesma te das tú, q*ue* podiéndolo celar e tenerlo en oculto, de tu propria voluntat lo acusas? Q*ua*nto más q*ue* a te saluar e fazer sin culpa de tal error, ayuda del todo la passada clara e limpia vida tuya: ca no*n* solament*e* en vista de la gente, mas en los secretos lugares de tu morada, siempre guardaste e honrraste la castidat, e lo q*ue* a muger digna de todo loor e al honor y estado de tu marido complía. (LB2-0ₐ)

Es de notar especialmente cómo se extiende en las alabanzas de la
castidad de Lucrecia, añadiendo detalles ausentes en el original,
como 'muger digna de todo loor', giro recurrente en la lírica cortés,

[9] Me remito al capítulo de mi tesis dedicado al *Razonamiento de Pere Torrella* para
un análisis pormenorizado de este debate.
[10] Virginia Brown edita *De claris mulieribus* con un breve pero intenso estudio
histórico.

o la referencia al 'honor y estado' del marido, muy acordes con la concepción cuatrocentista de la mujer como depositaria de la honra familiar.

Pero, retomando lo antes apuntado acerca del género literario de la *Declamación*, es fácil de ver que se trata de una obra perfectamente representable.[11] No resulta en absoluto inverosímil imaginarse un breve montaje teatral que dramatizara los sucesivos discursos del padre de Lucrecia y de la propia protagonista.[12] De la misma manera que la figura de Lucrecia era utilizada en las cortes italianas como fuente de inspiración y modelo a seguir por las cortesanas, resulta plausible imaginar que el texto del *Cancionero de Herberay* pudiera dedicarse a la lectura pública con fines ejemplarizantes (ver Franklyn 2002). Esta teatralidad se acentúa en el caso de la *Declamación* de LB2: la traducción puede seguirse frase por frase casi desde el principio hasta el final, pero el traductor añade un apunte final que no aparece en Salutati: 'E así poniendo una spada por sus fermosos pechos que de yuso su negro manto tenía scondida, rendió el *glorioso spíritu.*' La acotación parece destinada a ofrecer una imagen más vívida de cómo debe representarse el suicidio de Lucrecia. De esta manera, el *Cancionero de Herberay*, acaso desde el *primer arquetipo navarro-aragonés*, debió ser utilizado como un manual de entretenimiento constructivo, al modo de un guión del que se podrían sacar tanto canciones de amor decorosas como ejemplos de mujeres ilustres (nótese la coincidencia en esto con el *Razonamiento de Pere Torrellas*, que ofrece un ingente listado de mujeres virtuosas). El papel del compilador adquiere entonces una relevancia desconocida; por lo que sabemos de su vida y de sus ideas (a través de sus poemas y de su biografía), parece que esta intencionalidad está muy acorde con el programa ideológico de Hugo de Urriés.

La sencillez de la estructura de la *Declamación de Lucrecia* también contribuye a su adaptabilidad dramática. Es de notar el impacto que producirían en el espectador tanto los dinámicos argumentos esgrimidos por ambos personajes como el lenguaje descarnado que utilizan

---

[11] Sobre el paso de la comedia humanística al teatro representable, véase el libro de José Luis Canet Vallés 1993.

[12] Margaret Franklyn (2002) documenta cómo Lucrecia era un tema recurrente en las pinturas de los ciclos de *uomini famosi* en las cortes italianas del siglo XV. Se esperaba que su imagen sirviera de inspiración en la virtud a las mujeres que la contemplaban. Cabe, por lo tanto, valorar la posibilidad de que la *Declamatio* de Salutati y la *Declamación* de LB2 estuvieran destinadas a su representación o a su lectura pública con ambición edificante.

para defenderlos. El padre le recuerda a Lucrecia, con frecuentes interrogaciones retóricas y vocativos en segunda persona, todas las pruebas que ha dado de su virtud, y la anima a que viva para presenciar la venganza que sus familiares infligirán en la familia real:

> ¿Pues quieres tú agora corromper tu ignoçençia dándote la muerte? 3ᵛ Tu marido e padre, e tus más propinquos parientes los quales todos te absuleuen de la culpa e te vedan la muerte, ¿pues por qué quieres matando a ti mesma danyar e despreçiar el ju[i]zio de aquellos? Si te matas, piensa cómo encorres en la culpa que no tienes, la qual por tu muerte no fuyes. Ca nunca se pensará ser ignocente la persona que por sí mesma a la pena e turmento de los culpados se consiente.

Pero Lucrecia, en su respuesta, les informa de la firmeza de su decisión. Son frecuentes las exclamaciones e imprecaciones que, sin embargo, nunca llegan a romper la linealidad racional de su discurso; un mérito más de la impecable traducción del poeta de LB2:

> E dime tú, mi muy amado marido, ¿cómo podrás dexarte recebir en mis braços quando te recordare que no te abraça tu muger mas la mançeba de Tarquino? Esso mesmo tú, mi buen padre, ¿cómo me podrás llamar fija tuya pues la castedat que desde mi infancia e tiernos anyos yo prendí so tu muy santa e paterna diçiplina la perdí tan infortunadamente e con tanta injuria la corrompí? ¡O mezquina de mí! ¿E osaré yo mirar a mis fijos, el seno e primera morada de los quales amanzilló el adúltero?

Resulta de mucho interés la interpretación que ofrece Jed (1989) del cambio de foco argumental entre la leyenda originaria relatada por Livio y el diálogo dramático de la versión de Salutati: de una historia política se pasa a una historia humana. Más en concreto, a la historia de una mujer, de su dignidad y de su libertad para elegir sus valores morales sin tener que atender a la fuerte presión de su entorno patriarcal; de este modo, comprobamos cómo estos principios heroicos de Lucrecia dejan de ser una exigencia de un guión político escrito por Bruto (obviado en Salutati y en *Herberay*) para convertirse en un canto a la desgarradora belleza interior de una mujer que defiende su libertad del único modo en que la sociedad se lo permite: a través de la purificación que sólo la muerte le garantiza. Al igual que sucede en el *Razonamiento de Pere Torrellas*, en la *Declamación de Lucrecia* la mujer deja de ser depositaria pasiva de los valores superficiales de los hombres, y pasa a ser defensora activa de su propia dignidad humana: tan sólo una muestra del programa marcadamente humanista que impregna la ordenación y selección de contenidos en el *Cancionero de Herberay*.

OBRAS CITADAS

ARCHER, Robert, 2005. *The Problem of Woman in Late-Medieval Hispanic Literature*, CT, A214 (Woodbridge: Tamesis).

AUBRUN, Charles V., ed., 1951. *Le Chansonnier espagnol d'Herberay des Essarts (XVᵉ siècle)*, Bibliothèque de l'École des Hautes Études Hispaniques, 25 (Bordeaux: Féret et Fils).

BELTRAN, Vicenç, 2005. 'Tipología y génesis de los cancioneros: la reordenación de los contenidos', en *Los cancioneros españoles: materiales y métodos*, ed. Manuel Moreno & Dorothy S. Severin, PMHRS, 43, pp. 9–58.

BLAMIRES, Alcuin, ed., 1992. *Woman Defamed and Woman Defended: An Anthology of Medieval Texts* (Oxford: Clarendon Press).

——, 1997. *The Case for Women in Medieval Literature* (Oxford: Clarendon Press).

BROWN, Virginia, ed. & tr., 2003. Giovanni Boccaccio, *On Famous Women*, I Tatti Renaissance Library, 1 (Cambridge, MA: Harvard UP).

CANET VALLÉS, José Luis, ed., 1993. *De la comedia humanística al teatro representable: 'Égloga de la tragicomedia de Calisto y Melibea', 'Penitencia de amor', 'Comedia Thebayda', 'Comedia Hipólita', 'Comedia Serafina'*, Textos Teatrales Hispánicos del Siglo XVI, 2 (Madrid: UNED; Sevilla: Universidad; València: Universidad).

CROSAS LÓPEZ, Francisco, 1995. *La materia clásica en la poesía de cancionero*, Teatro del Siglo de Oro: Estudios de Literatura, 30 (Kassel: Reichenberger).

DUTTON, Brian, ed., 1990–91. *Cancionero del siglo XV, c. 1360–1520*, Biblioteca Española del Siglo XV, Maior, 1–7 (Salamanca: Universidad).

FRANKLYN, Margaret, 2002. 'A Woman's Place: Visualizing the Feminine Ideal in the Courts and Communes of Renaissance Italy', en *Gender in Debate from the Early Middle Ages to the Renaissance*, ed. Thelma S. Fenster & Clare A. Lees (New York: Palgrave), pp. 189–206.

JED, Stephanie H., 1989. *Chaste Thinking: The Rape of Lucretia and the Birth of Humanism* (Bloomington: Indiana UP).

LIDA DE MALKIEL, María Rosa, 1954. 'Juan Rodríguez del Padrón: influencia', *Nueva Revista de Filología Hispánica*, 8: 1–38.

LIVIO, Tito, 2005. *Ab urbe condita libri*, http//www.intratext.com/X/LAT0142. HTM#fonte .

MARINO, Nancy F., 1977. 'Hugo de Urriés: embajador, traductor, poeta', *Boletín de la Biblioteca de Menéndez Pelayo*, 53: 3–18.

MELE, Eugenio, 1938. 'Qualche novo dato sulla vita di Mossen Pere Torroella e suoi rapporti con Giovanni Pontano', *La Rinascita*, 1.4: 76–91.

MENESTÒ, Enrico, 1979. 'La *Declamatio Lucretiae* del Salutati: manoscritti e fonti', *Studi Medievali*, 3ª serie, 20: 917–24.

MORENO, Manuel, 2005. 'La variante en LB1: tres calas en el ms. Add. 10431 de la British Library', en *Los cancioneros españoles: materiales y métodos*, ed. Manuel Moreno & Dorothy S. Severin, PMHRS, 43, pp. 91–112.

NOVATI, Francesco, ed., 1891–1911. *Epistolario di C. Salutati*, Fonti per la Storia d'Italia, 15, 4 vols. (Roma: Istituto Storico Italiano).

PIZAN, Christine de, 1999. *The Book of the City of Ladies*, trad. Rosalind Brown-Grant (London: Penguin).

ROHLAND DE LANGBEHN, Regula, ed., 1997. Marqués de Santillana, '*Comedieta de Ponza', sonetos, serranillas y otras obras*, Biblioteca Clásica, 12 (Barcelona: Crítica).

ROVIRA, José Carlos, 1990. *Humanistas y poetas en la corte napolitana de Alfonso el Magnánimo*, Ensayo e Investigación, 31 (Alicante: Instituto de Cultura Juan Gil-Albert).

VENDRELL GALLOSTRA, Francisca, 1933. *La corte literaria de Alfonso V de Aragón y tres poetas de la misma* (Madrid: la autora). También en *BRAE*, 19 (1932) y 20 (1933).

WEICH-SHAHAK, Susana, ed., 1997. *La tradición musical en España: selección de romances sefardíes de Marruecos* (Madrid: Tecnosaga).

WELLES, Marcia L., 2000. *Persephone's Girdle: Narratives of Rape in Seventeenth-Century Spanish Literature* (Nashville: Vanderbilt UP).

WHETNALL, Jane L., 'Unmasking the Devout Lover: Hugo de Urriés in the *Cancionero de Herberay*', *BHS* (Liverpool), 74: 275–97.

Corn Lore at Cogolludo

EDWARD COOPER

(London Metropolitan University)

Medieval history is at first sight a poorly scripted drama with an inordinately long cast list of walk-on parts; the artistic creations, often unfinished, bafflingly anonymous and without an obvious audience. In the absence of documentation, the first step in elucidation is to identify related phenomena. Just such an unfinished artistic creation is the castle of el Real de Manzanares (Madrid), which formed part of a bloc of properties including Cogolludo (Guadalajara), dissipated by the father of the duchess of Arjona, Aldonza Mendoza, and which she unsuccessfully attempted to reconstitute prior to her death in 1436.[1]

El Real de Manzanares (Madrid), castle (c. 1479, Juan Guas). The right-hand range, with apse, was originally the Church of Santa María de la Nava (Cooper 1967)

---

[1] She is known to all connoisseurs of Castilian *estribillos* as the aggrieved party in no. 984 of the *Romancero general*, which has the portentous refrain 'De vós el duque de Arjona grandes querellas me dan' (Durán 1882: 46).

From the 'Cancioneiro da Vaticana' to the 'Cancionero general': Studies in Honour of Jane Whetnall, ed. Alan Deyermond & Barry Taylor, PMHRS, 60 (London: Department of Hispanic Studies, Queen Mary, University of London, 2007), pp. 127–42 ISSN 1460-051X. ISBN 0 902238 50 7.

What el Real and Cogolludo had in common by the end of the fifteenth century was sumptuous palatial late-medieval buildings whose ostentation and remote setting suggest rivalry. It is impossible to contemplate either building without thinking of the other. The first serious student of el Real de Manzanares, the architect Vicente Lampérez Romea, in 1916, attributed its construction unquestioningly to the duchess's step-brother, the marquis of Santillana, who died in 1458.[2] However, two sources record the construction by the marquis's son, Diego Hurtado de Mendoza, the first duke of el Infantado, brother of Pedro González de Mendoza, the Gran Cardenal. In one of them, the latter's will of 1475, the work is in progress (Cooper 1991: I, 176). Furthermore, the church of Santa María de la Nava was then still separate from the castle.

Palace of the dukes of el Infantado, Guadalajara, façade (Juan Guas, finished c. 1483). The pedimented windows are a later insertion. Others, introduced into the gallery, have been removed in the course of an extensive restoration. The heraldic panel over the portal was at one time moved upwards to make room for two such windows. The present positioning is debatable (Cooper 1986).

[2] Lampérez Romea 1916. The remains of an earlier castle, at the other end of the village, are also stylistically fifteenth-century, and could indeed be the work of the marquis, although he does not have a track record as a builder.

Not only was Santa María de la Nava subsequently incorporated, but this was done in a way that required a clear change of direction in the planning of the ensemble. This would suggest that the completion of the works was by the duke's successor in the possession of the property, his son, who took the title in 1479.

The second duke is also indisputably the author of the building most closely related to this second phase of el Real, not in fact the palace at Cogolludo, but the slightly earlier palace of the dukes in Guadalajara, designed by Juan Guas and completed around 1483. The galleries, although clearly by the same hand as those at el Real, are not absolutely identical: the palace is more elaborate than the castle and, presumably, a few years later. The castle is also related stylistically to two other castles, neither of which by any stretch of the imagination goes back to the lifetime of the marquis of Santillana, and much less to 1435 or even to 1445.

The most similar is Mombeltrán, built by the duke's brother-in-law Beltrán de la Cueva, and unlikely to have been started before 1462.

Mombeltrán (Ávila) castle of duke of Alburquerque (Juan Guas, c. 1462–64), detail (Cooper 1967)

Of known masons, Guas is stylistically the most likely to have designed this, mainly on the grounds of the similarity to el Real and to the palace. As at el Real, the ducal coronets are absent from the coats-of-arms even though the Alburquerque title was granted in 1464. Despite references to Guas as a mason from Toledo in documents of this period, he spent sojourns from 1458 to 1463, and 1467 to 1476, in Ávila, whence Mombeltrán was more or less accessible (Cooper 1991: I, 49).

The other castle is that of Belmonte (Cuenca), begun in the 1460s by Juan Pacheco, marquis of Villena, briefly married to the sister of the duke of el Infantado's first wife. Here the stylistic resemblance to el Real is less marked, although the plan, unique in Spain, may have been inspired by a drawing by Francesco di Giorgio Martini. Martini's manuscript has another drawing which presages the turret decoration at el Real, and Guas might have known about the similar finish to the *barrera* of Castilnuovo (Naples) co-ordinated by Guillem Sagrera (Alomar Esteve 1970).

Calahorra (Granada), castle of Rodrigo Mendoza, marquis of el Cenete
(Lorenzo Vázquez, 1509–11) (Cooper 2004)

The palace of the dukes of Medinaceli at Cogolludo, not initially part of this scenario, has been attributed not to Guas, but to the mason Lorenzo Vázquez, even though there is no documentary evidence of his authorship.[3] What militates against this identification is the total divergence between the style of the palace and that of the major known building of this type by Vázquez, the castle of la Calahorra near Guadix, built beween 1509 and 1511 by the marquis of el Cenete, Rodrigo Mendoza y Lemos, bastard son of the Gran Cardenal. Mysteriously, the latter does resemble another castle, Grajal, known to be the work of Lorenzo Donce (Cooper 1991:

[3] Pérez Arribas & Pérez Fernández 2000. As with other shadowy figures in the arts at this time, there is a temptation to prop up the attribution by boosting the image of the supposed author: of Vázquez 'nada cierto se conoce sobre su iniciación en las normas constructivas. No cabe duda, sin embargo, que su formación renacentista se vio favorecida por su estancia en Italia. Allí pudo admirar las magistrales obras de Brunelleschi, Michelozzo, Alberti y otros' (2000: 33). The first sentence is the truth. The second and third are flights of pure fancy.

II, 386). The stylistic examples that have been called in to link the palace with other documented works of Lorenzo Vázquez, in particular the Colegio de Santa Cruz in the University of Valladolid, which Vázquez built for the Gran Cardenal, turn out on scrutiny to be from a wave of Renaissance architectural sculpture that flourished in Castile at the end of the fifteenth century, with a family resemblance because of what it is: Renaissance sculpture.

Experience at matching tails of this type makes one extremely sceptical of jumping to conclusions over broad similarities.

A motif that masons tended to repeat mechanically was heraldic castles, even to the extent of copying them from each other or from a template, sometimes reversing them in the process.[4]

Mondéjar (Guadalajara, convent of San Antonio, *orla* of lions and castles on Acuña arms (Lorenzo Vázquez, c. 1510) (Cooper 2004)

[4] Cooper 2005: 430–33. Apart from common originals for dispersed derivatives (in all fields, not just ornamentation), and illustrated manuscript compilations, printing had been at the service of the diffusion of images since the publication at Verona in 1472 of Robert Valturius's *De re militari libri XII*, making precipitate latter-day assumptions of a common artistic identity progressively more hazardous. Indeed, the building that the Cogolludo palace unquestionably resembles, as is made clear by Margarita Fernández Gómez (1987), is the now vanished Banco Mediceo in Milan attributed to Michelozzo, depicted by Filarete in his *Trattato di Architettura* of c. 1460 (derided by Vasari as perhaps the stupidest set of books ever written). Of the various copies of the manuscript, the one with whose version of the Banco Mediceo the design of the Cogolludo Palace has most affinity is that formerly in Valencia University Library, lost in the 1950s (1987: 50). The author's hypothesis is that the copy came to Spain with the effects of the second count of Tendilla in 1488. This is less far-fetched than the notion of a sojourn in Italy of the architect of the palace in order to be familiar with the design.

Those on the *orla* of the Pacheco/Acuña arms on the known Vázquez convent of San Antonio at Mondéjar begun in 1497 are of an obviously less archaic pattern than the castles on the naceli heraldic *tondo* that dominates the façade of the palace, as well as being arguably not by the same hand.[5]

Palace of the dukes of Medinaceli, Cogolludo (Guadalajara, end of fifteenth century, authorship unknown), de la Cerda arms over portal (Cooper 2004)

Similar inconsistencies of criteria have dominated attempts to affix a precise date of construction to the palace. It is logical to suppose that it was born of a friendly rivalry with the Mendoza architectural hats-in-the-ring at el Real de Manzanares and Guadalajara, rather in the spirit of the literary *invenciones* of the period, with the result that a commencement date of c. 1479 has seemed plausible.[6] In this context, the Mendoza/Guas team

[5] Pérez Arribas & Pérez Fernández (2000: 41, lower) deviate slightly from this model, but do not approximate to those at Cogolludo either. The same is true of the sets of heraldic lions, equally susceptible to copying from templates, which at Cogolludo are unlike any of those at Mondéjar, although the differences are harder to observe. The convent is now a totally overgrown and fast collapsing midden of rats, wasps, carrion, and ordure. Entry is extremely dangerous.

[6] 2000: 41. This would rule out Vázquez as the architect. The study patiently tracks the eclectic nature of the decorative motifs referred to in the title, reinforcing, inadvertently, the impression that the palace of Cogolludo is not in the style of any individual designer.

comes off rather better, in that the results are stylistically more homogeneous, and of a recognizable character, albeit unequivocally *fin-de-siècle* Gothic. In comparison, the first duke of Medinaceli and his obstinately anonymous builder opt for what would today be called 'crossover', a mixture of imported, assertively mannerist, and scandalously costly, all-over Lombard rustication grafted on to *mudéjar* and *flamboyante* decorative detailing, and a penchant for the grotesques of the period which, to a lesser extent, can also be laid at Guas's door.

Palace of the dukes of Medinaceli, Cogolludo etc., façade (Cooper 2004)

The degree to which the result dazzled onlookers can be inferred from the much quoted return penned by the Mayor of Cogolludo, the Licenciado Zabala, on 3 January 1581, for Philip II's *Relaciones topográficas*:

La villa esta cercada de murallas de cal y arena y que es la mejor muralla que [his informants] han visto y han oido decir que es la mejor de España; que saben se hizo por mandato y costa del Ilustrisimo señor duque Luis, duque de Medinaceli, bisabuelo del duque Juan Luis de la Cerda que ahora es; que en el tiempo que el señor duque Luis labro e hizo labrar las murallas, labro tambien y construyo las casas y el palacio que el dicho duque mi señor tiene en las dichas villas que es una de las casas mas principales que hay en todo el reino, por tener mucho aposento, ser casa hermosa y fuerte y tener buen asiento. (44)

The perhaps excessively fulsome critical press that the palace has continued to attract ever since is partly due to its incongruity, in both sumptuousness and scale, alongside the humble surroundings of what has never been much more than a market-based enlarged village, albeit one with a castle and defensive wall. One can also postulate that the challenge implicit in its design at the end of its building period was not the one it started with.

Cogolludo was visited by Philip the Fair and Juana in October 1502. Earlier less specific references indicate that the palace was at least substantially complete by 1496, although building works were still going on in its grounds. From at least November 1492, Cogolludo becomes the administrative headquarters of the duchy of Medinaceli, and it is reasonable to assume that the palace was the building that came to house the ducal chancery. If this is sketchy, even more vague is the likely start date. 1479 does not correspond to any relevant biographical data, the earliest of which is the conversion by the duke of his Old Castile resources into a three-year fixed-income bond from January 1489, producing 1,500,000 maravedís per year; probably not enough to underwrite the building of the palace and the other developments in Cogolludo, but presumably supplemented by similar arrangements elsewhere (Pérez & Pérez 2000: 28–30).

Shortly before the installation of his *ménage* in Cogolludo, the duke of Medinaceli had instituted what looked on paper to be the eventual reincorporation of the town to the Mendoza patrimony, albeit not to the branch that held el Real. On 2 October 1492, he mortgaged Cogolludo to the marquis of el Cenete, Rodrigo Mendoza, as a dowry for the marquis's marriage to his daughter Leonor (the marquis was also his own cousin by another route). The Cardinal had been instrumental in dissolving the duke's unproductive first marriage and procuring his second.

If work on the ducal palace at Cogolludo was as advanced for the date as has been suggested (2000: 28), it is odd that neither the dowry transaction nor the wedding, celebrated in Medinaceli on 8 April 1493, took place there. Nor does Mendoza, already a bit on the well-thumbed side at 27, apart from his illegitimacy, look the ideal candidate. Apart from the dowry, the duke settled an absolutely colossal fortune on him, on the understanding that he would produce a male heir to fill the painful succession gap among the duke's otherwise inadequate offspring. 'Short change' would be an understatement for what actually ensued. From about 1494, the duke rebuilt the town walls of

Cogolludo, an indication that he expected trouble of some sort.[7] The longed-for heir died in early infancy, followed on 8 April 1497 by Leonor. On the demise of her offspring, and foreseeing her own, Leonor devolved her title to the throne of Navarre to her father.[8] The marital arrangement had no doubt turned sour well before this sad ending, and the now elderly duke had no option but to swallow his pride and belatedly marry his housekeeper Catalina 'del Puerto' Vique Orejón, in order to legitimize their son Juan.[9] His will, associated with this event, dated 11 November 1501, was drawn up, again, not in the palace, but in the cramped and spartan conditions of the castle of Cogolludo (Lampérez Romea 1916).

Having lost the ducal allowance and the conditional title to Cogolludo and, at least in his own mind, the prospect of ending up as king of Navarre, still independent at that date, the marquis of el Cenete may have harboured notions of grabbing the dukedom of Medinaceli for himself, when the duke died shortly after making his will. With his brother's father-in-law Íñigo López de la Cerda, younger brother of the deceased duke, the marquis besieged Cogolludo, in order to prevent it passing, with the dukedom, to the legitimized Juan (Fernández de Bethencourt 1904:

---

[7] Cooper 1991: doc. app. no. 210. Notwithstanding the eulogistic review of the Licenciado Zabala, the walls, far from being the best in Spain anyway, are likely to heve been already there. Pérez & Pérez suggest that the demolition of a section of town wall in 1496 was in order to accommodate the ducal gardens (26). However, had the palace been complete by 1492, as they believe, this would seem a long time to wait for such an operation. In fact if the demolition was related to the building of the palace, it is more likely that it was to facilitate access to the site, bringing the commencement date forward substantially.

[8] Her mother Ana, the duke's second wife, was the only, albeit illegitimate, offspring of Carlos, Prince of Viana. Fernández Gómez (1987: 45n7) reviews the several versions of her name while García Carraffa & García Carraffa, less helpfully, make Leonor the wife of the third duke of el Infantado (1927: 54).

[9] There is reason to suppose that she might have been a *conversa*, not an uncommon choice of mistress for an Old Christian, as the social displacement of *conversas* meant that they were available, with no strings attached, and they could bring no pressure on their paramours to make honest women of them. Of her sons only Juan de la Cerda was legitimized. His brother Alonso de la Cerda married María Gómez de Ciudad Real, of manifest *converso* lineage. His grandfather's step-brother, Juan de la Cerda, Luis de la Cerda Mendoza's son by his second wife Juana de Leiva, had a son, Juan de la Cerda, by a spouse or mistress whose identity is not recorded, an indication that she too was from a marginalized social group, as is the fact that their son Antonio de la Cerda married the widowed Inés Gómez de Ciudad Real, aunt of Maria Gómez (García Carraffa & García Carraffa 1927: 52–54).

401). The connection with el Real de Manzanares is underlined by
their lack of interest in any of the other Medinaceli possessions.[10]
The move was unsuccessful, and in 1503, by which time Íñigo
López de la Cerda was a widower (the date of his death is un-
known), Juan fortified the ducal castles of Somaén, Montuenga,
Arcos, Cogolludo, and Cihuela (Cooper 1991: 53).

For Cogolludo and Cihuela Juan de la Cerda employed Lorenzo
Vázquez as assessor of the work. This is the only documented en-
gagement of Vázquez by the Medinaceli regime, and certainly does
not prove that (as Pérez & Pérez contend, 2000: 45) the mason had
been in charge of work on the palace ten years earlier. It is also
strange that one of the outstanding Renaissance architects of the
time in Spain should undertake the humdrum chore of costing re-
pair work by mere *albañiles* on two mediocre castles. As far as can be
documented, until then the Mendozas had had a virtual monopoly
of Vázquez's services. Given that relations between the dukes of
Medinaceli and the Marquis of el Cenete and his circle had broken
down in the last five years of the fifteenth century, the Cogolludo
and Cihuela jobs may have been an act of ducal provocation.

Palace of the dukes of Medinaceli, Cogolludo,
etc., maize motif over portal (Cooper 2004)

[10] At some stage the loopholes in the *barrera* of the castle of el Real de Manzanares appear to have been altered to resemble the cross pertaining to the
cardinalate of Cenete's father (Cooper 1991: figs 72 i & ii). With regard to the
siege of Cogolludo, another possibility is that, knowing the value of the palace,
the marquis and his accomplice were, in effect, holding the duke to ransom by
threatening to bombard the building. As far as is known, it was not damaged.

If this is the case, it may explain why the marquis became so exasperated with Vázquez that he imprisoned him during the works on la Calahorra in 1509 (Gómez Moreno 1925: 34). Another oddity which may be related to the situation is the maize-plant motif in the original carving of the façade of the palace of Cogolludo.

Belmonte de Campos (Palencia), castle. The upper part of the fourteenth-century keep, where the stonework is clearly different, and much of the adjoining structure, were rebuilt, probably c. 1530, by Juan Manuel de la Vega (att. Juan Gil de Hontañón) (Cooper 1967)

The motif cannot, botanically, be earlier than 1493, and even that date is highly unlikely. The first duke of Medinaceli had a keen interest in Columbus's initiative, and wrote from Cogolludo to the Gran Cardenal on 19 March, to inform him of the mariner's arrival in Lisbon at the end of his first voyage.[11] It must be assumed that maize symbolizes, in a modest show of triumphalism, the duke's patronage of the discovery voyage. The most conspicuous placing of the motif, over the keystone of the doorway of the palace, is subtly composed so that from a distance it looks like a *fleur-de-lys*, heraldic device of the *apellido* de la Cerda, assuming its true identity only as one approaches. The *trompe l'oeil*

---

[11] Pérez & Pérez 2000: 16. They do not realize that the plants featured are maize, referring to them simply as 'palmetas'.

effect is on a par with the architectural joke of the early-sixteenth-century keep of the castle of Belmonte de Campos (Palencia), attributable to Juan Gil de Hontañón, which at first sight resembles any other late-medieval turreted Castilian *torre del homenage*, and turns out on closer inspection to be entirely composed of Renaissance detailing.

The maize plant appears again in the c. 1510 carving at San Antonio, Mondéjar (the known Vázquez work referred to earlier). The patron of the monastery, Íñigo López de Mendoza, the second count of Tendilla, was a cousin and ally of the marquis of el Cenete, and the use may be a further manifestation of the rivalry that had developed between the second duke of Medinaceli and the Mendozas.

Mondéjar (Guadalajara), convent of San Antonio etc., pediment with maize motif (Cooper 2004)

It is likely that the legitimization of Juan de la Cerda as second duke of Medinaceli was obtained by his brother-in-law Fadrique de Portugal, at the time bishop of Segovia. In 1512, the latter became bishop of Sigüenza, the diocese for Cogolludo as well as for Jadraque, inherited in 1495 by the marquis of el Cenete. There were to be six years of civil war in the diocese, between the supporters of Fadrique de Portugal and those of the disenfranchised schismatic cardinal of Santa Cruz Bernardino Carvajal, among them probably the marquis of el Cenete, whose father had been the previous Santa Cruz incumbent (Cooper 1991: doc. app. no. 412). All in all, Fadrique de Portugal is likely to have set foot in his new diocese for the first time no earlier than the end of March 1520. He left again almost immediately, to attend to the funeral rites of his mother. This was the official pretext for his absence, probably in Portugal, although the sojourn coincides almost exactly with the outbreak of the revolt of the *comuneros* of Castile, of whom his neighbour in Jadraque, the subversive marquis of el Cenete, was a sympathizer.

The bishop seems to have returned to his diocese as the rebellion was quelled, only to absent himself once again to Portugal at the end of 1521. A third recorded departure to the neighbouring country took place on 21 November 1523, to act as betrother of Charles V's sister to the king of Portugal (Minguella y Arnedo 1912: 212–14). As far as is known, therefore, Fadrique de Portugal was in his diocese at the time of the marquis's death, on 23 February 1523. The latter's successor was his daughter Mencía Mendoza y Fonseca. As she was then a minor, her tenure of her property depended on support from her relatives. The bishop exploited her vulnerability by immediately provoking an incident on the edge of her domains: on 4 July the Crown instructed the authorities of Jadraque to check the boundary with el Henajar, and to respond to the accusation from Jaime Romano, solicitor representing the dean and chapter of Sigüenza, that they had blocked the erection of a building there because they wanted the smallholdings to be let to the villagers of Huérmeces and not to those of Santiuste.[12] Hostilities then escalated:

don Carlos etc. a vos el [...] corregidor [...] de las villas de Atiença e Molina [...] salud e gracia: sepades que Anton de Atiença en nonbre de los vecinos e moradores de la villa de Xadraque y [...] de doña Mencia de Mendoça marquesa del Cenete cuya es la dicha villa [...] nos hizo rrelacion [...] que la clerezia y cabildo de la yglesia de Sygüença [...] contra voluntad de los dichos sus partes en el termyno que llaman de Vianylla cerca de unas montañas lugar e juridicion que diz que es de la dicha villa de Xadraque [...] an principiado e principian agora nuevamente a hazer e hazen una casa fuerte de cal y canto con grande muro cerca de la dicha montaña en lugar fuerte a manera de fuerça [...] que [...] desde la dicha fuerça se podria rrecrescer mucho daño a las nuestras salinas de Atiença

12 Archivo General de Castilla (Simancas), Registro General del Sello, July 1523, unfoliated.

que estan vna legua pequeña del dicho edeficio y muy cerca de dos ca-
mynos rreales por donde pasan muchos caminantes e mercaderes con
mercadurias [...] que van de Castilla a Aragon [...] por que vos mandamos
que [...] vades al dicho lugar de Vianylla [...] con [...] maestros de canteria
que sepan de semejantes obras [...] e [...] ayays ynformacion y sepays [...]
que es lo que mas cunple a nuestro servicio e al bien de la [...] tiera y co-
marca [...] e la ynformacion [...] la dad a la parte de la dicha villa de
Xadraque e su tiera para que la pueda traer e presentar ante nos en el
nuestro concejo [...] e sy hallaredes que es fortaleza o casa fuerte [...] e sy
la hacen syn nuestra licencia e mandado suspendays la dicha obra y edeficio [...] dada en Valladolid a nueve de jullio de Mdxxiij años arçobispo
de Granada Santiago Cabrero Gueuara Acuña Medina

registrada licenciatus secretario Luys Rramirez (ibid.)[13]

Mendoza had married a daughter of the unsuccessful rival claimant
to the dukedom of Medinaceli in 1501, Íñigo López de la Cerda,
and had built Almenara (Cuenca), one of the most heavily fortified castles in Castile (Cooper 1991: figs 148 & 154).

The first to spring to the defence of Mencía Mendoza, thus identifying the true issue at stake, had been a spokesman for the
inhabitants of Jadraque. The dean and chapter of Sigüenza re-
sponded with a complaint that the Alcaide of Jadraque, Vicente
Pérez de Albornoz, abetted by the villagers of Huérmeces, had
demolished houses belonging to their tenants in el Henajar.[14] The
Corregidor then summoned Mencía's uncle and guardian, Diego
Mendoza, lord of Almenara and count of Mélito.[15] Mendoza
complained about the fact that the Corregidor's deputy was
brother-in-law of a canon at Sigüenza cathedral, and the scrivener
on the case was a nephew of the latter; the official was told to review his personnel (Registro General del Sello).

It is likely that the first marriage of Mencía Mendoza to the
Flemish courtier Henry of Nassau, a friend of the ubiquitous
marquis of los Vélez, was sufficient to put paid to the conspiracy
of the duke of Medinaceli and his brother-in-law the bishop, although it is not known how the confrontation was resolved
formally. The palace of Cogolludo is perhaps the first sign of impending rivalry between the houses of Medinaceli and el

[13] The term *casa fuerte* signifies, at this period, a proscribed building of a fortified
nature and hints at the use of firearms.
[14] Royal command of 11 July, to the Corregidor of Molina de Aragón, to punish
those responsible.
[15] According to the royal instruction of Valladolid, 20 August, to the Corregidor
to deal with Diego Mendoza's agent (August 1523 unfoliated).

Infantado, represented by the flourishing of the maize plant and the enjoyment of the services of Lorenzo Vázquez. The desire of the duchess of Arjona to unify the domains of Cogolludo and el Real de Manzanares had cast a long and tortuous shadow.

WORKS CITED

ALOMAR ESTEVE, Gabriel, 1970. *Guillem Sagrera y la arquitectura gótica del siglo XV*, Publicaciones del Colegio Oficial de Arquitectos de Cataluña y Baleares: Colección de Estudios Históricos y Biográficos, 3 (Barcelona: Blume).

COOPER, Edward, 1991. *Castillos señoriales en la Corona de Castilla* (Valladolid: Consejería de Cultura y Turismo, Junta de Castilla y León).

——, 2005. 'Castillos toledanos en la Corona de Castilla', in *Congreso Espacios Fortificados en la Provincia de Toledo*, ed. J. Carrobles (Toledo: Diputación Provincial), pp. 423–39.

DURÁN, Agustín, ed., 1851. *Romancero general, o colección de romances castellanos anteriores al siglo XVIII*, II, BAE, 16 (Madrid: M. Rivadeneyra).

FERNÁNDEZ DE BETHENCOURT, Francisco, 1904. *Historia genealógica de la monarquía española*, V (Madrid: Enrique Teodoro).

FERNÁNDEZ GÓMEZ, Margarita, 1987. *Los grutescos en la arquitectura española del Prerrenacimiento* (València: Conselleria d'Obres Públiques, Urbanisme i Transports, Generalitat Valenciana).

GARCÍA CARRAFFA, Alberto, & Arturo GARCÍA CARRAFFA, 1927. *Enciclopedia heráldica y genealógica hispano-americana*, XXV (Madrid: Hauser y Menet).

GÓMEZ MORENO, M., 1925. 'Sobre el Renacimiento en Castilla: notas para un discurso preliminar, I: hacia Lorenzo Vázquez', *Archivo Español de Arte y Arqueología*, 1: 1–40.

LAMPÉREZ ROMEA, Vicente, 1916. *Los Mendoza del siglo XV y el castillo del Real de Manzanares* (Madrid: RAH).

MINGUELLA Y ARNEDO DE LAS MERCEDES, Toribio, 1904. *Historia de la diócesis de Sigüenza y de sus obispos*, II (Madrid: ptd Revista de Archivos, Bibliotecas y Museos).

PÉREZ ARRIBAS, Juan Luis, & Javier PÉREZ FERNÁNDEZ, 2000. *El palacio de los duques de Medinaceli en Cogolludo* (Guadalajara: Aache).

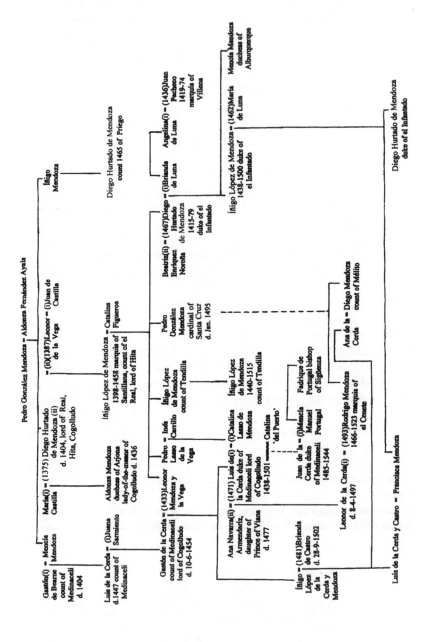

Baena's Ostriches

ALAN DEYERMOND

(Queen Mary)

Ruy Páez de Ribera's *Processo entre la Sobervia e la Mesura*, probably composed in 1408, is not, in general, an obscure poem; indeed, it is nearly always clear both in its words and in its larger units of speech.[1] Yet there is an exception, whose oddity has not been fully recognized by editors. Pride says to the narrator:

> Por mí fue venido el ángel de luz
> a poblar el fondo abismo infernal,
> el qual por boca de ombre carnal
> será por siempre llamado avestruz.
> (ll. 57-60; Dutton & González Cuenca 193: 493)[2]

This is puzzling both in its syntax and in its symbolism. The syntactical puzzle is the antecedent of 'el qual': is it 'ángel de luz' or 'abismo infernal'? Those with whom I have discussed this problem are divided (one changed his mind, so finely balanced are the arguments). Some think that the modern rule probably applies, and that the immediately preceding noun is the antecedent. Others point out that 'que' would have sufficed if 'abismo infernal' were the antecedent, and that the use of 'el qual' suggests the more distant noun (though that argument is weakened by the fact that 'el qual' has the

---

[1] There are three modern editions: Place 1946, Azáceta 1966, and Dutton & González Cuenca 1993. The poem is no. 288 in Dutton & González Cuenca (1993: 492–500; references are by line-number and page), and its ID is 0541. I give in the Appendix a brief account of work that has been done on this poet. 1408 is Dutton & González Cuenca's date (1993: 492). Edwin B. Place dates it at 1409 (1946: 35).

[2] In quotations from medieval Spanish I regularize the use of i/j, u/v, and $c/ç$, and I supply accents where necessary. I provide translations of Latin quotations from the *Aviarium*, but not of quotations that are easily accessible to those with a good command of Romance languages (the Vulgate and *Physiologus*). I use the thirteenth-century Castilian translation of Brunetto Latini's *Livres dou tresor*, and the fifteenth-century Catalan bestiary.

From the 'Cancioneiro da Vaticana' to the 'Cancionero general': Studies in Honour of Jane Whetnall, ed. Alan Deyermond & Barry Taylor, PMHRS, 60 (London: Department of Hispanic Studies, Queen Mary, University of London, 2007), pp. 143–60. ISSN 1460-051X. ISBN 0 902238 50 7.

right number of syllables for the line).[3] The only way to resolve this is, I think, by the sense of the passage.

Páez de Ribera tells us that 'ostrich' is commonly used ('por boca de ombre carnal') as an epithet for the Devil or, depending on our reading of the passage, for Hell. Is this true? The bird occurs regularly in medieval bestiaries and aviaries, with, as we shall see, conflicting meanings (though never, as far as I know, symbolizing the Devil or Hell). The most obvious place to find it if it was in common speech in early-fifteenth-century Spain is medieval proverbs, yet Eleanor S. O'Kane (1959), drawing on a wide variety of sources, has no entry for 'avestruz'. She finds six animals beginning with *a* (abeja, alacrán, ánsar / ansarón, asna / asno, ave, and avispa), but no ostrich.

The results of a search in medieval literature ('literature' in its restricted sense, excluding, for instance, bestiaries) are similar. It is at first surprising to find that the ostrich is not among the twenty-one birds of the *Divina commedia* (Holbrook 1902: 230–320), but Dante is not alone: no ostrich is to be found, for instance, in Chaucer or in *Celestina* (though twenty-five other birds are: see Blay Manzanera & Severin 1998: 33–37), or in most works of creative literature in the Middle Ages, though it is, as I have said, a regular feature of bestiary and aviary texts, and it is reasonably frequent in ecclesiastical iconography. I know of nine occurrences before the *Cancionero de Baena*. One is in the Portuguese *Orto do Esposo*, probably composed in the last decade of the fourteenth century, where chapter 13 of book IV tells us that a man who is tied to the things of this world does not have the freedom of a flying bird, but is like the ostrich. Another, describing a composite beast, is in a fragmentary fifteenth-century manuscript of the thirteenth-century *Historia de la Donzella Teodor* : 'un ave que bola por los montes [...]: su cuerpo es de ave estruz, e sus alas de águila, e sus cuernos de ciervo [...]' (Mettmann 1962: 158). The rest are purely zoological.[4] I

[3] I am grateful to Ian Macpherson, Ralph Penny, José Luis Pérez López, and Xelo Sanmateu for their comments.

[4] For instance: `tan grande commo un huevo de estrús' (*Libro del cavallero Zifar*; Wagner 1929: 260), or `Et las aves que son en parte aves et en parte vestias, pero semejan más a las aves; son los escrucies et los murciegos' (Juan Manuel, *Libro del cavallero et del escudero*; Ayerbe-Chaux 1989: 54). Other mentions are to be found in *General estoria* I & IV, *Picatrix*, *Libros del saber de astronomía*, and the *Crónica de Alfonso XI*. See Taylor 1990: 155–56.

cannot be sure that the ostrich does not occur in other *cancioneros* besides *Baena*, but I cannot recall seeing it, and it does not occur in the glossary to González Cuenca's edition of the *Cancionero general* (2004; surprisingly, it is not used in *invenciones* or *motes*: see Macpherson 1998 and 2004), nor is it found in the Galician-Portuguese *cancioneiros.*[5]

The *Cancionero de Baena*, in which the ostrich makes four appearances, is, therefore, exceptional. One of those appearances is, of course, in Páez de Ribera's poem; the other three are in poems by Alfonso Álvarez de Villasandino. The poetic use of the ostrich seems to be an idiosyncrasy of Villasandino's, probably adopted by Páez de Ribera. The former's pre-eminence among the poets of his time — 'fue esmalte e luz e espejo e corona e monarca de todos los poetas e trobadores que fasta oy fueron en toda España', says Juan Alfonso de Baena (Dutton & González Cuenca 1993: 11) — makes it natural that his example should be followed. Each of Villasandino's ostrich-bearing poems confronts us with problems of interpretation, and the relation of his use of the image to Páez de Ribera's is also problematic, since we do not have dates for the second and third of the former's poems. The first of them is dated by Dutton and González Cuenca at 1405, three years before Páez de Ribera's *Processo*):[6]

El sol e la luna esclarezcan su luz
por que Saturno amanse su saña
e sean movidas las partes d'España
en desfazimiento del gran avestruz [glossed as 'hipócrita, cruel'].
en cuanto atañe al pro de la cruz,
el alto Maestro ['Dios'] ampare e ordene
en tal guisa el mundo [...][7]

In the second poem we again find 'avestruz' used in a militantly religious context:

Manda que l' pongan la cruz

[5] I searched electronic files of the secular *cancioneiros* and of the *Cantigas de Santa Maria*, generously provided by J. M. Díaz de Bustamante. A full list of birds in the secular *cancioneiros* is to be found in Martínez Pereiro 1996: 225–29.

[6] Their reason for the date is that 1405 was the year in which Enrique III banished Pedro de Frías to Rome. Villasandino's poem seems likely to have been inspired by this event.

[7] *Profecía de Alfonso Álvarez contra el Cardenal [Pedro de Frías]. Baena* 115 (ID 1255), ll. 1–4; 1993: 147.

a los pies, ¡ved qué locura!,
el Alcorán, nescia escriptura,
en los pechos al marfuz;
el Atora, su vida e luz,
en la cabeça la quiere;
d'estas leys quien más podiere,
éssa lieve este avestruz ['hipócrita'].[8]

In the third poem the editors do not gloss 'avestruz':

Sube muy alto e non tartalea,
sigue tal regla como el alcaduz
que sube e desciende mejor que avestruz [...][9]

This passage does not have obvious relevance to the *Processo*. In
one sense the meaning is plain: 'sube e desciende mejor que
avestruz', because the ostrich is a flightless bird, a fact that was
well known in the Middle Ages ('Lo esturç sí és un gran oçell, e ha
alles, mes no pot volar [...]', says the fifteenth-century Catalan bestiary: Panunzio 1963–64: I, 126). Yet it is perhaps too plain, a
statement of the obvious (anything can rise and descend more easily
than the ostrich). I doubt whether this passage has anything to tell
us about Páez de Ribera's ostrich. It would be possible to make a
connection if we were to take 'el ángel de luz' as the antecedent of
'el qual' ('sube e desciende mejor que avestruz' = raised as high as
Lucifer, and its fall was as great), but that seems far-fetched. Let us,
therefore, concentrate on Villasandino's first and second ostriches.

In the second poem Villasandino accuses Alfonso Ferrández of
crypto-Judaism and, in the stanza I have quoted, of stipulating in
his will that the Cross should be put at his feet, the Koran on his
chest, and the Torah, 'su vida e luz', at his head. Here there is no
reason to dispute Dutton and González Cuenca's reading of
'avestruz' as 'hypocrite', but the first poem is a different matter.
They begin by emphasizing, and rightly so, the difficulties that
confront its readers: 'La complejidad de la teoría astrológica, su
proyección sobre la historia contemporánea y la permanente sospecha de corrupción del texto en PN1, hacen que este poema y
toda la serie 115–131 resulten de dificilísima interpretación' (1993:

[8] *Dezir por manera de testamento contra el dicho Alfonso Ferrández quando finó. Baena*
142 (ID 1282), ll. 25–32; 1993: 166.
[9] *Respuesta contra el dicho maestro Frey Lope* [de Monte]. *Baena* 346 (ID 1472), ll. 17–
19; 1993: 622.

147n). Yes, indeed. The one thing that seems clear is that 'hipócrita, cruel' is inadequate as a reading of 'avestruz', partly because of the preceding 'gran', but above all because the tone of this passage is so apocalyptic that to apply the image to any merely human target would be bathetic. The editors say in a footnote: 'El *avestruz* se refiere a Job 39.13–16 y *Lamentaciones* 4.3: "filia populi mei crudelis quasi struthio", de donde deriva el texto del *Bestiario*, incluido en el *Tesoro de Brunetto Latini*' (147n). In fact the bestiary is, as we shall see in due course, generally favourable to the ostrich, though the aviary is not.

José Guadalajara Medina's study of the prophecies of Antichrist in the Middle Ages (1996, revised 2004) can, I think, help us here. He points out that Villasandino makes use in several poems of Pseudo-Merlin apocalyptic and millenarian prophecies, following the tradition of Jean de Roquetaillade (Johannes de Rupescissa), and says that in our poem 'recurrirá Villsandino a exposiciones proféticas de factura merliniana, conjuntando, según los casos, figuras astrológicas y zoomórficas para representar los hechos del futuro' (1996: 311).[10] One of the 'figuras zoomórficas' is the ostrich, and it seems fairly clear that in this poem Villasandino is using it as a symbol of Antichrist.[11] That, and his prestige among the poets of his time, may explain why Páez de Ribera, three years later, sees the ostrich as diabolical.

How did Villasandino and Páez de Ribera come by the idea that the ostrich symbolized the Devil, or Hell, or Antichrist? There are two main traditions of ostrich symbolism in the Middle Ages, one contained in the bestiary, the other in the aviary. Both derive from the Old Testament, so that is where we must start. Roy Pinney observes: 'The ostrich is mentioned in the Bible more often than we might think. This is because three different Hebrew words have the primary meaning of "ostrich", although in many translations of the Bible they may be rendered as "owl" or "peacock"' (1964:

---

[10] This is a tradition with which Páez de Ribera also was familiar: one of his poems, 'en deuda con la tradición de Merlín, transmite una visión desoladora que recuerda las imágenes propias de los últimos tiempos' (1996: 312). The poem is the *Dezir como a manera de matáforas escuras quando andaba la división en el regno*: Baena 292 (ID 1422; Dutton & González Cuenca 1993: 517–18), composed in 1416. Animals play a large part in this poem: serpientes, dragón, pavón, grajas, bueitre, escorpión, elefante, girifalte (but no ostrich),

[11] For representations of Antichrist, see also Emmerson 1981: 21–24. It is worth remembering, in view of the glossing of 'avestruz' as 'hipócrita' by Dutton & González Cuenca, that Antichrist is often associated with hypocrites (see Emmerson 1981: 63, 64, 70, 95, 168, 169, 172, 192, & 211).

136).[12] Pinney says that the bird referred to in the Bible was probably a form of the African ostrich, *struthio camelus*, now extinct (1964: 136–38). Edwin B. Place, the only critic to offer an extended commentary on Páez de Ribera's poem, says that: 'In the Old Testament the ostrich is represented as cruel and unnatural [...]. The stupidity of the ostrich has long been proverbial' (1946: 36), and he refers readers to Covarrubias for the relevant passages. Covarrubias — who, surprisingly, takes it for granted that the ostrich signifies the Devil — did indeed make a good job of locating them (1943: 27–28). The most important is from Job 39:

> Penna struthionis similis est pennis herodii et accipitris. Quando derelinquit ova sua in terra, tu forsitan in pulvere calefacies ea? Obliviscitur quod pes conculcet ea, aut bestia agri conterat. Duratur ad filios suos, quasi non sint sui; frustra laboravit, nullo timore cogente. Privavit enim eam deus sapientia, nec dedit illi intelligentiam. Cum tempus fuerit, in altum alas erigit; deridet equum et ascensorem eius. (Job 39.13–18)

Job presents to us a forgetful, stupid bird, hardened against its young. In Lamentations 4.3 the hardness becomes cruelty: 'Sed et lamiae nudaverunt mammam, lactaverunt catulos suos: fili populi mei crudelis quasi struthio in deserto' (Lamentationes 4.3). A number of other Old Testament passages link ostriches with dragons (in all but the last quotation as dwellers in desolate places):

> Frater fui draconum, et socius struthionum. (Job 30.29).

> Sed requiescent ibi bestiae, et replebuntur domus eorum draconius, et habitabant ibi struthiones, et pilosi saltabunt ibi [...] (Isaias 13. 21)

> et erit cubile draconum, et pascua struthionum. (Isaias 34.13)

> Glorificabit me bestia agri, dracones, et struthiones [...] (Isaias 43.20)

> Propterea habitabunt dracones cum faunis ficariis, et habitabunt in ea struthiones [...] (Ieremias 50.39)

> faciam planctum velut draconum, et luctum quasi struthionum (Michaea 1.8)

One other passage is easily missed, because Jerome calls the bird 'milvus', the red kite (see George & Yapp 1991: 146–47), and editions of the Vulgate from 1592 onwards call it 'ciconia' (see

[12] The Hebrew words for 'ostrich' and their rendering into Latin — especially the use of *as(s)ida* — require a separate study by someone competent to undertake it. I am grateful to Susan Hook, Hilary Pomeroy, and Margaret Seccombe for essential information on this subject.

Voisenet 2000: 121n133) — hence the Authorized Version's 'stork'. However, the Vulgate's forerunner, the Vetus Latina, calls it, as Voisenet points out, 'asida', and it is this term that is picked up by *Physiologus* and passes thence into the Latin bestiaries (and some of the vernacular ones). Jeremiah 8.7 says:

> Milvus [sc. asida] in caelo cognovit tempus suum; turtur, et hirundo, et ciconia custodierunt tempus adventus sui; populus autem mus non cognovit iudicium Domini.

We have, then, three kinds of Biblical reference to the ostrich: the descriptions in Job 39 and, briefly, Lamentations 4; the five passages from Job, Isaiah, and Jeremiah that link it with the dragon; and Jeremiah 8. All of these except the last — which, as we shall see, becomes enormously influential — give an unfavourable picture of the bird, but none associates it with the Devil or with Hell. The association with dragons is, however, significant, given the frequent use in the Middle Ages of the dragon as a symbol for the Devil.

These Biblical ostriches are interpreted in two very different ways in patristic and medieval texts. The more widespread view is unfavourable. The mid-twelfth-century *Aviarium* that forms the first book of *De bestiis et aliis rebus*, attributed to Hugh of St Victor but probably, as Willene B. Clark has shown, by Hugh of Fouilloy, devotes a substantial chapter, deriving from Gregory the Great's *Moralia in Job* (Clark 1992: 20), to the ostrich. Most of the chapter is concerned with the bird as a symbol of hypocrisy, a vice which hardens the heart against one's children:

> Speciem namque phariseorum reprobans Dominus quasi strutionis pennam redarguit, quae in opere aliud exercuit, te in colore aliud ostendit, dicens, 'Vae vobis scribae et pharisaei, hypocritae', ac si diceret, 'Sublevare vos videtur species pennae, sed in infimis vos deprimit pondus vitae.' [...] Recte de hac strutione dicitur, quae derelinquit in terra ova sua. Curam namque filiorum hypocrita negligit, quia ex amore intimo rebus se exterioribus subdit in quibus quanto magis extollitur, tanto minus de prolis suae defectu cruciatur. [...] Unde adhuc struthionis sub specie subditur: duratur ad filios quasi non sint sui. (Chap. 142; Clark 1992: 188, 192, & 196) [For indeed, reproaching their pharisee-like appearance, the Lord shows it to be false like the wing of the ostrich, which in its action does one thing, in its appearance displays another, saying, 'Woe to you, scribes and pharisees, hypocrites' (Matt. 23.15), as if to say, 'The semblance of a wing seems to lift you, but the weight of life presses you down into the depths.' [...] What is said concerning this ostrich, which leaveth her eggs on the earth, is correct. For truly the hypocrite neglects the care of

his sons, because, through self love, he concerns himself with external things in which the more he is praised, the less he is pained by the failing of his offspring. [...] Whence the hypocrite is to this day placed in the guise of an ostrich: he is hardened to his sons as though they were not his. [...] (189, 193, & 197)]

The accusation of hypocrisy and cruelty spreads to include pride:

> Quas cum tempus fuerit in altum elevat, quia opportunitate comperta, eas superbiendo manifestat, alas in altum erigere est per effrenatam super-biam cogitationes aperire. (198) [The ostrich, given the opportunity, raises its wings, because when it sees its chance, it shows its wings in pride. To raise one's wings on high is to disclose one's thoughts through unre-strained pride. (197 & 199)]

What we do not find in the *Aviarium*, however, is the association of the ostrich with the Devil. On the contrary, the two are clearly distinguished:

> Obliviscitur etiam quod bestia agri conterat, quia nimirum si Diabolus, in hoc mundo saeviens, editos in bona conversatione illos rapiat, hypocrita omnino non curat. (194 & 196) [Indeed, the ostrich forgets that the beast of the field might crush the eggs, doubtless because if the Devil, raging about this world, should seize the sons produced in proper conversion, the hypocrite cares not at all. (197)]

Equally unfavourable, though differently weighted, is the ac-count given in Brunetto Latini's *Livres dou tresor* (the source for the animal chapters of the *Tresor* is *Physiologus*). The thirteenth-century Castilian version of Brunetto says:

> *Del estrución.* Estrución es una bestia muy grande, & á alas & plumas así commo ave, & pies commo camello. & non buela, ante es muy grave & muy pesada de conplisión, que la faze ser olvidadiza, en guisa que non le mien-bra de las cosas pasadas. [...] pone el estrución sus huevos, en manera que nunca torna a ellos ni se mienbra dellos. [...] Et quando los [pollos] fallan los padres, fázenles quanta crueldat pueden. Et sabet por la grant pereza que es en ellos [...]. & an sus estómagos, que son en la garganta, tanto calientes que comen el fierro & lo cuezen & lo consumen [...] (*Libro del tesoro*, chap. 142; Baldwin 1989: 82)

A composite beast (usually a warning sign), marked by forgetful-ness, cruelty, indolence, and the ability to digest iron: these present a fearsome picture of the ostrich. The account given in the Ara-gonese translation of the *Livres dou tresor* (*Libro del trasoro*, book I, chap. 172; Prince 1995: 65) differs in a number of respects, but the differences do not affect the overall impression.

It might seem impossible to construct a favourable picture out of the material presented in the Old Testament, but this was achieved by building on the enigmatic reference in Jeremehia 8. Version B of the Latin *Physiologus* says:

> Item est animal quod dicitur asidi, quod graeci struthiocamelon, latini struthionem dicunt. De isto animali Hieremias propheta dicit: 'Et *asida* in caelo cognovit tempus suum' [Hier. 8.7]. Physiologus dicit hoc quasi voltorium esse; habet quidam pennas sed non volat sicut caeterae aves [...]. Est enim hoc animal naturaliter obliviosum [...]. Si ergo asida agnoscit tempus suum et elevat oculos suos in caelum, et obliviscitur posteritatis suae, quanto magis nos oportet agnoscere tempus nostrum, oblivisci terrena et sequi caelestia, et elevare oculos cordi nostri? (chap. 27; Carmody 1939: 48–49).

The same interpretation is found in *Physiologus*'s twelfth-century descendants, the bestiary texts.[13] The fifteenth-century Catalan *Bestiari*, which has come from Latin via Tuscan, says:

> Lo esturç sí és un gran oçell, e ha alles, mes no pot volar, e ha fets los peus axí com a camell; e com fa sos ous, si·ls pon en la arena, e garda vers lo cel e té esment a una stela qui s'appella Virgo [...] Aquest sturç quant a açò que fa, si·ns mostra que nós deuriem fer lo semblant [...] (Text *A*, chap. 38; Panunzio 1963–64: I, 126)

This closely follows the text of chapter 60 of the second-family Latin bestiary, British Library MS Add. 11283, recently edited and translated by Clark (2006: 173). The interpretation of the ostrich as an example that we should follow is found also in vernacular bestiaries such as the *Bestiaire* of Philippe de Thaün (c. 1120–35) and, nearly a century later, the prose *Bestiaire* of Pierre de Beauvais (chap. 27; Mermier 1977: 81–82 & 143).[14] Philippe takes the rehabilitation of the ostrich further than his French successors: having followed the standard *Physiologus* / bestiary interpretation:

---

[13] Our information about the bestiary has been greatly increased in the last twelve years by three major books: Hassig 1995, Baxter 1998, and Clark 2006.

[14] My reference to Pierre de Beauvais is to the short version. The long version, as Florence McCulloch points out (1970: 146–47), describes the ostrich twice, once as 'ostruche' (chap. 29) and once as 'asida' (chap. 52). Like other bestiary descriptions, that of the ostrich and her eggs may be reinterpreted in an amatory context: for instance, in the anonymous late-thirteenth-century *Bestiaire d'amour rimé* (ll. 2697–2756; Thordstein 1941: 88–90). I cannot, however, see any evidence to support Alison Syme's opinion that 'Through the prominent rendering of and focus on eggs, the image [of the ostrich] depicts the necessity of symbolic castration for conversion' (2000: 169). The most obvious reason for rejecting this interpretation is, of course, that the bestiary account is chiefly concerned with the female ostrich.

E Ysaïas dit[15]
d'iceste en sun escrit
el ciel cunuist sun tens [...]
Saciez icest oisel
nus mustre essample.
(ll. 1253-55 & 1277-78; Walberg 1900: 47-48)

he adds a further parallel, recalling Jesus's injunction to let the
dead bury their dead (Matthew 8.22; Luke 9.60):[16]

si cum la beste fait
quant ele ses os lit.
E cist laissent al mort
ensevelir le mort
ki guerpissent le munt,
li richeises qu'il unt;
el ciel unt esperance
de regner senz dutance.
Deus duinst a tute gent
cest signifiement! (1293-1302; 48)

The most striking rehabilitation is iconographic: a German
blockbook of 1471, Franciscus de Retza's *Defensorium castitatis
Beatae Virginis Mariae*, printed at Ratisbon by Johann Eysenhut, in
which the ostrich hatching its eggs in the sun (not leaving them
unattended, as in all the texts I have cited) is paired with the lion
resuscitating its cubs (Franc 1940: 16). The latter, as everyone
knows, is a symbol of the Resurrection, so the ostrich, having got a
bad reputation by its Old Testament pairing with the dragon, is
now associated with the risen Jesus. This is not its only favourable
treatment in iconography: Beryl Rowland notes its use in medieval
heraldry (1978: 112; other favourable use in the Renaissance, 113).
An extensive survey of birds in European emblem literature in the
sixteenth and seventeenth centuries (García Arranz 1996) shows
frequent use of the ostrich, often in the ways with which we are
familiar from the bestiary and other medieval texts but also
— bringing it even closer to a display of resuscitating ability than

[15] He means Jeremiah 8.7.

[16] He seems to have taken this from *Physiologus*, since the passage is not present in the
twelfth-century Latin bestiaries. Version B of *Physiologus* ends its chapter on the ostrich
thus: 'Et dominus in evangelio dicit: [...] Dimitte mortuos sepelire mortuos suos, tu
autem veni sequere me' (Carmody 1939: 49). McCulloch says that Philippe's poem is
the 'oldest French bestiary and the one closest to the Latin *Physiologus* in some ways'
(1970: 47).

in the German blockbook — warming its eggs with the power of its eyes (1996: 234-35). The most striking case is that of the mid-thirteenth-century *Wartburgkrieg*, in which one of the participants 'would endow princes with the voice of the lion and the eyes of the ostrich, which hatches its eggs by gazing at them, so that they might rouse and animate their followers by word and look, inciting them to noble and knightly achievements' (Evans 1896: 94).

We have seen widely divergent interpretations of the ostrich in the Old Testament and in medieval literature and art, but nowhere outside the *Cancionero de Baena* have we seen an ostrich as the Devil or Hell or Antichrist. Is this an invention of Villasandino's, adapted by Páez de Ribera, or could the latter's assertion that 'el qual por boca de ombre carnal / será por siempre llamado avestruz' reflect a continuing belief? A clue may be found in a church at Eynesford, Bedfordshire, where there is a medieval carving of an ostrich with its head buried in the earth (Tisdall 1998: 178). This resembles Pliny the Elder's statement (*Historia naturalis*, X.1) that it buries its head in the undergrowth. Pierre Miquel, who notes this, adds that he cannot find the statement in patristic literature, and M. W. Tisdall says that he has been unable to find medieval literary references to this well known aspect of the bird's behaviour, though it 'is quoted as being in common parlance by 1563' (1998: 177). Could it be that the use of the ostrich as a symbol for the Devil or for the mouth of Hell, which Páez de Ribera tells us was also in common parlance, is another case of a popular belief that only occasionally comes to the surface in formal literature or art?

Let us now return to the problem of the antecedent of 'el qual'. There are some interesting observations in Gary D. Schmidt's *Iconography of the Mouth of Hell* :

> the influential images for the hell mouth were scriptural in origin [...]. The hell mouth represents the coalescence of four principal images: hell pictured as an open pit that swallows the unbeliever, Satan pictured as a roaring lion seeking souls to devour, Satan pictured as a dragon spouting infernal flames, and Leviathan as the great sea beast. (1995: 32).

> The [Old Testament] image of falling into a pit — a pit that seems to be in some sense conscious of the role it is playing — is emblematic of damnation. (33)

> Anglo-Saxon artists showed a propensity for converting the pit of hell into the mouth of hell. [... In] the *Paris Psalter* [...] the Anglo-Saxon artist has drawn hell in the shape of a pit. By curling the left edge in and curling the

right out, by adding an open eye and using flames to suggest teeth, the
artist has dramatically animated an inanimate pit. (35)

I believe that Páez de Ribera uses the image of the ostrich in a
similar way. One of the most widely held beliefs about this bird
in the late Middle Ages, a belief that was just as strong in the sixteenth century, was that it not merely swallowed iron but was
able to digest it, because of the intense heat of its throat. This belief, though absent from the bestiary, is of considerable
antiquity.[17] McCulloch suggests that it derives from a statement
by Pliny that the ostrich will digest anything (1970: 147n111). It
occurs, as we have seen, in the *Libro del tesoro*: 'an sus estómagos,
que son en la garganta, tanto calientes que comen el fierro & lo
cuezen & lo consumen [...]' (Baldwin 1989: 22). It seems to become entrenched in iconography earlier than in literature: an
ostrich holds a nail in its beak on the badge of Queen Anne, wife
of Richard II, and on the crest of the kings of Hungary and Bo-
hemia it holds nails, key, and horseshoe (Rowland 1978: 112). The
horseshoe seems to be favoured in English misericords: an ostrich
with one in its beak (Windsor, with an ibis, and Stratford-on-
Avon) and two ostriches holding horseshoes on either side of a
Rogationtide figure (Worcester Cathedral); the horseshoe appears
in drawings in Canterbury and Cambridge manuscripts and in
the Zwettle Abbey aviary, and various iron objects in sixteenth-
and seventeenth-century emblems.[18] The ostrich's ability to digest iron is mentioned in two sixteenth-century ballads: 'Digiero
yo tus desdenes / como el avestruz el hierro' and

> O si no pena y destierro
> en bien poco lo estimáis,
> pues como avestruz me dais,
> para que digiera yo el hierro. (Navarro Durán 1995: 30)

John Skelton, in *Phylyp Sparowe*, gives the explanation and the at-
tribute:

> The estridge that will eate
> An horshowe so great,

---

[17] It is found in a modified form in Vincent de Beauvais (see Robin 1932: 164), and
is rejected by Albertus Magnus (Malaxecheverría 1986: 112).

[18] See respectively Anderson 1938: 57; Tisdall 1998: 177 & 178 (also Anderson 1971:
plate 11); Yapp 1981: 55; George & Yapp 1991: 129–30; Clark 1992: fig. 9b; and
García Arranz 1996: 229–34.

In the stead of meate
Such fervent heat
His stomach doth freat. (Quoted by Robin 1932: 164)

Some of the evidence is later than Páez de Ribera's *Processo*, but taken as a whole it shows a continuing tradition over the centuries, which grows in popularity in the late Middle Ages and the Renaissance. That tradition makes the ostrich a particularly appropriate image for the mouth of Hell. One other point to bear in mind is that, if Páez de Ribera uses it in that way, the implied supernatural mouth balances the 'boca de ombre carnal'.

To conclude. The ostrich as symbol of the Devil makes sense only by association, through the dragon. It does not carry intellectual conviction or speak to the heart like the pelican as the crucified Christ or the phoenix or the lion cubs as the Resurrection. But the ostrich as the mouth of hell, swallowing and burning everything that comes its way, is satisfying both intellectually and emotionally.

Is this use of the image a rare literary manifestation of a popular and largely unrecorded tradition, passed on 'por boca de omne carnal ' and given written form by Páez de Ribera? Or did he take the ostrich's diabolical associations, used by Villasandino for Antichrist, and transform them into a vision of Hell, with gaping mouth and hot throat, that is waiting to swallow us — a stroke of individual genius? I leave that problem for Jane Whetnall to resolve, drawing on her unsurpassed knowledge of the manuscript *cancioneros*.[19]

[19] After correcting second proof of this article I saw Montero Curiel & Montero Curiel 2005. The authors devote five pages (217–22) to the ostrich in Páez de Ribera's poem and the three by Villasandino. They add little to the notes to these poems in Dutton & González Cuenca 1993 and the sources cited there, but they do refer to a mention of the ostrich in Ruy González de Clavijo's *Embajada a Tamorlán* (this needs to be added to p. 145, above), and they say (without discussing other possibilities) that in Páez de Ribera's poem 'el *avestruz* se presenta como símbolo del demonio' (221).

I am grateful to Victoria Prilutsky for bibliographical help, and to José Luis Pérez López for a number of valuable suggestions. Other debts are recorded in notes 3, 5, and 12, above.

APPENDIX

Páez de Ribera has received surprisingly little critical attention, given the high opinion of his quality expressed by Juan Alfonso de Baena, whose introduction to his poems says that 'era omne muy sabio entendido', and continues: 'todas las cosas qu'él ordenó e fizo fueron bien fechas e bien apuntadas' (Dutton & González Cuenca 1993: 492). Scholars in the mid-twentieth century agreed: Edwin B. Place, sixty years ago, called him 'the most stimulating poet of the Baena collection' (1946: 22), and Arnald Steiger concurred a few years later: 'destaca entre los autores del *Cancionero de Baena* por un sentimiento muy personal y por su verdadera originalidad' (1952: 7). The praise is, of course, not unanimous: Chandler Rathfon Post says of the *Processo*: 'The composition as a whole belongs to the large and dreary class of *débats*' (1915: 185), though that expresses distaste for a genre, not a balanced judgment on the poet's quality. But Post is in a minority among those who have read Páez de Ribera.

Those who turn to that indispensable research tool, the *Boletín Bibliográfico* of the Asociación Hispánica de Literatura Medieval, will find that most of the index entries under his name relate to his sixteenth-century namesake, the author of the chivalric romance *Florisando*. There are just three articles about this important poet (the two mentioned above and Pérez López 1991–92), though a number of scholars have devoted a few pages to him in the course of wider studies, notably José Amador de los Ríos (1864: 206–17); Post on the sources of his allegories (1915: 183–89); Pierre Le Gentil, who refers to his 'style d'une vigueur peu commune' (1949: 510); and Dorothy Clotelle Clarke on his metrics (1963: 152–58). The first of these is of particular interest to readers of the *Processo*: Amador de los Ríos devotes two and a half pages to 'su muy aplaudido *Proceso entre la Soberbia e la Mesura*', saying that 'dominan en esta composición las imágenes apacibles y risueñas' (211), and quoting lines 57–58, prefacing them with: 'la Soberbia, cuya satánica arrogancia se pinta en este bello rasgo' (212). It would have been interesting to have his reaction to the crucial lines 59–60.[20]

---

[20] See the account of Amador's life and work in Baasner & Moser-Kroiss 2007 (the invaluable work of reference that contains their article reached me as I was writing the present essay). He was painter, poet, dramatist, archaeologist, politician (Liberal Deputy 1864–65), and historian, as well as literary scholar. His output was prodigious: in addition to the *Historia crítica de la literatura española* he wrote two major books on the history and literature of Spanish Jews and *conversos*, and edited Santillana's works (his

In the first of the articles dedicated exclusively to Páez de Ribera, Place assesses what little information we have about the poet's life and family, and then provides a careful edition of the first of his poems in the *Cancio-nero*, the *Processo*. Steiger's article elucidates the difficult first four lines of the *Dezir contra la Pobreza*, but Pérez López returns to Place's model: after reassessing what is known and what has been surmised about the poet, he edits the *Proceso que ovieron en uno la Dolencia e la Vejez e el Destierro e la Pobreza*. It seemed for a time that there would be a full study of Páez de Ribera: Deborah Lloyd, a graduate student at the University of Kentucky, corresponded with me in 1979 about his suitability as a subject for a doctoral thesis. I encouraged her and sent some information, but within a few months a strong religious vocation led her to abandon graduate school. As far as I know, no one has since then taken up the idea.

edition reappeared pseudonymously in Clásicos Castalia, and was only recently replaced there by Kerkhof & Gómez Moreno 2003). No publisher would take the risk of his 4200-page *Historia crítica*, so he published it himself, financed by public subscription. Menéndez Pelayo was right to emphasize that this 'venerable monumento de ciencia y paciencia' is notable for its 'frecuentes aciertos de la crítica' (quoted by Baasner & Moser-Kroiss 2007: 83).

WORKS CITED

AMADOR DE LOS RÍOS, José, 1864. *Historia crítica de la literatura española*, v (Madrid: the author, ptd José Fernández Cancela).

ANDERSON, M. D., 1938. *Animal Carvings in British Churches* (Cambridge: UP).

———, 1971. *History and Imagery in British Churches* (London: John Murray).

AYERBE-CHAUX, Reinaldo, ed., 1989. *Juan Manuel, Cinco tratados*, Spanish Series, 51 (Madison: HSMS).

AZÁCETA, José María, ed., 1966. *Cancionero de Juan Alfonso de Baena*, Clásicos Hispánicos, 2.6, 3 vols (Madrid: CSIC).

BAASNER, Frank, & Judith MOSER-KROISS, 2007. 'Amador de los Ríos, José (1818–1878)', in *Doscientos críticos literarios en la España del siglo XX*, ed. Frank Baasner & Francisco Acero Yus, Anejos de *Revista de Literatura*, 70 = Akademie der Wissenschaften und der Literatur: Beiträge zur Romanistik, 11 (Madrid: Instituto de la Lengua Española, CSIC; Darmstadt: Wissenschaftliche Buchgesellschaft), pp. 79–84.

BALDWIN, Spurgeon , ed., 1989. *Brunetto Latini, 'Libro del tesoro': versión castellana de 'Li Livres dou tresor'*, Spanish Series, 46 (Madison: HSMS).

BAXTER, Ron, 1998. *Bestiaries and their Users in the Middle Ages* (Thrupp, Glos.: Sutton Publishing with Courtauld Institute).

BLAY MANZANERA, Vicenta, & Dorothy S. SEVERIN, 1999. *Animals in 'Celestina'*, PMHRS, 18.

CARMODY, Francis J., ed., 1939. *Physiologus latinus: éditions préliminaires, versio B* (Paris: E. Droz),

CLARK, Willene B., ed. & tr., 1992. *The Medieval Book of Birds: Hugh of Fouilloy's 'Aviarium'*, MRTS, 80 (Binghamton, NY: MRTS).

———, 2006. *A Medieval Book of Beasts: The Second-Family Bestiary: Commentary, Art, Text and Translation* (Woodbridge: Boydell Press).

CLARKE, Dorothy Clotelle, 1963. *Morphology of Fifteenth Century Castilian Verse*, Duquesne Studies: Philological Series, 4 (Pittsburgh: Duquesne UP: Louvain: Nauwelaerts).

COVARRUBIAS, Sebastián de, 1943. *Tesoro de la lengua castellana o española según la impresión de 1611, con las adiciones de Benito Remigio Noydens publicadas en la de 1674*, ed. Martín de Riquer (Barcelona: Horta).

DUTTON, Brian, & Joaquín GONZÁLEZ CUENCA, ed., 1993. *Cancionero de Juan Alfonso de Baena*, BFH, 14 (Madrid: Visor).

EMMERSON, Richard Kenneth, 1981. *Antichrist in the Middle Ages: A Study of Medieval Apocalypticism, Art, and Literature* (Seattle: Univ. of Washington Press; Manchester: UP).

EVANS, E. P., 1896. *Animal Symbolism in Ecclesiastical Architecture* (London: William Heinemann).

FRANC, Helen M., 1940. *The Animal Kingdom: An Exhibition of Manuscript Illuminations, Book Illustrations, Drawings, Cylinder Seals and Bindings* (New York: The Pierpont Morgan Library).

GARCÍA ARRANZ, José Julio, 1996. *Ornitología emblemática: las aves en la literatura simbólica ilustrada en Europa durante los siglos XVI y XVII* (Cáceres: Univ. de Extremadura).

GEORGE, Wilma, & Brunsdon YAPP, 1991. *The Naming of the Beasts: Natural His-*

tory in the Medieval Bestiary (London: Duckworth).

GONZÁLEZ CUENCA, Joaquín, ed., 2004. Hernando del Castillo, *Cancionero general*, Nueva Biblioteca de Erudición y Crítica, 26, 5 vols (Madrid: Castalia).

GUADALAJARA MEDINA, José, 1996. *Las profecías del Anticristo en la Edad Media* (Madrid: Gredos).

——, 2004. *El Anticristo en la España medieval*, Arcadia de las Letras, 26 (Madrid: Ediciones del Laberinto).

HASSIG, Debra, 1995. *Medieval Bestiaries: Text, Image, Ideology* (Cambridge: UP).

HOLBROOK, Richard Thayer, 1902. *Dante and the Animal Kingdom* (New York: Columbia UP).

KERKHOF, Maxim, & Ángel GÓMEZ MORENO, ed., 2003. Marqués de Santillana, *Poesías completas*, Clásicos Castalia, 270 (Madrid: Castalia).

LE GENTIL, Pierre, 1949. *La Poésie lyrique espagnole et portugaise à la fin du Moyen Âge*, I: *Les thèmes et les genres* (Rennes: Plihon).

MCCULLOCH, Florence, 1970. *Mediaeval Latin and French Bestiaries*, University of North Carolina Studies in the Romance Languages and Literatures, 33, 3rd ed. (Chapel Hill: University of North Carolina Press).

MACPHERSON, Ian, 1998. *The 'Invenciones y letras' of the 'Cancionero general'*, PMHRS, 9.

——, 2004. *'Motes y glosas' in the 'Cancionero general'*, PMHRS, 46.

MALAXECHEVERRÍA, Ignacio, tr., 1986. *Bestiario medieval*, Selección de Lecturas Medievales, 18 (Madrid: Siruela).

MARTÍNEZ PEREIRO, Carlos Paulo, 1996. *Natura das animalhas: bestiario medieval da lírica profana galego-portuguesa*, Campus, 2 (Vigo: A Nosa Terra).

MERMIER, Guy, ed., 1977. *Le Bestiaire de Pierre de Beauvais (version courte)* (Paris: A. G. Nizet).

METTMANN, Walther, ed., 1962. *La 'Historia de la Donzella Teodor': ein spanisches Volksbuch arabischen Ursprungs: Untersuchung und kritische Ausgabe der ältesten bekannten Fassungen*, Akademie der Wissenschaften und der Literatur, Abhandlungen der geistes- und sozialwissenschaftlichen Klasse, Jahrgang 1962, 4 (Wiesbaden: Franz Steiner, for Akademie der Wissenschaften und der Literatur in Mainz).

MIQUEL, Dom Pierre, 1991. *Dictionnaire symbolique des animaux: zoologie mystique* (Paris: Le Léopard d''Or).

MONTERO CURIEL, Pilar, & María Luisa MONTERO CURIEL, 2005, *El léxico animal del 'Cancionero de Baena'*, Medievalia Hispanica, 9 (Madrid: Iberoamericana; Frankfurt am Main: Vervuert).

NAVARRO DURÁN, Rosa, 1995. *La mirada al texto: comentario de textos literarios* (Barcelona: Ariel).

O'KANE, Eleanor S., 1959. *Refranes y frases proverbiales españolas de la Edad Media*, Anejos del *BRAE*, 2 (Madrid: RAE).

PANUNZIO, Saverio, ed., 1963–64. *Bestiaris*, ENC, A91–92 (Barcelona: Barcino).

PÉREZ LÓPEZ, José Luis, 1991–92. 'Un ejemplo de atribución múltiple en los cancioneros del siglo XV: el *Proçeso que ovieron en uno la Dolençia, la Vejez, el Destierro e la Proveza*, de Ruy Páez de Ribera, poeta del *Cancionero de Baena'*, *Dicenda*, 10: 219–40.

PINNEY, Roy, 1964. *The Animals in the Bible: The Identity and Natural History of All the Animals Mentioned in the Bible* (Philadelphia: Chilton Books).

PLACE, Edwin B., 1946. 'More about Ruy Páez de Ribera', *HR*, 14: 22–37.

POST, Chandler Rathfon, 1915. *Mediaeval Spanish Allegory*, Harvard Studies in Comparative Literature, 4 (Cambridge, MA: Harvard UP).

PRINCE, Dawn E., ed., 1995. *The Aragonese Version of Brunetto Latini's 'Libro del trasoro'*, Dialect Series, 15 (Madison: HSMS).

ROBIN, P. Ansell, 1932. *Animal Lore in English Literature* (London: John Murray).

ROWLAND, Beryl, 1978. 'Ostrich', in her *Birds with Human Souls: A Guide to Bird Symbolism* (Knoxville: Univ. of Tennessee Press), pp. 111–15.

SCHMIDT, Gary D., 1995. *The Iconography of the Mouth of Hell: Eighth-Century Britain to the Fifteenth Century* (Selinsgrove, PA: Susquehanna UP; London: Associated University Presses).

STEIGER, Arnald, 1952. 'Sobre algunos versos del *Cancionero de Baena*', *RFE*, 36: 6–30.

SYME, Alison, 2000. 'Taboos and the Holy in Bodley 764', in *The Mark of the Beast*, ed. Debra Hassig (New York: Routledge), pp. 163–84. First publ. as Garland Reference Library of the Humanities, 2076 (New York: Garland, 1999).

TAYLOR, Barry, 1990. Review of Ayerbe-Chaux 1989, *C*, 19.1: 148-59.

THORDSTEIN, Arvid, ed., 1941. *Le Bestiaire d'amour rimé, poème inédit du XIIIᵉ siècle*, Études Romanes de Lund, 2 (Lund: C. W. K. Glerup; Copenhague: Ejnar Munksgaard).

TISDALL, M. W., 1998. *God's Beasts: Identify and Understand Animals in Church Carvings* (Plymouth: Charlesfort Press).

VOISENET, Jacques, 2000. *Bêtes et hommes dans le monde médiéval: le bestiaire des clercs du Vᵉ au XIIᵉ siècle* (Turnhout: Brepols).

WAGNER, Charles Philip, ed., 1929. *El libro del cauallero Zifar (El libro del cauallero de Dios), Edited from the Three Extant Versions*, I: *Text*, University of Michigan Publications: Language and Literature, 5 (Ann Arbor: Univ. of Michigan).

WALBERG, Emmanuel, ed., 1900. *Le Bestiaire de Philippe de Thaün* (Lund: H. J. Möller; Paris: H. Welter).

YAPP, Brunsdon, 1981. *Birds in Medieval Manuscripts* (London: British Library).

Security and Surprise in the Versification
of the *Cancioneros*

MARTIN J. DUFFELL

(Queen Mary)

> Despite the tendency among critics to treat all the poetry of the 150-year period as an undifferentiated mass, great differences are apparent over time, from place to place, across genres, and even within the output of a given individual. (Jane Whetnall 2003: 293)

The profusion and variety that characterize *cancionero* poetry are consequences of the universal human need to be the same but different: it is usually safer for social animals to conform, but it is always more exciting for individuals to rebel. The need to do both prompts people to follow fashion, but to do so in ways that produce innumerable subtle variations: each individual seeks a unique expression of the current vogue. Composing poems was the height of fashion at the court of Castile between 1380 and 1530, and its composers chose to versify because every one else did so, and because it offered opportunities for self-promotion.[1] As Gerald Smith pointed out, writing a poem is one of the most remarkable things that humans do with their most distinctive property, language (2000: xli). An important component of poetic composition is metre, which can be concisely defined as the numerical regulation of the text (Lotz 1960: 135), and humans versify because their minds delight in patterns, their bodies crave rhythm, and their memories require aids in order to reproduce their favourite texts with accuracy. And, although metre is only one aspect of the *cancioneros'*

---

[1] More than 9,000 poems have survived from the period of the *cancioneros* (Dutton 1990-91), the great majority in Castilian; this corpus is almost four times the size of that of the Occitan troubadours (Ricketts 2001), and represents the work of more than 500 poets, but is probably only a fraction of what was in circulation at the time (Whetnall 2003: 293).

From the 'Cancioneiro da Vaticana' to the 'Cancionero general': Studies in Honour of Jane Whetnall, ed. Alan Deyermond & Barry Taylor, PMHRS, 60 (London: Department of Hispanic Studies, Queen Mary, University of London, 2007), pp. 161–76. ISSN 1460–051X. ISBN 0 902238 50 7.

profusion and variety, it is a feature that has the advantage of being verifiable by statistical analysis.

Verse, as Nigel Fabb notes (2002: 48-49), is characterized by counting, and by its division into lines, units that stretch from where the count begins to where it ends. While verse can be viewed as no more than 'language imitating itself' (Thompson 1961), it is a stylization of language that differs from normal speech or prose in that it contains more regularity, or *rhythm*.[2] We become accustomed to binary rhythms from our mothers' bipedal motion when we are in the womb, and they sustain us throughout our lives in the form of heartbeats, pulses, peristalses, and orgasms. The rhythms of language, and therefore poetry, are produced by events that characterize all utterances. These events are linguistic units that can be arranged hierarchically by size: phrases, words, syllables, feet, and moras (see Getty 2002: 7). The counting of one or more of these linguistic units forms the basis of every poem's lines, and gives the poetic discourse its regularity, or rhythm.[3] But, as Auguste Dorchain pointed out, audiences seek *surprise* as well as *sécurité* (1919: 22-23): they like to be soothed, but they also like to be stimulated (the need for both safety and excitement discussed in the opening paragraph of this article). The poet can meet this twin need by occasionally interrupting the verse's regularity, and when this tactic occurs within the line it is termed *tension* (see Allen 1973: 110-13). Tension involves delivering something that is not quite what the audience expects, and their expectation is based on the regularity of what precedes. For

---

[2] Rhythm may be defined as the recurrence of an *event* in time and rhythms may be subdivided into *primary* (one type of event) and *secondary* (two types), and into *simple* (occurring with one fixed interval) and *complex* (occurring at different intervals). For a detailed discussion of the physical properties of linguistic and poetic rhythm see Chatman 1965: 19-45.

[3] In ancient times Egyptian and Semitic poets counted phrases and Iranian poets counted syllables, while Germanic poets counted words and feet, and some Greek poets counted moras, as do Japanese poets to this day (see Duffell 2007: 19-26). A *foot* is the contrast between adjacent linguistic units, one of which modern metrists term *strong* and the other *weak* (see Jakobson 1960: 359); these units are often syllables, which in all languages are divisible into *light* (those of the minimum duration, or a single *mora*) and *heavy* (those of two moras). Heavy syllables either contain a long vowel / diphthong, or are closed by two or more consonants (Hayes 1995: 59-61); the English word *light* is thus heavy, while both syllables of the word *heavy* are light, and in moraic weight the two words are equal. For an analysis of syllable structure and weight in Spanish see Harris 1983: 1-80.

this reason all but the simplest verse contains tension, enough of it to add a pleasurable level of variety to its lines.[4]

There is another common way of providing variety in verse texts, and it involves the relationship between lines rather than the material within them. Versifying may be divided into two processes, which can be compared to architecture (the arrangement of lines into larger structures) and mechanical engineering (the construction of lines so as to produce rhythm): modern linguistic metrics terms these two processes strophe design and verse design.[5] The latter is the essential property of verse, and even the simplest is based on the concept of the line and the counting of linguistic material within it. Strophe design, however, is optional: lines may or may not be arranged in groups within a poem. The Ancient Greeks termed verse in which the lines were grouped in higher structures *strophic,* and verse in which they were not *stichic.* Thus Homer's *Iliad* and Virgil's *Aeneid* are stichic, while Pindar's and Horace's *Odes* are strophic, and Milton's *Paradise Lost* is stichic, while Dante's *Commedia* is strophic. *Cancionero* poetry is almost entirely strophic, because its poets cultivated rhyme (the repetition of phonemes in the nucleus and coda of the final accented syllables of lines); rhymed poems can be stichic only if a single rhyme runs through the whole poem. The *cancionero* poets were thus able to bring variety to their work in two ways, first by employing metres that had ample resources for tension within the line, and secondly by grouping their lines into a vast number of different structures, or strophes.

The key factors in *cancionero* strophe design are number, length, rhyme, and reprise: each strophe contains a specific number of lines, which are of specific lengths, and are linked by line-end rhyme; a strophe may also be linked to other strophes by the same rhymes, or by the repetition of rhyme words, or even whole lines. The number of strophes and these relationships between strophes determine what is termed *poem design.* The two categories of verse

---

[4] Nigel Fabb argues that tension emphasizes the boundaries of a metre, and that one of its purposes is to communicate the form to the reader (2001: 786).

[5] Modern linguistic metrics employs the terms of Jakobson 1960 to differentiate between actual lines (*verse instances*) and metres (*verse designs*). A verse design consists of a *template* (the pattern that underlies all verse instances) and a set of *correspondence rules* governing the linguistic material in instances that may correspond to each position in the template. The template comprises a number of *positions,* which may also provide strong/weak contrasts, again termed *feet.*

best represented in the *cancioneros* are the *canción*, or poem ostensibly a song, and the *decir*, or poem more patently composed for recitation; poems of the latter type were usually far longer than those of the former, but the underlying structure of their strophes shared some important features.[6] The *cancionero* poets employed a great variety of strophe designs, of which Ana Gómez-Bravo identifies and lists 2251 in her *Repertorio métrico* (1998).[7] This plethora of designs is deceptive, however, because the unique feature of many of the listed designs is one line of a different length or the repetition of a rhyme word. There were clearly firm favourites among the many poets whose work has survived: most *decires* have a strophe of eight lines (octaves), as do many *canciones*. Such octaves consist of two dirhyme quatrains with a limited number of possible rhyme schemes, and other strophe lengths can be created easily by the addition or subtraction of one or two lines.[8] The most popular rhyme schemes were given names, such as *copla castellana*, *copla de arte menor*, or *copla real* and many hundreds of the poems listed in the *Repertorio* belong to these categories.[9]

Verse design in the *cancioneros* was even more subject to fashion and the desire to conform: two metres so dominate the versifying that one was usually referred to as *el verso de arte menor* (the shorter

---

[6] The *cancioneros* also contain poems of other types, such as *romances*, *motes*, and *invenciones*, but in terms of the number of lines *canciones* and *decires* are clearly the most important. While *decires* usually comprised a series of octaves (often concluded by a quatrain), the strophes of *canciones* comprised a *cabeza*, one or more *mudanzas*, and *vuelta*, a subdivision that follows the two-melody structure of traditional sung lyric. As Jane Whetnall has pointed out, many *canciones* may never have been performed musically (1989: 204), and musical notation is found only in *cancioneros musicales* (2003: 293).

[7] Metrists employ formulae to help distinguish between strophe designs; for example, the formula a8 B4 b6 a8 a8 B4 b6 a8 describes a strophe in which lines 1, 4, 5, & 8 rhyme (a), as do 2, 3, 6, & 7 (b); while all its lines rhymed (a) have eight syllables (Spanish count), lines 2 & 6 have four, and 3 & 7 have six; lines 2 and 6 also end in the same word.

[8] Dirhyme quatrains can be divided into those with *rima cruzada* (abab) and those with *rima abrazada* (abba), and octaves built from them contain from two rhymes (e.g. abab baab) to four (e.g. abba cdcd). Omitting one of an octave's lines produces a septain, while adding one line produces a *novena*, and adding two produces a *décima*.

[9] Thus the *Repertorio* lists 3,000 *coplas reales* (abaab cdccd), 750 quatrains with *cruzadas dobles* containing only two rhymes (abab abab), and 700 *dodécimas* with *quebrados* like those of Manrique's *Coplas* (a8 b8 c4 a8 b8 c4 d8 e8 f4 d8 e8 f4).

line) and the other as *el verso de arte mayor* (the longer line).[10] In the surviving corpus poems in the shorter metre outnumber those in the longer by approximately 3:1, while poems in all other metres account for only two to three per cent of total. What was unusual about *cancionero* poetry was that the two dominant metres were of very different types: in *arte menor* the poets counted syllables, and in *arte mayor* they counted beats.[11] This ambivalence clearly caused many *cancionero* poets unease, because some sought to reform the situation by regularizing the number of syllables in their *arte mayor*, while others attempted to regularize the interval between beats (see Duffell 2007: 185-89). In *arte menor* the *cancionero* poets counted syllables to the final stress, which was on the seventh, and termed the metre an *octosílabo* because the default structure of Castilian words is *grave* (that is, there is a single post-tonic syllable).[12] In *arte mayor* these poets counted four (two-plus-two) beats, so that lines varied from nine to thirteen syllables in length. The *verso de arte menor* had became a strictly counted *octosílabo* only in the fifteenth century, since in the preceding century its lines had sometimes contained a syllable more or fewer (see Clarke 1964: 18–51). In contrast, around 1380 *arte mayor* had succeeded a syllable-counting

[10] It is not unusual for one or two verse designs to dominate a verse tradition: the French *alexandrin*, the English iambic pentameter, and the Italian *endecasillabo* are obvious examples of metres that have become canonical and that account for a very large proportion of all the verse composed in the language concerned. The French line contains six-plus-six syllables, the English five feet (strong/weak contrasts), and the Italian ten syllables subdivided into six plus four or four plus six.

[11] A *beat* is the simplest term for the strong element in a foot contrast: in verse instances a beat is normally represented by a syllable that is perceived as having more stress than its neighbours (see Liberman & Prince 1977). Derek Attridge explains the rhythms of English poetry entirely in terms of beats and *offbeats*, the latter being the linguistic material between beats and thus the weak element in the contrast (1982). Like their English contemporaries, the composers of Castilian epic poems such as the *Poema de Mio Cid* also seem to have counted beats (see Duffell 2002). The stressed syllables of languages with dynamic accent, such as Castilian and English, are louder and longer, and are delivered with a change in pitch (Fry 1958 and Penny 2002: 42-43). Compare the stress profiles of *hablo* and *insight* (strong/weak) with those of *habló* and *incite* (weak/strong)

[12] This essay employs the Spanish conventions for counting syllables and naming metres: an *octosílabo* contains seven syllables to its final stress and gains its eighth only when it ends in a *grave* word. I shall denote line lengths by the following abbreviations: 8G = an *octosílabo grave*; 8A = an *octosílabo agudo*; Q = *quebrado*, or severed line; Q4s & Q5s = *quebrados* of the two most common lengths; Q4A & Q4G = the two types of Q4.

(six-plus-six) metre (*cuaderna vía*), which had been introduced, probably from France, at the close of the twelfth century (see Duffell 2007: 109-43).

The metrical regularity of the *octosílabo* derives from the following features: (1) there is an interval of six syllables between line-final syllables, (2) line-final syllables carry phrasal stress (which may be monosyllabic), (3) they are also usually emphasized by rhyme, and (4) any line-final post-tonic syllable is extrametrical, or uncounted. The metrical variety found in *octosílabos* derives from its correspondence rules' allowing the poet a choice between the following options: (1) lines may be either *grave* or *agudo*, (2) any type of syllable may occupy the first six positions. This second option creates different rhythms within lines, in contrast to the rhythm between lines provided by the (rhymed) stress on every seventh syllable. Tomás Navarro refers to these different internal rhythms as *modalidades* (1973: 53-61), and a line with stress on syllables 1 & 4 he terms *dactílico*, a line with stress on 1, 3, 5, & 7 *trocaico*, and a line with stress on 2 & 4 *mixto*. A further source of variety is provided by minor variations in these rhythms where one or more of these stresses is replaced by a monosyllable or a syllable with secondary stress (termed by metrists *ictus promotion* or *erosion*). *Cancionero* poems in this metre invariably contain a mixture of *dactílico*, *trocaico*, and *mixto* lines (many with erosion), so that every poem comprises a unique mixture of rhythms.

The metrical regularity of the *verso de arte mayor* derives from: (1) each line contains four beats, divided into two plus two by a *caesura*, a mandatory word boundary between the second and third beat; (2) at least 80 per cent of beats are realized by the primary stressed syllables of polysyllabic words or by stressed monosyllables; (3) at least 80 per cent of the intervals between beats contain exactly two syllables, which gives the verse a predominantly triple-time (*dactílico*) rhythm. The metre's metrical variety derives from: (1) lines vary in length, usually between eleven and twelve syllables, although lines of nine and thirteen are possible;[13] (2) up

---

[13] This variability results from: (1) the first hemistich may be *agudo*, *grave*, or *esdrújulo*, and (2) either hemistich may be subject to the *anacrusic principle*, which follows the norm of musical rhythm (ABRSM 1958: 18) in allowing the first beat of an accentual metre to be preceded by one, two, or zero syllables. In effect this makes syllables before the first beat extrametrical, like those after the final stress in Romance metres.

to 20 per cent of beats are realized by atonic monosyllables or secondary stressed syllables; (3) up to 20 per cent of intervals between beats contain one or three syllables, producing a trochaic rhythm.[14] Note that of two adjacent stresses only one represents a beat, and a monosyllable may provide a beat rather than a neighbouring primary stress. Since the *verso de arte mayor* is a strongly divided line, hiatus is the normal treatment of adjacent vowels at the caesura, and the prevailing triple-time rhythm does not necessarily continue between the second and third beats of the line.

There was a further source of metrical variety available to *cancionero* poets, the *verso* (or *pie*) *quebrado* (henceforth *Q*), a term that is probably best translated as 'severed line'. The use of severed lines has an ancient pedigree: the Ancient Greek and Latin heroic couplet consisted of a line followed by two half-lines, and a number of other metres were used in strophes that contained a half-line: thus the Sapphic strophe, which in a late form supplied the metre of the medieval Iberian *Carmen Campidoctoris* (Montaner & Escobar 2001), comprised three lines and a half-line. Half-lines were also employed in early Romance verse, for example, the seven-syllable half-line (the first half of an *endecasillabo a maiore*) that Dante Alighieri (b. 1265, d. 1321) employed in sections VII, VIII, XII, XXIII, XXXI, & XXXIII of his *Vita nuova* (Chiappelli 1965). Even closer to the *Q* in structure is the severed line with which most English readers are familiar, that of a strophe popularized by Robert Burns (b. 1759, d. 1796): it rhymes aaabab, and each of the lines rhymed a contains four beats and each of those rhymed b contains two, making the latter half-lines.[15] The *Burns stanza* not only adds variety to iambic tetrameter verse, but it suits well that poet's predilection for pithy afterthoughts and cryptic comments (see Barke

---

[14] Fernando Lázaro Carreter (1972) argued that in *arte mayor* stress was wrenched in performance so as to produce a regular rhythmic triple-time delivery; I have argued that this is credible in Mena's *arte mayor*, where 3 per cent of hemistichs would require wrenching (Duffell 1999: 85), but not in the case of Santillana's *arte mayor*, where a much higher proportion of lines would require this treatment (see Duffell 2000: 121-22).

[15] Under French influence Middle and Early Modern English poets began to regularize the syllable count of their lines, which had always been accentual (see Duffell 2003): they did this by standardizing the size of the offbeats; thus in the lines of a *Burns stanza* each offbeat comprises one syllable, which combines with a following beat to produce what metrists term an *iambic* foot.

1960). The *cancionero* poets, however, employed the severed line more extensively than poets of other cultures (Clarke 1942: 340)

Overall, the sources of variety in *arte mayor* were greater than those in *arte menor* and the longer metre's irregularities were more striking. The *cancionero* poets took full advantage of this and developed individual styles of *arte mayor*, some of which were syllabic (with lines of 6 + 6 syllables), some stress-syllabic (lines of four *amphibrachs*, or dactyls), and some intermediate between the two categories (see Clarke 1964: 5-17). Although very few *arte mayor* compositions included severed lines, three of them can be found in the earliest surviving *cancionero* (c.1430), the *Cancionero de Baena* (henceforth *CB*; Dutton & González Cuenca 1993). The first is 'Aviendo grant quexa de vuestros porteros' (*CB* 202, ID 1342), by Alfonso Álvarez de Villasandino (b. c.1345, d. 1425). Its five strophes each comprise eleven lines containing twelve syllables and three lines containing six. Its metre may be classified as *arte mayor* because its hemistichs have two beats and a predominantly triple-time rhythm, but by eschewing the anacrusic principle the poet has transformed it into a *dodecasílabo* with Q6s.[16]

The second poem that combines *arte mayor* with Qs is 'Maestro esçelente, profundo letrado' (CB 379, ID 1504) by Juan Alfonso de Baena (b. c.1375, d. c.1434) and is datable to 1423. In each of its four strophes a severed line separates two quatrains of full lines, and the latter are more regular in syllable count than most *arte mayor* (only two out of thirty-six have zero anacrusis).[17] The four Qs, however, are not hemistichs of *arte mayor*, but a single syntagm (Q3G or Q4G): *de grado / eçelençia / cargado / o ruano*. The third poem, 'Muy alto señor, no visto aduay' (*CB* 452, ID 1580), is also by Baena. Its six strophes each comprise four lines of twelve syllables, followed by four Qs, and then three *octosílabos*. Here again, by eschewing the anacrusic principle, the poet has transformed *arte mayor* lines (recognizable by their four beats and prevailing triple-time rhythm) into as strict *dodecasílabos* as the *octosílabos* of the final tercet. (The poem's Qs, however, are either Q4G or Q5A, a combination I

---

[16] This poem, which is datable to 1418, is an extreme example of the greater syllabic and accentual regularity that typifies Villasandino's later verse (see Clarke 1964: 69-72).

[17] This proportion may be compared with the 33 per cent of lines with zero anacrusis in the most famous long poem in *arte mayor*, Juan de Mena's *Laberinto de Fortuna* (see Duffell 1999: 86).

shall discuss in detail later in this essay.) In all three poems the *arte mayor* is exceptionally regular, both in syllable count and rhythm, and this must be more than coincidence. It may be argued that these poems require *Q*s to provide variety and surprise, because they neglect the ample resources for both that can be found in other types of *arte mayor*.

In contrast to the longer metre, the *octosílabos* of the *cancioneros* seem to have needed the injection of an additional source of variety. Of almost 700 poems in the *CB* (or that part of it which is preserved in the Bibliothèque Nationale; PH1) fifty-one have *Q*s in their strophe designs. By my calculation there are 629 *Q*s in the fifty-one poems, and they occur in strophes of various lengths; the number of *Q*s in a strophe varies between one and eight, with an average of 2.5, but twenty poems contain only one; a *Q* may appear in any position in the strophe, but the final position is the most common (in 19 poems). Most remarkably, however, the *Q*s of the *cancionero* poets differ from the severed lines of other poetic traditions by varying in length. The following lengths occur among the 629 *Q*s of the *CB*: *Q3A* (2), *Q3G* (23), *Q4A* (80), *Q4G* (326), *Q5A* (168), *Q5G* (27), *Q6A* (2), and *Q6G* (1). Spanish metrists have noted this irregularity in the *Q*s of an otherwise strictly counted syllabic metre, and most have concluded that *Q4* is the norm and that *Q5*s occur under certain specific conditions. The first of these is when the preceding line is *agudo*, so that the extra syllable in the *Q* compensates for its predecessor's lack of a post-tonic syllable, and the second is when the *Q* opens in a vowel or diphthong and the preceding line closes in a vowel, so that interlinear synaloepha may occur (see Domínguez Caparrós 2004: 90). Note that in both cases the preceding line (8-1) and the *Q* (+5) combine to produce a count of 13 syllables, restoring regularity to the metre.

Other Spanish metrists, however, have elevated the fact that *Q5*s often occur in these conditions into a rule, a *regla de pie quebrado* (see Navarro 1974: 136-38), and in the remainder of this essay I shall test whether the *cancionero* poets' practice can reasonably be described as 'observing a metrical rule'. In discussing my research I shall employ the abbreviations *A+* (*agudo* + compensation) and *V-* (adjacent vowels, making interlinear synaloepha possible) to describe the two specific conditions under which *Q5*s should occur. The samples I have chosen for analysis total more than 1400 *Q*s and have been selected to represent the work of four different generations of *cancionero* poets. The first generation worked before the date of the *CB*'s compilation (1430), and in some cases considerably earlier; the second was active between 1430 and 1460; the third between 1460 and 1490, and the fourth worked after 1490 and well into the next century. The period before 1430 is represented by two samples consisting of 347 *Qs* from twenty-one poems in *CB*, ten (containing 147 lines) by Villasandino, and eleven by various other poets; the period 1430-60 is also covered by two samples: all 400 *Qs* of the *Proverbios* (Gómez Moreno & Kerkhof 1988) by the Marqués de Santillana (b. 1398, d. 1458), and the 168 *Qs* in the eight surviving poems (Pérez Priego 1989) that contain *Qs* by Juan de Mena (b. 1411, d. 1456); the third period is represented by one sample, the 160 *Qs* in the *Coplas a la muerte de su padre* (Beltrán 1993) by Jorge Manrique (b. c.1440, d. 1479); the final period is also represented by one sample, the 277 *Qs* of the *Bucólicas* (Rambaldo 1978) by Juan del Encina (b. 1468, d. 1529).[18]

Table 1 at the end of this essay shows the frequency with which *Q*4s and *Q*5s occur in each of the three possible environments, *A*+, *V*-, and *GC* (when the *Q* follows a *grave* line with an intervening consonant). The following lines from the *CB* (poem number), Santillana's *Proverbios* (*P*), and Manrique's *Coplas* (*C*) illustrate all the combinations of *octosílabo* and *Q*4/5 that are found in the samp les:[19]

A+ followed by *Q*4

(1)   la gen-til fres-cu-rᵃ y **tez**   / de la **ca**-ra   (*C*, 86-87)
(2)   que cuy-da ser per-fec-**ción** / tal pla-**zer**   (*P*, 279-80)
      A+ followed by *Q*5
(3)   si dis-cre-çión e sa-**ver** / non ha per-**di**-do?   (*P*, 11-12)
(4)   de-re-chos a sᵉ a-ca-**bar** / e con-su-**mir**   (*C*, 29-30)
      V- followed by *Q*4

---

[18] The *CB* numbers of Villasandino's ten poems are: 1 (ID 1147), 17 (ID 1164), 22 (ID 1167), 23 (ID 1168), 40 (ID 1183), 41 (ID 1184), 160 (ID1300), 194 (ID 1334), 209 (ID 1349), 256 (ID 0506); the *CB* numbers of the eleven other poems are: 307 (ID 0447), 311 (ID 1438), 327 (ID 1453), 328 (ID 1454), 344 (ID 1470), 385 (ID 1510), 386 (ID 1511), 387 (ID 1512), 398 (ID 1525), 452 (ID 1580), 463 (ID 1591). Dutton's number for Santillana's *Proverbios* is ID 0050; the poems with *Qs* attributed to Mena by Pérez Priego 1989 are ID 0337, ID 2329, ID 1804, ID 2327, ID 0853, ID 2235 (of which the odd-numbered strophes are in *arte mayor*), ID 6515, and ID 6516; Manrique's *Coplas* is ID 0277 and Encina's *Bucólicas* ID 4431.

[19] My samples employ the following typographical devices as an aid to scansion: (1) all words are double-spaced, (2) all syllables are hyphenated (3), mandatory stresses are marked in bold typeface, and (4) vowels not counted because of synaloepha are in superscript.

(5)   Fi-jo, sig^{ue} al en-ten-**di**-do/ e su **ley**   (*P*, 177-78)

(6)   syn re-par° e sin e-**mien**-da / es tal **da**-ño   (*P*,356-57)
       V- followed by *Q*5

(7)   re-buel-ve, tras-tor-na e **gir**^a / en-con-ti-**nen**-te   (*P*, 155-56)

(8)   el al-ma tan glo-ri-**os**^a / an-ge-li-**cal**   (*C*, 149-50)
       GC followed by *Q*4

(9)   có-mo, des-pués d^e a-cor-**da**-do, / da do-**lor**   (*C*, 8-9)

(10)   da-re-mos lo no ve-**ni**-do   / por pa-**sa**-do   (*C*, 17-18)
       GC followed by *Q*5

(11)   miem-bra-te de mí se-**ño**-ra   / por cor-te-**sí**-a   (307, 8-9)

(12)   ja-más non o-v^e a-le-**grí**-a / ¡Dué-le-te de **mí**!   (311, 9-10)

Table 1 shows that 73 per cent (146) of the 201 *Q*5s in these poems can be attributed to *A*+ and 20 per cent (40) to *V*-; but it also shows that only a minority of *A*+ and *V*- environments contain *Q*5s. Even if we accept a figure of 80 per cent (the figure for ictic stress or triple time in *arte mayor*) as being sufficient to constitute a norm, the *Q*5 figures for individual poets do not amount to norms: three poets employed *Q*5s in more than half of the cases of *A*+, Villasandino (61 per cent), Santillana (67 per cent), and Manrique (58 per cent); two employed *Q*5s in more than half of the cases of *V*-, Mena (63 per cent) and Manrique (70 per cent). What we can conclude from these figures is that Villasandino increased the use of *Q*5s in both environments, and that Santillana (in the case of *A*+) and Mena (in the case of *V*-) increased them still further. But only Manrique used *Q*5s in a majority of both special environments, while the ultra-methodical Encina rejected *Q*5s so totally that he seems even to have avoided adjacent vowels between full lines and the *Q*s that followed them.[10] The addition of an extra syllable to the *Q* in *A*+ and/or *V*-environments was therefore not a rule, but an option, one that different poets might choose to take on a different proportion of occasions. *Q*5s, unlike metrical rules, were features that gave versification an element of surprise, rather than security.

The fifteen *Q*5s that occur in other (*GC*) environments in my samples are all in the *CB*, where there are also a number of poems in which all the *Q*s are *Q*5 (usually *Q*5*A*). All these *Q*5s in other environments can be explained by two archaizing practices that lingered on from the versifying of the thirteenth and fourteenth centuries. The first was that some early Iberian poets counted actual, not notional syllables, so that 5*A* (not 4*A*) equalled 4*G* syllables, a method sanctioned by what modern metrists term the *ley de Mussafia* (see Domínguez Caparrós 2004: 216-18).[20] Although calling this practice a law does not mean that it was not a mistake, *cancionero* poets must have been well aware that tradition allowed counting in this way, because some of the earliest *octosílabos* in *CB* are 9*A*, not 8*A*. Another archaism may lie behind the presence of *Q5Gs*, because many of the poems with *Qs* of this length are composed, like examples (1) and (12) above, in Galician-Portuguese, the traditional language for lyrics at the court of Castile. They are among the earliest poems in *CB*, and date from the fourteenth century, a period when poets in Castile neglected syllable count, and composed what modern metrists term *verso fluctuante* (see Navarro 1974: 79 and Domínguez Caparrós 2004: 469-70). Thus in the lyrics of the *Libro de Buen Amor* (Gybbon-Monypenny 1988), which was completed in 1343, many full lines of the *verso común* (which later became the *octosílabo*) had seven or nine syllables, instead of eight, and similarly, some severed lines were *Q3s* or *Q5s*, not *Q4s* (see Duffell 2004: 71-74).

Each of the many *Qs* of anomalous length in the *cancioneros* may thus be attributed to one or more of four different technicalities: interlinear compensation, interlinear synaloepha, archaistic *Mussafia* counting, and/or the fourteenth-century *verso fluctuante*. But I should like to suggest two far simpler explanations. The first is that the *octosílabo* has no fixed caesura, unlike the Latin and Italian lines that are followed by half-lines. A caesura is a fixed position for the line's principal internal syntactic boundary (*colon*), but there is no such fixed point in the *octosílabo*; while most lines fall naturally into two syntagms, this divides them in a variety of ways. Since divisions into 4*G* + 3, 4*A* + 4, and 5*A* + 3 are all very common, it is not surprising that all these lengths appear as *Qs* in the *cancioneros*. Moreover, the very small number of *Q3s* and *Q6s* found in the *CB* also reflect possible subdivisions of the *octosílabo*, into 3*G* + 4, 3*A* + 5, and 6*A* + 2. The *Q* is thus not a

---

[20] The most convincing hypothesis on the rhythm of syllabic verse is that of Benoît de Cornulier, who argues that in a syllable-timed language the final stresses of lines and hemistichs fall at regular time intervals to create it (1995: 111-13). *Mussafia* counting, however, is antirhythmic, in that there is no regularity in the interval between final stresses or rhymes (see Duffell 2004: 73).

half-line, but a part-line of variable length, like the normal subdivisions of the *octosílabo*.[21]

My second simple explanation for the variability is that the *Q* reprises not the line's opening, but its close: it is an echo (or precursor) of a rhyme and the linguistic material that produces that rhyme. Since the first rule of versifying is that the counting must begin where the line begins, not where it ends, there is no reason why *Qs* should be counted, even though they are set within strictly counted syllabic verse. To employ a common image of truncation, the *Q* is not the female foreparts of the mermaid, but the fishy tail (the French meaning of my abbreviation). A distinctive shape, not a precise size, is the defining property of a tail, and *quebrados* are unmistakably short and rhyme-shaped. The *quebrado* not only provided an element of surprise within the reassuring familiarity of the *octosílabo*, it also had an intrinsic potential for variety — its length. It is therefore not surprising that so many poets employed this simple device to enrich and enliven their verse in the period's most overworked metre.

Table 1

Pentasyllabic *Quebrados* in Six Samples

sample	A+			V–			GC		
	Qs	*Q5s*	(%)	*Qs*	*Q5s*	(%)	*Qs*	*Q5s*	(%)
CB various	32	8	(25)	49	8	(16)	219	9	(3)
Villasandino	49	30	(61)	22	7	(32)	76	6	(4)
Santillana	112	75	(67)	38	88	(21)	250	0	(0)
Mena	31	11	(35)	16	10	(63)	121	0	(0)
Manrique	38	22	(58)	10	7	(70)	112	0	(0)
Encina	67	0	(0)	12	0	(0)	198	0	(0)
TOTAL	329	146	(44)	147	40	(27)	967	15*	(1)

---

[21] The only *octosílabos* in the *cancioneros* that are divided into half-lines are those with internal (*leonine*) rhyme, which is a feature of a number of poems, including *CB* 382-87 (ID 1507-12), *CB* 504 (ID 1630), and *CB* 506 (ID 1632). When these half-line rhymes are *grave* they are usually 4G + 4G, as in 'e faría / cortesía' (*CB* 504, 21); when they are *agudo*, however, they are always 5A + 5A, for example, 'cos natural / angelical' (*CB* 506, 9). The latter are *octosílabos* only according to the *ley de Mussafia*, and a few of the lines in these poems with internal rhymes are not octosyllabic at all; for example 'estrela / muy bela' (*CB* 504, 11) which is a *hexasílabo* of 3G + 3G.

Key

A+ sample: Qs following an *agudo* line; V- sample: Qs following a *grave* line that produces interlinear adjacent vowels; GC sample: Qs following a *grave* line separated by a consonant.

All fifteen of the Q5s that follow *grave* lines separated by a consonant are in the CB, which also contains ten Q3s and three Q6s.

WORKS CITED

ABRSM, 1958. *Rudiments and Theory of Music*, AB, 1197 (London: Associated Board of the Royal Schools of Music).

ALLEN, W. Sidney, 1973. *Accent and Rhythm: Prosodic Features of Latin and Greek: A Study in Theory and Reconstruction* (Cambridge: UP).

ATTRIDGE, Derek, 1982. *The Rhythms of English Poetry*, ELS, 14 (London: Longman).

BARKE, James, ed., 1960. *Poems and Songs of Robert Burns* (London: Collins).

BELTRÁN, Vicente, ed., 1993. Jorge Manrique, *Poesía*, Biblioteca Clásica, 15 (Barcelona: Crítica).

CHATMAN, Seymour, 1965. *A Theory of Meter* (Mouton: The Hague).

CHIAPPELLI, Fredi, ed., 1965. Dante Alighieri, *Vita nuova*, Grande Universale Mursia, ns, 7 (Milano: Mursia).

CLARKE, Dorothy Clotelle, 1942. 'The Fifteenth-Century *Copla de pie quebrado*', *HR*, 10: 340–43.

——, 1964. *Morphology of Fifteenth Century Castilian Verse*, Duquesne Studies, Philological Series, 4 (Pittsburgh: Duquesne UP; Louvain: Nauwelaerts).

CORNULIER, Benoît de, 1995. *Art poétique: notions et problèmes de métrique* (Lyon: Presses Universitaires de Lyon).

DOMÍNGUEZ CAPARRÓS, José, 2004. *Diccionario de métrica española*, 2nd ed., Biblioteca Temática, 8110 (Madrid: Alianza Editorial).

DORCHAIN, Auguste, 1919. *L'Art des vers*, 2nd ed. (Paris: Garnier). First ed. 1911.

DUFFELL, Martin J., 1999. *Modern Metrical Theory and the 'Verso de arte mayor'*, PMHRS, 10.

——, 2000. 'The Santillana Factor: The Development of Double Audition in Castilian', in *Santillana: A Symposium*, ed. Alan Deyermond, PMHRS, 28, pp. 113–28.

——, 2002. 'Don Rodrigo and Sir Gawain: Family Likeness or Convergent Development?', in '*Mio Cid' Studies: 'Some Problems of Diplomatic'*, *Fifty Years On*, ed Alan Deyermond, David Pattison, & Eric Southworth, PMHRS, 42, pp. 129–49.

——, 2003. 'The Iambic Pentameter and its Rivals', *Rhythmica*, 1: 61–85.

——, 2004. 'Metre and Rhythm in the *Libro de Buen Amor*', in *A Companion to the 'Libro de Buen Amor'*, ed. Louise M. Haywood & Louise O. Vasvári, CT, A209 (Woodbridge: Tamesis), pp. 71–82.

——, 2007. *Syllable and Accent: Studies on Medieval Hispanic Metrics*, PMHRS, 56.

DUTTON, Brian, ed., 1990-91. *El cancionero del siglo XV, c.1360–1520*, Biblioteca Española del Siglo XV, Serie Maior, 1–7 (Salamanca: Univ. de Salamanca).

——, & Joaquín GONZÁLEZ CUENCA, ed., 1993. *Cancionero de Juan Alfonso de Baena*, BFH, 14 (Madrid: Visor).

FABB, Nigel, 2001. 'Weak Monosyllables in Iambic Pentameter Verse and the Communication of Metrical Form', *Lingua*, 111: 771–90.

——, 2002. *Language and Literary Structure: The Linguistic Analysis of Form in Verse and Narrative* (Cambridge: UP).

FRY, Dennis, 1958, 'Experiments in the Perception of Stress', *Language and Speech*, 1: 126–52.

GETTY, Michael, 2002. *The Meter of 'Beowulf': A Constraint-Based Approach*, Topics in English Linguistics, 36 (Berlin: Mouton de Gruyter).

GÓMEZ-BRAVO, Ana M., 1998. *Repertorio métrico de la poesía cancioneril del siglo XV*, Poetria Nova, Serie Maior, 1 (Alcalá de Henares: Univ. de Alcalá).

GÓMEZ MORENO, Ángel, & Maxim P. A. M. KERKHOF, ed., 1988. Marqués de Santillana, *Obras completas*, AH, 146 (Barcelona: Planeta).

GYBBON-MONYPENNY, G. B., ed., 1988. Arcipreste de Hita, *Libro de buen amor*, CC, 161 (Madrid: Castalia).

HARRIS, James W., 1983. *Syllable Structure and Stress in Spanish: A Non-Linear Analysis*, Linguistic Monographs, 8 (Boston: MIT Press).

HAYES, Bruce, 1995. *Metrical Stress Theory: Principles and Case Studies* (Chicago: Univ. of Chicago Press).

JAKOBSON, Roman, 1960. 'Closing Statement: Linguistics and Poetics', in Sebeok 1960: 350–77.

LÁZARO CARRETER, Fernando, 1972. 'La poética del arte mayor castellano', in *Studia hispanica in honorem R. Lapesa*, I (Madrid: Gredos & Cátedra-Seminario Menéndez Pidal), pp. 343–78.

LIBERMAN, Mark Y., & Alan Prince, 1977. 'On Stress and Linguistic Rhythm', *LIn*, 8: 249–336.

LOTZ, John, 1960. 'Metric Typology', in Sebeok 1960: 135–48.

MONTANER, Alberto, & Ángel ESCOBAR, ed. & tr., 2001. *Carmen Campidoctoris, o poema latino del Campeador* (Madrid: España Nuevo Milenio).

NAVARRO (TOMÁS), Tomás, 1973. *Los poetas en sus versos desde Jorge Manrique a García Lorca* (Barcelona: Ariel).

——, 1974. *Métrica española*, 4th ed. (Madrid: Guadarrama).

PENNY, Ralph, 2002. *History of the Spanish Language*, 2nd ed. (Cambridge: UP).

PÉREZ PRIEGO, Ángel, ed., 1989. Juan de Mena, *Obras completas*, AH,175 (Barcelona: Planeta).

RAMBALDO, Ana María, ed., 1978. Juan del Encina, *Obras completas*, I: '*Arte de poesía castellana' y poemas religiosos y'Bucólicas'*, Clásicos Castellanos, 218 (Madrid: Espasa-Calpe).

RICKETTS, Peter, 2001. *Concordance of Medieval Occitan* (Turnhout: Brepols).

SEBEOK, Thomas A., ed., 1960. *Style in Language* (Boston: MIT Press).

SMITH, Gerald, 2000. 'Russian Poetry: The Lines or the Lives' (Presidential Address of the MHRA), *Modern Language Review*, 95: xxix–xli.

THOMPSON, John, 1961. *The Founding of English Meter* (London: Routledge & Kegan Paul; New York: Columbia UP).

WHETNALL, Jane, 1989. 'Songs and *Canciones* in the *Cancionero general* of 1511', in *The Age of the Catholic Monarchs, 1474-1516: Literary Studies in Memory of Keith Whinnom*, ed. Alan Deyermond & Ian Macpherson (Liverpool: UP), pp. 197–207.

——, 2003. '*Cancioneros*', in *Castilian Writers 1400-1500*, ed. Frank A. Domínguez & George D. Greenia, Dictionary of Literary Biography, 286 (Detroit: Thomson Gale), pp. 288–323.

Firing Blanks: Sexual Frustration and Crossbow Imagery in *Cancionero* Poetry

KIRSTIN KENNEDY

(Victoria and Albert Museum)

Cancionero poets liked talking about sex, and having it as well.[1] The 'velado erotismo', in the late Keith Whinnom's phrase, which pervades these compilations is created by the ambiguity of verbs such as 'acometer', 'cabalgar', 'justar', 'perder', and 'tirar', which as well as their literal meanings are also used to refer to the sexual act (Whinnom 1981: 36). Thanks to the penetrating intellect of twentieth-century scholars, *cancionero* euphemisms for the act of coitus and its orgasmic result are now familiar to modern readers, who have rightly become sceptical of earlier interpretations of these poems as repetitive examples of 'insípida y artificial galantería', and of greater historical than literary interest.[2] Some poets, indeed, are neither gallant nor subtle in their double-entendre. Take, for instance, the short poem by Guevara dedicated, as the rubric helpfully explains, 'a su amiga estando con ella en la cama':

> ¡Qué noche tan mal dormida!
> ¡Qué sueño tan desvelado!
> ¡Qué dama vos, tan polida!
> ¡Qué ombre yo, tan penado!
> ¡Qué gesto el vuestro, de dios!
> ¡Qué mal el mío, con vicio!
> ¡Qué ley que tengo con vos!
> ¡Qué fe con vuestro servicio!
> (González Cuenca 2004: II, no. 210)

Guevara's paradoxical recollection of his night of love-making is couched in terms of religious worship, a frequent device in *cancionero*

---

[1] See Whinnom 1981, Macpherson 1985, Macpherson & MacKay 1993, Deyermond 1978, Vasvári 1999, and Moreno 2001.

[2] The verdict of Marcelino Menéndez Pelayo in his *Antología de poetas líricos castellanos*, cited in Whinnom 1981: 9-10.

From the 'Cancioneiro da Vaticana' to the 'Cancionero general': Studies in Honour of Jane Whetnall, ed. Alan Deyermond & Barry Taylor, PMHRS, 60 (London: Department of Hispanic Studies, Queen Mary, University of London, 2007), pp. 177–90. ISSN 1460-051X. ISBN 0 902238 50 7.

poetry. He presents the woman as a pure, even divine, creature and himself as her tormented servant. His torment, however, is his desire for her, a desire which in this poem is satisfied and which, Guevara implies, is mutual. Lines 5 and 6, which focus on the lovers in bed, contrast her god-like countenance with his 'mal', or suffering, lustful state.[3] It is a contrast in keeping with the antithetical imagery of the poem which places Guevara in a subservient position to his lady. However, her divine expression could also be interpreted as one of the sexual ecstasy attendant upon Guevara's adoration or 'servicio', and so the poem commemorates not just the poet's orgasm but his prowess at lovemaking as well.

A celebration of orgasm (usually from the male perspective) is not the only sexual subject to be found between the covers of *cancioneros*, although to date it is one which has attracted the most critical attention. The same mixture of explicit and allusive language is also used to ponder the causes and frustrations of male impotence.

Contemporary writers and physicians had supplied various explanations for the problem. Age was an obvious reason, although the difficulty was not exclusive to those with white hair and beards. The anonymous author of the *Carajicomedia* also considered younger men who ejaculated without achieving a full erection, and those who '[dan] cojonadas aprisa sin tiento' (*Carajicomedia* 1995: 79–80) equally impotent. Medical wisdom provided further explanations. Bernardo de Gordonio gave a detailed account in his 1305 *Practica dicta Lilium medicine*, and his advice still circulated, this time in printed Spanish translation, in 1495 (Gordonio 1991: Book VII). The reasons for the problem were manifold, and could include the woman herself if she was old, ugly, menstruating, or smelly. Men, though, were also to blame: those who were young, too old, too drunk, or who, indeed, had too much sex, would find themselves incapable. Likewise psychological states affected performance: 'los melancólicos no cobdician ni naturalmente pueden' (Gordonio 1991: 302).

The successful achievement of coitus, Gordonio observed, required a combination of physical and psychological factors:

---

[3] Antonio de Nebrija (1516) gives the Latin equivalent of 'vicio' as 'luxus, luxuria', while 'luxus' is sternly defined by Alfonso de Palencia as 'delectaçion dissoluta, o abundançia demasiada dende se dize luxuria, que es la mesma dissoluçion fea' (Palencia 1490: I, sub nomine).

en el coitu son tres cosas necessarias, conviene a saber, calor e ventosidad e humidad. E assí segund Avicena el sentido viene del celebro, e el espíritu e el viento del coraçón, e la sangre e el desseo del fígado. En tal manera que el desseo natural en parte es delos riñones e del fígado, e el complimiento viene del coraçón. (Gordonio 1991: 301)

Sexual desire required a positive mental state and full post-prandial digestion for success. These conditions fulfilled, only then could a man (as Gordonio puts it) '[echar su] simiente enla madre tan solamente; e en ninguna manera en otro agujero'.[4]

Unsurprisingly, these theories and diagnoses are reflected with varying degrees of subtlety in *cancionero* references to impotence.[5] In some instances, the poets are in no doubt that it is the woman who is to blame. Diego López de Haro uses a branch of broom to symbolise his frustrated desire because his lady is menstruating (Kennedy 2002: 168). Aires Telez, on the other hand, receives an acorn ('boleta') from his lady and complains that his 'grande mere-cimento / tam pequeno fruito daa' (Resende 1990-98: IV, no. 766). The gift was presumably also meant to be read on a medical level. Acorns assisted retention of bodily fluids (*Tacuinum* 1996: colour plate XV, Gordonio 1991: 297 & 336), so it seems the lady in ques-tion was also keen to discourage ejaculation in her admirer.

Other poets suffered impotence brought about by their own physical or mental state. A group of *motes* and replies composed around 1510 by Fadrique Enríquez de Cabrera, Admiral of Castile, on behalf of a series of courtiers, imagines both the Count of Benavente and Pedro Girón with kidney and kidney-related com-plaints which, it is implied, have affected their sexual performance. Cabrera also imagines their ladies' responses:[6]

---

[4] *Cancionero* poets, though, refer to other aspects of forbidden sexuality, such as the intriguing series of questions about sexual identity addressed by four male courti-ers to 'ūa dama que refiava e beijava dona Guiomar de Crasto' (Resende 1990-98: III, no. 586). On female desire where the object is male, see Deyermond 1978. Mean-while, studies on homosexuality in early Iberian poetry have tended to focus on the thirteenth-century *cantigas d'escarnho e maldizer*, on which see Lopes 1994 and Black-more 1999.

[5] Perhaps the most extensive survey of medical aspects of *cancionero* poetry has been that by Maximiano Lemos (1920) who published, in instalments, an article identifying physicians, surgeons, and the complaints they treated. His focus was Resende's *Cancioneiro Geral*.

[6] Intriguingly, the rubric to the *motes* adds a note on their provenance: 'dizen que se fallaron escriptos en vn meson'. This suggests they may have formed part of after-dinner entertainments.

El conde de bena vente que sirve a doña ysabel de salazar y es enfermo de los riñones:
Lo mas grave de mis penas
es corrimiento de arenas.

Su amiga
Villalobos sabra çierto
quel dolor os tiene muerto

don pedro giron por que es enfermo dela yjada
No tiene amores quien ama
por que nel mal dela yjada tiene
mayor fuerça quando viene.
Su amiga
Lo que mi servidor siente
curalo vn paño caliente.
(Dutton 1990-91: I, 372)

The Count's imagined affliction is ironic in the circumstances. Although a source of acute pain, kidney stones could give young men an erection according to Gordonio, because of the heat they generated (Gordonio 1991: 293). Isabel de Salazar's reference to 'Villalobos' conceals a level of wit now lost to us: the scribe has seen fit to add a marginal note that 'este villalobos es vn fisyco de la corte', but this does not explain the humour behind the assertion. Pedro Girón, meanwhile, is unable to consummate his love because of the even more pressing pain he suffers in his side. To cure the problem, his lady proposes applying a hot towel to his side. This would counteract the impotence-inducing coldness afflicting an area (stomach and kidneys) which, as we have seen, was thought to play a key role in a man's sexual well-being.

Other poets are less explicitly physiological and more allusive in the description of the condition, playing with terms such as 'gloria' and 'muerte' more familiar to modern readers in accounts of sexual triumphs. The following *canción* by a poet identified simply as 'Tapia' is an illustration not only of the ambiguous language used by these poets, but also of a distinctly unclimactic level of meaning:[7]

Ninguno tenga esperança
que en el mal de amor hay medio,
porque es cierta su mudança
y es incierto su remedio.
Y si Amor y su belleza
os hiziere amar forçado,

---

[7] On the identity of this shadowy figure, see Giuliani 1991.

no os dure más el cuidadoque le dura la firmeza.
No os engañe su esperança,
que al comienço, al fin y medio
es muy cierta su mudança
y es incierto su remedio.
(González Cuenca 2004: II, no. 311).

On one level, Tapia is expounding standard characteristics of love, using standard vocabulary, to present the paradox that the only constant aspect of this emotion is its inconstancy.[8] There is, he says, no stability ('medio') associated with this ever-changing emotional situation which is, he implies, imposed upon its unwilling victim ('Y si Amor y su belleza / os hiziere amar forçado'). The advice he offers, that the smitten person's amorous torment should not last longer than his feelings of constant love for the lady ('no os dure mas el cuidado / que le dura la firmeza'), continues the paradox by contrasting the lover's shifting emotional state with his constant loyalty. This portrayal of love as an irrational force which brings false hope and uncertainty is one found in many other poems of the period (Rodado Ruiz 2000). However, the language which Tapia uses to describe the paradox in which the lover finds himself can also be read in such a way as to alter the subject of the whole *canción* from a general observation on love to a specific observation on the capriciousness of the male member. The choice of 'forçado' as the adverb to describe the way in which love and beauty make a person fall in love implies not only an involuntary, irrational element, but also a physical, sexual one. This physical subtext continues in the next two lines, where 'durar' of course has a temporal sense — but used here in conjunction with 'firmeza', it is difficult to ignore echoes of the adjective 'duro': 'hard'. In this context, then, the sense of 'firmeza' is subverted: it suggests not only the lover's constant loyalty, but a consequence of it, namely an erection. Read in this way, Tapia's advice that 'cuidado' should not outlast 'firmeza' is not simply a continuation of the paradox of love as a constant inconstant. Instead, he is offering the practical tip that the man should not let his passionate thoughts last longer than his erection. Reading the first four lines of the second stanza in this way also alters completely the way in which the other lines of the *canción* are understood. The opening reference to 'mal de

---

[8] Compare, for example, Jorge Manrique's poem 'diziendo qué cosa es amor', in Manrique 1993: no. 3.

amor' becomes specifically physical rather than abstract; the 'mudança' which Tapia says is characteristic of this 'mal' becomes a reference to the problem of impotence.

Luis de Bivero, on the other hand, suffers from what appears to be a bout of personal melancholy in the following *canción*:

Temor, Dolor se combaten,
Seso con Amor guerrea,
Coraçón, Fuerças, debaten:
ninguno vence pelea.

Temor pierde la victoria,
Dolor huye de la llaga,
el Seso niega la gloria,
el Amor falta a la paga,
La Razón manda se maten.
Por lo que el uno dessea,
Coraçón, Fuerças, debaten:
ninguno vence pelea.
(González Cuenca 2004: II, no. 269)

The poem addresses the poet's internal struggle to achieve orgasm. His endeavour ends in failure because his mind ('seso') blocks 'la gloria' which is orgasm. The crucial role played by the imagination in man's ability to act was outlined by Galen and later by Gordonio, who explained how this higher faculty warmed the lower organs (including, of course, the penis) into action (Gordonio 1991: 303). Thus any mental uncertainty would lead to impotence because it would paralyse movement in the limbs. Bivero's hesitant condition, his 'temor', may be equated with Gordonio's definition of 'tremor', which equally includes the metaphor of internal conflict:

Tremor es menguamiento de la virtud motiva [...] o el tremor es batalla de la virtud voluntaria que mueve a las partes de arriba e de la enfermedad moviente a las partes de baxo [...] La causa d'esto es todo aquello que enflaquesce la virtud [...] como imaginaciones temerosas. (1991: 126)

Bivero's brother Alonso Pérez, second Viscount of Altamira, also considered the topic of impotence in an exchange with Garci Sánchez de Badajoz, but their perspective is a broader, and unusual, one:

Otra del vizconde de Altamira	Respuesta de Garci Sánchez de Badajoz
Pues este mundo traviesso	Son tales la llave y huesso
es terrero do tiramos	de esta ballesta que armamos
y el blanco el bien que esperamos,	que quando al blanco apuntamos
¿por qué echamos tan aviesso,	hazen el dexo tan tiesso
pues tanto precio jugamos?	que por desarmar erramos.
Gran aparejo tenemos	Y esto haze que no havemos
para que el precio ganemos	plazer dando do acertemos,
de la gloria prometida,	mas ser cosa dessabrida,
pues la ballesta es la vida,	y el errar que nos combida
tiros, obras que hazemos,	inclinación en que fuemos
do ganamos o perdemos.	nascidos para que erremos.
(González Cuenca 2004: II, no. 698.1)	(González Cuenca 2004: II, no. 698.2)

These two poems are included in Castillo's *Cancionero* as part of a section entitled 'Aqui comiençan todas las preguntas de este cancionero'. As Keith Whinnom observed, the poems grouped here are intended to 'despistar a los lectores y sugerirles una lectura obscena cuando la que ofrece el malicioso autor es aparentemente inocente' (1981: 67). While this is certainly true in the case of this particular exchange, the Viscount's poem is not really a riddling question which demands that Garci Sánchez de Badajoz identify a particular object in his response, as Whinnom suggests. Instead, the exchange is, ostensibly, about man's faltering attempts to gain a place in heaven, to which Sánchez de Badajoz concludes that to err is innate to mankind. However, these moralizing sentiments are belied by the conceit of the crossbow which is used to express them. The crossbow firing arrows from a worldly firing range at a target in order to win heavenly glory has clearly phallic overtones, emphasized by Altamira's concern that the arrows from the crossbow sometimes miss their target, despite great preparation. This can be interpreted as a gloomy observation that sex is not always orgasmic. Garci Sánchez de Badajoz's reply, meanwhile, develops the image of the crossbow in an emphatically phallic way by beginning with a reference to the trigger, or 'llave', and the 'huesso', or nut, the catch on which the spanned bow-string is caught behind the arrow until released by the trigger (Martínez de Espinar 1644: fol. 13r; Payne-Gallwey 1903: 97-98).[9] Keys are a common image in the language of erotic euphemism, and are usually inserted into equally suggestive locks (Vasvári 1999). This 'llave', however, does

---

[9] A slightly abbreviated English translation of Martínez de Espinar's technical account of the construction of the crossbow (1644: fol. 13r) is found in Payne-Gallwey 1903: 149-52.

not unlock doors (or women). Instead, according to Sánchez de
Badajoz, it is a trigger which, along with the nut that it comes into
contact with when the crossbow is fired, consistently shoots off
badly-aimed arrows because it makes the bow over-taut.[10] The
metaphorical outcome is that 'no avemos / plazer dando do acer-
temos', and the over-stiffness of the euphemistic crossbow can be
read as the all-too-human error of premature ejaculation. The
crossbow, moreover, is an appropriate weapon to be associated
with this particular range of sexual imagery. In one popular four-
teenth- and fifteenth-century method of spanning the bow the
crossbowman placed his foot in a stirrup to hold the tiller down
and used the strength of his upper body to pull back the string using a belt at his waist (Alm 1994: 40-41). The archers in the
foreground of the Pollaiuolo brothers' 1490s painting of *The Martyrdom of St Sebastian* (in the National Gallery, London), span their
bows in just this way. Alfonso Bivero and Garci Sánchez de Badajoz are imaginative in their choice of metaphor. The verb 'tirar' is
found as a metaphor for ejaculation in Pero d'Ambroa's scurrilous
thirteenth-century *cantiga* about a shooting competition between
the courtesan Maria Balteira and a group of crossbowmen (Lopes
2002: no. 327; cf. Julian Weiss's comments, p. 252, n.9 below), but in
general crossbow imagery seldom appears in *cancionero* poetry.
When it does, its erotic significance is only occasionally exploited, as
for example in this sixteenth-century refrain to a *villancico rústico*
which is based on the sexual undertones of the hunt:

Ándome en la villa,
fiestas principales,
con mi ballestilla
de matar pardales.
(Alzieu, Lissorgues, & Jammes 1984: no. 48)

By contrast, in one of only two other references to crossbows in
the list of key words in proverbial phrases in Dutton's monumental edition of *cancionero* poetry (1990–91, VII: 597–609), the Count of

---

[10] 'Dexo', defined as 'fin de cada cosa' (Nebrija 1516), must mean bow in this context. In the operation of actual crossbows, over-tautness was a problem caused not
by the trigger and nut, but by incorrect spanning of the bow so that it pressed
against the upper surface of the tiller. The bow then came into contact with the nut at
a lower angle when released by the trigger, and as a consequence the arrow was
propelled by an unequal force so that 'no va derecho, sino culebrando': Martínez de
Espinar 1644: fol. 16r; Payne-Gallwey 1903: 150–151. I am grateful to Angus Patter-
son, of the Victoria and Albert Museum, for showing me examples of sixteenth-
century crossbows.

Oliva uses the sexual innuendo of the hunting image to very different effect. In his poem describing a dream of an encounter with a hermit, the mood is one of suppressed eroticism, as the hermit instructs the love-sick author to inure himself to sexual temptation. The obvious implication of the (loaded) crossbow in the proverbial advice offered by the hermit is that it be fired to test the weapon's mettle, but in fact the context of the poem twists this reading to mean the opposite:

> Y pues tu suerte dichosa
> te hizo nascer catiuo
> no hagas cosa viciosa
> sufre muerte tan honrrosa
> muriendo quedas biuo
> No busques en tus afanes
> que la fin sea muy presta
> que mejor es que no sanes
> 'quel pasar los gauilanes
> se prueua bien la ballesta'.
> (Dutton 1990-91: v, 453)

The other reference to a 'ballesta' is also found in the context of a proverb, and it has a moralizing rather than a sexual meaning. Gómez Pérez Patiño dedicated a 'muy sotil & escuro' *dezir* to Leonor López de Córdoba on her departure from Queen Catherine's service. Among the adages he used to structure his composition was one involving a crossbow, a reference included to demonstrate the maxim that words are harmless weapons: 'dela ballesta El sueno / espanta pero es palo' (Dutton 1990-91: III, 243).[11]

This essay has argued that the treatment of sexual relations in *cancionero* poetry extends to meditations on impotence and its causes. The topic is frequently presented allusively, enabling the author to play with expectations about the sense of words. While it is unsurprising that this double-entendre often appears in love poetry, I should like to conclude by suggesting that this theme can be profitably explored in works that are ostensibly religious and which have so far been interpreted as such. Take, for example, the short poem by Juan de Tapia:

---

[11] Neither of these proverbs appears in Santillana's near-contemporary collection, although his anthology does include three that refer to a 'ballestero'. See López de Mendoza 1995: *sub letra*.

Fortuna sobre la tierra
me ha girada la faz,
mal me fallo con la guerra,
mucho peor con la paz.

El evangelio de sant Johán
non lo entiendo, en verdat,
el Apocalipsi con afán,
mucho más la Trinitat.
Pues que Amor me destierra
bolviéndome la su faz,
mal me fallo con la guerra,
mucho peor con la paz.
(Tapia 2004: no. xv)

The modern editor of this text, Luigi Giuliani, draws attention to
'la desorientación y sufrimiento del poeta' in the work, noting also
that the refrain contains an echo of a sonnet in Petrarch's *Canzoniere* (Tapia 2004: 88). Yet I suggest that the poem allows us to
explore the reasons for Tapia's 'desorientación y sufrimiento', and
that this, as it turns out, has a definite physiological origin. The
clue to this reading lies in the references to the gospel and the Trinity. The choice of St John's gospel is made not just because its
exegetical challenges prompt Tapia's perplexity but more importantly, I think, because John is the poet's namesake. When he has
thus written himself quite definitely into the poem, the other two
religious references equally invite an interpretation personal to the
author. The dire resonance of the Apocalypse is perhaps obvious
enough, but the mention of the Trinity plays on a tradition of literary double-entendre. The symbolism of the number three as a
reference to male genitalia is found in the twelfth-century Latin
comedy *Babio* where the protagonist is castrated (Bate 1976: 59),
and the sense was still current in fifteenth-century Castilian *cancionero* poetry. In one of a series of scurrilous verses aimed at a
man identified as the 'Almirante', the poet Soria takes as his subject the Admiral's 'baxa trinidad', a clear reference to his
genitalia.[12] Juan de Tapia, then, experiences difficulty not just in

---

[12] '*Soria al Almirante que le imbio una rrana y un sapo y un mochuelo*: / Otra trinidad
hallamos / aca baxo en este suelo / de rrana sapo y mochuelo / y esta en uos la
contemplamos / ay otra dificultad / sin rremedio / que en la baxa trinidad / no
sois uno sino medio' (Dutton 1990-91: II, 452). Soria questions the masculinity of
the Almirante's 'baxa trinidad' by his reference to toads and frogs (creatures contemporaries associated with the vagina because they dwell in wet, cold
environments) and the term 'medio' (used here in the double sense of 'moderation'
and 'vagina').

understanding the mysteries of the Trinity. He is also unable to comprehend his difficulty in achieving an erection. This reading brings the meaning of his refrain more sharply into focus. Drawing on the standard sexual undercurrents present in words associated with war and peace, Tapia laments his inability to perform during intercourse ('la guerra') and his subsequent anguish: 'Mal me fallo con la guerra, / mucho peor con la paz'. Moreover, if this refrain is indeed intended as an echo of Petrarch's 'Pace non trovo, et non ò, da far guerra', then it is an ironic reworking.[13] The original is a line in a sonnet characterized by the poet's expression of the conflicting emotions which his desire for Laura has aroused in him. Tapia, on the other hand, is perplexed only by himself.

Impotence might seem a surprising theme for the lotharios of the *cancioneros*. However, as I have tried to show, it was simply another topic which enabled poets to display their ingenuity to subtle or satirical effect (there is no reason to presume that literature necessarily reflected life). The wit of *cancionero* poets is often neutered by literal readings, despite the fact that their texts are pregnant with different levels of meaning. This essay has tried to suggest one approach, but it seems to me that there are many more related to love and sexuality still to be uncovered.

188   KIRSTIN KENNEDY

WORKS CITED

ALM, Josef, 1994. *European Crossbows: A Survey*. Tr. H. Bartlett Wells, ed. G. M. Wilson, Royal Armouries Monograph, 3 (Dorchester: Henry Ling).

ALZIEU, Pierre, Yvan LISSORGUES, & Robert JAMMES, ed., 1984. *Poesía erótica del Siglo de Oro: Floresta de poesías eróticas del Siglo de Oro con su vocabulario al cabo por el orden del a.b.c.*, 2nd edn (Barcelona: Crítica).

BATE, Keith, ed., 1976. *Three Latin Comedies*, Toronto Medieval Latin Texts, 6 (Toronto: Pontifical Institute of Medieval Studies).

BLACKMORE, Josiah, 1999. 'The Poets of Sodom', in *Queer Iberia: Sexualities, Cultures, and Crossings from the Middle Ages to the Renaissance*, ed. Josiah Blackmore & Gregory S. Hutcheson (Durham, NC: Duke UP, 1999), pp. 195-221.

Carajicomedia 1995. *Carajicomedia: texto impreso*, ed. Álvaro Alonso (Madrid: Aljibe).

DEYERMOND, Alan, 1978. 'The Worm and the Partridge: Reflections on the Poetry of Florencia Pinar', *Mester* (Los Angeles), 7: 3-8.

DURLING, Robert M., ed. & tr., 1976. *Petrarch's Lyric Poems: The 'Rime sparse' and Other Lyrics* (Cambridge MA: Harvard University Press).

DUTTON, Brian, & Jineen KROGSTAD, ed., 1990-91. *El cancionero del siglo XV, c. 1360-1520*. Biblioteca Española del Siglo XV, Serie Maior, 1-7 (Salamanca: Universidad).

GIULIANI, Luigi, 1991. 'Tapia y Juan de Tapia: un caso de homonimia en los cancioneros', *Anuario Brasileño de Estudios Hispánicos*, 1: 49-62.

GONZÁLEZ CUENCA, Joaquín, ed., 2004. Hernando del Castillo, *Cancionero general*, Nueva Biblioteca de Erudición y Crítica, 26, 5 vols (Madrid: Castalia).

GORDONIO, Bernardo, 1991. *Lilio de medicina: un manual básico de medicina medieval, edición crítica de la versión española, Sevilla 1495*, ed. John Cull & Brian Dutton, Medieval Spanish Medical Texts Series, 31 (Madison: HSMS).

KENNEDY, Kirstin, 2002. 'Inventing the Wheel: Diego López de Haro and his *Invenciones*', *BHS* (Liverpool), 79: 159-74.

LEMOS, M., 1920. 'A medicina no *Cancioneiro de Garcia de Resende*', *Arquivos de História de Medicina Portuguesa*, ns. 11.3: 93-96, 4: 113-28, 5: 145-53, 6: 161-76.

LOPES, Graça Videira, 1994. *A Sátira nos Cancioneiros Medievais Galego-Portugueses*, Imprensa Universitária, 102 (Lisboa: Editorial Estampa).

——, 2002. *Cantigas de Escárnio e Maldizer dos Trovadores e Jograis Galego-Portugueses* (Lisboa: Editorial Estampa).

LÓPEZ DE MENDOZA, Íñigo, Marqués de Santillana, 1995. *Refranes que dizen las viejas tras el fuego*, ed. Hugo Óscar Bizzarri, Teatro del Siglo de Oro: Ediciones Críticas, 56 (Kassel: Reichenberger).

MACPHERSON, Ian, 1985. 'Secret Language in the *Cancioneros*: Some Courtly Codes', *BHS*, 62: 51-63.

——, 1998. *The 'Invenciones y letras' of the 'Cancionero general'*, PMHRS, 9.

——, & Angus MACKAY, 1993. '"Manteniendo la tela": el erotismo del vocabulario caballeresco-textil en la época de los Reyes Católicos', in *Actas del Primer Congreso Anglo-Hispano*, I: *Lingüística*, ed. Ralph Penny (Madrid: Castalia), pp. 25-36.

MANRIQUE, Jorge, 1993. *Poesía*, ed. Vicente Beltrán, Biblioteca Clásica, 15 (Barcelona: Crítica).

MARTÍNEZ DE ESPINAR, Alonso, 1644. *Arte de ballestería y montería* (Madrid: Imprenta Real).

MORENO, Manuel, 2001. 'El dulce placer de significar agudamente lo que se quiere decir', *BHS* (Liverpool), 78: 465-87.

NEBRIJA, Antonio de, 1516. *Vocabulario de Romance en latin [...] nueuamente corregido* (Salamanca: Juan Varela).

PALENCIA, Alfonso de, 1490. *Uniuersal vocabulario en latin y en Romance*, 2 vols (Sevilla: Paulo de Colonia).

PAYNE-GALLWEY, Ralph, 1903. *The Book of the Crossbow* (London: Longmans, Green). Reprint, with *Appendix to the Book of the Crossbow and Ancient Projectile Engines* (1907) (New York: Dover Books, 1995).

PETRARCA, Francesco, 2000. *The Canzoniere (Rerum vulgarium fragmenta)*, tr. Frederic J. Jones, I (Leicester: Troubadour).

RESENDE, Garcia de, 1990-98. *Cancioneiro Geral de Garcia de Resende*, ed. Aida Fernanda Dias, 5 vols (Lisboa: Casa da Moeda).

RODADO RUIZ, Ana M., 2000. *Tristura conmigo va: fundamentos de amor cortés*, Humanidades, 49 (Cuenca: Universidad de Castilla-La Mancha).

Tacuinum 1996. *The Medieval Health Handbook: 'Tacuinum sanitatis'*, tr. Oscar Ratti & Adele Westbrook (New York: George Braziller).

TAPIA, Juan de, 2004. *Poemas*, ed. Luigi Giuliani, Textos recuperados, 23 (Salamanca: Ediciones Universidad de Salamanca),.

VASVÁRI, Louise O., 1999. *The Heterotextual Body of the 'Mora morilla'*, PMHRS, 12.

WHETNALL, Jane, 2007. 'Las transformaciones de Petrarca en cuatro poetas de cancionero: Santillana, Carvajales, Cartagena y Florencia Pinar', *Cancionero General*, 4 (2006 [2007]): 81-108.

WHINNOM, Keith, 1981. *La poesía amatoria de la época de los Reyes Católicos*, Durham Modern Languages Series: Hispanic Monographs, 2 (Durham: University).

Verba volant, scripta manent: The Metamorphosis of Oral *Lyra Minima* East and West

STEPHEN RECKERT
(Institute of Romance Studies, London)

I ought to say at the start that this is more an anthology with running commentary than a proper essay. Most of my Iberian examples of the transformation of oral into literary *lyra minima* are from Margit Frenk's *Nuevo corpus de la antigua lírica popular hispánica* (2003) and Rip Cohen's critical edition of *500 Cantigas d'Amigo* (2003).[1] Wherever practicable I reduce essentially minimalist lyrics expanded by devices such as parallelism or refrains to their primitive semantic nuclei, tacitly abbreviating parallel verses and eliminating the repetition of refrains.

My East Asian examples come from two collections, respectively the earliest documents of Chinese and Japanese poetry: the 'Classic of Songs' or *Shi Jing* (Waley 1954), with 305 texts dating from about 1000 to 600 BCE, and the monumental *Man'yōshū* or 'Collection for 10,000 Ages' (*MYS*), with some 4500 poems from the seventh and eighth centuries. Over 300 of these derive from folk songs of the far Northeast of the country, the primitive region celebrated a millennium later by the *haiku* master Bashō in the diary of his 800-mile walking tour of the 'narrow roads of the interior' (*Oku no Hosomichi*, elegantly translated by Octavio Paz and Eikichi Hayashiya (1970) as *Sendas de Oku*). These songs are transcribed in a relatively impenetrable kind of Japanese *sayagués* (impenetrable at least to me, since half the key words are missing from my trusty *Kenkyūsha* dictionary). But just as there are traditional-style *cantigas de amigo* by Kings Dinis and Alfonso the Wise, and court poets and nobles like the Admiral of Castile, Pae Gomez Charinho, or the

[1] I have standardized accents, punctuation, and word division in both these editions. As Cohen implies (2003: 31), the classification of the cantigas d'amigo as originally oral is justified by the fact that however much the feminine voice we hear in them may have been manipulated by male, literate poets, 'archaic social, linguistic and musical features [...] suggest that it is genuine in its origins'.

From the 'Cancioneiro da Vaticana' to the 'Cancionero general': Studies in Honour of Jane Whetnall, ed. Alan Deyermond & Barry Taylor, PMHRS, 60 (London: Department of Hispanic Studies, Queen Mary, University of London, 2007), pp. 191-200. ISSN 1460–051X. ISBN 0 902238 50 7.

Count of Barcelos, the *Man'yōshū* contains, along with the North-eastern quatrains and other anonymous ones, popular-style verses by poets of the nobility and even princes and emperors. A distinctive feature (apparently belying the image of Japan as a paternalistic and *machista* society) is the number of poems by princesses, empresses, and ladies of the Court. But if the greatest period of Japanese poetry (from the ninth to the eleventh century) is the only 'Golden Age' in any literature, Eastern or Western, ever dominated by women, it is because 'serious' literature (meaning essentially prose) was written in Chinese, which, like Latin in medieval Europe, was not for the ladies. To moisten one's brush on the ink-stone and dash off the occasional *tanka* in Japanese was admissible provided one fulfilled one's proper duty to be decorative and keep the servants in order, but more than that was not quite seemly.[2] Ironically, the very survival of vernacular Japanese literature has been attributed to this male chauvinist prejudice against the education of women.

With our four anthologies, we have at our disposal an intimidating total of some 4800 East Asian and 2900 Iberian poems. About 90% of the songs in the *Man'yōshū* are five-line *tankas* of 5-7-5-7-7 syllables; for our purposes we can discount almost 500 in other forms, including 260 so-called 'long poems' or *chōkas*, roughly comparable in form and function to Iberian *romances*.[3] The Iberian corpus, for its part, contains many courtly *cantigas* that as well as not being minimalist have nothing traditional about them, so we are left with a slightly less alarming aggregate. For the *Man'yōshū* I use the Nippon Gakujutsu Shinkōkai edition, and for the Chinese text of the *Shi Jing* that of the eminent Victorian James Legge. My own version owes much to Arthur Waley's fine translation and little to Legge's mock-Tudor rhymes.

The basic cast of characters in the Eastern and Western traditions is the same: an *amiga*, her *amigo*, and her mother. In the West there are also her own not always trustworthy *amigas*; and a rival may lurk in the wings. The usual backdrop for the protagonists' love

---

[2] Anne Birrell (1998: 58–59) notes that even before Confucius education in China was primarily restricted to upper-class males, with literature more or less their exclusive preserve, and in the Táng dynasty (7th–10th centuries) the life of women poets combined the world of the courtesan with that of the literary elite; or in the words of Dachs & Suárez (2004: 14), 'debemos a monjas, aristócratas y cortesanas los relativamente pocos poemas de autora conservados'.

[3] The longest *chōka* in the *Man'yōshū* has fewer than 150 lines.

spring, riverbank, lakeside, or seashore, or by the wandering moon; in the West the scene may also be a sanctuary or the *amiga*'s own home. Secondary characters in the form of symbolic representatives of Nature often intervene: the mysterious phallic stags in Pero Moogo's seven poems; the timeless and immortal cicada; or birds of omen like those that sang of love in Nuno Fernandez Torneol's best-known *cantiga* (Cohen 2003: 126) until the faithless *amigo* dried up the springs wherein they drank, or those in Fernand' Esquio's 'Vaiamos, irmana, vaiamos dormir / nas ribas do lago' (2003: 530), which the *amigo*, bow already in hand, spares because of their sweet singing. Or like those in this anonymous *tanka*:

I'll think of you, my love,
on evenings when the grey mist
floats above the rushes,
and the voice of the wild ducks sounds chill. (*MYS* 860)

The greatest and most prolific of the *Man'yōshū* poets, Kakinomoto no Hitomaro, uses the same motif to evoke the familiar theme of the lover's insomnia in what we may call a *tanka de amor*:

Sleepless with longing, I see the daybreak.
Ah, those wild ducks flying past:
could they be her messengers? (*MYS* 16)[4]

These two *tankas* help to shed light on the symbolism of the mysterious and immensely popular seventeenth-century *copla* of the two (or sometimes three) wild ducks that cause a *niña* such pain:

Dos ánades, madre,
que van por aquí
mal penan a mi. [...]
Al campo de flores
yvan a dormir.
Mal penan a mi. (Frenk 2003: 182B)

When it is the *amigo* who is in pain, his beloved may take his threats of imminent *Liebestod* for mere rhetoric, as in a *cantiga de escarnio* by Garcia de Guilhade in which she says she does not believe his story, but he is welcome to go ahead and die 'se lhi prouguer, / e a mi praz de coraçon / por veer se moire, se non' (Reckert & Macedo 1996: 90–91), Hitomaro complains wryly of the same treatment

---

[4] The great Welsh poet Dafydd ap Gwilym, a contemporary of King Dinis and Chaucer, similarly invokes the thrush (y ceiliog), the seagull (yr wylan), and the lark ascending (yr ehedydd) as lovers' messengers: Bromwich 1985: 72–79.

in another *tanka de amor*:

> As if to say 'feel free to die,
> if it's because of me',
> that pert miss strolls,
> provocative, past my gate. (*MYS* 160)

But the *trovador* Roi Queimado takes revenge on another pert miss, flouting the courtly taboo against the naming of names to warn her that once she realizes just what she has done, her present triumphalism will give way to rueful awareness of her guilt: 'Pois que eu ora morto for, / sei bem ca dira mia senhor: / "Eu som Guiomar Afonso!"; but 'Pois souber mui bem ca morri / por ela [...], filhara / enton o seu queixo, e dira: / "Eu som Guiomar Afonso..."' (Reckert & Macedo 1996: 92). A resourceful Japanese suitor, anticipating the Provençal cliché of *amor de lonh* by half a millennium, gets a dusty answer when he too threatens to die of love, but for a woman he has never seen, and his Jaufre Rudel gambit miscarries:

> You'll have to get a better story:
> who on earth, since the beginning of time,
> has ever heard of anyone who died
> for someone he's never laid eyes on? (*MYS* 937)

The Galician Airas Carpancho imagines another possible dénouement, with the *amiga*'s remorse for her disdain provoking a role reversal: now it is she who is dying of love:

> Madre velida, meu amigo vi:
> non lhi falei e con el me perdi,
> non lhi falei, ca o tiv' en desden,
> e moiro agora, querendo-lhi ben! [...] (Cohen 2003: 143)

Here again is Hitomaro, with a special dilemma that can present itself to a polytheist suitor:

> What might be the name of the god
> I must invoke with offerings
> if I am ever to see my love,
> even though only
> in my dreams? (*MYS* 161)

For Galician *amigas*, the name problem does not arise: the whole *santoral* is on call (and much of it is called on). One such, in a *cantiga* by Pae Gomez Charinho (Cohen 2003: 303), invokes an obvious local favourite: 'Ai, Santiago, padron sabido, / vos mh'adugades o meu amigo'; but other useful allies are not far to seek. Pero Viviaez depicts the confidence of an ingenious *amiga* who devises a scheme to attract suitors: as our mothers are going to San Simon de Val de Prados to light votive candles, she says, we *meninhas* can go along too, 'e nossos amigos todos la iran' to see us dance in our light summer dresses (223). In one of the Orense *xograr* Johan Servando's eighteen songs referring to his namesake's shrine, though, a less fortunate *meninha's* attempt to emulate this stratagem fails to work: 'Fui eu a San Servando por veer meu amigo, / e non o vi na ermida nen falou el comigo, / namorada!' (379); and even the best candles are not always effective: a disenchanted supplicant in a *cantiga* by Nuno Treez declares that as San Clemenço do Mar has ignored her pleas to bring back her *amigo*, he will get no more *candeas de Paris* from her: cheap tallow ones will do nicely (*CDA* 435).

The Iberian *pastorela*, as essentially a variant of the *cantiga de amor*, depicts a prettified rustic damsel in an idyllic setting, courted by a chivalrous aspirant to the status of *amigo*; and the class difference is conveniently elided. In contrast this poignant anonymous *tanka*, by inverting the protagonists' roles, actually stresses the difference, implicitly recognizing the impossibility of a happy ending:

My hands, so chapped
from husking rice:
again tonight he'll hold them,
sighing —
my young lord. (MYS 850)

Translation can hardly capture the effect of the adroit placing, in the original, of the key words 'lord' and 'sighing' (*tono* and *nagekan*) respectively at the beginning of the next-to-last line and as the last word of the poem.

Four of Martin Codax's seven *cantigas*, all set on the banks of the ría of Vigo, treat the ubiquitous motif of impatient waiting for a rendezvous by the water: 'Ai ondas que eu vin veer, / se me saberedes dizer / porque tarda meu amigo / sen min?' (Cohen 2003: 519). This *tanka* deals with the same predicament, in a similar scenario but with the characteristic Galician melancholy replaced by the annoyance of a spirited Japanese *amiga*:

Where willows overhang the winding stream,
I wait and wait for you,
drawing no water,
only pacing to and fro
stamping my foot with impatience. (*MYS* 856)

In an unconventional variation on this theme, a laid-back ancient Chinese *macho* coolly deflates its romantic *angst*. The spring evoked here, Arthur Waley points out, is being recommended not, as usually assumed, just for its salubrious water: such places are also handy for casual pick-ups:

> Down by the town gate
> it's easy to loiter.
> Down where the spring flows by,
> it's not hard to get what you're looking for. (Waley 1954: 13)

If Love and Death, Time and Nature, are the primary colours on the palette of all poetry, Love and Nature may be the brightest, but it is Time that takes precedence over all the others, ageing and finally destroying the lovers, bringing leaves to the trees in spring only to strip them again in autumn, making the moon wax and wane and the tides ebb and flow. A universal archetype of timelessness, conforming, in its ignorance of its own death, to Schopenhauer's criterion for immortality, is the cicada.[5] A *haiku* by Bashō, beautifully translated by the apostle of Brazilian Modernism, Manuel Bandeira (1958: 442), makes the point:

> A cigarra... ouvi:
> nada revela em seu canto
> que ela vai morrer.

For Bandeira (1958: 211–12), hearing cicadas that are the same yet not the same as those he heard as a boy, their very timelessness serves to remind him that man is a hostage to Time: 'ó cigarras que zinis, / não sois as mesmas que eu ouvi menino [...]. / Dêem-me as cigarras que eu ouvi menino.'

In medieval Japan the same symbolic connotation is implicit in this *tanka de amigo*:

> Cicadas chirp
> at my bedside,
> but I am sick at heart.
> Sleepless, I stay up,
> with you always on my mind.   (MYS 929)

Another *tanka*, in a variation on the theme of sleepless waiting, adds the moon:

> While with my sleeve

---

[5] I discuss cicada symbolism at greater length in Reckert 1978: 31–43.

I smooth my bed
and sit up
waiting for you
the moon has set.⁶   (*MYS* 950)

Here the absent moon is a symbolic proxy for the lover, as in a sixteenth-century *villancico* where it stands not for the *amigo* but for his *amada*:

¡Ay, luna que reluzes,
toda la noche me alumbres! [...];
Amada que reluzes,
toda la noche me alumbres.   (Frenk 2003: 1072)

It is again the *amada* who speaks in this poem from the *Shi Jing*, and this time her waiting has been rewarded: the imperative of the *villancico* is replaced by a triumphant present indicative:

Eastward the moon is high.
That lovely man
is in my bower.
He is in my bower:
his foot is on my threshold.⁷   (Waley 1954: 4)

Bed is of course the obvious place to wait for a lover, but a peculiarity of early East Asian poetry is the fastidious discretion with which it shuns explicit sensuality. There are no *teticas agudicas que el brial quieren romper*, or pleas of *no me los amuestres más, que me matarás*; and if a *casada* has *pechos hermosos* the poet will not say so, because she will be his own wife. Married love is indeed a norm, and the fizzing hormones of youth and the subterfuges of adulterous courtly lovers alike are absent. The only overt object of eroticism, amounting almost to a fetish, is woman's hair, which has to do duty for all the physical attributes that go unmentioned.⁸

Trichinophilia is hardly less familiar to the Iberian tradition.⁹ 'Cabelos,

---

⁶ I have translated *orishi* (literally 'I kneel'), as 'I sit', because the usual way of 'sitting' in much of East Asia is kneeling, which therefore does not necessarily imply any religious or reverential significance, and in terms of a Sino-Japanese gestural semiotics would constitute a *degré zéro* or 'unmarked' form.

⁷ James Legge (1967:108), perhaps thinking of Wyatt's mistresses who sometime did him seek, stalking with naked foot in his chamber, misses the point and translates *zu* ('a gentleman; complimentary designation of men sometimes used of women' according to Matthews 1981) as 'that lovely girl'.

⁸ Edwin A. Cranston (1975: 78) remarks that ladies of the Heian court (8th–12th centuries) 'were proud of wearing their hair to the floor' (surely a more aesthetic as well as less inconvenient fashion than the Chinese custom of foot-binding).

⁹ For this motif see my commentary on Joan Zorro in Reckert & Macedo 1996: 181; Sleeman 1981.

los meus cabelos', an ingenuous girl tells her mother in a *cantiga* by
Johan Zorro: 'el rei m'enviou por elos: /   madre, que lhis farei?';
and the mother, aware that the king's demand is a synecdoche, can
only answer resignedly, 'Filha, dade os a el rei' (Cohen 2003: 390).
The washing of hair is a special topos: in one of Pero Moogo's stag
poems (422) an *amiga* has seen the *cervos bravos*, 'e con sabor delos
/ lavei meus cabelos [...]. Des que los lavei [...], d'ouro los liei, / e
vos asperei, / meu amigo'; and another, in a *cantiga* by Johan
Soarez Coelho (174) proudly tells her mother that after washing
her hair at the spring, 'alo achei, madr', o senhor deles / e de mi'.
The mood is quite different in the implicit praise of a young nun's
beauty, with an equally implicit lament for its wilful misuse, in
this anonymous quatrain:

> ¡Cómo lo tuerce y lava,
> la monjita el su cabello!
> ¡Come lo tuerce y lava!
>   y luego lo tiende al hielo.   (Frenk 2003: 18)

For Japanese love poetry, however, it is uncombed hair (*midare-
gani*) that is a specific topos, as in a celebrated 'tangled-hair' *tanka* by
the passionate Heian court poet Izumi Shikibu (fl. c. 970–1030):

> I fling myself down
> careless of the tangles
> of my raven hair,
> longing again for him
> who stroked it smooth.[10]

Yet another Japanese variation on the theme of waiting for a lovers' rendezvous evokes the ominous drumbeat that is a reminder
of the passing of Time:

> The watchman's drum
> tells me it's time
> for us to meet:
> how strange

Sleeman 1981.

[10] For Cranston (1975: 78–79), 'the most striking objective analogue of the internal
turmoil of love is the image of tangled hair', which 'often implies the abandon of a
night of love'. On the celebrated (not to say notorious) Lady Izumi — like Murasaki Shikibu, author of the greatest Japanese novel, *The Tale of Genji*, a member of
the Empress Akiko's salon — see Carter 1991: 119–24. 'Shikibu' was a sobriquet
rather than a personal name, it being socially not done to record the names of well-
born ladies (cf. Murasaki 1976, I: vii–viii).

And this pair of anonymous Castilian quatrains (Frenk 2003: 568BC) joins the same motif of the lovers' failed meeting with that of the unfaithful *amigo*:

Tañen a la queda;	A la queda han tocado,
y mi bien no viene:	mi amor no viene:
otros nuevos amores	algo tiene en el campo
me lo detienen.	que lo detiene.

Here for the last time is Hitomaro, confronted as before with the problem of access to his love:

With her loving mother
keeping her cooped up at home
like a butterfly in the cocoon,
how shall I ever manage
to find a way to see her? (*MYS* 168)

The solution, as a defiant *menina* warns her mother in a *cantiga* by King Dinis, is up to the butterfly herself:

Que coita ouvestes, madr' e senhor,
de me guardar que non possa veer
meu amig' e meu ben e meu prazer,
mais se eu posso, par Nostro Senhor [...],
guisar-lho ei, e pes a quen pesar. [...]   (Cohen 2003: 618)

I end with an anonymous *tanka* (anonymous only in the sense that I have never known who wrote it). It was sung sixty-four years ago by an *amiga*, who was no Madame Butterfly in her cocoon but a young Japanese language assistant at Yale, as I was no Lieutenant Pinkerton, only a sergeant technician. Two winters before, her picture had been on Tourist Board posters all over Japan, skiing on the slopes of her native island of Hokkaidō. In this very different New England winter she taught me more about Japanese on long walks in the snow and at parties in friends' flats (or parties *à deux* in her own) than in class. In the spring I was called to active service, but throughout the summer we met whenever I had a weekend pass, and then again in September for one last time.[11] This is the *tanka* she sang the night before I embarked for this blacked-out and beleaguered island to be a Japanese translator, seconded to the RAF, at Bletchley Park:

Matedo, kurasedo	Waiting, enduring:
konu hito no	loneliness

[11] I have written about Eiko before, under the patronym Frederick Carlson, in a 'palm-of- the-hand story' (the *fabula minima* genre invented by the Nobel laureate Yasunari Kawabata): Reckert 1994.

yoi-machi gusa no[12]　　　　　　of a flower that waits in the night
yaru senasá.　　　　　　　　　for one who never comes.
Ko yoi wa, tsuki mo,　　　　　Tonight, it seems
de nu sō na.　　　　　　　　not even the moon will come.

WORKS CITED

BANDEIRA, Manuel, 1958. *Poesia e Prosa,* I: *Poesia* (Rio de Janeiro: Aguilar).

BASHŌ, Matsuo, 1970. *Sendas de Oku [Oku no Hosomichi]*, tr. Octavio Paz & Eikichi Hayashiya (Barcelona: Barral).

BIRRELL, Anne, 1998. 'Canonicity, Micropoetics, and Otherness in the Eighteenth-Century Anthology of Medieval Chinese Poetry, *Three Hundred Poems of the T'ang'*, in *One Man's Canon: Five Essays on Medieval Poetry for Stephen Reckert*, ed. Alan Deyermond, PMHRS, 16, pp. 51–68.

BROMWICH, Rachel, ed. & tr., 1985. Dafydd ap Gwilym, *A Selection of Poems* (Harmondsworth: Penguin).

CARTER, Steven D., ed. & tr., 1991. *Traditional Japanese Poetry* (Stanford: UP).

COHEN, Rip, ed., 2003. *500 Cantigas d'Amigo*, Obras Clássicas da Literatura Portuguesa: Literatura Medieval, 1 (Porto: Campo das Letras).

CRANSTON, Edwin A., 1975. 'The Dark Path: Images of Longing in Japanese Love Poetry', *Harvard Journal of Asiatic Studies*, 35: 60–100.

DACHS, Ramon, & Anne-Hélène SUÁREZ, 2004. *De la China a al-Andalus* (Barcelona: Azul).

FRENK, Margit, ed., 2003. *Nuevo corpus de la antigua lírica popular hispánica (siglos XV a XVII)* (México: Univ. Nacional Autónoma de México, Colegio de México, & Fondo de Cultura Económica).

LEGGE, James, ed. & tr., 1967. *The Book of Poetry [= Shi Jing]: Chinese Text with English Translation* (New York: Paragon).

MATTHEWS, R. H., 1931. *A Chinese-English Dictionary* (Shanghai: China Inland Mission Press).

MURASAKI Shikibu, 1976. *The Tale of Genji*, tr. Edward G. Seidensticker (London: Secker & Warburg).

MYS 1965. *The Man'yōshū: The Nippon Gakujutsu Shinkōkai Translation of 'One Thousand Poems'*, with the Texts in Romaji, ed. W. T. De Bary, introd. Donald Keene (New York: Columbia UP).

RECKERT, Stephen, 1978. 'O Cisne e a Cigarra', in Stephen Reckert & Y. K. Centeno, *Fernando Pessoa: Tempo • Solidão • Hermetismo* (Lisboa: Moraes), pp. 17–43.

—— (as Frederick Carlson), 1994. *Três Contos da Palma da Mão: 1. Nem a Lua Saiu,* suppl. to *Colóquio/Letras,* 132-33.

——, & Helder MACEDO, 1996. *Do Cancioneiro de Amigo*, Documenta Poética, 3, 3rd ed. (Lisboa: Assírio & Alvim).

SLEEMAN, Margaret, 1981. 'Medieval Hair Tokens', *Forum for Modern Language Studies*, 17: 322–36.

WALEY, Arthur, tr., 1954. *The Book of Songs [= Shi Jing]*, 2nd ed. (London: George Allen & Unwin).

---

[12] *Yoi-machi gusa* (the 'night-waiting herb') is in fact the name of a species of night-flowering plant, used here as a *kake-kotoba* or punning metaphor for the woman.

Isabel la Católica en el cine: el ciclo colombino

XELO SANMATEU

(Queen Mary)

En las siguientes páginas haré un recorrido cronológico por las apariciones de Isabel la Católica en el cine en general y me detendré después en un ciclo en particular, el de las películas de temática colombina — y excepcionalmente haré alguna breve referencia a sus intervenciones para televisión.[1] Quedaría para otra ocasión el estudio de dos grupos de películas con presencia isabelina: las que recrean la obra de Tamayo y Baus, *La locura de amor*, y las que tratan aspectos de su biografía, aunque comento brevemente una de ellas: *La reina Isabel en persona*. Por lo que se refiere a las de tema colombino, a los títulos que ahora comento habría que añadir en el futuro los de aquellas películas que me ha sido imposible visionar hasta el día de hoy; en cualquier caso, en la filmografía que incluyo al final pueden verse los detalles de éstas, así como de las que trato con alguna extensión a lo largo del ensayo.

Un repaso rápido a la filmografía pronto deja ver que la reina Isabel aparece prácticamente siempre en papeles secundarios, y que en ellos ha sido interpretada por actrices muy diferentes. Esta diferencia es notoria en la muy dispar apariencia física de las actrices que han dado vida al personaje y es probablemente resultado de la asunción por parte de los cineastas de que el público no posee un conocimiento previo de los rasgos fisonómicos de la reina, entre otras cosas porque no ha existido una tradición cinematográfica que ayudara a difundir su imagen. Esta ausencia de familiaridad con el personaje se debe en parte, como señala Mercedes Águeda Villar, a que España carece de una tradición de novela histórica que popularice a

---

[1] Quisiera dar las gracias a todos aquellos que han dedicado parte de su tiempo a hacerme llegar el material que he utilizado en el presente trabajo: películas, referencias bibliográficas y artículos, sin los cuales me hubiera sido imposible escribirlo.

From the 'Cancioneiro da Vaticana' to the 'Cancionero general': Studies in Honour of Jane Whetnall, ed. Alan Deyermond & Barry Taylor, PMHRS, 60 (London: Department of Hispanic Studies, Queen Mary, University of London, 2007), pp. 201-24. ISSN 1460–051X. ISBN 0 902238 50 7.

grandes personajes históricos — al estilo de las tradiciones de Francia o Gran Bretaña, de autores como Scott y Dumas — cuyos caracteres se han dado a conocer primero gracias a la obra literaria original o sus traducciones, y después gracias a las adaptaciones cinematográficas de dichas obras (2003: 38).

El hecho de que la llegada de Colón a América se produzca auspiciada precisamente por la corona de Castilla y la misma trascendencia del acontecimiento hacen que Isabel, personaje indispensable para la consecución de la empresa, siempre ocupe un lugar secundario respecto al almirante, protagonista indiscutible de la hazaña. Así, si la figura de Isabel es conocida entre el público más allá de las fronteras españolas, lo es fundamentalmente en función de la epopeya, y su aparición en la pantalla va ligada la mayoría de las veces a la recreación de dicha gesta.

En la década de los cuarenta, y a pesar del encumbramiento de su figura en el universo mítico del franquismo, la reina no tiene ningún papel de protagonista. Será en la década siguiente en una cinta dirigida por Orduña, cuando la reina tenga su intervención más notable dentro del período de la dictadura, en un film épico de temática colombina: *Alba de América*, de 1951, la contestación del régimen a la película inglesa *Christopher Columbus* de 1949.[2]

Tras más de dos décadas de ausencia, el personaje hace de nuevo acto de presencia en la pantalla en *La espada negra*, producción de 1976 de Francisco Rovira Beleta. Este film trata sobre el matrimonio

---

[2] Según Rafael de España la inseguridad del régimen ante el futuro de las fuerzas del Eje contuvo los entusiasmos patriótico-imperiales de la industria cinematográfica en los años cuarenta, además de las limitaciones presupuestarias que impedían tras la guerra derroches en producciones de alto presupuesto: 'Por paradójico que resulte, el cine histórico del franquismo descuida muchísimo la visión "heroica" del pasado nacional. Entre los grandes films históricos españoles del periodo 1942–51 es muy difícil encontrar auténticas exaltaciones de la España imperial, e incluso en ocasiones las referencias son francamente contradictorias: no hay films sobre los Reyes Católicos, pero sí sobre su escasamente presentable hija Juana la Loca (*Locura de amor*, 1948), tampoco sobre Carlos I ni Felipe II, y sin embargo se recurre a personajes más difíciles de adaptar a los lugares comunes de la retórica patriotera, por ejemplo los Comuneros en *La leona de Castilla* (1951) o el primer Borbón en *La princesa de los Ursinos* (1947), por no hablar de todos los melodramas de ambientación decimonónica ajenos a cualquier coartada patriótica' (de España: 2002). Sea como sea, es difícil ignorar los tintes de exaltación del pasado imperial en *Locura de amor*, y desde luego en producciones como *Alba de América*; no obstante, sí es cierto que las figuras imperiales se quedaron al margen de los papeles protagonistas.

de Isabel y Fernando, y las circunstancias poco comunes en las que su unión tuvo lugar.[3]

Llama la atención que hasta hoy no se haya rodado ningún *biopic* — uno de los géneros históricos por excelencia — sobre Isabel la Católica, que recoja su faceta como reina o como princesa, lo que aún sorprende más si pensamos en los numerosos avatares de su existencia (materia prima de primer orden para guionistas). Sin embargo, la reina hubiera conseguido su papel estelar a principios de los setenta si el productor norteamericano, afincado en España desde la década anterior, Samuel Bronston hubiera podido sacar adelante su proyecto *Isabel de España / Isabella of Spain*, al que la prensa llegó a dar cierta difusión.

Hasta 2000 no aparece la reina como protagonista absoluta de ninguna película. Ese año se estrenó la película *La reina Isabel en persona*, dirigida por Rafael Gordon, un monólogo en el que la reina, interpretada por Isabel Ordaz, único personaje del film, ayudada por unas pocas piezas de atrezzo y ligeros cambios de vestuario, va repasando momentos de su existencia y comentando sus aciertos y desaciertos en los asuntos de gobierno y en su vida personal. Algunos de los aspectos que trata son poco conocidos para el público en general, como su patronazgo de las artes, su creación de hospitales de campaña o la regulación de las jornadas de trabajo de los indígenas de las colonias. También repasa algunas facetas de su vida más personales, y también poco conocidas, como las desventuras de sus hijos, sus partos o la enfermedad que la llevó a la muerte. Al hilo de estos comentarios, la reina va insertando referencias a los grandes hitos de la historia de la humanidad, por ejemplo: el lanzamiento de la bomba de Hiroshima, la guerra de Vietnam, la llegada del hombre a la luna o el descubrimiento de la penicilina. La mención de acontecimientos de la Edad Contemporánea le permite crear paralelos entre situaciones presentes y pasadas, como es el caso de la expulsión de

---

[3] Mis comentarios sobre esta película se basan en las filmografías que he consultado y en los artículos que dan cuenta de ella y que aparecen en la bibliografía: Clemente de Pablos 2004: 38 y José Manuel Rodríguez García 2001–02. Por lo que se refiere a las circunstancias del matrimonio a las que se hace referencia, éstas tienen que ver con el hecho de que Isabel y Fernando contrajeron matrimonio sin esperar a la llegada de la dispensa papal (usaron una versión falsificada de la misma, a la espera de que llegara la auténtica) que les permitía contraer matrimonio, a pesar de su grado próximo de consanguinidad (tenían un bisabuelo en común, Juan I de Castilla, 1358–90). Además, Isabel carecía del permiso de su hermano Enrique IV, que poseía su tutela y que por tanto debía acceder a la celebración del matrimonio antes de que éste tuviera lugar, así como del visto bueno del Consejo Real (Fernández-Armesto 1975: 40–43).

los judíos en el año 1492 y la Ley de Extranjería, que regulaba la presencia de emigrantes en España.[4]

La película, a pesar de tratarse de un monólogo, posee cierto dinamismo gracias a la banda sonora de Eva Gancedo y a los movimientos de cámara. De cualquier forma, es posible que el espectador no familiarizado con la figura de la reina se extravíe en algún momento entre las alusiones que ésta hace a su vida y a su tiempo. Podemos asumir por el tipo de género escogido — el director declaró repetidamente que no quería hacer un film histórico: 'tenía que decidirme a contar la historia como si la Reina Isabel fuera el compendio de toda la aventura humana' (*La reina Isabel en persona*, el monólogo de una monarca': 2007) — que la película tendrá difusión entre un público muy reducido y, de hecho, su estreno fue muy limitado.[5]

Por lo que se refiere al ciclo colombino en particular, voy a comentar cuatro películas bastante dispares. Parece difícil trazar una línea que conecte todas las representaciones de la reina, más allá de las referencias comunes a los datos biográficos — legendarios o históricos — que comparten las producciones. Como es de esperar, la reina siempre ocupa un segundo plano respecto a Colón, pero en este papel secundario lo interesante es ver cómo su personalidad va cambiando: cuánto está en función del personaje de Colón y del carácter del propio actor que lo interpreta. Más allá de esto, y también por lo que se refiere a las relaciones de Isabel con otros

[4] Éste es uno de los momentos de la película en los que la reina tiene dificultades para explicar los motivos de sus actos (como parece que le ocurrió al director-guionista cuando estaba tratando este punto): 'Todos firmamos ese decreto, pero fuimos todos juntos, ¿se pretendía evitar para siempre las persecuciones que terminaban en sangre?, ¿se les expulsaba para poseer sus riquezas?, lo único que tenía claro es que la expulsión no fue por motivos racistas; el racismo es un complejo de inferioridad que ni yo ni mi pueblo padecemos [...] tres palabras que hacen que Europa y el resto del mundo estén unidos por la misma ignorancia a lo desconocido ... tres palabras que son: el eterno decreto de expulsión que yo firmé hace quinientos años, son tan sencillas, imprescindibles, tres palabras que nos hacen a todos sangre del mismo animal humano, de sus miedos: Ley de Extranjería. La tolerancia sólo es un sueño. Si no se acata la ley, se aplica la ley. Estamos donde estábamos en 1492 [...] Identificamos nuestra identidad personal con el destino de nuestra nación y de ahí nace la fatalidad, imprevisible. La civilizada Alemania del siglo XX lanza todo el fuego del infierno sobre Londres ... Si ya sé, error colectivo ... El miedo es el mismo, la injusticia mayor ... Fuimos Caín y que el señor nos libre de volver a serlo nunca más.'

[5] En 2001 se estrenó *Juana la loca*, dirigida por Vicente Aranda, en la que la reina aparece brevemente, pero presentando una imagen bastante realista (ver Águeda Villar 2003: 39).

personajes, llaman la atención las variaciones que sufre el personaje del rey. Fernando padece como nadie los avatares de los guiones, hasta el punto de quedarse sin decir ni una sola palabra en la película *1492, The Conquest of Paradise*, de Ridley Scott. En las páginas siguientes repasaré estos puntos y haré mención de algunos otros detalles propios de cada una de las producciones.

A finales de los 40 y principios de los 50 se dan dos producciones en las cuales el papel de la reina tiene cierta importancia. Se trata de la película inglesa *Christopher Columbus* (David MacDonald, 1949), inspirada en el relato *Columbus, a Romance*, de Rafael Sabatini — quien inicialmente había escrito el guión de la película — y, su respuesta peninsular, *Alba de América* (Juan de Orduña, 1951). *Christopher Columbus* forma parte de un reducido número de films espectaculares de los Estudios Gainsborough que rompían con su línea más tradicional de producciones históricas o los 'costume dramas', en un intento de atraer al mercado americano. Con ese propósito Arthur Rank había contratado a Sydney Box, después del éxito que éste obtuvo con *The Seventh Veil* en 1945, con la esperanza de que le ayudara a salir del bache económico en el que se encontraba en ese momento.[6] Desafortunadamente para los estudios, la película fue un rotundo fracaso, a pesar de todos los esfuerzos por recrear fielmente la época en la puesta en escena, la intervención de actores de prestigio y de una cantidad respetable de extras, y el uso del technicolor. El resultado final fue una sucesión

---

[6] No queda del todo claro en las fuentes que he podido consultar hasta ahora, cuál fue la motivación primera de este proyecto. Susan Harper afirma por una parte que: 'After 1945 Rank began to experience severe economic difficulties. He made unsuccessful attempts on the American market' y no es descabellado pensar que quizás la historia de *Christopher Columbus* fue elegida porque su argumento podía tener cierto atractivo para el público estadounidense. Pero, también según Harper: 'Box had a perfectly good script for *Christopher Columbus* [escrito antes de llegar él], which he proceeded to tear apart and rewrite with his wife and co-producer Muriel Box. [...] With Christopher Columbus, Box attempted a reorientation. The American actor Fredric March was imported and the film's script is essentially a paean to America' (1994: 21 & 134). Muriel Box, en su autobiografía, comenta al respecto: 'Our most ambitious production at Gainsborough, *Christopher Columbus*, starring Fredric March, was also our worst flop and fully justified the fears we had before embarking on it. The Rank Group insisted on making this because a large sum of money had already been expended on the purchase of the story rights, also a screenplay by the author, Rafael Sabatini, before we arrived at the studio. After a good deal of research I found this long script both inaccurate and inferior in quality. I passed on my opinion to Sydney and we asked to be excused from producing it, but to no avail. The initial outlay had to be recouped no matter what and so we went ahead with the film and a costly affair it proved.' (1974: 196–97).

de cuadros estáticos en los que los personajes parecían atrapados. La trama, que cubre la vida de Colón desde su llegada a La Rábida hasta su vejez (el relato de Sabatini sólo cubre hasta el regreso de Colón de su primer viaje) se desvía en la primera parte de la película hacia las intrigas palaciegas que precedieron al viaje del almirante y, como dijo uno de los críticos, 'by the time everybody got around to the discovery of America the audience interest had slackened to the point of no return' (Quirk 1971: 199).

Por lo que se refiere a la actuación de Florence Eldridge en el papel de Isabel, quizás el término que mejor podría calificarla sería el adjetivo inglés: 'unremarkable'. Es una actuación comedida, plana, poco expresiva. Medio siglo después de que la película fuera estrenada, este comedimiento aún llama más la atención tras haber visto reinas cuya caracterización está mucho más marcada, en parte gracias a la actuación de quienes las interpretan: bien poseen una fuerte personalidad como es el caso de Amparo Rivelles (*Alba de América*) o Sigourney Weaver (*1492, The Conquest of Paradise*) o por lo contrario, son demasiado ingenuas o hasta infantiles, como Rachel Ward (*Christopher Columbus, The Discovery*). A raíz del estreno de *Christopher Columbus* los críticos comentaron: 'Even Miss Eldridge, sterling artist that she is, and who could usually be relied upon for a distinctive performance, managed to be no more than dignified and stately as the monarch who, at long last, sent Columbus voyaging' (Quirk 1971: 199); 'As Queen Isabella, Florence Eldridge seems a bit less lively than Her Majesty was reported to have been' (crítica de *The New Yorker* citada en Quirk 1971: 200).

La reina tiene un papel importante en la consecución de la empresa colombina y su intervención es indispensable para resolver el conflicto que plantean los escarceos amorosos de Fernando — escarceos que aunque tienen una base histórica, se exponen en la película por las implicaciones que tienen para Colón. Aunque su caracterización recoge algunos de los detalles de su leyenda, no profundiza en el personaje histórico; en ese sentido puede considerarse una más del repertorio de reinas que aparece en los films históricos o de aventuras, muy populares en su momento, y quizás la actriz así lo percibió.

Algunas particularidades del personaje, sin embargo, llaman la atención: la mayoría de las intervenciones de la reina se producen cuando se encuentra sentada, frente a una mesa de trabajo llena de papeles, lo que puede explicar en parte el estatismo de la interpretación. Es un personaje que no mantiene demasiado las distancias. En la primera entrevista con Colón le dice: 'Come closer, I dislike to speak to people at a distance.' La impresión de este primer encuentro es que Isabel parece estar siempre ocupada: 'Talk to me freely, but briefly', le dice a Colón, y ante la ansiedad que éste manifiesta por creer que necesitará más tiempo le responde: 'I am indulging myself as it is, now briefly.'

La reina de Florence Eldridge es una especie de sensata madre de familia que necesita tener su casa en orden y no tiene tiempo para distracciones. Atender a los planes de Colón forma parte de sus quehaceres. Habiendo leído ya sus documentos, lo insta a hablar de lo que no está escrito: 'What is it that you imagine, what is it that you see?' El diálogo muestra a un Colón visionario, muy del gusto decimonónico (y probablemente resultado de su propia autopropaganda): 'I was elected, preordained, inspired', y aunque la reina parece interesada en su empresa, sobre todo por la posibilidad de recuperar las tierras que están en manos de los infieles, no se deslumbra demasiado con sus impulsos, al revés que otras reinas del repertorio: 'You have heard that the noblest aims can cause men to twist the facts to serve their theories.' La reina, con un aire de familia casi protector, le aconseja a Colón antes de despedirse: 'You must curb your impatience and wait, it's good for the soul!' Llega incluso a sorprender su familiaridad cuando al final de la primera entrevista le pregunta: 'Are you married?' La pregunta, inesperada en el contexto en el cual se produce, no sorprende tanto cuando vemos la importancia que las cuestiones familiares tienen en el film.

En la primera parte de la película, la vida de Colón se mueve entre la tentación de abandonar su proyecto, casarse y tener una vida familiar convencional, y el empeño obstinado en fraguar su empresa. Son el propio empecinamiento del almirante y los consejos de Beatriz Enríquez: 'Marriage is difficult enough when two people want it badly', lo que hace que se decida a optar por lo segundo, con lo que se desbaratan los ilícitos planes de Beatriz de Bobadilla que lo tienta con la comodidad de la vida en la corte: 'You could have a position at court, money, security!'

El episodio enlaza con una escena que pone en evidencia los deslices del Rey Católico con Beatriz de Bobadilla.[7] En la escena,

---

[7] Fernández-Armesto comenta que en 1480 la reina, ante los escarceos amorosos de Fernando con Beatriz de Bobadilla (no la Marquesa de Moya, sino su prima del mismo nombre), hizo casar a ésta con Hernán Peraza, un conquistador de la Gomera que se encontraba en la corte para responder a la acusación de haber matado

Colón ve a un individuo intentando forzar a Beatriz a que lo bese, se abalanza sobre él y lo tira al suelo. El villano resulta ser el propio rey Fernando. La reina, que es testigo de los hechos, despachará el problema con rapidez, con sentido práctico: 'Of course you must make clear to your cousin [le dice a Francisco de Bobadilla–Francis L. Sullivan, primo de Beatriz] that no blame attaches to her. She cannot help her beauty any more than the king can help noticing it.' Isabel, que ya había enviado a Beatriz de Bobadilla al exilio en Canarias diez años antes (y sabemos por Joanna de Torres–Nora Swinburne que: 'The queen has a long memory, especially when her husband is concerned'), decide volver a hacerlo: 'As a mother myself I know how painful it is to be separated from your own children [por el diálogo nos hemos enterado de que Beatriz tiene dos hijos]. Tell her that she has our permission to return to the Canaries, at once!' Cuando Francisco de Bobadilla le pregunta a la reina cuál será el castigo del navegante por agredir al rey, ella responde: 'I am sure he [the king] has forgotten all about it.' La inclusión de este episodio permite ver a la reina lidiar con una situación de su vida privada y al margen de las cuestiones de Estado, aunque respecto a éstas mantiene el mismo espíritu práctico. Una vez Isabel ha decidido respaldar la empresa de Colón, se da cuenta de la carga económica que supone su financiación y, ya que tiene sus joyas a mano, las recoge todas y dice a Santángel–Abraham Sofaer: 'Raise what is necessary on this!', a lo que Santángel responde con la consabida negativa.[8] ¿Qué cineasta renunciaría a la tentación

a un correligionario, con la intención de mandarlos después a ambos de vuelta a las Canarias, en un intento de alejar la tentación de su afectuoso marido. Peraza murió en una insurrección en las islas en 1488. Según Fernández-Armesto, después de 'a celebrated amorous encounter with Columbus', Beatriz volvió a casarse con Alonso de Lugo (1975: 108–09).

[8] Parece, según la opinión más difundida, que la reina no empeñó las joyas: 'La reina no podía pignorar sus joyas porque hacía tiempo que las tenía empeñadas a los jurados de Valencia como garantía de un préstamo para financiar la guerra de Granada. Y tampoco conviene olvidar que el viaje no supuso un coste importante' (Varela 2006). La leyenda, que fue perpetuada por el padre de las Casas, la creó el propio hijo de Colón, Hernando, que en *La Historia del Almirante* incluyó el siguiente pasaje: 'Visto por San Ángel [sic] el favor que le hacía la Reina en aceptar lo que por consejo de tantos había desestimado, la respondió que no era necesario empeñar sus joyas, que él serviría á su alteza prestándola el dinero' (Colón 2006: 72). De cualquier modo, Peggy Liss no encuentra del todo descabellado el episodio: 'Did Isabel indeed offer to pawn her jewels? Probably, for that was one of the reasons rulers owned jewels and the sum was small and reimbursement anticipated. Her gesture need not be viewed as a tremendous commitment to Columbus' project, for in any case she was not offering prized possessions so much as a customary collateral. Many of her

de incluir el episodio? Nadie lo hace hasta Ridley Scott.

La película muestra una actuación de la reina mucho más conte-
nida por lo que se refiere a su relación con Colón que otras
producciones posteriores. De todas formas, la cercanía del personaje y su ánimo protector hacia el almirante se mantienen hasta el
final de la película, cuando se pone en pie para ayudarlo a levan-
tarse después de que éste llegue encadenado ante su presencia, o
cuando le da el último consejo casi maternal: 'Now we think that it
is best that you should rest for a while.'

Dos años más tarde, *Alba de América* mostrará a Isabel y a Colón
compartiendo una común visión mesiánica. Dirigida por Juan de Orduña en 1951, es la réplica española a *Christopher Columbus*, una
respuesta airada producida por CIFESA, que con ella añadía un título
más a su ciclo de producciones históricas.[9] Según Carlos F. Heredero:

> Se trata de un intento de revisar el descubrimiento de América a la luz de
> la doctrina nacionalista: denunciando las intrigas del banquero judío Isa-
> ac con el francés Armagnac y el rey de Portugal (lo que el régimen
> llamaba la 'conspiración judaica internacional') para hacerse con el secre-
> to de Colón y contraponiendo el afán de títulos y riquezas que exhibe el
> descubridor (a quien también se presenta como un héroe predestinado)
> con el limpio objetivo de la reina católica de 'ganar almas para el cielo' y
> de llevar a las nuevas tierras 'sangre generosa para alumbrar la noble fa-
> milia de las Españas'. (1993: 175)

Amparo Rivelles despliega en esta película una interpretación que
está en el polo opuesto a la de Florence Eldridge. En este caso, la reina
parece vivir en una especie de continuo arrobamiento casi místico.
Esta tensión en la interpretación se explica no sólo porque la reina
carga con el peso del inconmensurable deber de la evangelización,
sino por toda la acumulación de facetas que se aglutinan en el personaje y contribuyen a exponer tanto sus comentarios como los de

---

jewels, among them the ruby and pearl necklace that was her wedding gift, were
already in pawn in Santángel's Valencia, and not for the first time [...] In her sugges-
tion to Santángel, therefore, she may have been indulging in some kind of irony, for
the sum was scarcely worth the jewels. [...] Nor did Santángel respond as gallantly
as to open his own purse. Rather, he advanced funds from crown monies to which
he had access.' (1992: 89–90).

[9] Fèlix Fanés recoge las palabras de Orduña respecto al film inglés en una conversación con José María García Escudero: 'El Rey Católico era un muñeco al que Colón
abofeteaba, se ponía en ridículo a la reina, se denigraba España y a la gesta [...] de los
Reyes Católicos' (1989: 252). Además la película acababa con las desencantadas — e
inaceptables a oídos españoles — palabras de Colón, refiriéndose a los Reyes Católicos: 'I will never recover from such ingratitude... People will remember me long after
they are dead and forgotten'.

otros personajes. La reina es auxiliadora de los soldados heridos o enfermos, a los que limpia la frente con su pañuelo: '¡Sois el ángel que vela por nuestros soldados!' y el alma caritativa que socorre a sus familias: '¡Que de nuestra tesorería se atienda a las familias de estos soldados!'; la gala de sus capitanes: 'La reina visitará el campamento, debemos darle una buena jornada de armas', el timonel visionario del futuro imperial-católico de la patria: 'la veo aquí entre nosotros, contemplando lo que siempre adivinó', y continuamente se la identifica con la patria misma: 'Lleva la bandera de la reina ¿Cómo podéis llamarlo extranjero [a Colón]?' Tal concentración de atributos, que hace rayar al personaje en la santidad, requiere una pareja intensidad en la interpretación que condense la enormidad de los deberes que el personaje carga sobre sus hombros.

Como era de esperar, tal carga trascendió lo puramente visual y permeó la lengua de la reina hasta hacerla hablar con un enrevesado estilo y una sintaxis que abusa del hipérbaton: 'Sea nuestra su esperanza'; 'por todos los caminos anda Dios'. Su elevado registro, todo hay que decirlo, está muy en consonancia con el del resto de los personajes.

La concepción del film en conjunto, tal como la explica José Luis Téllez, propicia, o quizás requiere, y emplaza perfectamente la actuación:

> Es un caso extraordinario de film casi experimental, realizado dentro de la industria y con todo el aparato oficial tras de sí. *Alba de América* es un trabajo insólito de pura enunciación, que construye cada plano en razón de una suerte lógica significante interna (y abstracta) y que, en cierta manera, prescinde enteramente de la narratividad. [...] Lo único que parece interesar a Orduña es la organización del encuadre considerado como un todo autosuficiente, desdeñoso de la progresión del relato en la que se inscribe: punto límite que articula el devenir fílmico como una sucesión de deslizamientos, de *tableaux-vivants* narcisísticamente cerrados sobre sí mismos. (Téllez 1990: 54)

La convergencia de elementos en un film de esta naturaleza — una puesta en escena antinaturalista (con el agobiante espesamiento visual de los decorados de Sigfrido Burman, arrancados de la pintura histórica decimonónica); la caracterización hagiográfica de la reina: 'Her looks clearly imitate classic iconography in diverse images of the Virgin Mary' (Mira 2004: 70); y la carga de la misión histórica encomendada — acabaría justificando el cuasi permanente trance en que parece estar la Reina Católica que interpreta

Amparo Rivelles.[10]

La película no tuvo éxito en el momento en que se estrenó. El público le dio la espalda, al revés de lo que había hecho tres años antes con *Locura de amor*, film basado en la vida de Juana la Loca que adolecía de semejantes excesos dramáticos.[11] No es extraño que películas con tamaño nivel de dramatismo acabaran saturando al público. La reina no volverá a asomarse a la pantalla hasta años más tarde; cuando lo haga ya habrá perdido los ropajes pesados con que la invistieron el franquismo y el cineasta que mejor llevó su imaginario a la pantalla.

Las producciones que se estrenaron en 1992 iban por derroteros bien distintos a los de *Alba de América*. Mientras la figura de Colón era objeto de toda suerte de revisiones históricas que cuestionaban el carácter heroico y la grandeza de su aventura, el gobierno español preparaba una plétora de celebraciones del Quinto Centenario que difundiera la imagen de una España liberada de las telarañas de la dictadura (Lunenfeld 1992: 141). Tanto el proyecto de Scott como el producido por Salkind (dirigido finalmente por Glen, aunque con anterioridad se pensó en el propio Ridley Scott y después en George Cosmatos: Mitchell & Gorman 1991: 4) gozaron de las subvenciones del Ministerio de Cultura y de la Comisión del Quinto Centenario, respectivamente.[12] Según Peggy K. Liss, la erosión del mito de Colón no afectó

[10] En efecto, los poetas de la corte de Isabel la Católica ya la habían equiparado a la Virgen (Lida de Malkiel 1977). El análisis de las actuaciones de Amparo Rivelles, ha llevado a Jo Labanyi a ponderar otras facetas de la actriz pero a hacer una lectura muy negativa de sus papeles como heroína histórica: 'In a few films, the female protagonist's public prominence is undercut by the melodramatic excess of the performance style, verging on hysteria and reinforcing the traditional notion that women, being bound up in the world of private emotion, are incapable of an impartial sense of justice. The casting of Amparo Rivelles, whose star image was based on her roles in the nineteenth-century domestic melodramas, as the Catholic Queen in *Alba de América / American Dawn* (1951), a ghastly biopic of Columbus, and as the widowed leader of the sixteenth-century Comuneros' Revolt in *La Leona de Castilla / The Lioness of Castile* (1951), is disastrous both for the political message and for the representation of gender. Her pouting tantrums and fragile beauty undermine her authority as historical leader, suggesting that women are unfit for political leadership' (Labanyi 2000: 174).

[11] 'La operación fracasa triplemente: por lo acartonado de su discurso político (que incluso dentro del régimen hallaba detractores, como el ya mentado García Escudero [a la sazón Director General de Cinematografía], por su imposibilidad absoluta como empresa comercial (se trata de un film tan fascinador como plúmbeo) y por su planteamiento puramente formalista, ilustrativo a ultranza' (Téllez 1990: 54).

[12] 'Certainly in Spain we had enormous financial aid from the Ministry of Culture,

demasiado a la figura de la reina: 'Isabel has emerged oddly un-scathed, very much a part of America's historical past, if still a shadowy figure'(2003: 69); 'Isabel's seemingly assured place in his-tory may involve her having become an enigmatic icon, one ringed with sufficient ambiguity to accommodate a number of imagined or useful labels' (2003: 78n37).

La ambigüedad o la oscuridad del personaje permitió que *1492, The Conquest of Paradise* y *Christopher Columbus, The Discovery* ofre-cieran imágenes bien dispares de la reina, pero no más dispares de lo que ambas películas eran entre sí. Ninguna reveló gran interés por la verdad histórica: 'Historical personages are revised, deified or demonized, conflated or created from whole cloth to serve the director's will' (Rahn Phillips & Phillips 1995: 62).[13]

En ambas producciones el papel de la reina está en función del personaje de Colón. En *1492, The Conquest of Paradise* en particular, el papel de la reina, y hasta cierto punto la elección de la actriz, pare-ce haber dependido del actor que lo representaba: Gerard De-pardieu. En el caso de *Christopher Columbus, The Discovery*, el papel de la reina está además en función de su marido Fernando — Tom Selleck.

Como en las otras producciones, el personaje de Isabel de *1492, The Conquest of Paradise*, aun siendo secundario, está por encima de los otros personajes secundarios, incluido el de Beatriz Henríquez, in-terpretado para la ocasión por Ángela Molina. Tanto ella como Sigourney Weaver — actrices a las que solemos ver en papeles pro-tagonistas y no de repertorio — exhibieron diferentes estilos de belleza gracias a escotados vestidos que les permiten lucir los hom-bros al aire, a pesar de los rigores del clima (Rahn Phillips & Phillips 1985: 64). En múltiples escenas de gran opulencia y enorme atractivo visual destaca la figura de Isabel, luciendo una larga y rizada melena, vestida en tonos dorados atenuados por la penumbra: un contraste bastante grande, como ya ha señalado Mercedes Águeda Villar, 'con la leyenda tradicional de su austeridad' (2003: 93).

Esta discrepancia con la leyenda tradicional se extiende a la figura de Colón. El navegante es un personaje en conflicto con su propio

---

which was planning the celebration three years ago. There was no real problem with the Ministry in terms of accuracy of the story other than minor requests. I guess we were well-rehearsed' (Bahiana 1992: 35).

[13] Los espectadores con más expectativas podrían seguir los consejos de estos críticos: 'The casual viewer would do well to disbelieve every word and virtually every scene in both films' (1995: 62).

carácter — tiene accesos de cólera que no puede reprimir — y en conflicto con la superstición y el fanatismo que son el signo de su tiempo. Inmerso en esta conflictividad, el personaje se muestra difícil, irascible; en palabras de Scott: 'a strong, physical man, driven by his emotions and instinct, a strong orator with the personality to persuade men to follow him' (Bahiana 1992: 35), ¿ y quién mejor que Depardieu para interpretarlo?: 'His natural character seems to dove-tail into my perception of who Columbus may have been' (Bahiana 1992: 34–35).[14] Dicho esto, surge inmediatamente la pregunta de quién podría estar a la par con 'the great hulking figure of Mr. Depardieu', que además 'can suggest passions that the screenplay never pursues with any consistency' (Canby 1992a). Aparte de esto, era un reto también encontrar una actriz que no se viera bajita frente a la corpulencia del actor francés (Weaver mide 1m 85cm).[15]

La primera entrevista entre la reina y el navegante exige del espectador que prescinda de cualquier preconcepción sobre la distancia que podía separar dos personas de rango tan distinto:

Isabella: They believe the Ocean is uncrossable, señor Columbus.
Columbus: What did they say about Granada before today? (La reina se da la vuelta y lo mira)
Isabella: That it was impregnable, hm… (La reina se levanta y lo mira frente a frente). I cannot ignore the verdict of my Council.
Columbus: Surely you can do anything you want. (La reina camina)

---

[14] Peter Wollen en su comentario de la película para *Sight and Sound,* vio en el subtítulo *The Conquest of Paradise,* una referencia al libro del mismo título de Kirkpatrick Sale, fundador del Partido Verde americano, inmisericorde con la figura de Colón a quien hace responsable de las masacres y catástrofes que han ocurrido desde el tiempo de la conquista (Wollen 1992: 22). Nancy Griffin califica la visión de Scott y de la periodista Roslyne Bosch, ambos responsables del guión, como: 'a portrait of the explorer that falls between his once-heroic image and the censure that has recently been brought upon him by revisionists such as Kirkpatrick Sale' (Griffin 1992: 92). Sin embargo, la opinión del director no podría estar más alejada de ello: 'There is a book by Patrick [sic] Sale which is *completely* damning on every level about Columbus as a seaman, as a cartographer, he virtually calls him a buffoon' (Salisbury 1992: 88). Si la personalidad del carácter, por sus extremos, se aleja un poco de la leyenda más tradicional en la película de Scott, quizás sea más por el intento de subrayar su empecinamiento y la singularidad de su visión del mundo, que por ofrecer una visión de la historia en la línea del libro de Sale. No obstante, *1492, The Conquest of Paradise,* hace algunas calas en lo políticamente correcto, así Santángel al llegar a Granada después que la ciudad ha caído, dice: 'It is a tragic victory for us, we are losing a great culture!'

[15] Ridley Scott pensó en Angelica Huston para el papel, quien también posee un tipo físico que podría medirse con el de Depardieu. En las declaraciones del director respecto a la elección de la actriz no queda claro por qué Huston quedó descartada (Salisbury 1992: 88).

Isabella: How little you know! (Pausa) Why should I believe in you, señor Columbus?

Columbus: May I speak freely? (Se miran cara a cara)

Isabella: You show no inclination to speak otherwise.

Columbus: I know what I see, I see someone who doesn't accept the world as it is, who's not afraid. I see a woman who thinks, what if...

Isabella: (Interrumpiendo) A woman?

Columbus: Forgive me, but you are the only queen I know.

Isabella: Then that makes us equal, you are the only navigator that I know. (Pausa) How old are you, señor Columbus?

Columbus: Thirty-nine, your majesty. And you?

Isabella: I am forty. (Pausa) You will be informed of our decision. (Vuelve a su escritorio y se sienta. Pausa.)

Columbus: Actually, I thought you were younger than I. (Se va, después que la reina se da la vuelta y lo mira)

Este entretenido diálogo tiene lugar entre una reina que se hace la interesante y un Colón cuya desfachatez y osadía parecen deslumbrarla. En la familiaridad que llegará a haber entre ambos personajes, Peter Wollen (1992) vio una remota referencia a la novela de Alejo Carpentier *El arpa y la sombra*, novela en la que el navegante confiesa haber mantenido una relación amorosa con Isabel, además de referirse a algunos otros escarceos amorosos de la reina.[16] Sea como sea, el film, como ocurrirá también con *Christopher Columbus, The Discovery*, acorta las distancias entre Colón y la reina, tanto en las entrevistas que tienen lugar en privado como en los actos públicos. En Barcelona, entre humaredas — tan del gusto de Ridley Scott — los reyes reciben al navegante en el interior de la catedral. En un más que osado plano, la reina, que para la ocasión viste sus más suntuosas galas reales, le ofrece la mano a Colón para que la guíe en la procesión. Tras unos pasos, la cámara discurre de Colón a Isabel, después a Fernando y de nuevo a Colón, y el espectador pudo sacar sus propias conclusiones de lo que esto significa.[17]

[16] 'También ella acababa de cumplir cuarenta años [...] Y, aquel día, movido por una audacia de la que me hubiese creído incapaz, pronuncié palabras como dichas por otro — palabras que no repetiré en mi confesión — que me hicieron salir de las estancias reales cuando empezaban a sonar las dianas de los campamentos. Y desde esa noche venturosa, sólo una mujer existió para mí en el mundo que esperaba *por mí* para acabar de redondearse' (Carpentier 1990: 284–86).

[17] Aunque la escena no le resta mérito a la película, al contrario, le añade esplendor (y de paso gracias a ella podemos ver al rey que sigue sin decir palabra), lo cierto es que tal recibimiento probablemente nunca tuvo lugar tal como se presenta en el film: 'Pese a todas las descripciones que nos dejaron los cronistas, de ninguna manera hemos de pensar que Colón recibió en Barcelona un recibimiento apoteósico por la sencilla razón de que de haber sido así, no hubieran dejado de señalarlo los

Pero quizás la escena más osada del film tiene lugar durante el banquete que sigue casi inmediatamente a la procesión. Colón da a probar a los invitados un cigarro — y vemos a la reina toser — y comenta que los indígenas van desnudos como Dios los creó. La reina pregunta entonces: 'Which God?' El pie es sólo una excusa para que Colón desarrolle sus pensamientos sobre cierto panteísmo que parece habitar la conciencia de los indígenas, pero aun así, resulta demasiado difícil imaginar a una reina católica formulando semejante pregunta. La pregunta extraña incluso en el contexto de este film en el que la reina claramente se desmarca del consejo de los clérigos (y no olvidemos que pronto su tesorero Gabriel Sánchez–Armand Assante advierte a Arojaz–Kario Salem del peligro que corre su posición si se empeña en oponerse a sus deseos) y en el que la Iglesia se identifica con el fanatismo y la ignorancia. Prueba de ello es el tono intimidatorio del clérigo Arojaz presidiendo el consejo de sabios que juzga el proyecto de Colón.[18] Las terroríficas escenas de la muerte en la hoguera de una hereje, al principio de la película, son una temprana condena de ese fanatismo y de la Iglesia que en buena medida lo propicia. El banquete termina con unos planos de la reina que, en un arranque de coquetería, se tapa la cara con una pequeña careta de oro traída con otras joyas del Nuevo Mundo y sin apartársela le dice a Colón: 'We are more than gratified, Cristóbal!'

El último encuentro entre la reina y Colón tiene lugar después de que Sánchez le haya hablado a ella de la necesidad de reemplazar al almirante como gobernador de las colonias. La reina, que tiene piedad de Colón, le concede su deseo de volver a viajar, pero esta vez sin sus hermanos. Cuando al final Isabel profiere las improbables palabras: 'The New World is a disaster', Colón la reta de nuevo diciéndole: 'And the old one, an achievement?'

Varias intervenciones de la reina en la película revelan facetas del personaje que otros films no dejan ver: su sentido del humor al

dietarios y los libros de ceremonias barceloneses que callan la estancia de Colón en la ciudad condal. El encuentro, sin duda emotivo y cordial, hubo de limitarse a un sencillo acto cortesano' (Varela 2006).

[18] Respecto a este tema, la película de nuevo se toma alguna que otra libertad con la historia: según Joseph Pérez, Colón era un autodidacta que carecía de una formación sólida con la que respaldar su proyecto. Aunque los cálculos de Marino de Tiro que Colón defiende habían sido refutados varias veces por los expertos (Pérez 2006: 130–31), la película lleva a pensar que es la respuesta a las trampas teológicas que le tienden los clérigos lo que hace que éstos no den su aprobación al proyecto, y no las lagunas científicas del navegante.

reírse de un Colón que le dice a Sánchez querer hacerse monje si su proyecto no sale adelante, mientras lo espía desde otro aposento; o cierto desaliento cuando, aunque sin suspirar, alude a la distancia que separa la apariencia y la realidad de su existencia en el comentario: 'How little you know'. Gracias a su poco convencional relación con Colón se revelan rasgos de su personalidad que no se manifestarían, suponemos, en su relación con otros personajes.

Christopher Columbus, The Discovery, cubre la empresa de Colón sólo hasta que éste regresa de su primer viaje. Los títulos de crédito de la película se abren con Marlon Brando (Torquemada) y Tom Selleck (Fernando). El nombre de la actriz que interpreta a la reina, Rachel Ward, sigue al de George Corraface (Colón) al que interpretó al almirante 'as a fellow who smiles a lot, has a set of extremely white teeth, enchants the ladies and is handy with a sword' (Canby 1992b). Rachel Ward, que tenía varios títulos cinematográficos en su haber en 1992, era conocida en aquellos momentos sobre todo por su aparición en la serie australiana de televisión *The Thorn Birds*.

Aunque la Iglesia tiene, por supuesto, un papel importante en las otras producciones, la Inquisición, y sobre todo el inquisidor general, Tomás de Torquemada, están imbricados en la trama general del film como no lo están en otras películas. La inclusión del personaje de Torquemada fue probablemente la manera gracias a la cual los productores pudieron justificar la presencia de Brando en el reparto, y con ello dar cierto marchamo de prestigio a la película (un poco en la línea de *Superman* (Richard Donner, 1978), que comparte guionista, Mario Puzo, con esta producción). El resultado, sin embargo, es que el film se mueve en un espacio difuso entre la épica histórica, de alto presupuesto, con estrella de primera categoría en el papel de una figura histórica notable; y el film de aventuras (el proyecto se conocía como 'Indiana Jones Columbus': Klady 1991: 7), con actores de cierto renombre, pero sin la talla de Brando. Algunos de ellos no acaban de estar del todo en su papel, bien por su apariencia o porque su trayectoria profesional los ha marcado con las trazas de otros tipos de personaje, cuyo caso más flagrante es Tom Selleck. En último término, el intento de combinar las dos categorías genéricas, además de la presencia de actores interpretando personajes a contrapelo, dan al traste con la cohesión de la película.

En este marasmo de interpretaciones está la de Rachel Ward– Isabel que — apoyada por un guión poco consistente — personifica a una reina casi infantil y dependiente de su esposo. En sus entrevistas con Colón, Isabel habla siempre en terminos de sueños, para cuyo cumplimiento necesita la intervención de Fernando: 'It has always been my dream, should God give me the crown of Castilla, I might one day recapture all of those domains for Christendom; with the good right arm of the church and my husband's bravery in the battlefield, God may yet grant me that dream.'

La intervención de los otros personajes ayuda también a aligerar el carácter de la reina. Así Torquemada tras la caída de Granada dice con aire complacido: `He [God]'s given Spain to his Son in answer to the prayers of a young girl. God is great, and our debt to him is infinite.' A la falta de 'gravitas' propiciada por el guión, habría que añadir también el tipo físico de la actriz: 'Rachel Ward is too pretty to represent Queen Isabel at thirty-seven, who had at least ten pregnancies and a hard life in the saddle behind her' (Rahn Phillips & Phillips 1995: 63), y un vestuario, que si a Fernando lo hace parecer un rey de la baraja de Fournier, a ella la ha provisto de unos pendientes largos en forma de cruz que combinan bien con su larga y juvenil melena. La presencia del personaje de Torquemada–Brando en la producción da pie a tratar el problema del antisemitismo y la cuestión de la expulsión de los judíos, pero la película no se ocupa de las relaciones de la reina con Tomás de Torquemada (cuya intervención en la gestación de los viajes de Colón es más bien dudosa, aunque esa es una cuestión al margen); como mucho, en un gesto que muestra la propensión al coqueteo del personaje más que su autoridad real, la reina le pide al inquisidor que abandone la sala para entrevistarse a solas con Colón. Torquemada obedece con cierta disimulada sorpresa y con una sonrisa desdeñosa y sardónica, muy propia de Brando.

La otra figura sin paralelo en producciones anteriores es la de Fernando. Según Rahn Phillips & Phillips, el papel del escéptico Fernando se acerca bastante a la figura histórica (y al Fernando de *Juana la loca* de Vicente Aranda, podría añadirse).[19] Tampoco la recreación de la relación de la reina con el rey alcanza grandes honduras, aunque sí pone de manifiesto un fuerte contraste entre sendas personalidades: el carácter soñador de Isabel contrasta fuertemente con el espíritu práctico y materialista de Fernando.

---

[19] 'Isabel sees great advantages for Christianity in Columbus's proposal, despite the skepticism of her husband, Ferdinand of Aragon (Tom Selleck), and Tomás de Torquemada (Marlon Brando), Head of the Spanish Inquisition. That these three pivotal figures are portrayed fairly accurately represents a rare victory for the film's historical advisers' (Rahn Phillips & Phillips 1995: 63). Los asesores de la producción fueron Juan Gil y Consuelo Varela.

En la primera audiencia concedida a Colón, Fernando hace preguntas y comentarios propios de una entrevista de trabajo: 'The wealth may well be beyond imagining, but the cost would be considerable. What exactly is your background, señor Colón? [...] In Genoa, what rank was your father?' En la segunda entrevista, Fernando intenta definir los términos del contrato: 'As a master of this enterprise, what rewards do you expect, señor Colón? [...] Until now, I questioned your mathematics, señor Colón, but I see that was a mistake [...] Modify your requests, we all know your condition.' En el recibimiento de Colón, poco antes de que éste aparezca le dice a la reina: 'Had I known he would succeed ... To bestow such an honour on a Genoese!' Y tras lidiar con los formalismos, añade: 'Admiral Colón, you have earned our respect and admiration, now, where is my gold?' La reina deja las cuestiones económicas en manos de su esposo. A ella le interesan las almas y al rey el oro. Cuando con aire despreocupado dice: 'I am in debt to God, I intend to carry his word to the Indies, if I must pawn my own crown jewels to do so!', no la vemos descender al terreno de lo práctico, sino hacer una concesión al legendario motivo de las joyas. La financiación del viaje de Colón claramente preocupa a Fernando. Isabel sin embargo piensa en el resultado último de la empresa: la evangelización (y con ello está más cerca de la Isabel de Orduña que de la de Scott, definitivamente). Al dejar en manos de su marido el asunto de la financiación, situándose en un segundo plano por lo que se refiere a la negociación, renuncia definitivamente al 'Tanto monta'.

Por último, y también como muestra de un guión que socava la autoridad de la reina por todos los frentes, la reina exhibe una ligereza coqueta en el trato con Colón — nada regia y menos católica — que cabría esperar del otro personaje femenino de importancia: Beatriz Henríquez, interpretada por Catherine Zeta-Jones. Las libertades en términos del guión en esta dirección llevan a Isabel a decir: 'Señor Colón, you look splendid!' o 'You have a way with women, Colón' (al entregarle su cruz al marino). La respuesta de Colón se encuentra a la altura de las circunstancias: 'I'm from Genoa, your majesty.' La conversación, que le da un aire humorístico a la película, al final va en perjuicio del propio personaje de la reina, que, dicho sea de paso, carece casi por completo de carácter regio.

Tras este extenso repaso por la filmografía isabelina podría concluirse que la exaltación de la figura de la reina en la tradición tardorromántica y su posterior apropiación por el franquismo, ejemplificada por las películas de Orduña, probablemente impidieron que durante décadas su figura se tratara en la pantalla española, dada la carga ideológica nacional-católica que el personaje llevaba adscrita. Cuando el personaje volvió a aparecer, lo hizo en una película, *La reina Isabel en persona*, cuya difusión ha sido muy limitada, o en un papel muy breve, como en el caso de la película de Aranda, que aquí sólo se ha mencionado. Ninguna producción reciente ha popularizado demasiado la figura de la reina, aunque lo que han podido dar a conocer sobre ella tiende a acercarse más al personaje histórico que las anteriores.

Por lo que se refiere a las películas estrenadas en el 92, y a pesar de la sincronía de su producción, Isabel recibe tratamientos muy distintos. Scott creó un personaje a la altura y en función de Colón-Depardieu; Glen quiso crear una reina de película de aventuras sin grandes honduras, y hasta cierto punto más próxima a la que interpreta Florence Eldridge. La ambigüedad genérica de *Christopher Columbus, The Discovery*, película que intentaba mostrar la grandeza de la empresa y a la vez presentaba a uno de sus máximos responsables como una reina jovial casi infantil, le restó al personaje toda credibilidad.

FILMOGRAFÍA

Ésta es aún una relación incompleta de las películas en las que parece la reina, dividida en tres partes: dos apartados según su temática y el último, el de las películas cómicas atendiendo al género, que no he estudiado hasta ahora, pero que merece la pena señalar al menos, porque gozaron de cierto éxito entre el público. Por su temática, podrían aparecer también en los apartados precedentes, aunque posean una tónica bastante distinta al resto de las producciones.

Algunos títulos se encuentran seguidos por un asterisco, bien porque no he podido constatar la presencia del personaje — aunque ésta parece probable dado el argumento — o porque el personaje no aparece pero se hace referencia a él.

Películas de temática colombina

1912 *The Coming of Columbus*, dir. Colin Campbell, EE.UU, Selig Polyscope Company.*

1916 *La vida de Cristóbal Colón y su / el descubrimiento de América (La vie de Christophe Colomb)*, dir. Émile o Gérard Bourgeois y guión Charles Drossner, 1917 (1916), prod. Argos Films y subvencionada por el Estado / (Francia), copr. Films Cinematographiques (aparece en algunas filmografías datada en 1917). Isabel: Léontine Massart. Película de alto presupuesto, un millón de pesetas que, según Julio Pérez Perucha, tuvo un resultado muy mediocre (1995: 79-80). Las abundantes imágenes exteriores que aparecen fueron rodadas en España y según Mercedes Águeda Villar, su escenografía 'tuvo en cuenta alguna de las imágenes más famosas de los cuadros de historia de nuestro siglo XIX' (2003: 39).[20] Se filmó con actores franceses: Georges Wage representó a Colón, y Léontine Massart, que ya había hecho el papel de Margarita de Navarra en *La Reine Margot* de Pathé Frères en 1914, interpretó a la reina española.

1923 *Columbus*, dir. Edwin L. Hollywood, 1923, Chronicles of America Pictures, Production Company, distribuida por Pathé Exchange. Isabel: Dolores Cassinelli. La actriz era conocida en su época como 'The Cameo girl of the movies'. En ese mismo año interpretó a Pocahontas en la película *Jamestown*, del mismo director. Colón fue interpretado por Fred Erich y el rey Fernando por Robert Gallard. El guión está basado en la novela de quien también fue el guionista de la película Irving Berdine Richman: *The Spanish Conquerors, a Chronicle of the Dawn of Empire Overseas* (New Haven, 1919). En la película se muestran los problemas de Colón en la corte portuguesa y cómo la intercesión del confesor de Isabel hace posible que Colón consiga una audiencia. La reina que simpatiza con su causa, vende sus joyas en secreto para financiar su empresa. Colón después de viajar con tres barcos, llega a las Antillas. La película pertenece a un ciclo llamado 'Chronicles of America Pictures'. En 1923, Yale University Press decidió llevar a la pantalla los cincuenta volúmenes de su serie 'Chronicles of America', aunque sólo se llegaron a producir quince, el último de los cuales es *Columbus*. La película se califica en la base de datos del British Film Institute como 'instructional', y quizás podría incluirse en la categoría de documental.

1949 *Christopher Columbus*, dir. David MacDonald (Macdonald en la película, también en *Variety Movie Guide* y en *Biopics* de George

---

[20] Carlos Reyero ofrece un exhaustivo repaso de los cuadros decimonónicos que popularizaron la imagen de Colón en su artículo 'La iconografía de Colón' (2006: 424-41), dividido en núcleos temáticos, y que dedica un apartado en particular a Colón e Isabel y Fernando: 'Colón y los Reyes Católicos: al servicio del nacionalismo español' (2006: 436-439).

F. Custen), 1949, Gainsborough. Isabel: Florence Eldridge.[21]

1951 *Alba de América*, dir. Juan de Orduña, Cifesa. Isabel: Amparo Rivelles.

1985 *Christopher Columbus*, dir. Alberto Latuada, Francia, Italia / EE.UU. / República Federal Alemana. Radiotelevisone Italiana Clesi Cinematografica Production en asociación con Antenne 2-Bavaria Atelier and Lorimar. Isabel: Faye Dunaway.[22]

1992 *Christopher Columbus, The Discovery*, dir. John Glen, Estados Unidos, Peel Enterprises. Isabel: Rachel Ward. *1492, The Conquest of Paradise*, dir. Ridley Scott, Estados Unidos. Touchstone. Isabel: Sigourney Weaver.[23]

Biográficas[24]

1976 *La espada negra*, dir. Francisco Rovira Beleta, Óscar Producciones Internacionales, SA. Isabel: Maribel Martí.

2000 *La reina Isabel en persona*, dir. Rafael Gordon, Producciones Rafael Gordon. Isabel: Isabel Ordaz (premio a la mejor actriz en el Festival de Toulouse).

[21] De esta década son las siguientes producciones a las que simplemente quiero hacer referencia aquí, hasta que pueda comprobar detalles específicos de las mismas y , por tanto, si tiene sentido incluirlas en la filmografía sobre Isabel la Católica:
1943–*Cristóbal Colón / La grandeza de América*, México, Columbus Films (Ges) / Producciones Ormaechea, con música de Rodolfo Alter y dirigida por director español José Díaz Morales refugiado de la Guerra Civil de España en México. Su primera película fue *Jesús de Anisarte*.
1945–*La carabela de la ilusión / Villa Rica del Espíritu Santo*, Dir. Benito Perojo (¿?), 1945, Argentina, Pampa Film, con guión de Hugo McDugal y Benito Perojo.

[22] Esta miniserie de televisión merece una mención especial, aun en esta filmografía fundamentalmente cinematográfica. Cubre la vida de Colón desde antes que éste conozca a Felipa, su esposa, es decir, periodos de su vida que no se ven en otras producciones. Faye Dunaway es quizás la reina más cabal de todas y la serie quizás ofrece las imágenes más bellas de la empresa colombina.

[23] Como contrapunto a las películas de alto presupuesto que se estrenaron en el año del Quinto centenario, suele señalarse *La marrana*, dirigida por José Luis Cuerda (Central de Producciones Audiovisuales / Antea Films). En la película no parece Isabel la Católica, pero la acción tiene lugar en el contexto de su reinado, y por tanto contiene referencias a acontecimientos como el viaje de Colón y la expulsión de los judíos.

[24] Las filmografías de Clemente de Pablos (2004: 38) y Rodríguez García (historiamedieval.temalia.com) incluyen los siguientes títulos, pero hasta el momento no puedo asegurar que deben incluirse dentro de la filmografía sobre la Reina Católica.
1946–*El doncel de la reina*, dir. Eusebio Fernández Ardavín, Onuba.
1952–*Catalina de Inglaterra*, dir. Arturo Ruiz-Castillo, 1952, Valcázar Producciones Cinematográficas. Trata sobre el matrimonio de la hija de los Reyes Católicos con Arturo, el príncipe de Gales y después con su hermano el futuro Enrique VIII.

The Royal Diaries: Isabel, Jewel of Castilla, EE.UU, Scholastic Pro-ductions.[25] Isabel: Lisa Jakub. Producción para televisión que existe en DVD, pero no se distribuye en Europa. Basada en el li-bro de Carolyn Meyer, es la historia de Isabel como una princesa jovencita que escribe en un diario cuánto le acontece: cuando su hermano Enrique intenta casarla, ésta busca formas ingeniosas para zafarse del matrimonio hasta poder decidir por sí misma quién será su esposo. Fernando es interpretado por Christopher Ralph. La obra de Meyer pertenece a la serie *The Royal Diaries*, diarios de personajes históricos femeninos, que comprende títu-los como: *Anastasia, the Last Grand Duchess*, de la misma autora, y otros como *Victoria, May Blossom of Britannia*, de Anna Kirwan, y *Elisabeth, the Princess Bride*, de Barry Denenberg.

Cómicas

1982 *Cristóbal Colón, de oficio descubridor*, dir. Mariano Ozores, Constan Films, SA. Isabel: Fiorella Faltoyano.

1992 *Carry on Columbus*, dir. Gerald Thomas, Reino Unido, prod. Is-land World / Productions / Comedy / House production / En aso-ciación con Peter Rogers Production. Isabel: June Whitfield.[26]

OBRAS CITADAS

ÁGUEDA VILLAR, Mercedes, 2003. 'Imagen de Isabel la Católica en la cinemato-grafía', *CDL (Boletín del Ilustre Colegio Oficial de Doctores y Licenciados en Filosofía y Letras y en Ciencias, Colegio Profesional de Educación)*, 147: 38–39.

BAHIANA, A. M., 1992, 'Ridley Scott', *Cinema Papers*, 90: 32–35.

BOX, Muriel, 1974. *Odd Woman Out* (London: Leslie Frewin).

CANBY, Vincent, 1992a. 'Review / Film: Gerard Depardieu as Columbus: Ide-alist, Dreamer and Hustler', *The New York Times, nytimes.com*, 9 Octubre. Consultado: 30 de abril de 2007.

——, 1992b, 'Review / Film: It's Goodbye, Columbus, as Torquemada Waves', *The New York Times, nytimes.com*, 22 Agosto. Consultado: 30 de abril de 2007.

---

[25] He incluido este título televisivo por tratarse quizás del único que muestra a Isabel como princesa.

[26] Otro título no confirmado sería: *Delirios de grandeza*, dirigida por Gerard Oury, en 1971 (1972). Se trata de una producción de: España, Italia, Francia, y Alemania, (con Louis de Funes), producida por Rafael Gil Álvarez / Gaumont Internacional / Mars Film Paramount / Orion Film Produktion. En una categoría distinto podría situarse *Torquemada*, dirigida por Stanislav Barabas y estrenada en 1988. Se trata de una producción hispano-británica rodada en alemán, producida por Cine Interna-cional, y según los críticos españoles bastante desafortunada.

CARPENTIER, Alejo, 1990. *Obras completas*, IV: *La aprendiz de bruja, Concierto barroco, El arpa y la sombra* (México: Siglo Veintiuno).

CLEMENTE DE PABLOS, Miguel, 2004. 'Isabel de Castilla en el cine', *Patrimonio*, 17 (Especial V Centenario de la Muerte de Isabel la Católica: *La herencia de la reina de Castilla*, Fundación del Patrimonio Histórico de Castilla y León): 38–39.

COLÓN, Fernando, 2006. *Historia del Almirante Don Cristóbal Colón: edición facsímil* (Alicante: Biblioteca Virtual Miguel de Cervantes; Madrid: Biblioteca Nacional). Edición digital basada en la de Madrid, [Tomás Minuesa], 1892. Localización: Biblioteca Nacional (España) sig: HA/15548.] http://www/cervantesvirtual.com/FichaObra.html?Ref=21388 Consultado: 29 de mayo de 2007.

DE ESPAÑA, Rafael, 2002. 'El camino de las Indias: una perspectiva franquista ("La nao capitana" de Florián Rey)' (Alicante: Biblioteca Virtual Miguel de Cervantes). Edición digital basada en la publicada en 1995 en *Actas del V Congreso de la Asociación Española de Historiadores del Cine* (A Coruña: CGAI), pp. 211–18, http://www.cervantesvirtual.com/FichaObra.html?Ref=5223. Consultado: 4 de julio de 2007.

FANÉS, Fèlix, 1989. *El cas Cifesa: vint anys de cine espanyol (1932–1951)* (València: Filmoteca de la Generalitat Valenciana).

FERNÁNDEZ-ARMESTO, Felipe, 1975. *Ferdinand and Isabella* (New York: Taplinger Publishing Company).

GRIFFIN, Nancy, 1992. 'Columbus Discovering', *Premiere*, 6.2: 88–92.

HARPER, Susan, 1994. *Picturing the Past: The Rise and Fall of the British Costume Film* (London: British Film Institute).

HEREDERO, Carlos F., 1993. *Las huellas del tiempo: cine español 1951–1961* (Valencia: Filmoteca de la Generalitat Valenciana).

KLADY, Leonard, 1991. 'Salkinds' Columbus May Sail Straight onto Small Screen', *Screen International*, 822 (30 August): 7.

LABANYI, Jo, 2000. 'Feminizing the Nation: Women, Subordination and Subversion in Post-Civil War Spanish Cinema', en *Heroines without Heroes: Reconstructing Female and National Identities in European Cinema, 1945–51*, ed. Ulrike Sieglohr (London: Cassell), pp. 163–82.

LIDA DE MALKIEL, María Rosa, 1977. 'La hipérbole sagrada en la poesía castellana del siglo XV', en sus *Estudios sobre la literatura española del siglo XV*, ed. Yakov Malkiel (Madrid: José Porrúa Turanzas), pp. 291–309.

LISS, Peggy K., 1992. *Isabel the Queen: Life and Times* (New York: Oxford UP).

——, 2003. 'Isabel, Myth and History', en *Isabel la Católica, Queen of Castile: Critical Essays*, ed. David D. Boruchoff (New York: Palgrave Macmillan), pp. 57–78.

LUNENFELD, Marvin, 1992. 'What Shall We Tell the Children? The Press Encounters Columbus', *The History Teacher*, 25.2: 137–44.

MIRA, Alberto, 2004. 'Spectacular Metaphors: The Rhetoric of Historical Representation in Cifesa Epics', en *Spanish Popular Cinema*, ed. Antonio Lázaro Reboll & Andrew Willis (Manchester: UP).

MITCHELL, Angus, & Paul GORMAN, 1991. 'Columbus All at Sea as Salkinds Sue Cosmatos', *Screen International*, 825 (20 September): 4.

PÉREZ, Joseph, 2006. 'Cristóbal Colón y los Reyes Católicos', en *Cristóbal Colón*, ed. Carlos Martínez Shaw & Celia Parcero Torre (Salamanca: Junta de Castilla y León), pp. 129–38.

224

XELO SANMATEU

PÉREZ PERUCHA, Julio, 1995. 'Narración de un aciago destino (1896–1930)', en Román Gubern, José Enrique Monterde, Julio Pérez Perucha, et al., *Historia del cine español* (Madrid: Cátedra), pp. 19–45.
QUIRK, Lawrence J., 1871. *The Films of Fredric March* (New York: The Citadel Press).
RAHN PHILLIPS, Carla, & William D. PHILLIPS, 1995. 'Christopher Columbus: Two Films', en *Past Imperfect: History According to the Movies*, ed. Marc C. Carnes (London: Cassell).
REYERO, Carlos, 2006. 'La iconografía de Colón', en *Cristóbal Colón*, ed. Carlos Martínez Shaw & Celia Parcero Torre (Salamanca: Junta de Castilla y León), pp. 423–41.
RODRÍGUEZ GARCÍA, José Manuel, 2001–02. 'Los Reyes Católicos en el cine', aparecido originalmente en historiamedieval.temalia.com y ahora en http:// usuarios. lycos.es/ historiador1969.cinereyes.htm Consultado: 29 de mayo de 2007.
SALISBURY, Mark, 1992. 'In Nineteen Hundred and Ninety Two', *Empire*, 41: 84–90.
TÉLLEZ, José Luis, 1990. 'De historia y de folklore: notas sobre el 2º período Cifesa', *Archivos de la Filmoteca*, 4: 50–57.
VARELA, Consuelo, 2006. 'Isabel la Católica y Cristóbal Colón' (Alicante: Biblioteca Virtual Miguel de Cervantes). http://www.cervantesvirtual.com/Ficha Obra. html/Ref=18873 Consultado el 29 de mayo de 2007.
WOLLEN, Peter, 1992. 'Cinema's Conquistadors', *Sight and Sound*, 2.7: 20–23.

The Four Recensions of Fray Íñigo de Mendoza's *Vita Christi* with Some Unpublished Stanzas

DOROTHY SHERMAN SEVERIN

(University of Liverpool)

A preliminary analysis of the electronic collation of all the currently known extant *cancionero* versions of Fray Íñigo de Mendoza's *Vita Christi*, now available in the various Salamanca manuscripts which formerly were difficult to access, reveals, as suspected, a history of authorial revision, both for manuscript circulation during the reign of the Catholic Monarchs, and for public consumption in print. Because of the political nature of the poem, and the need for revision of the work to reflect the changing situation during the period of consolidation of power of the Catholic Monarchs, I am dividing the manuscripts into four recensions, which show careful and critical revisions of the text. Each recension has a number of manuscript witnesses that differ between themselves, reflecting the vagaries of manuscript transmission. In an earlier analysis of my own (Severin 2004), I distinguished simply between the longer and shorter versions represented by HH1 (now defined as the first recension) and LB3 (the second recension), and the printed versions (the fourth recension), without discussing the third recension as represented in texts SA4a and EM6 (see below).

The manuscripts, roughly in order of the age of the version (not necessarily the age of the manuscript) are:

1. Original recension

1.1 HH1, the *Cancionero de Oñate Castañeda*, the only extant complete original version with the attack on Henry IV and the grandees in the correct location. Harvard University Houghton Library, fMS Span 97, fols 314^v-44^v.

From the 'Cancioneiro da Vaticana' to the 'Cancionero general': Studies in Honour of Jane Whetnall, ed. Alan Deyermond & Barry Taylor, PMHRS, 60 (London: Department of Hispanic Studies, Queen Mary, University of London, 2007), pp. 225–34. ISSN 1460-051X. ISBN 0 902238 50 7.

2. Second recension

2.1. PN11, a complete early version with the attack on the grandees retrieved and written at the end of the poem. Paris, BN Esp., fols 118^r–95^v.

2.2 LB3, the *Cancionero de Egerton*, a shorter old version with the attack on the grandees excised, but related to the older tradition and with similarities to PN11 in the stanza sequence at the end of the poem. British Library, Egerton 969, fols 59^r-82^v.

2.3 SA4b, a shorter version with some unique stanzas, related to the early manuscript tradition. Salamanca, Universitaria 2139, fols 5^v-30^r.

2.3 NH2, the *Cancionero de Vindel*, a fragmentary version related to the early versions. New York, Hispanic Society of America, B2280, pp. 1-19.

2.4 SA4c, a fragment in Salamanca 2139, fols 34^r-37^v, retrieving the attack on the grandees which is missing from both full versions of the poems in this important manuscript. There are blank pages at fols 30^v-33^v, between SA4b and SA4c.

3. Third recension

3.1 SA4a, used as base text (along with the earlier excised stanzas from HH1 and other sources, in correct order and numbered additionally) for the electronic edition in preparation and available from autumn 2007. This is the longest version of the revised manuscript, which circulated in the courts in the late fifteenth century. It has been extensively rewritten in parts with most of the political commentary excised. It was not, however, the version used for printing. In Salamanca 2139, fols 71^r-122^r. Despite extensive rewriting it has a similar number of stanzas to HH1. Its supposedly unique last two stanzas are also found as the first two stanzas of ID 7815 at fol. 119^r; see also SA9, below.

3.2 EM6, a version very closely related to SA4a, missing the last two rewritten stanzas in SA4a, but featuring three stanzas from the earlier tradition which are missing in SA4a, two of which find their way into the printed tradition. Escorial K-III-7, fols 1^r-97^r.

4. The Printed Tradition

4.1 ML1, derived from the printed tradition; it seems to be a copy of 95VC (Zaragoza: Hurus), the only copy of which is in Rome,

Alessandrina, inc. 382, fols 2^r-31^r. Curiously, it has a small number of stanzas from the original tradition (HH1) missing from the Third recension (SA4a, EM6). Madrid, Fundación Lázaro Galdiano MS 30, fols 2^r-41^r.

4.2   SA9, related to the printed tradition; this is another Salamanca manuscript previously unavailable (MS 2762, fols 1^r-27^r.) A slightly later hand also writes in four *Vita Christi* stanzas, 382-85 in my numbering, at fol. 29^r. This manuscript also repeats the two final stanzas of SA4a as the first two stanzas of ID 7815 at fol. 27^v.

As Keith Whinnom pointed out years ago (1962, 1963, and 1977), the main difference in the narrative of the Passion story is that the presentation in the temple (Simeon and the *Nunc dimittis*) occurs at an earlier point in the narrative in HH1 and related texts, after the circumcision. In the later tradition the *Nunc dimittis* comes after the Magi and before the flight into Egypt. Almost as interesting is the fact that the Third recension (SA4a, EM6) supplements the missing HH1 stanzas with new stanzas, some in praise of the Virgin, so that all of the longer versions of the poems tend to be around 390 to 392 stanzas. However, the conflated base texts with all surviving stanzas contain 510 stanzas. This makes it the longest single Spanish poem of the fifteenth century.

Although I speculate, it seems logical that the long revision of the Third recension was undertaken by the author, perhaps at the behest of the Queen, after the civil war was ended in the late 1470s and a policy of reconciliation with old enemies had been inaugurated. The date of HH1, possibly as early as 1479 or 1480, places it on the cusp of this period. The direct attack on the Queen's enemies, the Girón-Pacheco-Carrillo brothers (especially the last one, the bishop), in the offending stanzas was no longer politic after the end of the war. Whether the author also undertook the revision for printing is also a moot point, but the early date of the *cancionero* editions of his poetry after 1480 (the first *cancioneros* to be printed) would argue for a revision by the poet himself.

The stanzas which I have been unable to find in the Rodríguez Puértolas editions (1968a and 1968b) are mainly from SA4b, a treasure-trove of new stanzas (numbering of the electronic edition):

1.   121-1 to 121-9 (SA4b), an attack on bad priests;
2.   161-1 to 161-3 (SA4b, also 161-2, fragmentary in EM6, ML1, SA9),

additional stanzas in the interlude of the shepherds;

3. 200-1 to 200-9 (SA4b); an attack on the church hierarchy;
4. 204-1 and 204-2 (SA4b), extra stanzas in the 'circumcision of Cas-
    tile' attack, these against the civil servants of the King;
5. a rewrite of 226 (SA4b);
6. 361-1 and 361-2 (LB3, PN11, SA4b), transitional to the massacre of
    the Innocents;
7. 374-2 (LB3, PN11);
8. 390-1 to 3 (HH1), conclusion;
9. 391-92 (SA4a, also found as part of ID7815 elsewhere in SA4 and
    in SA9).

I print these new stanzas below, using the base text for the electronic
edition which has had contractions resolved and long ſ replaced. I
think that we can speculate that, since many of these are anti-clerical
(or at least are against the abuse of position), these were also excised
by the author well before the revision for printing. However, some of
his other poems, notably his 'Razón contra sensualidad' (ID 2901), are
equally outspoken.

<S 121-1>
dexad a la castidad
que guardar no se supiera
es virtud que la umildad
y la pobre pobredad
no cunplen desta manera
que dello son mercadores
muy avarientos logreros
otros son arrendadores
de la codiçia amadores
no desechan los dineros

<S 121-2>
estos no son castellanos
que usan tal decretal
ni menos son çibdadanos
toledanos seuillanos

a nuestros son de portogal
mas esta alta consejuda
desaire ca me entended
y dise la viegesuda
a ti lo digo fijuda
y vos nuera lo entended

<S 121-3>
so dixeren el tropel
de sus obras no las diesmas
Responde por que papel
no basta ia para el
avnque pasan de mill tres mas
mas dire de bigardones
que se llaman en el a cuervos
vnos frayles terçerones
que handan por los mesones

y son desperados syervos

<S 121-4>
en achaque de santuarios
san laçaro & san anton
traen vnos corralarios
fechos en los sermonarios
daca para san ayron
con los milagros conpuestos
qual les syna vy escrivano
sacan los dineros prestos
de los que quedan por çestos
en los dar al tal tirano

<S 121-5>
este los Rudos escanta
con que esta sacalina
y con la bos quebranta
saca el cabeçal o manta
y la casa con la vina
arracadas & brodaduras
saca de las aldeanas
las bronchas & flocaduras
con palabras de blanduras
Roban las synples serranas

<S 121-6>
estes no curan tomar
la Regla de san benito
san françisco semejar
mas su propio Remidor
es a satanas maldito
estos tienen su traslado
sy sus obras cotejasen
de contrafecho moldado
con pinsel ansy pintado
en estos pienso fallarse

<S 121-7>
[first line cut]
de las coplas de mingo Rebulgo

el frayle bien pareçe
dentre en su Religion
y a los canpos pertenesçe
donde el feligres ofreçe
diga la pedricaçion
y cada vno que guarde
lo que tiene prometido
de obrar bien no se tarde
de virtud no covarde
en el mundo no metido

<S 121-8>
a los que estas arguyçiones
algo tocare o convenga
echaren maldiçiones
yo fago Renuçiaçiones
& digo sostera los venga
tal que enmienden sus vidas
la Razon ansy consiente
aquestas sean Ronpidas
para faser alguna quedas
y a mi digan maldiziente

<S 121-9>
da fin a lo dicho

quien desta ya va tocado
por ventura se syntiere
de oyr este tratado
pesare mal pecado
sy dentro del se viere
sy disen son estremas
& alguno fuere corrido
sy dellas ficiere remas

te diran tu que te quemas
ajos as comido
{SA4b}

****

<S 161-1>
fabla el otro pastor

daca daca tu minguillo
la yesca y los pedernales
y lle vemos al chiquillo
en tu firmo soçarronillo
do sy corderos Reçentales
y lle vale tres ancharones
& aderesca tu mamoria
aqui tangas bien los sones
que estos nuestros çamarrones
oy saltaran en la gloria

<S 161-2>
non miras los tres ping{?}
que salen de aquellos Cantos
yo juro que son santos
todos aquellos pastores
escucha amigo sy espantos
ay de dios y que gasajo
avras mingo si le escuchas
ni comer mjgas con ajo
ni borregos en tasajo
ni sopar huerte las puchas

<S 161-3>
fabla el otro pastor

los pastores conbidados
daquestas personas tales
y dellos mucho amediantados
y desigualmente espantados
en plaseres desyguales

en saltos y enbaylar
y con mucha alegria
començaron de cantar
vn canto muy syngular
benedita eres maria

<S 200-1>
o uos papas cardenales
o dehanes arçobispos
estados saçerdotales
personas conventuales
y uos priores & obispos
mirad el muy alto grado
que dios a uos quiso dar
ca el mismo consagrado
de vuestras manos tratado
es contino en el altar

<S 200-2>
o ministros camareros
de la trenidad conplida
de la iglesia tesoreros
del pulgatorio porteros
por que en la pena se oluida
por quien nuestro fee se alça
vos hereges son feridos
por quien la iglesia se alcança
& tienen della esperança
los que della van perdidos

<S 200-3>
lo que veo ya no dades
a sabios Aministrados
benefiçios dinidades
mas fazes muchos abades
que son mas torpes que letrados
y mas sy son favoridos

avnque sean todos neçios
dona pimona & partidos
garçi sobaco conplidos
tratan con uos sus preçios

<S 200-4>
el evangeljo leystes
y no se sy lo guardastes
pues de graçia Reçebistes
lo que del señor ovistes
de graçia lo donasys?
a sus deçipulos fablando
por esto les castigar
a uosotros no olvidando
mas aquello confirmando
por vuestro deveys tomar

<S 200-5>
a estos grandes dexando
& aqui fizme mi nonbre
destas mas non proçesando
nin sus virtudes contando
pues que dellos no me asonbre
de capellanes & caras
que biven en las aldeas
presenta se sus mas duras
de sus obras mucho feas

<S 200-6>
este sy promesas fazen
quales son los que las guardan
pues sus voluntades aplazen
al señor mucho desplazen
en pecados enbueltos andan
& sabre otras alvriçias
que mas procuran fravdar
para su hermana avariçias

terçias diezmos & premençias
o por las almas Resar

<S 200-7>
mas procuran tresquilar
los feligreses no viçios
que las misas çelebrar
los maytines enpeçar
con malditos exerçiçios
Revelados treyntanarios
Resan en los breviarios
aun todos son devoçion
estes y los no venarios
por acortar la liçion

<S 200-8>
el Resar de contrayçion
en çima de los finados
con el criste eleyson
dada el bodigo y el lechon
y las blanades y los cornados
el que esta çerca de su mano
para que le de el ysopo
al sobrino de su hermano
non su fijo publjcano
esto por que no se sopo

<S 200-9>
muy poco onesta son ama
prima hermana o sobrina
que la tienen & la llama
ella es prima de cama
verdadera concupina
y algunos a sus conpadres
diz que llevan el portasgo
enel ventajas las comadres
avnque sean sus cofadres

afirman el con padrasgo

****

<S 204-1>
secretarios y escrivanos
çircunçiden su mal modo
çircunçiden con sus manos
de fazer fechos tiranos
no pagen despues por todo
çircunçidense sederos
consejeros delos Reyes
non dar al Reyno dolores
pues en todos son primeros
non le quebranten sus leyes

<S 204-2>
çircunçidense seruidores
las sus caras con doss fazes
guarden se de ser traydores
a sus Reyes & señores
non tengan modo Rabazes
pues ayan tomen tal consejo
çircunçiden mal fazer
mudan su mal pellejo
& su consejo es de tener

****

<S 226>
Conparaçion

Como haze la candela
quando alunbra las conpañas
que con su luz los consuela
syn que de su mal le duela
pues se queman las entrañas
ansy letor sy lo vereys
aquestas gentes ebreas

se quemaron con sus leyes
dando grand luz a los Reyes
con su profeta micheas

<S 226a>
Y non seades la candela
que esta puesta en el candelar
que da luz aquien la vela
y ella de synon se Reçela
como sea de quemar
y nos mirad bien esta luçerna
avnque paresçe no agra
que ella quema la linterna
y su alma mucho ynferna
del que en pecado consagra

****

<S 361-1>

torna a la estoria

dexemos agora esto
y Reboluamos la mano
escreuir por orden puesto
el fecho muy desonesto
de aquel erodes tirano
por quien la cruel fazaña
la pena del obrador
a los señores de españa
faze enfrenar su saña
con barnada temor

<S 361-2>
Comiença la estoria

asi fue que ofresçidos
en el santo portalejo
los dones y Resçebidos
los tres Reyes despedidos

de la madre fijo y viejo
ya todos acordados
de tornar por do boluieron
desque fueron acostados
por el angel auisados
por estas palabras fueron

****

<S 374-2>
y desta cruel conquista
para ver lo verdadero
vayamos al coronista
apostol y euangelista
de todos quatro el primero
este llaman sant mateo
el qual sy lee quienquiera
fallaran segund yo creo
el tirano fecho feo
pasar por esta manera

****

S 390-1>
fin de los ynoçentes

O muy mas cruel que nero
Rey tirano enponçoñado
entre los fieros mas fiero
tan sangriento carrniçero
que ensangrientas mi tratado
queda quedate maldito
que pongo ffin a tu estoria
por torrnarme con mi escrito
para la tierra de egibto
tras el señor de la gloria

<S 390-2>
Ofreçer a mi memoria
en ffin del cuento tan triste

que en aquesta tu vitoria
a los Roçines de añoria
mucho erodes pareçiste
que piensan que van derechos
y andan al derredor
asy caminan tus fechos
por que mas tomes apechos
el degollar del Señor

<S 390-3>
oraçion de doña juana

Si por vno de los santos
ante dios son acabados
nuestros Sospiros y llantos
quanto mas seran por tantos
cuantos oy son degollados
pues por su mereçimiento
te pido niño diuino
que te fallen por çimiento
mis obras mi pensamiento
mi Reposo mi camino

****

<S 391>
muy alto & muy poderoso
prinçipe Rey y señor

las graçias mas espeçiales
los yngeños mas delgados
con vuestra alteza son tales
como los onbres codales
con gigantes cotejados
como negro etiopiano
delante lindo aleman
como en corte el aldeano
como paresçe el milano
delante del gauilan

<S 392>
mas por que el loor grosero
es a la virtud perfeta
como entiznado espolero
de quien toma el cauallero
espuelas con que arremeta
delibera mi Rudeza

muy magnifico señor
de loar a vuestra alteza
mas contra ajena pereza
que para vuestro loor

muy alto & muy poderoso
prínçipe Rey

WORKS CITED

RODRÍGUEZ PUÉRTOLAS, Julio, 1968a. *Fray Íñigo de Mendoza y sus 'Coplas de Vita Christi'*, Biblioteca Románica Hispanica, 4.5 (Madrid: Gredos).

——, ed., 1968b. Fray Íñigo de Mendoza, *Cancionero*, Clásicos Castellanos, 163 (Madrid: Espasa-Calpe).

SEVERIN, Dorothy Sherman, 2004. 'Las tres versiones de la *Vita Christi* de Fray Íñigo de Mendoza', in her *Del manuscrito a la imprenta en la época de Isabel la Católica*, Estudios de Literatura, 86 (Kassel: Reichenberger), pp. 47-67.

WHINNOM, Keith, 1962. 'The Printed Editions and Text of the Works of Fray Íñigo de Mendoza', *BHS*, 39: 137-52.

——, 1963. 'MS Escurialense K-III-7, el llamado "Cancionero de Fray Íñigo de Mendoza"', *Filología*, 7 (1961 [1963]): 161-72.

——, 1979. 'Fray Íñigo de Mendoza, Fra Jacobo Maza, and the Affiliation of Some Early MSS of the *Vita Christi*', *Annali di Ca' Foscari*, 16 (1977 [1979]): 129-39.

The Lady Is (in) the Garden: Fray Pedro de Valencia, 'En un vergel deleitoso' (*Baena* 505)

BARRY TAYLOR

(British Library)

Este dezir fizo e ordenó el dicho Maestro Fray Diego por amor e loores de una donzella que era muy fermosa e muy resplandeçiente, de qual era muy enamorado

1   En un vergel deleitoso
fui entrar por mi ventura,
do fallé toda dulçura
e plazer muy saboroso;
5   .... oso
la entrada fue escura,
morar muy peligroso.

En muy espessa montaña
10   este verger fue plantado,
de todas partes çercado
de ribera muy estraña;
al que una vez se baña
en su fuente perenal,
15   según curso natural,
la duçura lo engaña.

Pumas e muchas milgranas
lo çercan de toda parte,
non sé ome que se farte
20   de las sus frutas tempranas;
mas, amigos, non son sanas
para quien d'ellas mucho usa,
que usando non se escusa
que non mengüen las mançanas.

25   Calandras e ruiseñores
en él cantan noche e día,
e fazen gran melodía
en deslayos e discores;

From the 'Cancioneiro da Vaticana' to the 'Cancionero general': Studies in Honour of Jane Whetnall, ed. Alan Deyermond & Barry Taylor, PMHRS, 60 (London: Department of Hispanic Studies, Queen Mary, University of London, 2007), pp. 235–44. ISSN 1460–051X. ISBN 0 902238 50 7.

     e otras aves mejores,
30   papagayos, filomenas;
     en él cantan las serenas
     que adormeçen con amores.

     La entrada del vergel
     a mí fue siempre defesa,
35   mas, amigos, non me pesa
     por saber quanto es en él;
     es más dulce que la miel
     el roçío que d'él mana,
     que toda tristeza sana
40   el plazer que sale d'él
     (Dutton & González Cuenca 1993: 348–49; ID 1631).

Fray Pedro de Valencia de León (c. 1350–1412) has forty-three poems in the *Cancionero de Baena*. For Baena, this poem is in praise of a maiden, presumably human. However, we should not feel constrained by rubrics (cf. Gornall 1998 and 2004, Kennedy 2006). I think it is beyond doubt that this poem combines elements of courtly love and the love-cult of the Virgin Mary, derived from Christian readings of the Song of Songs; the question is the role and relative importance of these traditions. In this article I shall test four possible interpretations in which these two elements are present in varying proportions, in which the garden described refers to religion, the religion of love, a general description of the lady, or a sensual description of her body.

1. The Virgin

The Bride of the Song of Songs is called 'hortus conclusus' (4.12). By the fourth century Christian exegesis understood the Bride, and hence the garden, to be a figure of the Virgin Mary (Winston-Allen 1993: 155). By the later Middle Ages the image had been re-eroticized, as secular poets likened their earthly ladies to the Mother of God (Huizinga 1924: 136–59, Whetnall 1995).

In Spanish the best-known example of the garden as an image of Mary is the Prologue to Berceo's *Milagros* (Drayson 1981, Bayo 2005). The fountain, the fruit, the musical birds are found in both Fray Diego and Berceo. 'Pumas' and 'milgranas' are the fruits and pomegranates of Song 4.13: 'Emissiones tuae paradisus malorum punicorum [=milgranas], cum pomorum [=pumas] fructibus, cypri cum nardo' ('Thy plants are an orchard of pomegranates, with pleasant fruits; camphire, with spikenard', AV). 'Fuente' (14) reappears in an unambiguously Marian poem by Fray Diego, 'Virgen santa muy pura' (*Baena* 505) in which he calls Mary 'fuente perenal / do mana toda mesura' (ll. 7–8). The 'roçío' of l. 38 is also an image of Mary (Salzer 1886: 40–42 & 550–51). When Fray Diego says he may only contemplate the garden from a distance (33–40), he may be recalling that Mary is *hortus conclusus*.

However, the poet's acceptance of his exclusion sits ill with the concept of Mary as intercessor between man and God: as Berceo says with the voice of orthodoxy:

Ella es dicha puerta en sí bienençerrada,
pora nós es abierta por darnos la entrada
(*Milagros* 36ab, cited Bayo 2005: 57)

More importantly, the presence of various negative terms militates against a Marian reading: 'peligroso' (8), 'engaña' (16), 'non sanas' (21).

2. The Religion of Love

Wolf-Dieter Lange (1971: 122–24), following F. Bliss Luquiens (1905: 308) and Pierre Le Gentil (1949–53; I, 250–53), identifies Fray Diego's garden with the garden of love in the *Roman de la Rose*, lines 1330–32. (Charles F. Fraker, reviewing Lange, thought he makes the association 'too exclusively', 343.) Lange argues that at line 33 the poet 'turns away from his model [the *Roman de la Rose*] and spiritualizes the erotic situation in a Christian sense' (125), and relates the poem to medieval Spanish didactic works in which personifications inhabit a garden. This 'elevation of the context' is 'presumably explicable through the allegorizing model and the Christian tendencies of *amor cortés*' (125). However, Fray Diego does not make his didactic meaning explicit, nor does Lange.

3. The lady in the garden

Criticism has pointed out a parallel with the latter section of 'O comes amoris, dolor', preserved in the *Carmina burana*.[1]

1   O comes amoris, dolor,
     cujus mala male solor,
          An habes remedium?

4   Dolor urget me, nec mirum,
     quem a praedilecta dirum,
          En vocat exilium,

---

[1] I cannot find where I read this.

7   Cujus laus est singularis,
       pro qua non curasset Paris
              Helenae consortium.

10   Sed quid queror me remotum
       illi fore, quae devotum
              me fastidit hominem,

13   Cujus nomen tam verendum,
       quod nec mihi praesumendum
              Est ut eam nominem?

16   Ob quam causam mei mali
       me frequenter vultu tali
              Respicit, quo neminem.

19   Ergo solus solam amo,
       cujus captus sum ab hamo,
              Nec vicem reciprocat.

22   Quam enutrit vallis quaedam,
       quam ut paradisum credam,
              In qua pius collocat

25   Hanc creator creaturam
       vultu claram mente puram,
              Quam cor meum invocat.

28   Gaude, vallis insignita,
       vallis rosis redimita,
              Vallis flos convallium.

31   Inter valles vallis una,
       quam collaudat sol et luna,
              Dulcis cantus avium.

34   Te collaudat philomena,
       vallis dulcis et amoena,
              Maestis dans solacium.

Love's sorrows

[1] O sorrow, love's companion, whose ills I suffer ill, hast thou no remedy?

[4] Sorrow overwhelms me, and no wonder, since dread exile summons me from my beloved,

[7] whose renown is so matchless that for it Paris would have been indifferent to Helen's company.

[10] But why do I grieve that I shall be so far away from her who disdains me, the devoted vassal

[13] of one whose name is so much to be revered that I must not presume to name her,

[16] and who, because my love for her causes my misery, gives me a look such as she gives to no one else?

[19] So I alone love her alone on whose hook I am caught and who does not return my affection.

[22] Now some valley, which I would call Paradise, sustains her, in which the loving creator places

[25] this creature, lovely in countenance and pure in soul, whom my heart entreats.

[28] Rejoice, noble valley, valley covered with roses, valley the flower of valleys,

[31] the only valley among all valleys, which sun, moon, and the sweet song of birds extol together.

[34] The nightingale extols thee, sweet and pleasant valley, that givest comfort to the sorrowful. (Brittain 1962: 262–63)

At line 22, the Latin poet's attention shifts from the unfeeling lady to the valley which she inhabits. The valley is praised in the terms of the Song of Songs, but there is no reason to detect a religious subject here. Also in accordance with the Marian model, the valley functions as a metonym for the lady. The parts of the valley (roses, sun, moon, birds, nightingale) seem not to bear any specific meaning. This raises a general methodological point to which I shall return: must every element in an allegory have a specific meaning?

4. Carnality: the lady is the garden

Our poem displays a high percentage of language which may be interpreted as sensuous: 'deleitoso' (1), 'dulce' (3, 16, 37), 'plazer' (4, 40), 'saboroso' (4), 'natura, natural' (8, 15), 'fartarse' (19), 'frutas' (20).[2]

'Mana' (38) is an illogicality which validates the search for a hidden meaning: dew does not well up; it is 'the moisture deposited by minute drops upon any cool surface by the condensation of the vapour in the atmosphere; plentiful in the early morning. (Formerly supposed to fall softly from the heavens.)' (OED, s. v. dew). Elsewhere Fray Diego speaks of plants (514.7–8) and 'mesura' (503, cited above) which 'manan' from a 'fuente'. Although both expressions are metaphorical, the idea that such things rise up is consistent with literal hydraulics.

To my mind there are parallels with an English poem of the seventeenth century: William Cavendish, Duke of Newcastle, Love's Flowers:

[2] José Luis Gavilanes Laso 1999 proposes a sexual reading of the poem which seems to me under-documented.

From your lips I will pluck
Fresh roses, kisses suck,
And blow those budding leaves,
Rob you and so disseaves
5   Those odiferous
Fragrant love's flowers, thus.

It is no theft, for when
I kiss, you take't again
And doth your lips renew
10 with your own honied dew
And natural showers got
from your tongue's water-pot.

When my lip, heated, seeks
Love's cooler walks, your cheeks;
15 Or wandering loves to rove
In thickets, your hair's grove;
Or on love's mounts that's fair,
Your panting breasts, gives air;

Or bathe me in love's pool
20 My heated love to cool;
Or in love's grotto shun
your eyes, each a hot sun:
Fresh fountains there will please me,
With sweet fanned air to ease me.
(Broadbent 1974: II, 327–28)

Newcastle's editor glosses 'pool' as 'navel' and 'grotto' as 'vulva', although without supporting references. His interpretation is logical: the lover's kisses move from love's walks (14), love's grove (16), and love's mounts (17), all clarified as cheeks, hair, and breasts, to the veiled love's pool and grotto (19, 21).

In the light of Newcastle's *dew*, *pool* and *grotto*, we might add *fuente* (14) and *rocío* (38) to our list of possible sexual terms. These intuitions need to be objectified. The main Spanish source for verifying carnal meanings is *Poesía erótica del Siglo de Oro* (*PESO*) (Alzieu et al. 2000). This work, which gathers a corpus of anonymous works from 1580 to 1700, stands out from other work on sexual language such as Cela's *Diccionario secreto* in its mature attitude to the subject and its no-nonsense clarity, albeit couched in the decent obscurity of a dead language. All too often studies of sexual language can be both prurient and twee. *PESO*, first published in 1975, complements the conclusions of Keith Whinnom (1970 and 1981) on the fifteenth century, although the authors do not seem aware of his work (Whetnall 2007).

Djordjina Trubarac, in her study of the golden apples, remarks of Fray Diego:

> no resulta difícil reconocer detrás de ese paradisíaco 'vergel' y sus 'alre-
> dedores', una posible descripción de la fisionomía femenina. En nuestro
> caso, de mayor interés que el 'vergel' serían sus 'alrededores', puesto que
> en ellos es donde aparecen las granadas y las manzanas sin que se men-
> cionen los frutales. Las frutas eróticas, como naranjas y limones,
> identificadas con las partes del cuerpo femenino, son bien conocidas en la
> lírica española y de muchos otros pueblos. Parece ser que que el poeta (no
> olvidemos que se trata de un fraile), quiere expresar la admiración por los
> encantos de su amada, pero a la vez quiere exculpar el hecho de rehuirla,
> diciendo que ese atractivo puede ser engañoso respecto a la vida eterna y
> por lo tanto, peligroso. (2001: 321-22)

To Trubarac's comments we may add the following data from *PESO*.

huerto: nos 88, 137; huerta 79; jardín 114a

deleite: 5, 14, 16, 40; deleitoso 11.

dulce: nos 11, 25, 40, 61, 94, 98, 100, 101, 124a, 136, 136a, 143(18).

sabroso: 2, 25, 40, 49, 64, 85, 94, 98, 138.

natura: 2a, 22, 79, 109, 118. 'Natura' can be *cunnus*, but I think here it has the association with Aristotelian materialism (Scaglione 1963; Rico 1985). Elsewhere in Fray Diego 'natura' seems to mean 'body':

> pues es su natura muy floxa e blanda,
> dezidles que usen de poca vianda
> ca d'esta figura Ipocras lo manda.
> (*Baena* 509.25; ID 1635)

manzanas: not in *PESO*, but cf. 'fruta' which can be male or fe-male: 79, 85, 117.

rocío: 79, 80[3]

manar: 136a; agua: 139.

PESO then supplies sensual meanings for a number of words in Fray Diego's poem; all these words also have innocent meanings, most obviously *dulce*, a staple of the literature of love and of reli-gion. Indeed, in order for allusive and playful writing to make its effect, it is essential that such terms should be ambiguous. The evidence in *PESO* can only support a sensual reading but not clinch it. Back to the text. In the light of the material gathered here, I propose this reading. The garden means the lady, who incarnates

---

[3] See also Deyermond in press.

sensual pleasures ('deleitoso', 'dulçura', 'plazer saboroso') (1–8). Her body, a work of Nature, is also dangerous (7–8). Lines 13–16 make the same point: her fountain (a part of her body), also a work of Nature, is treacherous. ('Fuente' I think is *cunnus*, but it is not documented.) Lines 21–24 mean: these fruits are not good for the health of him who makes much use of them, for by using them he cannot avoid the apples becoming wasted/depleted (his *testes* will wither from over-exertion). The sweet dew which flows from the garden is her *lubricatio*. The 'espessa montaña' is likely *pubes*, but I have not been able to document this reading.

What of the flora and fauna, the *pumas* and *milgranas* (17) and *calandras*, *ruiseñores* etc. (25–32)? In my reading, the relationship between lady and garden varies from a general parallelism to a detailed correspondence of parts: *frutas* are general, *mançanas* are specific; *calandras* seem general, *vergel* specific. In properly Marian allegory (as in Berceo), the fruits etc. have specific meanings. In 'O comes doloris' they seem not to. Nor do they in Fray Diego. Does this indicate a difference between the workings of Biblical exegesis, which is required to be comprehensive, and non-Biblical poetry which is not?

5. Conclusion

My reading of this poem agrees only in part with Baena's rubric: 'Este dezir fizo e ordenó el dicho Maestro Fray Diego por amor e loores de una donzella que era muy fermosa e muy resplandeçiente, de qual era muy enamorado.' Its subject is 'amor' (the word 'amores' appears in line 32), in the sensual meaning. Fray Diego's sly references to the sexual organs make his poem more burlesque than a paean 'de loores'.

WORKS CITED

ALZIEU, Pierre, Robert JAMMES, & Yvan LISSORGUES, ed., 2000. *Poesía erótica del Siglo de Oro*, 2nd ed., Biblioteca de Bolsillo, 42 (Barcelona: Crítica). First edition 1975.

BAYO, Juan Carlos, 2005. 'La alegoría en el prólogo de los *Milagros de Nuestra Señora* de Berceo', in *Transformaciones de la alegoría*, ed. Rebeca Sanmartín Bastida & Rosa Vidal Doval (Madrid: Iberoamericana; Frankfurt am Main: Vervuert), pp. 51–69.

BRITTAIN, Frederick, ed. & tr., 1962. *The Penguin Book of Latin Poetry* (Harmondsworth: Penguin).

BROADBENT, John, ed., 1974. *Signet Classic Poets of the 17th Century*, 2 vols (New York: New American Library).

DEYERMOND, Alan, in press. 'The Wind and the Small Rain: Traditional Images in a Late-Medieval English Court Song and their Contemporary Castilian Analogues'.

DRAYSON, Elizabeth, 1981. 'Some Possible Sources for the Introduction to Berceo's *Milagros de Nuestra Señora*', *MAe*, 50: 274–83.

DUTTON, Brian, & Joaquín GONZÁLEZ CUENCA, ed., 1993. *Cancionero de Juan Alfonso de Baena*, Biblioteca Filológica Hispana, 14 (Madrid: Visor).

FRAKER, Charles F., 1974. Review of Lange 1971, *HR*, 42: 341–43.

GAVILANES LASO, José Luis, 1999. 'El sexo femenino como "locus amoenus": Fray Diego de Valencia de León y otros ejemplos', in *Amor y erotismo en la literatura, congreso internacional, Salamanca 1988* (Salamanca: Caja Duero), pp. 385–94.

GORNALL, John, 1998. 'How Reliable is a *Razo*? Attribution and Genre in *Baena* 40/556 and 557',*C*, 26.2: 227–41.

——, 2004. 'How Far Should We Trust Rubricators? Three *Invenciones* from the *Cancionero general* of 1511 Re-examined', *BSS*, 81: 363–67.

HUIZINGA, Johann, 1924. *The Waning of the Middle Ages: A Study of the Forms of Life, Thought and Art in France and the Netherlands in the Fourteenth and Fifteenth Centuries*, tr. F. Hopman (London: Edward Arnold).

KENNEDY, Kirstin, 2006. 'Do Cancionero Rubrics Help Solve *Invenciones?*', *Proceedings of the Thirteenth Colloquium*, ed. Jane Whetnall & Alan Deyermond, PMHRS, 51, pp. 137–46.

LANGE, Wolf-Dieter, 1971. *El fraile trobador: Zeit, Leben und Werk des Diego de Valencia de León (1350?–1412?)*, Analecta Romanica, 28 (Frankfurt am Main: Vittorio Klostermann).

LE GENTIL, Pierre, 1949–53. *La Poésie lyrique espagnole et portugaise à la fin du Moyen Âge*, 2 vols (Rennes: Plihon).

LUQUIENS, F. Bliss, 1907. 'The *Roman de la Rose* and Medieval Castilian Literature', *Romanische Forschungen*, 20: 284–320.

RICO, Francisco, 1985. '"Por aver mantenencia": el aristotelismo heterodoxo en el *Libro de buen amor*', *El Crotalón: Anuario de Filología Española*, 2: 169–98.

SALZER, Anselm, 1886. *Die Sinnbilder und Beiworte Mariens in der deutschen Literatur und lateinischen Hymnenpoesie des Mittelalters: mit Berücksichtigung der patristischen Literatur: eine literar-historische Studie* (Linz: K. K. Ober-Gymnasium).

SCAGLIONE, Aldo, 1963. *Nature and Love in the Late Middle Ages* (Berkeley: University of California Press).

TRUBARAC, Djordjina, 2001. 'Las manzanas de oro: un motivo en las líricas populares española y serbia', *Dicenda*, 19: 315–36.

WHETNALL, Jane, 1995. 'El *Cancionero general* de 1511: textos únicos y textos omitidos', in *Medioevo y literatura: Actas del V Congreso de la Asociación Hispánica de Literatura Medieval (Granada, 27 septiembre – 1 octubre 1993)*, ed. Juan Paredes (Granada: Universidad, 1995), IV, pp. 505–15.

——, 2007. 'Whinnom and the *Cancioneros*', in *Keith Whinnom after Twenty Years: His Work and its Influence*, ed. Alan Deyermond, PMHRS, 53.

WHINNOM, Keith, 1970. 'Hacia una interpretación y apreciación de las canciones del *Cancionero general* de 1511', *Filología*, 13 (1968–69 [1970]): 361–81.

——, 1981. *La poesía amatoria en la época de los Reyes Católicos*, Durham Modern Language Series, 2 (Durham: University of Durham).

WINSTON-ALLEN, Anne, 1993. '"Minne" in Spiritual Gardens of the Fifteenth Century', in *Canon and Canon Transgression in Medieval German Literature*, ed. Albrecht Classen, Göppinger Arbeiten zur Germanistik, 573 (Göppingen: Kümmerle), pp. 153–62.

Other Lost Voices: A Note on the *Soldadeira*

JULIAN WEISS

(King's College London)

The desire to recover a literary landscape and identify the traces of the writers and texts that populate it has been a constant inspiration in Jane Whetnall's work, in particular in her ground-breaking research on the late-medieval Castilian lyric. Though it was never published, her Cambridge PhD thesis (1986) marked a significant step in the revisionist readings of the once scorned *cancionero* verse which gathered momentum in the 1980s. Indeed, one might characterize this process of recovery as, first and foremost, the recuperation of lost voices. Throughout work published over three decades, we see an interest in voice in several senses of the term. First, there is a fascination for voice as such: the literal — and now for the most part lost — voicing of the lyric, the song as recorded in and transformed by writing. To illustrate the span of this interest, one only has to set her 1989 study on the *canción* alongside her 2005 article on intercalated quotations. In the former, she examines the tension inherent in the *canción* as, by the end of the Middle Ages, it acquired an increasingly textual status and distanced itself from its vestigial musicality. Published in 2005, '"Veteris vestigia flammae": a la caza de la cita cancioneril' picks up threads from her earlier study (1989: 199–201), though ultimately its roots lie deeper, in her 1986 thesis. In this essay, the implications of which I shall discuss below, she explores the power of music to cross frontiers, carrying fragments of text with it. Secondly, there is voice as source. In her remarkable 2006 essay, she uncovers the traces of a dialogue between *cancionero* poets and Petrarch: findings that are possible only to someone with a formidable command of the textual evidence and an ear finely tuned to poetic nuance. In this essay one of the poets studied is Florencia Pinar, which illustrates a third aspect of Jane Whetnall's interest in voice: the fact that it is

From the 'Cancioneiro da Vaticana' to the 'Cancionero general': Studies in Honour of Jane Whetnall, ed. Alan Deyermond & Barry Taylor, PMHRS, 60 (London: Department of Hispanic Studies, Queen Mary, University of London, 2007), pp. 245-56. ISSN 1460–051X. ISBN 0 902238 50 7.

gendered, and that women's voices have consistently been silenced or marginalized.

Symptomatic of both research agenda and method is 'Isabel González of the *Cancionero de Baena* and Other Lost Voices' (1992). This pioneering and judicious study is a fundamental point of reference for anyone interested in women's role in the production of late-medieval Castilian court poetry, and my own debt to it should be evident from my title.[1] In it, Jane Whetnall surveys the extant written record for the traces of female-authored texts, and considers various factors that led to the exclusion or marginalization of women as poets. These range from a particular compiler's embargo on women's poetry to the more covert, but equally disabling, masculinist literary conventions of the literary establishment, which make woman the object but never the active subject of courtly desire, or which marginalize the popular verse forms — ballad and folksong — most closely associated with the feminine, whether through composition or transmission. It is highly characteristic of her work that she never presents a one-sided formulation of the problem; she never regards women as victims, either of their own incapacity or of male conspiracy:

> None of these women are [...] isolated, lone voices (though there is every reason to believe that they were isolated in respect of each other): male sympathy and, effectively, patronage undoubtedly played an essential part in the preservation of poems that circulated only in the private sphere. (1992: 73)

The parenthetical remark is worth glossing. Though she recovers a range of textual evidence for female authorship, she is reluctant to cluster it together as a network or reconstruct it as a tradition. To be sure, there were female voices, and women had an active role and presence in the literary world, but the texts penned by women could not coalesce into anything as coherent and ideologically effective as a tradition, which might enable them to overcome the misogynist assumptions that made an oxymoron out of 'female authorship', and to collaborate on equal footing with men. They were 'full participants in the literary life of the court' (73), but as unequal members of a hierarchy.

---

[1] It has also been a foundational study for my other contributions to the field, e.g, most recently 2006b. Another early example of her research on the connection between gender and genre is her study of the *lírica femenina* (1984).

As this summary indicates, Jane Whetnall's research obviously goes beyond the important archeological recovery of empirical evidence. Hers is an archeology of a cultural context, recovering documents and placing them, through an act of creative interpretation, back into the social and cultural relations in which they were produced. This interpretative move returns us to her abiding interest in two of the three aspects of voice mentioned above: the voice of woman as author and the voice of the poem as sound and music. As I mentioned above, in the essay '"Veteris vestigia flammae": a la caza de la cita cancioneril' (2005) we trace back to its French roots the fragmentary quotation of a song woven into a Castilian poem by the Leonese poet Juan de Tapia, who wrote in the Neapolitan courts of Alfonso el Magnánimo and his son, Ferrán. What in other hands might have been a rather sterile exercise in source hunting becomes the solid foundation for some highly suggestive speculations on the more intangible domains of cultural research. These quotations, she writes:

> son una muestra del poder de la canción para cruzar fronteras, sean de tiempo o de espacio, y para traspasar los límites de la comprensión lingüística [...]. Es un poder del que carece la letra de un poema por sí sola. Aun cuando la melodía se haya perdido irremediablemente, no nos desanimemos, no debería importarnos demasiado: podemos suplirla con un esfuerzo de la imaginación. Hacer caso omiso de tales canciones significa renunciar a una fuente riquísima y sugerente. (2005: 190)

Linking this interest in song to the problem of women's role in the (re)production of court culture leads us to the shadowy figure of the female minstrel, who, like her male counterpart, was instrumental — indeed literally so — in enabling music and text to 'cruzar fronteras [...] de tiempo o de espacio'.[2]

Long ago, Ramón Menéndez Pidal pointed out a paradox at the heart of one area of the written record concerning the female minstrel, or *soldadera*, one of the amorphous category of singers, dancers, musicians, acrobats, and mimes that drew such opprobrium from medieval moralists for their capacity to inspire lewdness. Speaking of Maria Pérez, la Balteira, the most infamous of the *soldadeiras* of the Galician-Portuguese tradition, he observed that:

---

[2] The international character of minstrelsy was emphasized by Menéndez Pidal 1942, in what remains the basic point of departure for research into the *juglares*. For more recent studies, with ample bibliographies, see Rodríguez Velasco 1999 and Filios 2005; I return to the latter work below.

Todo cuanto ella hacía caía en gracia y era motivo de chacota; mas de sus
habilidades artísticas en el canto o en el baile ninguno dice una palabra, y,
sin embargo, esas habilidades eran las que le daban entrada en la corte.[3]

The contradiction is thrown into relief by the number of satirical
poems about male *juglares*, which, besides the usual array of invectives that target various forms of social, sexual, and moral
inadequacy, explicitly engage with their role and conduct as performers and aspiring composers. A useful taxonomy of these social
and literary conflicts has been compiled by Joaquim Ventura (1993:
545–46), who also makes passing note of the silencing of the
woman's role as performer (539).

Amongst those who have written on the literary representation
of the *soldadeira*, Denise K. Filios has done most to explore the gap
between historical profession and poetic portrayal (2005: esp. 1–82;
see also Filios 1998). There is not the space here to summarize this
major book in the detail it warrants, but her attempt to resituate
the surviving poetic texts in the context of their thirteenth-century
performance is methodologically analogous to the impulse that
drives some of Jane Whetnall's research into the later period. This
is to say that besides drawing on documentary evidence, an eclectic range of modern critical approaches, and close textual analysis,
her attempt to reconstruct the ways in which the *soldadeiras* par-
ticipated in the performance of invectives about themselves is also
a self-conscious product of 'un esfuerzo de la imaginación' (Whetnall 2005: 190). Filios draws a speculative, but compelling, picture
of the *soldadeira* as a 'ritually deviant insider' (2005: 36), who enacts
misogynist fantasies of womanhood even as she might often undermine male fantasies through mime, tone of voice, and ironic
gestures, in the process underscoring the fact that many invectives
of these camp-followers, or prostitute-singers, are already indis-
solubly linked to mockery of men's own vice and inadequacy.

In general terms, the satirical representation of the *soldadeira*
starts with an anecdote. Given a tendency to read some invectives
as historically accurate, it is worth pointing out that although they

[3] 121–35, at p. 135. This scholar's biography of her, based on the evidence of the
cantigas d'escarnho, needs to be revised in the light of Carlos Alvar's historical research, which demonstrates that there were at least two Marias Pérez (1985: 11–
20). I was unable to locate this article, but I am deeply grateful to the author for
providing a detailed synopsis. For an important recent general study of Galician-
Portuguese invective, see Liu 2004, and for a comprehensive bibliography see
Wright 1998: esp. 116–18.

purport to be inspired by actual events and conduct, this anecdotal character is not a mimetic exercise — a drawing from life — but a display of the poet's ability to embellish established rhetorical and thematic convention.[4] In large measure, these conventions derive from the storehouse of medieval misogyny: female deceit, cunning, insatiable sexual desire, garrulousness mingled with various other manifestations of immorality, such as irreligiosity, superstition, gambling, and vanity.

The insatiable, castrating female is a prominent motif, and it expresses a typically masculine anxiety over sexual and social mastery, albeit expressed in self-consciously comic mode. The sexual competitiveness that underpins many an invective aimed at the *soldadeira* can be interpreted on various levels. For example, in Alfonso X's *cantiga* 11 (*Cantigas* 1965; Paredes 2000), we see Joan Rodríguiz measuring beams to rebuild Maria Balteira's house. Balteira, with undisguised pride, declares that to give satisfaction the beam needs to be of the broadest girth possible: 'Esta é a medida d'Espanha, / ca non de Lombardia nen d'Alemanha' (ll. 16–17). The rather obvious phallic pun evokes the physical as well as the libidinal sexual capacity of the female, and although in other poems this capaciousness inspires masculine nervousness and wonder, here it is the occasion for Alfonso X to suggest that Spaniards can measure up, unlike their courtly counterparts in Lombardy and Germany. It is no coincidence that these two countries are those mentioned in the exordium of the *Razón de amor* as the *fons et origo* of courtliness. Through the imagined speech of Balteira, Alfonso X, like so many other medieval poets, plays with the boundary separating — and linking — refined sexual conduct and unrestrained desire.

This is one of the few *cantigas* in which the *soldadeira*'s voice is poetically represented (see also *Cantigas* 1965, nos 14, 191, 313, and 1, which I discuss below). But even so, she is still far from being explicitly acknowledged as court entertainer and performer. What matters is her body, the reactions it inspires, and its symbolic potential. To illustrate the symbolic and ideological nexus between the grotesque female body and the silencing of her minstrelsy, we can simply point to one of the more aggressively obscene invectives in the corpus, written by Afonso Eanes do Coton: 'Marinha, en tanto folegares' (*Cantigas* 1965: no. 52). Here, the poet expresses bewildered

---

[4] For examples of the tendency to reconstruct historical reality on the basis of poetic fiction see Rodrigues Lapa's notes to poem 425 (*Cantigas* 1965).

astonishment that, in the act of copulating, Marinha does not burst ('rebentar'), even though he has covered up each of her orifices (mouth, nostrils, ears, eyes, vagina and rectum). This extraordinary poem has been discussed by various scholars, who read its portrayal of sexual rivalry from different perspectives and with different emphases.[5] It is a graphic representation of the female body as orifice, which man inevitably strives to plug, albeit with greater urgency and uncomprehending desperation than in Alfonso's poem. If Marinha is indeed a *soldadeira*, we do not have to read this poem in narrowly sexual terms, and we might legitimately wonder about the kind of connection that could be drawn between her insatiable orifices and her role as singer/ entertainer.[6]

Why the body? Feminist scholars, drawing on medieval medical, moral, and philosophical evidence, have long established the ideological association between a woman's physiology and her speech. When woman speaks, often though not exclusively in the more carnivalesque literary modes, it is 'bodytalk', to borrow the title of Jane Burns's book on Old French literature (1993; see also Filios 2005: 27-28). Thus, the poem about Marinha could perhaps be read figuratively as an expression of man's frustrated desire to control female speech: he can shut her up, but there is something resistant about her body/talk that escapes his understanding. And yet, in this poem, and in the case of the *cantigas d'escarnho* more generally, I think there are more precise ideological pressures at work. The links between female performers and perceived sexual availability are widely acknowledged and amply documented. I would argue, therefore, that these poems represent the consequences of female minstrelsy — the lust, the degradation, the grotesque physicality thought to be produced when a woman performs.[7] In short, performance is textually

---

[5] See Filios (2005: 33-35), who gives references to other interpretations, and my own brief note in 2006a: 194.

[6] Marinha, also the name of the protagonist of nos 225 and 341, is never actually named as a *soldadeira*, although in his notes to these poems Rodrigues Lapa suggests that she may be one. The looseness with which the term is applied raises a question that cannot be properly explored here, namely that the satire directed at some women is aimed at courtly ladies, as in the later traditions of Castilian *cancionero* verse (the 'burlas provocantes a risa') or sixteenth-century anti-Petrarchism.

[7] Typical of ecclesiastical attitudes is Martín Pérez's *Libro de las confesiones* (XIVc), on which see Filios 2005: 15-16. Later, Filios suggests that 'perhaps anxiety about the potentially polluting effect of soldadeiras' offstage performances caused their onstage acts to be passed over in silence' (44). I think she is right, but I would add that the onstage performances are of equal concern at an ideological level.

there, but only as an embedded effect. To portray this effect explicitly as the result of a female minstrel singing, accompanying, or dancing would be counterproductive, since it would call into question the ethical basis of court performance itself, which relied so heavily on professional minstrels. As is well known, these were welcomed as essential members of court society, even as their suspect and dangerous presence was invigilated and regulated by lawmakers and moralists (Menéndez Pidal 1942: 41–64; Filios 2005: 16–18 & 38–42).

The ambivalent general status of minstrelsy itself helps explain why the body of the *soldadeira* inspires such a mixture of fascination and loathing. But there is also ambivalence on a more particular level, given the bonds that tied poet to minstrel in an unequal though mutually dependent relationship. If the *juglar* depended upon the court poet for his livelihood, the latter depended upon him for bringing his verse to life in song and performance, enabling it, as Jane Whetnall observed, to 'cruzar fronteras [...] de tiempo o de espacio' (2005: 190). Given prevailing patriarchal attitudes, one can understand the ideological pressures to silence the singing voice and physical performance of the *soldadeira*.

These hypotheses can be explored through textual analysis of an invective that happens to be, significantly perhaps, the very first poem in Rodrigues Lapa's collection (*Cantigas* 1965; poem 364 of the *Colocci-Brancuti* songbook). It is the first of Alfonso X's *cantigas* about Maria Balteira — at least we presume it is she, although the first line is missing.[8]

> [Maria Pérez vi muita' assanhada,]
> por que lhi rogava que perdoasse
> Pero d'Ambroa, que lo non matasse,
> nen fosse contra el desmesurada.
> E diss' ela: 'Por Deus, non me roguedes,
> ca direi-vos de min o que i entendo:
> se ũa vez assanhar me fazedes,
> saberedes quaes peras eu vendo.'

The poem's position and the missing line make it doubly symbolic of the ambivalent status of the *soldadeira* in court society: at once symbolically central and anonymous. This dual status is also reflected in the poem's content. This is one of the very few poems

---

[8] The poem is unique to *Colocci-Brancuti,* and it heads the sequence of satires and invectives composed by the Wise King. The identification of Maria Balteira is plausible on internal grounds. See also Filios (2005: 64–67), whose reading differs from mine in several respects.

in which the *soldadeira*'s voice is represented. Following the out-
burst quoted above, the remainder of the poem (three and a half
stanzas) is a lively tirade against the King for having interceded on
behalf of the insolent Pero d'Ambroa. According to Rodrigues Lapa, Maria's indignation is provoked by two of Pero d'Ambroa's
mocking invectives found elsewhere in the *Cancioneiro*.[9] Leaving
aside the difficulties of textual identification, the woman's speech
is, as I have suggested, marked by an oxymoron, or a contradictory
binarism of presence and absence. This is to say that although the
fictional voice of Maria is marked by self-righteous anger and confidence in her rhetorical power to put people in their place, her
actual verbal prowess is put in abeyance: it is a threatening, yet
forever unrealized, potentiality. Her real power is hidden away,
and her answering back is postponed.

Alfonso's representation of this angry female also dwells on her
assumed emancipation from the courtly bonds of *mesura*. As we
have seen, in the opening stanza she has brushed aside the royal
plea not to be 'desmesurada' (l. 4), and in the second she justifies
her rage in no uncertain terms. Not only does she assert that the
King's own request is inappropriate ('desguisada'), but she also
questions his own role as arbiter of courtliness: 'e non sei eu quen
vo-lo outorgasse' (l. 10) and declares once again that the King (and
presumably his entire court) fails to recognize her true self: 'pois
vejo que me non conhecedes' (l. 13). These details, and others like
them, show how the King uses this poem as a vehicle for fairly
conventional representation of the symbolic feminine: woman as a
trope for excess, the unknown, the chaotic, and the contestatory.

Alfonso fleshes out his otherwise stereotypical portrait with
some interesting touches, which lends Maria's voice a more nu-
anced tone. At the very centre of the poem we read the following
declaration of proud autonomy: 'E, se m'eu quisesse seer viltada, /
ben acharia quen xe me viltasse' (ll. 17–18). This amusingly ironic
detail — 'I'll choose who I am going to be insulted by' — marries
the contradiction between her freedom (to choose) and her fate (to
be degraded). The words and posture attributed to this woman

[9] Rodrigues Lapa cites nos 341 and 342, although these numbers do not coincide
either with the numeration of *Colocci-Brancuti* or with his own, which record five
cantigas in which Pero d'Ambroa attacks women: 329, 331, 333, 335, and 337. Of
these, two name Balteira explicitly (329 and 335), one cites Maior Garcia (333), with
the other two women being anonymous. Poem 335 is thematically linked to Alfonso's poem, since it also refers to Balteira's injured honour.

remind me of a *mote* composed centuries later by one of the female correspondents of Fernando de la Torre, who signs her often con- flictive exchange of epistles with this courtier with the opaque phrase 'Ni quiere quien puede'. Jane Whetnall was the first to draw out the meaning and implications of a conceit that expresses the anonymous woman's desire to demonstrate that she under- stood the rules that enabled her participation in the literary game, but also her reluctance to be utterly governed by them.[10]

The other more noteworthy element is the refrain that ties to- gether the various strands of this vision of injured female pride: 'se ũa vez assanhar me fazedes, / saberedes quaes peras eu vendo'. This recognition of the female propensity to talk back bears two markers of social class. First, there is the colloquialism that, as Rodrigues Lapa points out in his notes, evokes a contemporary popular proverb: '"Com teu amo não jogues as peras", isto é, "não te metas com ele, que ficarás mal"' (*Cantigas* 1965: 1). At the risk of forcing the interpretation, Alfonso's adaptation of the proverb, turning it into what Filios calls the protagonist's 'personal motto' (2005: 65), may also be significant. These 'peras', the symbols of Maria's superior retaliatory powers, are for sale. As figurative merchandise, they evoke not just any speech but a minstrel's per- formance of invective, bought and sold on the courtly market.[11]

To sum up these notes, we can move forward four centuries to another fictional *soldadera* whose voice is for hire: La Chispa, from Calderón's *El Alcalde de Zalamea*. The fact that this camp-follower is portrayed explicitly as a singer, and not primarily as a whore, is an indication of the cultural changes that have enabled *soldaderas* to be at least culturally visible as performers, even if not morally and socially respected (e.g. the spread of female literacy, the popularity of *lírica femenina*). And yet it is a sign of the enduring power of this fictional type and the patriarchal attitudes that underpin it that Calderón's portrayal of La Chispa bears such a strong affinity with the invectives written four centuries earlier. Quick-tempered, cun- ning, witty, fond of gambling and drink, and handy with a knife, she is endowed with an inexhaustible supply of song. Beyond her

---

[10] See Whetnall (1992: 73–74), further glossed by Weiss (2006b: 1148–49). Similarly, Filios points out that *soldadeiras* 'played along with their assigned role of deviant insider [in order to] maintain a place at court' (2005: 30).

[11] For Alfonso X's strictures against the commercialization of verse, see Filios (2005: 13 and 28).

characterization, it is her social and thematic function that provides the most telling comparison with the representation of the earlier *soldadeiras*. Though she sells her voice to Don Álvaro and joins the plot to carry off Pedro Crespo's daughter, her songs also provide an ironic and critical commentary on the actions of her superiors. Her songs, therefore, are both complicit in and independent of dominant aristocratic values — they are those of a deviant insider, to borrow Filios's epithet. Before Pedro Crespo turns to address the audience, she is given the final words of the play, in which she recalls her willingness to confess her role in the rape when faced by the instruments of torture. Unlike her companion Rebolledo, she resolutely insists that she will continue to sing out, 'cuantas veces a mirar / llegue al pasado instrumento' (2763–64; Calderón 2000). In a play whose themes cluster around the nature of truth — is Crespo's execution of Don Álvaro justice or revenge? — it is no accident that the dilemma finally converges on the singing of this socially marginal yet symbolically central figure. The concluding pun on 'cantar' — irrepressible truth-telling or contemptible entertainment — neatly encapsulates the *soldadera*'s necessary though unsettling and ambiguous presence in official culture.

WORKS CITED

ALVAR, Carlos, 1985. 'María Pérez, Balteira', *Archivo de Filología Aragonesa*, 36–37: 11–40.

BURNS, E. Jane, 1993. *Bodytalk: When Women Speak in Old French Literature* (Philadelphia: Univ. of Pennsylvania Press).

CALDERÓN DE LA BARCA, Pedro, 2000. *El garrote más bien dado o El Alcalde de Zalamea*, ed. Ángel Valbuena Briones, Letras Hispánicas, 67 (Madrid: Cátedra).

Cantigas 1965. *Cantigas d'escarnho e de mal dizer dos cancioneros medievais galego-portugueses*, ed. M. Rodrigues Lapa (Coimbra: Galaxia).

FILIOS, Denise K., 1998. 'Jokes on *Soldadeiras* in the *Cantigas de escarnio e de mal dizer'*, *C*, 26.2: 29–39.

——, 2005. *Performing Women in the Middle Ages: Sex, Gender, and the Medieval Iberian Lyric* (New York: Palgrave Macmillan).

LIU, Benjamin, 2004. *Medieval Joke Poetry: The 'Cantigas d'Escarnho e de Mal Dizer'* (Cambridge, MA: Dept of Comparative Literature, Harvard University).

MENÉNDEZ PIDAL, Ramón, 1942. *Poesía juglaresca y juglares: aspectos de la historia literaria y cultural de España*, Colección Austral, 300 (Madrid: Espasa-Calpe).

PAREDES, Juan, 2000. *Cantigas de escarnio y maldecir de Alfonso X: problemas de interpretación y de crítica textual*, PMHRS, 22.

RODRÍGUEZ VELASCO, Jesús D., 1999. *Castigos para celosos, consejos para juglares* (Madrid: Gredos).

VENTURA, Joaquim, 1993. 'Sátira e aldraxe entre trobadores e xograis', in *O cantar dos trobadores: Actas do Congreso celebrado en Santiago de Compostela entre os días 26 e 29 de abril de 1993*, Colección de Difusión Cultural, 2 (Santiago de Compostela: Xunta de Galicia), pp. 533–50.

WEISS, Julian, 2006a. *The 'Mester de Clerecía': Intellectuals and Ideologies in Thirteenth-Century Castile*, CT, A231 (Woodbridge: Tamesis).

——2006b. 'What Every Noblewoman Needs to Know: Cultural Literacy in Late-Medieval Spain', *Speculum*, 81: 1118–49.

WHETNALL, Jane, 1984. '*Lírica femenina* in the Early Manuscript *Cancioneros*', in *What's Past is Prologue: A Collection of Essays in Honour of L. J. Woodward*, ed. Salvador Bacarisse et al. (Edinburgh: Scottish Academic Press), pp. 138–50 & 171–75.

——, 1986. 'Manuscript Love Poetry of the Spanish Fifteenth Century: Developing Standards and Continuing Traditions', PhD thesis (Univ. of Cambridge).

——, 1989. 'Songs and *Canciones* in the *Cancionero general* of 1511', in *The Age of the Catholic Monarchs, 1474–1516: Literary Studies in Memory of Keith Whinnom*, ed. Alan Deyermond & Ian Macpherson (Liverpool: UP), pp. 197–207.

——, 1992. 'Isabel González of the *Cancionero de Baena* and Other Lost Voices', *C*, 21.1: 59–82.

——, 2005. '"Veteris vestigia flammae": a la caza de la cita cancioneril', in *I canzonieri di Lucrezia / Los cancioneros de Lucrecia: Atti del convegno internazionale sulle raccolte poetiche iberiche dei secoli XV–XVII*, Ferrara, 7–9 ottobre 2002, ed. Andrea Baldissera & Giuseppe Mazzocchi (Padova: Unipress), pp. 179–92.

——, 2006. 'Las transformaciones de Petrarca en cuatro poetas de cancionero: Santillana, Carvajales, Cartagena y Florencia Pinar', *Cancionero General*, 4: 81–108.

WRIGHT, Janice, 1998. 'Reference Bibliography', *C*, 26.2: 91–129.

Note on the Illustrations

p. 190   Crossbowmen practising at the target; trained dogs retrieving the arrows.

p. 244   *Le Roman de la Rose, aultrement dit le songe du vergier* (Paris, c. 1520).

p. 254   *Soldadeira* (with drum) and acrobat.

p. 256   Above, male and female *juglares*, with musical instruments (from the *Cantigas de Santa Maria*, Escorial MS b-I-2). Below, *trovador, juglar* with vihuela, and singer with drum (from the *Cancioneiro da Ajuda*).

Index of *Cancionero* Numbers

Index of ID Numbers
Only numbers given in the text, not those of poems
whose numbers are not given, are indexed here.

Index of First Lines

Index of Scholars

Names of scholars are indexed when their work is quoted, summarized, or discussed (however briefly), but not when there is merely a bibliographical reference. Entries for Jane Whetnall's publications refer to the list on pp. 13–14, above. The index includes translators of literary works.

Subject Index

Alberto Latuada: 221; David MacDonald: 205, 220; Juan de Orduña: 202, 205, 209, 218, 219, 221; Gerard Oury: 222n26; Mariano Ozores: 222: 222; Benito Perojo: 221n21; Francisco Rovira Beleta: 202; Arturo Ruiz-Castillo: 221n24; Ridley Scott: 205, 209, 211, 213, 214, 218, 219, 221; Gerald Thomas: 222

SCRIPTWRITERS ETC: Rodolfo Alter (music): 221n21; Sigfrido Burman: 210; Charles Drossner: 219; Eva Gancedo (soundtrack): 204; Mario Puzo: 216; Irving Berdine Richman: 220

PRODUCERS: Muriel Box: 205; Sydney Box: 205; Samuel Bronston: 203; Rafael Gil Álvarez: 222n26; J. Arthur Rank: 205; Ilya Salkind: 211

COMPANIES: Antea Films: 221n23; Argos Films: 219; Central de Producciones Audiovisuales: 221n23; Chronicles of America Pictures: 220; Cifesa: 209, 221; Cine Internacional: 222n26; Columbus Films: 221n21; Constan Film: 222; Films Cinématographiques: 220; Gainsborough Studios: 205, 221; Gaumont International: 222n26; Island World: 222; Mars Film Paramount: 222n26; Onuba: 221n24; Orion Film Produktion: 222n26; Óscar Producciones Internacionales: 221; Pathé Exchange: 220; Pathé Frères: 220; Peel Enterprises: 221; Peter Rogers Production: 222; Producciones Ormaechea: 221n21; Producciones Rafael Gordon: 222; Radiotelevisione Italiana Clesi Cinematografica: 221;

Scholastic Productions: 222; Selig Polyscope Company: 219; Touchstone: 221; Valcázar Producciones Cinematográficas: 221n24

fin'amors: see courtly love
Finch's restaurant: 19
flight into Egypt: 227
Flor de paradís: 39, 47n19
Florence: 55, 116, 122, 124
Fonseca, Alonso de, Archbishop of Seville: 91
formalism: 17
foundation myths: 119
France: 104
Franciscans: 45n15
franquismo: 202, 211, 218
French music: 104; poetry: 46, 50–51, 167n15, 247; song: 17
Frías, Pedro de, cardinal: 145
Froissart, Jean: 104

Galen: 182
Galician-Portuguese lyric: 9–10, 71, 145, 172
Galve, Juana, Marchioness of Pescara (mother of Costanza d'Ávalos; and of the poet Rodrigo d'Ávalos?): 97n10, 100
Garcia, Maior (soldadeira): 252n
Garcia, Martí (poet): 106n5
García Escudero, José María, Director General de Cinematografía: 209n9, 211n11
Garcilaso de la Vega: 15–16
garden: 10, 235–44
Garí, Joan, legend of: 39, 40n7
Garret, Benet, il Cariteo (poet): 100
gaya ciencia: 57n4, 58, 59
generations of poets: 169–70
George of Trebizond: 119
Germanic poetry: 162n3
Germany: 249
Girón, Pedro, Master of the Order of Calatrava: 179–80, 227
Girón de Rebolledo, Fernando,

Tabula gratulatoria

Jareer A. Abu-Haidar
Dana Allen
Rosamund Allen
Álvaro Alonso
Katy Amberley
Robert Archer
Samuel G. Armistead
Jon Arms
Gemma Avenoza Vera
Lola Badia
David Barnett
Francisco Bautista
Rafael Beltrán
Vicenç Beltran
Andrew M. Beresford
Barbara Bisegna
Roger Boase
Julia Boffey
Álvaro Bustos Táuler
Lluís Cabré
Miriam Cabré
Axayácatl Campos García Rojas
Rosanna Cantavella
Derek C. Carr
Dee Charnley
Antonio Chas Aguión
María Clitherow
Geraldine Coates
Juan-Carlos Conde
Carlos Conde Solares
Edward Cooper
Alex Coroleu
Don W. Cruickshank
Trevor Dadson
Patricia D'Allemand
Trudi L. Darby
Catherine Davies
Departamento de Filología Española y Latina, Universi-
dade da Coruña
Alan Deyermond
Enric Dolz i Ferrer
Martin J. Duffell
Peter Evans
Josep-Anton Fernàndez
José Manuel Fradejas Rueda
Chiharu Fukui
Leonardo Funes
Montserrat Galí Morales
Miguel García-Bermejo Giner
Lucía Medea García López
Robert Gillett
Nigel Glendinning
Esther Gómez Sierra
Lucila González Alfaya
Elena González-Blanco García
Luis González Fernández
George D. Greenia
Richard Haigh
Ciara Jean Hand (RIP)
Marta Haro Cortés
Ieuan Harries
Annie Harris
Louise M. Haywood
Ann Henderson
David Henn
Richard Hitchcock
David Hook
Michael Hunter
Lynn Ingamells
Diana Ivanova
Paula Jojima
Kirstin Kennedy
Maxim. P. A. M. Kerkhof
Kauser Khan
Pamela King
Tess Knighton
Eukene Lacarra
Jeremy Lawrance

Sue Lewis
C. Alex Longhurst
Santiago López-Ríos
David McGrath
Ian Macpherson
Laura Catherine Madden
Fiona Maguire
Nancy F. Marino
Sadurní Martí
Giuseppe Mazzocchi
Olga Cecilia Méndez González
Rafael M. Mérida Jiménez
Roger Middleditch
Laura Mier
Carlos Mota
Cristina Moya García
Marina Núñez Bespalova
Terence O'Reilly
Stephen Parkinson
Ralph Penny
Óscar Perea Rodríguez
Chris Pountain
Victoria Prilutsky
Rafael Ramos
Real Biblioteca, Madrid
Stephen Reckert
Peter T. Ricketts
Montserrat P. Robinson
Rebecca Frances Rogers
Regula Rohland de Langbehn
Pilar Rose-Alcorta
Concepción Salinas Espinosa
Rebeca Sanmartín Bastida
Xelo Sanmateu
Connie L. Scarborough
Dorothy S. Severin
Harvey L. Sharrer
Alison Sinclair
Fotini Skarlatou
Margaret Sleeman
Joseph Snow
Phil Swanson
Cleofé Tato
Barry Taylor

María Isabel Toro Pascua
Isabel Torres
Lesley Twomey
University of Durham Library
University of Exeter Library
Louise O. Vasvári
Rosa Vidal Doval
Elina Vilar Beltrán
Julian Weiss
Barbara F. Weissberger
Geoffrey West
Tristán White
Roger Wright

Notes on Contributors

Robert Archer studied at the Universities of Durham and Oxford, and taught at La Trobe University (Melbourne) before his election to the Chair of Spanish at Durham and then the Cervantes Chair of Spanish at King's College London. He works mostly on fifteenth- to seventeenth-century Spanish and Catalan literature. He has published critical editions of the complete works of Ausiàs March (1997) and of Pere Torroella (2004) and a monograph on March's imagery (1985), and has worked in recent years on medieval misogyny and defence of women: *Misoginia y defensa de las mujeres: una antología de textos medievales* (2000) and *The Problem of Woman in Late Medieval Hispanic Literature* (2005).

DAVID BARNETT, who took his first degree in Classics at Cambridge, worked as a teacher and translator in Barcelona before returning to England to work as a lexicographer. He then studied for a BA and MA in Hispanic Studies at Queen Mary, and is in the final year of his PhD work, under Jane Whetnall's supervision; his thesis is a study and edition of a collection of Marian miracle stories in a fifteenth-century Catalan manuscript. He has published 'The Voice of the Virgin: Accessible Authority in the Visitation Episode of Isabel de Villena's *Vita Christi*' (2006).

FRANCISCO BAUTISTA is a Research Fellow in the Department of Spanish Literature, Universidad de Salamanca. From 2004 to 2006 he was a Postdoctoral Fellow at Queen Mary, and he has taught at the University of Pennsylvania and the University of Cambridge. He is the author of *La 'Estoria de España' en época de Sancho IV: sobre los reyes de Asturias* (PMHRS, 50, 2006), and edited *El relato historiográfico: textos y tradiciones en la España medieval* (PMHRS, 48, 2006). He has published articles on historiography, epic, and romance, is preparing an edition of the *Crónica carolingia* for Textos Recuperados, and is collaborating with Inés Fernández-Ordóñez on an anthology of the *Estoria de España* and with Alberto Montaner on a book on the epic. He is Secretary of the Sociedad de Estudios Medievales y Renacentistas.

ANDREW M. BERESFORD, who gained his doctorate at Queen Mary and Westfield College, is Senior Lecturer in Spanish in the University of Durham. His articles are chiefly on medieval Spanish hagiography and debate poems, but their subjects also include *Celestina* and *cancionero* poetry. He has published *The Legends of the Holy Harlots: Thaïs and Pelagia in Medieval Spanish Literaure* (Tamesis, 2007) and *The Legend of Saint Agnes in Medieval Castilian Literature* (PMHRS, 59, 2007). He is now preparing a third book, on the origin and diffusion of the cults of Saints Agatha and Lucy.

ROGER BOASE is an Honorary Research Fellow in the Department of Hispanic Studies, Queen Mary. He was previously Professor of English at the University of Fez. His research interests are in the expulsion of the Muslims from Spain and in *cancionero* poetry. He is the author of *The Origin and Meaning of Courtly Love: A Critical Study of European Scholarship* (1977), *The Troubadour Revival: A Study of Social Change and Traditionalism in Late Medieval Spain* (1979), and, with Aisha Ahmad, *Pashtun Tales from the Pakistan-Afghan Frontier* (2003); most recently, he has edited *Islam and Global Dialogue: Religious Pluralism and the Pursuit of Peace* (2005).

LLUÍS CABRÉ teaches medieval Catalan literature at the Universitat Autònoma de Barcelona. From 1990 to 1993 he was Lecturer in Catalan at Queen Mary and Westfield College, and he returned as Batista i Roca Visiting Research Fellow in 1994-95. His publications include a critical edition of Pere March's *Obra completa* (1993), an edition and Catalan translation (with Josep Batalla & Marcel Ortín) of Ramon Llull's *Rhetorica nova* (2006), and a number of articles on medieval Catalan poetry, notably 'El conreu del lai líric a la literatura catalana medieval' (1987) and 'Aristotle for the Layman: Sense Perception in the Poetry of Ausiàs March' (1996).

CARLOS CONDE SOLARES took his first degree at the Universidad de Oviedo, and is now writing, under Jane Whetnall's supervision, a PhD thesis on 'The *Cancionero de Herberay* and the Literary Court of John II of Navarre'. He teaches language classes at Queen Mary, where he co-organizes the Hispanic Studies Departmental Research Seminar. He is co-editing the *Proceedings* of the XVII and XVIII Colloquia, and has an article on Juan and Francisco de Villalpando in press. His translation of Anthony Close's *Cervantes and the Comic Mind of his Age* was published in 2007.

EDWARD COOPER was Reader at London Metropolitan University, and is an Honorary Research Fellow in the Department of Hispanic

Studies, Queen Mary. Among his publications are *Castillos señoriales de Castilla de los siglos XV y XVI* (1980), *Castillos señoriales en la Corona de Castilla* (1991), *La mitra y la roca: intereses de Alfonso Carrillo, Arzobispo de Toledo, en la Ribera del Ebro* (with Salvador Mirete Mayo, 2001), and research papers on the revolt of the Comunidades de Castilla in 1520–21. He is a Corresponding Fellow of the Real Academia de Alfonso X el Sabio, and Visiting Lecturer in the Department of Mineralogy and Crystallography of the Universidad Complutense.

ALAN DEYERMOND, FBA, is a Research Professor at Queen Mary. He founded the Medieval Hispanic Research Seminar at Westfield College in 1967. He has been a Visiting Professor at the University of Wisconsin, the University of California (Los Angeles and Irvine), Johns Hopkins, and Princeton, and is a Corresponding Fellow of the Medieval Academy of America. He was President of the Asociación Internacional de Hispanistas, and received the Premio Internacional Elio Antonio de Nebrija in 1994. His books include *The Petrarchan Sources of 'La Celestina'* (1961), *Epic Poetry and the Clergy: Studies on the 'Mocedades de Rodrigo'* (1968), *A Literary History of Spain: The Middle Ages* (1971), *La literatura perdida de la Edad Media castellana: catálogo y estudio*, I (1995), and *The 'Libro de Buen Amor' in England* (2004).

MARTIN J. DUFFELL is an Honorary Research Fellow in the Department of Hispanic Studies at Queen Mary, an Honorary Fellow of the college, and an Honorary Companion of the University of Manchester. After taking a BA in Classics he made his career in international business (latterly combining that with research on metrics). Until he took early retirement in 1995 he was Head of Management Recruitment at Unilever. He was the founding Editor-in-Chief of the *Hispanic Research Journal*, 1998–2002. He is the author of thirty articles on English, Romance, and comparative metrics, and of *Modern Metrical Theory and the 'Verso de arte mayor'* (PMHRS, 10, 1998), *Syllable and Accent: Essays on Medieval Hispanic Metrics* (PMHRS, 56, 2007), and *A New History of English Metre* (in press).

KIRSTIN KENNEDY is research fellow and curator (Renaissance) at the Victoria and Albert Museum, where she is working on the redisplay of the European medieval and Renaissance collections. She was a British Academy Postdoctoral Fellow at King's College London from 2000 to 2003. She has published articles on Alfonso X and on *cancionero* poetry, and is preparing a study of Alfonsine manuscripts for publication by Editorial Nausicaa (Murcia).

GIUSEPPE MAZZOCCHI teaches Spanish in the Dipartimento di Lingue e Letterature Straniere Moderne of the Università degli Studi di Pavia. He edited the poetry of Alonso Pérez de Vivero in *Poeti 'cancioneriles' del secolo XV* (Giovanni Caravaggi et al., 1986). His books include an edition of the Comendador Román, *Coplas de la Pasión con la Resurrección* (1990), an edition and translation of Diego de San Pedro, *Cárcel de Amor* (2002), and an edition of Fray Luis de Granada, *Guía de maravillas* (2006); among recent articles are 'I sonetti agiografici del Marchese di Santillana' (2002), '"Vestirme quiero mañana": un decir burlesco di Guevara (?), e qualche riflessione ecdotica' (2004), 'La *Vida de Aristóteles* di Bruni: edizione e studio' (with Olga Perotti, 2004), and 'I manoscritti nella trasmissione della "novela sentimental" castigliana' (2004).

STEPHEN RECKERT, FBA, held the Chair of Spanish at University of Wales, Cardiff, and the Camoens Chair of Portuguese at King's College London. Since he took early retirement he has divided his time between Lisbon (where he was a Research Fellow of the Gabinete de Estudos de Simbologia) and London (Honorary Senior Research Fellow of the Institute of Romance Studies). His first article was 'Alcuni parallelismi fra i simboli concreti della *Divina Commedia* e del *Pilgrim's Progress*' (1948). His masterpiece, *Beyond Chrysanthemums: Perspectives on Poetry East and West* (1993), has been translated into Portuguese and amplified in Spanish. Other books include *Vida y obra de Medrano*, II: *Edición crítica* (with Dámaso Alonso, 1958), *Do cancioneiro de* amigo (with Helder Macedo, 1976), *Gil Vicente: espíritu y letra* (1977), and *From the Resende Songbook* (PMHRS, 15, 1998).

XELO SANMATEU is a Senior Language Instructor in the Department of Hispanic Studies at Queen Mary, where she gained an MA in Medieval Studies, and is now preparing a doctoral thesis on the Middle Ages in Hollywood film. She has published articles in this and related fields, and also a monograph on John Boorman's *Excalibur* (2001).

DOROTHY SHERMAN SEVERIN, OBE, Lecturer in Spanish at Westfield College from1969 to1982, has since then been Gilmour Professor of Spanish in the University of Liverpool, where she was the first female Pro-Vice-Chancellor (1989-92). She has published two editions of

Celestina (1969 and 1987) and five editions of *cancionero* poetry: Diego de San Pedro (1974 and, with Keith Whinnom, 1979), *Martínez de Burgos* (1976), *Oñate-Castañeda* (with Michel Garcia & Fiona Maguire, 1990), and *Colombina* and *Egerton* (2000). She is now directing a project for internet publication of all *cancionero* manuscripts. Her books include four monographs on *Celestina* and, most recently, *Religious Parody and the Sentimental Romance* (2005). She was the founder of Women in Spanish, Portuguese and Latin-American Studies (WISPS).

BARRY TAYLOR taught at Westfield College and the University of Exeter before taking up a post at the British Library, where he is now Curator of Hispanic Collections, 1501–1850. He has edited and translated Alonso de Cartagena (?), *Cathoniana confectio* (2004), and his articles on *cancionero* poetry include 'Juan de Mena, la écfrasis y las dos fortunas' (1994), 'Cota, Poet of the Desert: Hermits and Scorpions in the *Diálogo entre el Amor y un viejo*' (1997), 'Mena y Lucano' (1998), and 'Santillana and Allegory' (2000). Among his recent articles on other subjects are 'Versiones largas y breves de textos castellanos medievales y áureos' (2000), 'La *fabliella* de don Juan Manuel' (2000), 'En busca de la variante de autor en los textos medievales españoles' (2001), '*Exempla* and Proverbs in the *Libro de Buen Amor*' (2004), and 'The Tale of the Half Friend (Aarne-Thompson 893) in Some Hispanic Witnesses' (2005).

JULIAN WEISS is Professor of Medieval and Early Modern Spanish Studies at King's College London, where he is Director of the Centre for Late Antique and Medieval Studies. He previously taught at the University of Virginia and the University of Oregon. His teaching and research interests include gender and cultural studies, and the history of literary theory. In addition to numerous articles on these topics, he is the author of two monographs: *The Poet's Art: Literary Theory in Castile, c. 1400-60* (1990) and *The 'Mester de clerecía': Intellectuals and Ideologies in Thirteenth-Century Castile* (2006). He has also edited or co-edited several volumes of essays. With Antonio Cortijo, he is currently completing a critical edition of Hernán Núñez's Renaissance commentary on *El laberinto de Fortuna* by Juan de Mena.

55. Juan Miguel Valero Moreno, *Las transformaciones del discurso historiográfico: el caso de Eutropio como modelo*. 2006, 117 pp. ISBN 0 902238 32 9

56. Martin J. Duffell, *Syllable and Accent: Studies on Medieval hispanic Metrics*. 2007, 226 pp. ISBN 0 902238 35 3

57. Aengus Ward, *'Sumario analístico de la Historia Gothica': Edition and Study*. 2007, 118 pp. ISBN 0 902238 36 1

58. Thomas R. Hart, *Allegory and Other Matters in the 'Libro de buen amor'*. 2007, 101 pp. ISBN 0 902238 42 6

59. Andrew M. Beresford, *The Legend of Saint Agnes in Medieval Castilian Literature*. 2007, 103 pp. ISBN 0 902238 43 4

60. *From the 'Cancioneiro da Vaticana' to the 'Cancionero general': Studies in Honour of Jane Whetnall*, ed. Alan Deyermond & Barry Taylor. 2007, 290 pp. ISBN 0 902238 50 7

Orders to: PMHRS, Department of Hispanic Studies,
Queen Mary, University of London,
Mile End Road,   London E1 4NS